Congenial Souls

MEDIEVAL CULTURES

SERIES EDITORS

RITA COPELAND
BARBARA A. HANAWALT
DAVID WALLACE

*Sponsored by the Center for Medieval Studies
at the University of Minnesota*

Volumes in the series study the diversity of medieval
cultural histories and practices, including such inter-
related issues as gender, class, and social hierarchies;
race and ethnicity; geographical relations; definitions
of political space; discourses of authority and dissent;
educational institutions; canonical and noncanonical
literatures; and technologies of textual and visual
literacies.

CONGENIAL SOULS

READING CHAUCER FROM
MEDIEVAL TO POSTMODERN

STEPHANIE TRIGG

Medieval Cultures, Volume 30
University of Minnesota Press
Minneapolis
London

A portion of chapter 4 has been published as part of "Discourses of Affinity in the Reading Communities of Geoffrey Chaucer," in *Rewriting Chaucer: Culture, Authority, and the Idea of the Authentic Text, 1400–1602*, ed. Thomas A. Prendergast and Barbara Kline (Columbus: Ohio State University Press, 1999), 270–92. Reprinted by permission of Ohio State University Press.

Published by the University of Minnesota Press
111 Third Avenue South, Suite 290
Minneapolis, MN 55401-2520
http://www.upress.umn.edu

Library of Congress Cataloging-in-Publication Data
Trigg, Stephanie.
Congenial souls : reading Chaucer from medieval to postmodern /
Stephanie Trigg.
     p. cm. — (Medieval cultures ; v. 30)
Includes index.
ISBN 0-8166-3822-5 (alk. paper) — ISBN 0-8166-3823-3 (PB : alk. paper)
1. Chaucer, Geoffrey, d. 1400—Criticism and interpretation—History.
2. Chaucer, Geoffrey, d. 1400—Appreciation—Great Britain.
3. Authors and readers—Great Britain—History.
4. Criticism—Great Britain—History.
5. Middle Ages in literature.
6. Canon (Literature)
I. Title. II. Series.
PR1924 .T69 2001
821'.1—dc21   2001002129

Printed in the United States of America on acid-free paper

The University of Minnesota is an equal-opportunity educator and employer.

12 11 10 09 08 07 06 05 04 03 02   10 9 8 7 6 5 4 3 2 1

For Paul

Contents

ACKNOWLEDGMENTS

This book has been a very long time in the making. I have been sustained throughout by the Department of English with Cultural Studies at the University of Melbourne, a most extraordinary cluster of reading communities. Under the various headships of Stephen Knight, Terry Collits, Ken Ruthven, and Simon During, the department has always been a challenging and exciting place to teach and work as I wrote this book. I am deeply grateful to my colleagues and students there for providing the kind of environment that has made me constantly rethink this project.

I have received research support from the English department, the Arts Faculty, the University of Melbourne, and the Australian Research Council, and I am glad to express here my gratitude to those bodies. They have enabled me to work with Melissa Raine, Ros Harris, and Helen Hickey, and it's a great pleasure to thank them, Helen in particular, for tireless and productive efforts in support of this project.

Papers from sections of this book have been given at the universities of Melbourne, Adelaide, Western Australia, and Sydney. I am grateful to my colleagues for their responses, and to Tom Burton, Andrew Lynch and Philippa Maddern, and Margaret Clunies-Ross for these opportunities.

For giving me materials and references, I am most grateful to Geraldine Barnes, John Bowers, John Ganim, the late Beverly Kennedy, Glending Olson, and Ken Ruthven. I also wish to thank librarians at a number of institutions: the British Library, Cambridge University Library, the Beinecke Manuscript and Rare Book Library at Yale University, the Huntington Library, and the Victorian State Library in Melbourne. I would especially like to thank the Inter-Library Loan service at the Baillieu Library at the University of Melbourne for invaluable assistance.

More specific and more personal thanks go to the individuals who have counseled, assisted, and challenged me in a variety of ways—intellectual, familial, and personal—as I wrote this book: Diana Barnes, Marion Campbell, Eva Christoff, Peter Christoff, Sheila Delany, Robyn Eckersley, Elizabeth Fowler, Kerryn Goldsworthy, Helen Groth, Kristin Headlam, Kevin Hart, Graeme James, Jean James, Stephen Knight, Henry Krips, Valerie Krips, Andrew Lynch, Bernard Muir, Peter Otto, Kim Phillips, Elizabeth Robertson, Ken Ruthven, Fiona Trigg, Una Trigg,

Wesley Trigg, Clara Tuite, Chris Wallace-Crabbe, Jocelyne Wilson, and the members of the Medieval Round Table at the University of Melbourne. I would also like to offer warm thanks to Rita Copeland for her thoughtful encouragement of this project.

Joel Trigg has lived with this book all his life, and deserves special thanks for his forbearance as I worked on chapter after chapter. Paul James, my most subtle and most demanding reader, has been helping me finish this book for what must seem like a very long time indeed. I dedicate it to him with love, and with joy in our lives together.

Abbreviations

BL	British Library
CUL	Cambridge University Library
EETS	Early English Text Society
JEGP	*Journal of English and Germanic Philology*
LRB	*London Review of Books*
MED	*Middle English Dictionary*
MLA	Modern Language Association
MLQ	*Modern Language Quarterly*
MP	*Modern Philology*
NLH	*New Literary History*
NM	*Neuphilologische Mitteilungen*
PLL	*Papers in Language and Literature*
PMLA	*Publications of the Modern Language Association*
PQ	*Philological Quarterly*
RES	*Review of English Studies*
SAC	*Studies in the Age of Chaucer*
SAQ	*South Atlantic Quarterly*
THES	*Times Higher Education Supplement*
TLS	*Times Literary Supplement*

INTRODUCTION

THE CONGENIAL SOULS OF CHAUCER
AND HIS READERS

The cover of the Riverside paperback edition of Chaucer's works features a famous fifteenth-century image of pilgrims on horseback. The group rides out beyond the city walls; the bright reds and blues of their clothes and the elaborate detail of their horses' trappings gleam against the background of soft green grass. The top third of the picture is divided into three receding and overlapping planes: a building in warm ochre, then the walls of the cathedral town in the soft gray of distance, and finally, a range of blue hills and smaller villages against a horizon breaking into dawn. Our eye returns to the pilgrims. We can see four of them completely, and only the torsos of two other men whose horses are barely visible: it is clear that this frame shows us only part of a much longer string of riders. They spread across the page, gesturing at one another in attitudes of public or confidential appeal.

The picture is a perfect choice for the cover of Chaucer's *Works*. It combines the gorgeous detail of the medieval illuminated manuscript with a flattering confirmation of all that is most recognizable and appealing of what we remember about the *Canterbury Tales*, Chaucer's most famous work. The sober figure in the middle of the painting who seems to be listening attentively to a man of impressive demeanor might well be Chaucer himself.

That, at least, is how the reader is invited to read the illustration, an image that often adorns the covers of books on Chaucer and that comes from a manuscript of John Lydgate's *The Siege of Thebes* (BL, MS Royal 18 DII, f. 148). In his prologue to *The Siege*, Lydgate explains how he chanced to meet up with Chaucer's pilgrims as they lodged at Canterbury, though Chaucer himself is dead and buried. He agrees to accompany them as they return to London and tells "The Siege of Thebes" as the first tale of the homeward journey, reactivating the narrative contract drawn up by the host in Chaucer's *General Prologue*, whereby each pilgrim will tell two tales on both legs of the journey. In this prologue, Lydgate praises Chaucer's poetic skills but simultaneously inscribes

THE RIVERSIDE
CHAUCER

NEW EDITION

'This is the best edition of Chaucer in existence'
Anthony Burgess

Cover of the paperback edition of *The Riverside Chaucer*.

himself in Chaucer's place. Like Chaucer, he is both observer and par-
ticipant, another poet-pilgrim. Lydgate pays stylistic homage to Chaucer's
work in his own voice, yet his fiction of the return journey underlines
and compensates for its narrative deficiencies, its incomplete state. *The
Siege of Thebes,* moreover, seems designed generically to complement or
rival the *Knight's Tale,* the first of Chaucer's outbound stories, in that it
recounts the history of Thebes up to the point where the *Knight's Tale*
begins, with Theseus's return to Athens.

Because it illustrates Lydgate's preface, this picture stands as a curi-
ous supplement to Chaucer's work, for it depicts a moment that is de-
pendent on but conspicuously absent from *The Canterbury Tales.* Chaucer
notoriously shows us his pilgrims approaching, but not arriving at, the
end of their pilgrimage. There is no hint, apart from the Host's ambi-
tious plan for the story-telling competition, that he might ever describe
the return journey. This picture shows the moment of departure from
Canterbury, not London, while its central sober figure, we now realize,
signifies not only Chaucer but also Lydgate in his monk's habit, his
"cope of blak" (prologue to the *Siege of Thebes,* line 73).[1]

The most seductive aspect of the Riverside cover is its combination
of realism and wish-fulfillment. The Royal manuscript satisfies the de-
sire that Chaucer's work and its manuscripts consistently frustrate: the
desire to witness the poet in the prime imaginative site of the *Tales,*
meeting and speaking with his fictional creations. It goes much further
than the portraits in the Ellesmere manuscript, for example, in satisfy-
ing doubting speculations as to how the pilgrimage and the dynamics of
its narrative exchanges might really have worked. Would it have been
possible to *hear* a story told on horseback? This manuscript shows us
how. We see the horses in more realistic proportion, too; and the whole
scene is far more elaborate and less stylized than the Ellesmere illustra-
tions. And yet it enacts what can be only a fantasy of telling stories from
horseback to a company of thirty-odd people.

Taken from its context in a single copy of a supplementary poem by
Lydgate and used to herald a standard edition of the monumental *Works
of Geoffrey Chaucer,* the picture's register changes dramatically. As an
emblem of the edition it introduces, it promises nothing less than a ful-
fillment of our unspoken and increasingly unspeakable desire to see and
speak with Chaucer, to recapture an elusive, virtually forbidden moment
of authorial presence. The figure in red and white is engaged in precisely

that activity, speaking as if in private confidence with the monk-poet, who inclines sympathetically toward him. This speaker may be designed to represent the Host, who, on the eve of the journey, addresses Lydgate in familiar terms and offers counsel for his health. In any case, it is a private and intimate moment; the man in orange to the left claims the attention of the pilgrims riding ahead, while the man in blue to the right appeals back to those who follow. At the heart of this public, or communal, scene, then, with its glimpses of complex urban and rural societies, we find the possibility of a private moment shared with the author. This more intimate reading generates its own losses, though, as the fantasy of horseback narration collapses: three of the six riders are speaking at once.

Like other early poets, editors, and commentators, Lydgate regarded the *Canterbury Tales* as an open, unfinished text, a text that needs more work. Its generic opposite, the modern edition, makes a virtue of offering textual closure in the form of an authoritative, established text that constrains, even prohibits, any work of reconstruction by the reader. This jewel-like illustration, this pristine medieval artifact, is an attractive emblem of unmediated historical authenticity, the guarantee embodied in the edition (though in fact the image has been increased in size by almost one-third, and its colors deepened and enriched in reproduction). What is this cover but a confident promise of immediate communication with the author, as if it is we who are speaking with Chaucer, we who are riding by his side? The image smooths the path of our approach to the poet, precisely—and perversely—through its own mediated historicity, its context as a marginal illustration to Lydgate's parasitic text. Chaucer's complex reception history of imitation, commentary, and editorial reconstruction is thus embraced, but transcended.

The Royal manuscript is a more inviting induction to the Chaucerian community than are several other familiar fifteenth-century images of Chaucer. Unlike the famous Corpus Christi frontispiece to *Troilus and Criseyde,* where the richly dressed aristocratic audience is silent and passive, or the tradition of Chaucerian portraiture exemplified by the manuscript portrait in Hoccleve's *Regement of Princes,* where the poet's audience is invisible, the Royal manuscript as cover illustration offers the modern reader a place from which to listen and, most important, from which to "speak" to the author. It's even easier to imagine ourselves here as readers of Chaucer or, indeed, as members of his original audience, since the pilgrims are not distinguished one from another by the traditional iconography of costume or physiognomy. We may like to think ourselves into some kind of medieval mind-set in order to read Chaucer, but we don't often dress up as the Wife of Bath or the Miller in order to do so. On the contrary, the ideal position for reading Chaucer has often been to become as much like Chaucer as possible. Lydgate is the first to discern this advantage when he puts himself in Chaucer's place on the return journey to London, riding Chaucer's horse, as it were, in order to write his own Canterbury tale.

There remains to make one obvious point about this front cover illustration: as an image of an exclusively male company of pilgrims, it implies a male readership. For the Royal illuminator, characterization might be dispensable, but gender is not. It is a measure of Chaucer's reputation as a generalist, as a writer interested in women, if not, indeed, as an androgynous writer, that the absence of women does not stand in the way of this appealing representation of the Chaucerian community and the welcome it seems to extend to the prospective reader or buyer, of the book and the academic and cultural capital it signifies.[2]

It would be narcissistic and "presentist" in the extreme to expect the fifteenth-century illuminators to furnish an image or series of images that would reflect Chaucer's readers to themselves in all their changing forms and ideals across the centuries. My interest in this book design stems less from the possibilities of critique than from those of analysis: this image beautifully encapsulates many of the relationships among Chaucerians that are my central concern. The Riverside cover offers a very typical form of invitation to the world of Chaucerian scholarship and criticism, an invitation that is both individualized ("Place yourself in the company of Chaucer") and socialized ("Place yourself in the company of other Chaucerians").

Congenial Souls tracks the dynamics between the various forms of readership that cluster around Geoffrey Chaucer at different times in his long reception history. It analyzes the discursive patterns in which Chaucerians speak and write of Chaucer, with a special interest in uncovering the way they establish various forms of affiliation and affinity with him, with his work, and with other Chaucerians. This project is both historical in its coverage and political in its concerns, since it will challenge the attractive fiction of the Chaucerian community as an inclusive, unproblematic point of entry to Chaucer studies. Tracing the history of Chaucerian critical discourse and its present manifestations also forces us to ask questions about the future of Chaucerian studies. How, and how often, will we speak and write of Chaucer in the new millennium?

Congenial Souls starts from the assumption that Chaucer is an exemplary figure of canonical authorship for English literary tradition and that the historical patterns of his reception and his present study are instructive for both the past and the future of literary studies. From Chaucer's early commentators we learn about the making of English authorship in the humanist tradition and about the early forms of literary studies in English, while his current situation might also prove to be exemplary in another fashion. Chaucer is a prime site on which to consider the critical future of texts and authors who have traditionally formed the core of the canon of English literature, especially in the education sector. In this book I bypass the question of whether Chaucer should be included in any particular syllabus or curriculum: this is not really an issue for students of canonical authors to determine in isolation from specific pedagogical contexts. Instead, I examine the relation between his canonical status and the discursive forms in which his readers and the institutions of criticism have sustained that status, particularly in the face of current critiques. The question of canonicity is not solely concerned with what to teach and read; it is also about *how* we read and write and, crucially, the subjectivities we invite our students to perform.

One of the most powerful imperatives of traditional literary criticism is the metaphysical fiction of authorial presence, sustained by the possibility of the reader identifying with the author, the better to hear their words directly. Chaucer studies provides the exemplary model for such identifications. Chaucer is exemplary, in the sense that as the first English writer to receive the formative attentions of humanist textual criticism in the sixteenth century, he becomes a model for the making of literary authorship. Chaucer's own works also invite sympathetic readerly identifications, through the attractive narrative voices he constructs for himself. The image of the Canterbury pilgrimage—a group of diverse characters with a common aim—will prove to be one of the most important means of imagining such identifications, both with Chaucer and with other Chaucerians, among his various reading communities.

It is true that in the most recent Chaucer criticism, these patterns of identification play a vastly reduced role, but in the final chapter I will suggest that they persist, not merely as vestigial, often embarrassed, traces of earlier, less self-conscious modes, but indeed, as structural features of modern criticism. In that respect, they continue to maintain and reproduce the community of readers that constitutes the audience for all monographs and articles on Chaucer, no matter how transgressive their intent or how trenchant their critiques.

This book makes no claim to exhaust the history of Chaucer's reception as a narrative of changing images or representations of the poet, nor does it attempt to survey the enormous critical variety of Chaucerian interpretation. It takes for granted that canonical authors are reinterpreted and reinvented to suit the tastes and interests of subsequent centuries and the changing demands for different forms of cultural capital. I examine the media of Chaucerian representation; the forms, the genres, and the discursive voices of Chaucer criticism; and the institutions that sustain those discourses. Poetic voice is a privileged topic in Chaucer studies, usually organized around issues of authorial intention and dramatized characterization or, in more recent years, of writerly play and the dispersal of authorial voice into impersonated or dialogic voices. Instead of trying to "hear" Chaucer's voice more accurately, I approach this topic from the opposite angle, studying the various attempts of Chaucer's readers to voice what *they* see as an appropriate "Chaucerian" tone in criticism and, in so doing, to become model Chaucerians. While at times my analysis will touch on the influence of Chaucer on his poetic followers and moments of popular reception, I am principally concerned with the greater gap his prose critics must bridge between themselves and the medieval poet and with the functions of imitation, dialogue, and conversation in the project of critical commentary.

I take my title from John Dryden and the defense of his "improvements" and "additions" to Chaucer when he translates several tales into his *Fables Ancient and Modern* in 1700: "And to this I was the more embolden'd, because (if I may be permitted to say it of my self) I found I had a Soul congenial to his, and that I had been conversant in the same Studies."[3] Dryden *writes* Chaucer (translating, adding, improving) on the strength of his exemplary *reading*. His direct knowledge of Chaucer derives not only from a spiritual capacity (as a poet, he is born into the same race, or family, as Chaucer), but also from an apprenticeship in learning comparable to the medieval poet's. The two poets reflect well on each other, while philology and poetry—scholarship and inspiration—are still at this point perfectly compatible. At the midpoint of Chaucer's six-hundred-year reception history, the preface consolidates a number of strands in the late medieval and early modern response to Chaucer. It also provides a founding moment for modern criticism. Dryden's combination of historicism (reading Chaucer well by replicating his own studies) with formalism (responding to the long-dead poet with a comfortable, and comforting, familiarity) will be crucially enabling for modern criticism, as we will see in chapter 5.

For the moment, though, "congenial" is my key term, since it embraces the two senses in which readers have traditionally established a relationship with Chaucer.[4] First, in Dryden's primary sense, it invokes a brotherly, even spiritual companionship in poetry and learning: a relationship between two bookish yet compatible individuals across a substantial historical gap. It's a relationship that takes flattering echoes from the word's roots in the Latin *genius:* "guardian spirit," but also "enjoyment, inclination; talent." But there is no restriction on the number of readers who can claim a congenial soul with a dead author; and the convivial Chaucerian personality eases such identifications. In this second sense, Chaucer is less the solitary bookish figure than the jovial companion on pilgrimage. And while Dryden's invocation of a Chaucerian spirit at this point in his preface is more individual than communal, the congenial society of pilgrims—the most idealized drinking companions in English literature—is not very far away. Writing of Chaucer's naturalism, he comments, "I see . . . all the Pilgrims in the *Canterbury* Tales, their Humours, their Features, and the very Dress, as distinctly as if I had supp'd with them at the *Tabard* in *Southwark*" (4:1450–51).

In my title, the idea of Chaucer and his readers as "congenial souls" condenses a number of influential patterns and traditions in Chaucerian reception. Both the key aspects of those patterns—the individualized and the socialized forms of Chaucerian identity—derive from moments in his works and long-established understandings of those passages. From the early dreamer alone with his books to the amorous aspirant who serves love from afar to the quiet observer with his head cast down on the Canterbury pilgrimage, Chaucer appears as a solitary figure, a flattering image for readers who encounter his works alone in their own studies or libraries. "The existence of a scholar can be a lonely one: too often he must sit, hermit-like, at his books 'also domb as any stoon.' An irrepressible zest for life and the ability to communicate it are rare qualities." Beryl Rowland's remarks in honor of Rossell Hope

Robbins epitomize this model of the scholar who transcends "his" nec-
essary, readerly solitude with an equally "Chaucerian" love of life.[5] But
the vision of Chaucer as a congenial member of the Canterbury pil-
grimage, laughing with, not at human weakness, is a powerful social
complement to this solitary model: Chaucer's readers over many cen-
turies have taken pleasure in picturing themselves among his compan-
ions at the Tabard Inn. In recent years, this is more often than not done
ironically, but it is still done and plays an important, if indirect, role in
"training" new Chaucerians.

A third, less obvious, but just as powerful, image of communication
in Chaucer's writing is found in his addresses to his own friends: Buk-
ton, Scogan, Strode, and Gower. It is an image supported, though not
unequivocally, by other instances of brotherly friendship in his fictions:
Pandarus and Troilus, Palamon and Arcite, Aleyn and John. These also
assist the male reader wanting to place himself close to Chaucer, want-
ing to imagine himself as a member of Chaucer's first audience of
friends and fellow poets, sharing the poet's sensibilities and frames of ref-
erence. That these ideals of solitary reading and spiritual communion,
of conviviality, and of amity are nearly always exemplified as masculine,
or more directly homosocial, is only one difficulty faced by Chaucer's
modern readers.[6] We have learned subtle ways, however, to negotiate or
transcend the critical heritage we must embrace, in order to find differ-
ent kinds of affinity with writing that is in many regards *un*congenial to
modernity and postmodernity. These maneuvers are not unique to
Chaucer's readers, but their history is more distinctly legible here than
in most other traditions of English literary studies. Shakespeare tradi-
tion is the most obvious comparison, but Chaucer studies has more in
common with many other fields in that Chaucer's texts provide many
images of the poet himself at work, reading, talking, and writing, images
that are particularly enabling for readers wishing to place themselves in
Chaucer's company or in a company of Chaucerians. For example, con-
sider the ease with which Leigh Hunt "hears" *Troilus and Criseyde* as if it
were addressed personally to himself. Where the narrator comments,
"Thow, redere, maist thiself ful wel devyne" (5.270), Hunt annotates his
copy: "There is something singularly pleasing, flattering, and personally
attaching in finding one's self thus personally addressed by such a man
as Chaucer, even under an individual designation so generalizing."[7]
This uninhibited desire to hear Chaucer directly, while repressed from

modern scholarly decorum, still resonates through much of our work, despite our best professional intentions.

None of these desires, or the strategies to fulfill them, is straightforward or unproblematic, and my work in this book is to explore their contradictions. I argue that we need to pay particular attention to the ways in which we currently define ourselves as "Chaucerians" and the ways we invite, or teach, our students to take up that identity, to join that increasingly professionalized community. If the possibility of direct access to the canonical writers of the past looks less and less feasible—and desirable—in a postmodernist academy, can we conceive a form of Chaucer studies independently of these structures of identification and affinity with the author? What if these structures turn out to be a necessary condition for the study of canonical authors from the past?

Congenial Souls starts by considering Chaucer's status as an exemplary canonical author for English literary tradition, and the more specific formation of Chaucerian "tradition" as a means of bridging the gap between the medieval and the modern, while introducing the ideas of community and Chaucerian identity in greater detail. Chapter 2 considers the question of where the Chaucerian text begins and ends and the nature of the Chaucerian signature: what are we responding to when we read "Chaucer"? I turn in chapter 3 to look at a number of early readings of the Chaucerian text as still open, where reading Chaucer is, literally, to write Chaucer. Chapter 4 considers the reinvention by humanist textual criticism of Chaucer as an object of both scholarship and affection among restricted communities of readers. Chapter 5 revisits the crucial moment of Dryden's translations and commentary on Chaucer and examines the importance attributed to this text by later Chaucerians, especially the dynamic it establishes between loving and criticizing Chaucer. In chapter 6, I examine the early academic writing about Chaucer in the late nineteenth and early twentieth centuries, focusing less on the familiar work of the early professionals than on some of the more popular "amateur" kinds of writing that have now fallen out of favor. Chapter 7 considers a number of recent attempts to "reform" Chaucer studies and the Chaucerian community and examines their effect on mainstream Chaucer studies, in the present and into the future of Chaucer criticism and medieval studies.

Congenial Souls traces patterns that I argue are extensive and wideranging over the long traditions of Chaucer studies. It plots a selective rather than an inclusive trajectory and tends to focus on those moments when the tradition turns to analyze its own history, since my primary concern is with the way Chaucerian readers imagine and write about their relationship with each other and with their predecessors. My method is unapologetically historical in its concerns for origins, as I aim to demonstrate the influence of some of the earliest forms of response to Chaucer on later discussions and the importance of Chaucer and Chaucer studies for the history of modern English literary criticism. It's a further project of this book, however, gradually to politicize our current readings of Chaucer—indeed, the reading of Chaucer in general—in relation to the discourses by which we make ourselves Chaucerian(s). The history of Chaucer criticism is still being made, after all.

Since I began work on this project almost ten years ago, there has been a discernible tonal shift in Chaucer criticism, comparable with many other areas of literary studies. The voices of Chaucer studies are in process of undergoing a transformation that responds to the major changes in literary studies, tertiary education, and the traditional distribution of cultural capital in our communities, as well as other factors. I have sought to articulate those changes as they affect Chaucer studies, tracing the history of a tradition through some of its most important transitional moments.

Some of these moments will be familiar; others, less so. For example, American readers may have already experienced an unusual kind of alienation when I began by writing of the paperback edition of the *Riverside Chaucer*. This edition is the standard text for readers in the United Kingdom and many Commonwealth countries, but has never been published in the United States. The Houghton Mifflin Company first published the Riverside Chaucer in 1987. In the following year, they licensed Oxford University Press to produce a paperback edition, on condition that it would not be sold in the United States. This agreement revived the spirit of the British Traditional Market Agreement of 1947 (rescinded in 1976), whereby U.K. and U.S. publishers agreed to divide the English-speaking book market into two: the United Kingdom, along with (former) members of the Commonwealth, and the United States, along with its dependencies.[8] Houghton Mifflin reserved the right to publish a paperback version for sale in the United States, but have never exercised that right, while even the Canadian office of Oxford University Press has no right to distribute the paperback title. It's worth noting how the structure

of colonialist capitalism has affected the distribution of the most fre-
quently cited Chaucer text. This becomes a rather different narrative
from that suggested by the "Anglo-American collaboration" in scholar-
ship praised on the back cover of the paperback edition, and reminds us
that we rarely, in fact, all read the same "Chaucer." It will be a recurrent
theme of this book that the international community of Chaucerians is
not always as homogeneous as some members of that community like
to imagine it.

Nor, it must be admitted, are Chaucer studies so central to literary
studies as they once were. While the influence of Chaucer and Chauce-
rians on the structure of author studies in English literary criticism is
immense, it is also the case that such studies are currently being dis-
placed from the academic curriculum. Where does this leave Chauceri-
ans and their relation to their past? It may be time to refigure both our
understanding of the past and our relation to the future of literary stud-
ies. This should not imply the end of Chaucer or of Chaucer studies, but
it may involve a kind of closure to the Chaucer tradition, to our long-
cherished notions of Chaucer's centrality to literary tradition, and ulti-
mately, it may transform what it means to be Chaucerian at all.

1

SPEAKING FOR CHAUCER

CANON AND COMMUNITY

In 1980, Charles Muscatine addressed the New Chaucer Society. "While it does look," he remarked, "as if it would be highly un-Chaucerian to be too solemn or too pious about Chaucer scholarship, none of us is under the obligation, after all, to be Chaucerian. Chaucer would have been the first to insist, rather, on our being ourselves, and doing well what our talents and temperaments fit us for."[1] Muscatine's delicious paradox is fitting from a scholar who has been so influential in teaching the twentieth century how to read Chaucerian ambiguity and irony; that is, as undermining any tendency toward solemnity and piety. Releasing us from the obligation to be Chaucerian, he instantly reintroduces Chaucer as a moral authority, directing us to discover our own individuality. It is an ethical paradox fit for a postmodern age: wanting release from the compulsory identification with the author, we look to the author for permission. So if we still harbor the desire to follow Chaucer, to do as Chaucer says, it's fortuitous, in an era of self-fashioning, that we can embrace a reading of Chaucer that encourages us to "be ourselves."

Muscatine appeals to one of the most powerful structuring fictions of literary studies, that in reading literary works we might gain access to the imaginative consciousness behind or beyond those works, a consciousness we can then release from its social, historical, and cultural context. In its psychological anachronism, Muscatine's vision of Chaucer counseling us to "be ourselves" is a perfect illustration of the attractive fiction by which the canonical author can be made to speak outside or beyond his works (and in this case, beyond any likely medieval formulation of selfhood). It is also a fiction that bolsters the authority of the

1

critic who can make the author "speak" in this way. In speaking for Chaucer, Muscatine becomes the exemplary Chaucerian, conjuring up the poet in a manner that depends only vestigially on a reading of his works but that also depends on codes only the initiated members of the Chaucerian community can comprehend.

Muscatine's remarks are clearly prefatory, an informal, opening gambit in a presidential address to a sophisticated "New" society of Chaucerians who will take his invocation of Chaucer's spirit only half seriously. In its more general form, however, the possibility of identification between author and reader on which his ironic gesture depends is an important structural feature of traditional reading practices, and one that underlies much of the work of canonical literary studies. Assuming that the text reflects authorial expression and experience, this model teaches the reader how to replicate that experience as closely as possible, by attentive and sympathetic reading and a kind of immersion in the authorial voice in question.

This book will offer many examples of this implicit invitation to identify with Chaucer, as a means of becoming an exemplary Chaucerian and an exemplary *teacher* of Chaucer. Here is Larry D. Benson editing a collection of essays in honor of B. J. Whiting: "[T]hose whose works appear in this volume are but a small percentage of his many friends, students and colleagues who would have liked to demonstrate their affection in this way. For a time we thought of calling this volume *Chaucer and His Friends,* since most of his students develop the conviction that Mr. Whiting *is* Chaucer, and all are his friends eager to pay him honor."[2]

These customary identifications are one of the easiest targets of attack in current critiques of literary studies. Antony Easthope's neat characterization of this model shows how it can be turned against itself:

> As the presiding pedagogic discourse for literary study, literary criticism aims to re-create together the author's experience, the text itself, and the reader's re-creation of that text in a triune of transparencies. The reader as subject of this discursive practice, this deployment of knowledge and power, is to be confirmed as a simple unity in imaginary plenitude, invited into a position of identification with the author.[3]

Easthope generalizes to make a strategic point: this description is a significant starting point for a series of distinctions he draws between the object, the subject, and the relations between them in literary and in cultural studies. Characterizing literary studies in this way makes it easy for Easthope to draw a contrast between the two disciplines. In Easthope's analysis of its objects and its subjects, cultural studies is revealed as more diverse, less hegemonic, less restricted than literary studies to the intimate dyad, the very restricted economy of individual author and reader: "While the discursive operation of literature exercises power by interpellating its subject in an imaginary unity, cultural studies works to compel its subject into a dispersed, relative and partisan identity." As has become typical in many accounts of cultural studies, Easthope defines the new field at the expense of the old, characterizing literary studies in its least progressive or interrogative mode. Contending that the shift from literary *into* cultural studies is a paradigm shift, he draws a sharper contrast than one that accurately reflects all versions of literary studies.[4]

By 1991, however, when Easthope was writing, overt readerly expressions of identification with the author had long been edited out of most versions of literary studies and were rarely expressed as the conscious aim of criticism, pedagogy, or theory. Debates about the canon, about pedagogy, about the relations of literary with historical or anthropological studies, and about our various psychological and political investments in the way we do literary studies are now far more likely to dominate discussion than is the best way to internalize authorial point of view. Even the category "author" has been profoundly theorized and historicized as a contingent, not a necessary, condition of writing or reading. No longer is the author seen as the inevitable starting point of discussion; in fact, the debate over the canon and the curriculum of literary studies has virtually inverted the model of the reader absorbing the wisdom of the great authors. Instead of reflecting the author's experience, it is increasingly argued that the objects of literary analysis and study should reflect the reader's experience; that literary syllabuses should "represent"—in both senses of the word—their reading constituencies.[5] The emphasis on the works of historically distant authors who belong to culturally dominant groups (the "dead white males" of popular currency) is one of the first points of attack of feminist, postcolonial, and multicultural studies and of other movements concerned to expose the hegemonic cultural politics of a traditional criticism that implicitly or explicitly claimed to be concerned with aesthetic and moral "value" alone, independently of the social and historical context of author or reader.

For Easthope, however, the concerns of the 1980s and 1990s with theory, politics, and their effects on criticism are merely symptomatic registers of the crisis in literary study, a moment that is now passing as the "fresh paradigm" emerges. It is beyond the scope of this study to anticipate the long-term future of literary and cultural studies, although I do think the paradigms are not quite so discrete as Easthope maintains. Conversely, it is hard to deny that, faced with the emergence of cultural studies, the traditions of literary studies are in process of radical change, far greater and more momentous than the many alterations and changes brought about *within* literary studies by the interpretive and critical battles waged at different times in this century, and especially since the 1980s. These struggles and their contested histories are in danger of being elided in accounts, like Easthope's, that operate by opposing cultural studies against literary studies. Easthope's diagnosis, however, is typical of many critiques and analyses of a moribund literary studies, and so worth considering in any study concerned, as this one is, with the immediate future of the canonical text in the contemporary academy.

Easthope's characterization of the "presiding pedagogic discourse" is accurate insofar as it describes a long tradition in literary studies that focuses on an idealized relation of intimacy between author and reader. Yet that discourse "presides" in complex and sometimes contradictory ways. Muscatine, for instance, cites rather than fully enacts this practice, invoking its rhetorical power to address the Chaucerian community. Yet it has also been substantially modified in a postmodernist era that is increasingly suspicious of both the metaphysics and the politics of authorial presence and readerly identification with that presence. Chaucer studies reveals a full range of attitudes and practices in such identifications, as his readers speak to Chaucer and make Chaucer speak, while increasingly raising doubts about those very possibilities.

At this transitional moment in Chaucer studies, I seek to trace the history of a pattern whose closure I also mark. The history of Chaucer studies is usually read as a history of changing images of the poet and competing fashions in interpretation, although more recent studies have begun to focus on the implicit and explicit politics of the dominant institutions and critical practices of medieval studies. My project works principally at the level of discourse analysis, concerned with the relations between Chaucer and his readers, and also among those readers. It is less interested in the specifics of textual interpretation and more concerned with the discourses of affinity, as I call them, by which Chaucer's readers write themselves into relationships of intimacy with the poet and with his various reading communities. Yet it is also a book deeply concerned with the theory of literary studies and of medieval studies and with the interesting position of Chaucer studies at their intersection, at a time when both fields are reexamining their traditional claims to cultural authority.

In one sense, of course, Charles Muscatine is right: there is something very "un-Chaucerian" about discussing Chaucer criticism. It's a frequent, if barely publishable, joke among Chaucerians to wonder what Chaucer would make of our speculations and struggles over his work. That joke is itself part of my study, however, as is the idea of the Chaucerian community that produces the joke and for whom it is funny. In the sense in which his readers are all Chaucerians, there is nothing *more* Chaucerian—certainly nothing more characteristic of the modern professional—than to study the critical and discursive patterns of Chaucer scholarship. The canons of literature produce special objects of criticism, but they also produce very distinctive subjects.

This chapter examines the twinned constructions of Chaucer as a canonical and as a medieval author; as well as his status as an exemplary figure for both those traditions, before turning to the concept of tradition itself as an important sustaining feature for modern Chaucer studies. Chaucer tradition is structured around the knowledge of Chaucerian voice: this very complex, yet distinctive medieval voice is the focal point for a number of images of community. The final section of this chapter begins the work of tracing the origins of both the intimate and the communal responses to Chaucer in some of his shorter poems.

Exemplary Chaucer:
Canonicity and Philology

Chaucer becomes the exemplary instance of English authorship only gradually. The discourses of authorship are barely available to him—as we will see in chapter 2—and it is only after his death that Chaucer is recognized and written about decisively as an object of these emergent regimes. Chronologically prior among them is the discourse of praise among Chaucer's poetic successors, who quickly move from acknowledging his name as worthy of recall to finding his work worthy of imitation. Chaucer is not the only poet to inspire such praise by the writers and poetic genealogists of the fifteenth century, but he generates a much more complex response among his imitators and followers than do his contemporaries and near-contemporaries Gower and Lydgate. In Seth Lerer's analysis, for example, Chaucer is installed as author, laureate poet, and "father" of poetry in English by poets infantilized by and subjected to the reading positions already established in Chaucer's own poetry.[6]

Since this elevation at the expense of his contemporaries, Chaucer's place at the chronological head of the canon of English literature has remained undisputed.[7] Historical tastes in literature might vary—Chaucer certainly goes through a period of disfavor in the eighteenth century, and different poems move in and out of favor at different times—but his name has always headed up any list or summary of the canonical authors of English tradition. While we continue to ask questions about the value of such lists, Chaucer's name always appears in any syllabus or publisher's list that aims at "coverage." As a material example of Chaucer's popularity at the college level in the United States, at least, let me cite a list published in 1994 of the top-selling titles among Cliffs Notes.[8] The volume on *The Canterbury Tales* comes in at number six, behind *The Scarlet Letter*, *Macbeth*, *Hamlet*, *The Odyssey*, and *The Adventures of Huckleberry Finn*. These lists also have their counterparts in more popular traditions of recognition by academic and nonacademic institutions. Chaucer is named (erroneously) by Dryden as the first poet laureate, while his burial in Westminster Abbey as a tenant inspired the subsequent inauguration of Poets' Corner there.[9] Students at Christ Church, Oxford, in the 1720s had to purchase a copy of John Urry's unpopular edition of Chaucer's *Works* as a condition of enrollment.[10] Most recently, the purchase by John Paul Getty Jr. of a copy of Caxton's first edition of *The Canterbury Tales* for U.S.$7.58 million (a price record, as of 1998, for any printed book) through a Christie's auction testifies to the ease with which symbolic capital can sometimes be converted directly into economic capital, though symbolic value in this case also resonates with nationalist value: the volume will remain in Britain. British anxiety about "ownership" of Chaucer is also reflected in Richard Beadle's review of the recent Ellesmere facsimile.[11] Of the first facsimile produced by Manchester University Press in 1911, he writes that this was "made hardly a moment too soon, as the original was, shortly afterwards, in 1917, sold to Henry E. Huntington, along with the rest of the Bridgewater library, and shipped off to California." It's a wonderful image of the manuscript being "transported," like a guilty convict, as if from the center of empire to its frontiers.

Chaucer's history, then, will be instructive in all kinds of ways for the history and politics of literary canons. Even though Chaucer remains a poetic figure of some importance to modern writers,[12] it is really the Chaucer of literary history who provides a model for literary criticism and whom this book takes as its main concern. Chaucer is singled out by English scholars in the sixteenth century as the medieval poet most worthy of scholarly attention, the most appropriate site on which to develop the new humanist textual criticism. Its discursive genres and material practices—the edition, the biography, the commentary, the glossary, and so on—develop independently of the poetic traditions of imitation, praise, and rivalry, and gradually produce a different kind of Chaucer as the object of scholarship, evaluation, and commentary. Correspondingly, his readers in this sphere constitute themselves not as poets, but as editors, scholars, biographers, and critics of a writer of historical, national, and aesthetic importance. The articulation of a range of narrative and rhetorical subject positions—scribe, editor, printer, bookseller, publisher, commentator—around the text of Chaucer is crucial for the differences between author, editor, and critic on which our own critical institutions and practices still depend. Chaucer's critics come to "speak" less directly to Chaucer and in Chaucer's voice than do his poetic successors, gradually displacing this desire onto a plenitude of informed and knowing commentary, filling up the spaces around the texts with answers to the questions those texts seem to pose, and inviting other readers to do the same.

While this book will concentrate on the traditions of Chaucer scholarship and criticism, it will also focus on the margins of those literary traditions, margins that I argue are often indicative of Chaucer's broader, more general reception. One instance of Chaucer's exemplary authorship is provided by a foundational moment in Australian university tradition. The motto of Macquarie University, founded in 1964 in northern Sydney, is "And gladly teche." The motto was suggested by the first chancellor, A. G. Mitchell, the author of *Lady Meed and the Art of Piers Plowman* (1957). The university's historians comment on his "suggestion of genius":

> "In words of great simplicity and directness," Mitchell told the
> Council, "it describes the two inseparable interests and respon-

sibilities of the university scholar." To select part was not to obliterate the rest of the line but to adopt a device long familiar among classical scholars, in quotation from the scriptures and in modern English poetry—"that of quoting part of a line of verse, or part of a sentence and leaving to the reader the pleasurable satisfaction of supplying the context." . . . He was offering the Clerk of Oxenford as the institution's ideal and symbol.[13]

The Clerk has always been an important figure for Chaucerians seeking to find an image of themselves in Chaucer's poetry. Robert Longsworth, for example, introduces his study of the Clerk thus: "Chaucer's Clerk is a man of learning, and learned men have customarily written of him with fraternal sympathy. Whether he be measured by his preference for the bookshelf above the fiddle, by his genteel poverty, or by his Oxonian dignity, his mien and manner have endeared him to his latter-day colleagues."[14] And in Melbourne, in 1994, Jennifer Strauss, Monash University medievalist and union official, read the description of the Clerk to rousing applause at a Trades Hall meeting during a strike organized to resist government restructuring of university research budgets. It has been a fundamental platform of university teachers in Australia, as elsewhere, that teaching and research should be inseparable activities. Chaucer's clerk, who would gladly teach *and* learn, was the obvious model for Mitchell's desire "to recognise the significance and challenge of good teaching, but not to downgrade learning or research."[15]

The embedded citation in the Macquarie motto indicates Chaucer's status as cultural icon and the manner in which the canonical text invites recognition and completion in a complex model of social relations. Chaucer provides the focal point for the university's potential to imagine its relationship to tradition by recognizing and completing a Chaucerian text. At the same time, Macquarie was being established as a comparatively radical institution of tertiary education, giving due importance to new subject areas and the breakup of traditional disciplinary formations. Chaucer serves as a reassuring link to an older world of scholarship.[16]

Of course, a position of such prominence can also be a liability. For if Chaucer is the exemplary author, he is therefore also the exemplary, or at least original, dead white male. In casual discussion, though never in print, Chaucer is sometimes dismissed as "irrelevant" to contemporary theory and criticism precisely because he exemplifies canonical tradition and scholarship so purely. Chaucer studies are named, moreover, by Gayatri Spivak (this time, in print) as an instance of the author-based disciplines for which there is no longer automatic space in the academy, no matter how revivified by avant-garde literary theories.[17]

And yet from within Chaucer studies, the impact of this challenge registers less severely. There seems to be little diminution in the number of studies being published or reviewed, while Chaucerians demonstrate a prodigious capacity to reinvent themselves in response to current debates in critical theory and practice and, indeed, to reflect on those changes.[18] Spivak questioned the possibility of postcolonial readings of Chaucer: "Are there those?" she asked in disbelief. Not only were there a number of such readings already published or in preparation as she wrote, but her essay also proved the specific point of genesis for another, and it has now developed into a minor theme in contemporary Chaucer studies.[19]

The canonical text, by definition, can absorb the most profound critiques both from within and from outside its own well-established traditions. The six centuries of critical response to Chaucer's works reveal dramatic reversals in taste and interpretation, while more recently, these texts have been read and studied through a wide variety of critical and theoretical approaches: historicisms old and new; formalist and structuralist stylistics; Marxist and new historicist contextual studies; source and translation studies; textual and manuscript studies; feminist, psychoanalytic, deconstructive, and queer studies; even postcolonial and cultural critiques of the very institutions of medieval studies. If canonical reception has a determining structure, it is a structure geared to accommodate rather than to resist radical change and variety. Leaving aside, for the moment, the threat to the *teaching* of Chaucer and medieval literature in the university system, the Chaucer research that *is* being done has been able to absorb most of the challenges thrown up by contemporary developments in literary and critical theory. After all, it is in the interests of both conservative and radical readers to maintain a structure that licenses such interpretive variety and that celebrates such plurality.

These competing perspectives have never been regarded as an embarrassment; rather, the diversity of interpretations of particular works and our constant modifications of our idea or image of Chaucer are widely celebrated as signs of his inexhaustible richness and as support for his claims to remain at the chronological head of the canon of English literature.[20] Far from exhausting Chaucer or the critical enterprise, the wealth of this tradition seems to guarantee its very future. Other critical histories—Shakespeare's, for example—may rival Chaucer's in volume, but for sheer age and continuity, this is one of the most remarkable sequences in literary criticism, not least because it discloses a full range of late medieval and Renaissance critical responses to early English poetry.

Like many reception histories, however, this story is mostly told from an omniscient perspective of benign disengagement, as if it had no bearing on the current business and crisis of criticism; as if it were a separate story. The practical difficulties of describing the modern wealth and diversity of Chaucer criticism often result in the impression that Chaucer's "reception" stops at a given point and modern (professional) "criticism" takes over. This bifurcation is another marker of the canonical text: a long reception history testifies to the text's heritage value as cultural capital, while a thriving contemporary criticism testifies to its continued relevance and value as object of exchange across a range of cultural fields.

There is also another kind of split between the general and the specialist aspects of Chaucer's reception. These are absolutely crucial to each other, though their relationship is not without contradiction. By far the majority of writing and original research on Chaucer is performed by scholars whose primary institutional identity is that of medievalist and whose work is directed to each other or to students entering the field of medieval studies. Indeed, academic Chaucerians sometimes lament the sheer size and diversity of their own enterprise. Reviewing a cluster of books on Chaucer in 1996, for example, Peter Mack comments: "What Chaucer needs is intelligent popularization and a good television adaptation: what he has got is a thriving sector of an academic industry."[21]

As Steve Ellis has recently demonstrated, however, Chaucer does have an important life in the imagination of poets and other writers outside the academy of specialists,[22] though this life is rarely represented in published commentary. An important and vocal exception is Harold Bloom, who ingenuously describes himself "only as a general critic of literature, and as a common reader of Chaucer."[23]

When Chaucer is read primarily as a canonical author by writers such as Bloom, he is placed at the head of a continuous tradition of English poetry, part of the "natural" literary heritage of the educated classes, to be read with effortless ease. His texts are seen to embody timeless values and perspectives of easy relevance to modernity (witness the sequence of "Tales" in the *Los Angeles Times* describing the "latter day pilgrimage" of Democrat supporters to attend President Clinton's inauguration in 1993).[24] In this model, the qualities, in all senses, of the Chaucerian corpus are self-evident. The Chaucerian text embodies a range of beneficial effects: human wisdom, complexity, and variety; a generalized notion of "tradition"; and, though less often now, a certain notion of Englishness. The "general reader" who consumes this Chaucer is sustained by an informed interest in and love of literature, needing no special training or very specific knowledge of the text to participate in this literary heritage.

As a part of medieval studies, however, Chaucer is subject to a much different kind of scholarly regime, one that is often characterized by its insistence on a discontinuous linguistic and historical past, approachable only through specialist training. Whether that past is seen as culturally, socially, and theologically homogeneous or heterogeneous (and I acknowledge here the complexity of this question), the historical specificity of the medieval past throws doubt on the easy modernity of Chaucer. In this aspect at least, the medieval Chaucer is in direct contradiction to the canonical Chaucer.

These dual dispensations also present Chaucerian language differently. As the source of poetry in English, Chaucer's language is simply a pleasantly archaic version of modern English. As a medieval writer, however, Chaucer's English becomes a philological phenomenon, legible only through a study of Middle English dialects and semantics. The medievalist is trained in, or trains others in, a very specialized form of reading in English.

These two understandings of Chaucer are conceptually quite discrete and speak to separate cultural and educational agendas, which often exist in some tension with each other. In Pierre Bourdieu's terms, the general and the specialist receptions of Chaucer represent the general and restricted fields, respectively, of cultural production.[25] Bourdieu defines the relationship between these fields as one of rivalry over the process of cultural consecration: that is, the bestowal of value on particular instances of art, literature, and intellectual or cultural capital.

The two fields in which Chaucer is reproduced are often brought together, however, by the material considerations of publication. Let me return to the Riverside Chaucer discussed in the introduction, a text that is typical of modern editions in its attempt to bridge, even to exploit, the opposition between these two traditions of reading Chaucer.

The cover illustration of the Canterbury pilgrims clearly signals the "medieval" nature of the text it introduces, but the book also engages our attention as a "classic" production, a text of high culture marketed at the general reader, as well as the student. It is described as "[t]he third edition of the definitive collection of Chaucer's Complete Works," while the "dramatic increase" in Chaucer scholarship is welcomed as enabling scholars, the "team of experts at the Riverside Institute," to "re-create Chaucer's authentic texts." Thus, the Chaucer tradition celebrates itself. In what other sense could Robinson's work still be regarded as "definitive" now that it has gone into a third, completely revised edition? The blurb goes on: "In short, *The Riverside Chaucer* is the fruit of many years' study— the most authentic and exciting edition available of Chaucer's Complete Works." Lest we feel overwhelmed by the weight of the authorities before us, and all their tiresome years' study, the repetition of "authentic" promises an unmediated path of access to Chaucer, while the adjective "exciting" surprises us into a sense of newness. More important, reassurance comes from a different kind of authority, that of the well-informed general reader, a role played here by Anthony Burgess, who writes:

> The Riverside Chaucer, like its predecessor and companion the Riverside Shakespeare, is beautiful to look at and a sensuous delight to handle. . . . The linguistic, historical and literary scholarship are a masterpiece of Anglo-American collaboration. The reading of Chaucer is made into an exquisite pleasure not a philological chore. This is the best edition of Chaucer in existence.

Burgess's remarks about the sensuous pleasure of reading this book apply only to the hardback edition that he must have been reviewing— the paperback edition is practical and affordable, but hardly delightful to handle—but the opposition between the direct, pleasurable accessibility of the canonical text and the necessary anxiety of philology could not be revealed more clearly. Tim Machan similarly comments that the bulk of the material in the Riverside edition, its notes, commentary, bibliography, and glossary

proclaim the scholarly thoroughness with which it was pre-
pared and offer the reader . . . many of the requisites for gain-
ing a broadly based historical sense of Chaucer's works. On the
other hand, this same material seems forbiddingly to say,
"Abandon all hope, ye who enter here," since if this material is
necessary for the modern reader to understand and appreciate
Chaucer, then Chaucer by implication is very far indeed from
the modern reader and the modern world.[26]

Similarly, Burgess's concession that reading Chaucer might other-
wise be "a philological chore" opens up an enormous gap between the
work that scholars do and the pleasure experienced by the general reader.
The Riverside reader is absolved from all that specialist training and is
invited simply to listen, to speak, to be with Chaucer, as if Chaucer schol-
arship—and Chaucer scholars—were irrelevant to the personal, imme-
diate pleasure of consuming the text. The scholar or student, on the other
hand, is reassured that this will be the standard, quotable text of Chau-
cer, obviating the need to mess around with manuscripts and variants.

Responding to the very authority of the texts presented in this edi-
tion, it is fashionable now among Chaucer scholars to express their dis-
satisfaction with the Riverside Chaucer and similar editions that insist
on presenting a text that is so very clean, whose spelling and punctua-
tion are so firmly modernized, and that effaces so effectively the manu-
script marginalia and all the traces of its editors' passing. Manuscript
specialists are not content with this compromise between the two dis-
pensations, and calls are increasingly being heard for editions that fore-
ground the textual uncertainty that has historically constituted and
produced Chaucer's work. Proposals are heard for unedited transcrip-
tions of variant manuscripts, for separately bound fragments of the *Can-
terbury Tales*,[27] or even the "Chaucer box" advocated by Russell Potter,
whereby Chaucer's separately bound tales *and* other works could be as-
sembled by the reader "in whatever order seemed to her meaningful or
significant."[28] For Ralph Hanna III, too, the very convenience of the sin-
gle-volume edition of *The Works* of Chaucer "addresses a professional
necessity which is ours and neither the author's nor scribes'."[29]

Such critiques foreground the genuine disjunction between this
specialist audience and the more popular or general readership of Chau-
cer. As most of these scholars concede, to represent Chaucer's text in

these historically purer forms would price them out of the reach of stu-
dents and would alienate the general reader unconcerned with the tex-
tual scruples of the professional Chaucerian. Conversely, Helen Cooper
remarks on the choice of the roundel from the *Parliament of Fowls* as one
of the hundred "Poems on the Underground" in London: "It is one of
the ironies of the history of editing Chaucer that his most widely dis-
seminated poem should be a conjectural reconstruction of a stanza
never known in any form to most of his medieval readers."[30] In all like-
lihood, fully digitized and hypertext editions such as those produced by
The Canterbury Tales Project under the direction of Peter Robinson and
N. F. Blake, which can incorporate multiple variants, glosses, and anno-
tations, will remain the province of specialists with the confidence to ne-
gotiate the dizzying range of possibilities newly on offer.[31] Even though
digital technology may make such a text feasible, the authoritative struc-
tures of scholarly tradition and the desire for authenticity will not be dis-
solved so quickly.[32] Indeed, in a report in the *Times Higher Education
Supplement* on the digitized Chaucer, Tony Durham and the subeditor
are most excited about the possibility of authenticity, not textual frag-
mentation and uncertainty. The article is headed "Traces on Vellum
Offer Clues to the Definitive Chaucerian Text," while Durham draws at-
tention to "the exciting possibility that we possess a text that Chaucer
himself could have seen."[33]

Many of these proposals for different kinds of texts, however, do in-
dicate a crucial concession on the part of professional Chaucerians,
who now seem willing to make it more difficult to read Chaucer, to hear
Chaucer's voice. This is a dramatic departure from the textual tradi-
tions prevailing until recently, which have aimed to transcend the his-
torical distance between Chaucer's voice and our own. There is no
doubt that editions that disperse the authorial voice into its variants and
annotations make it much harder to cherish the illusion of hearing that
voice directly.[34]

Scholarly willingness to let go of the fiction of Chaucerian voice at
this very significant point—where students and other readers are first
introduced to Chaucer—may be the clearest indication yet of the clo-
sure, if not the final end, of the regime of authorial presence.

The Chaucer Tradition

I love to call him old Chaucer. The farther I can throw him back into the past, the dearer he grows; so sweet is it to mark how his plainness and sincerity outlive all changes of the outward world.

James Russell Lowell, *Conversations on Some of the Old Poets*, 1845

It is a measure of the radical changes in the decorum of literary criticism over the last century that I can quote James Russell Lowell's affectionate veneration of Chaucer in a spirit of amused condescension, confident that my readers will respond in a similar way. It is because Lowell's founding premises seem so alien, so historically distant from my own, and because I want to examine such undiluted expressions of affection toward Chaucer that I can quote him at all, to introduce this discussion of Chaucerian scholarly tradition. And yet there are enough similarities between Lowell's discussion of Chaucer in this brief quotation and my invocation of Lowell to trouble the intended irony of this citation. For even though we make opposite points—for him, Chaucer remains stable beyond "all changes of the outward world," while for me, Lowell typifies those very changes—I have enacted the same distancing effect on a writer from the past. By quoting his remarks, so evocative of an earlier, more informal discourse of literary criticism than my own, I have rehearsed the same gesture; only this time it is he, the critic, who is "thrown back into the past." This act of citation exemplifies some of the difficulties and challenges of speaking about Chaucerian reception and the traditions of Chaucer studies in a book so clearly situated in that field.

As we might expect, however, the Chaucer tradition itself provides a path out of this potential impasse, by embracing the very idea of tradition and foregrounding its own history. Chaucer's reception is frequently celebrated as a venerable tradition that is productively superseded by modern criticism. Its exponents and practitioners can thus claim historical mastery over the past five or six hundred years of commentary on Chaucer, without being exhausted by the weight of that commentary, since modern criticism is so clearly distinguished from the work of past generations. Moreover, as with all canonical texts, the tradition itself is a measure of the symbolic and cultural capital long invested in the text. The currency of Chaucer criticism, in this metaphor, is "old money."

Chaucer's reception is frequently charted and documented in encyclopedic style and scale, and its dominant features are lovingly rehearsed and critically analyzed, just as the lives and personalities of its most influential writers themselves often become the subjects of discussion, in all their seriousness or eccentricity. Through the work of the three most important collections of documents, edited by Caroline Spurgeon, J. A. Burrow, and Derek Brewer, respectively, the overall narrative of changing representations and reading of Chaucer has become a familiar one.[35] An attentive reading of these documents shows, however, that critical readings and models of interpretation do not simply succeed one another in gentlemanly fashion, though some versions of tradition would encourage this perception.[36] Rather, particular readings struggle against others to gain acceptance, and we need to read this "tradition" both for what it manifests and also for what it seeks to repress. We might borrow Gerald Bruns's formulation: "In a critical theory of tradition, tradition is not the persistence of the same; on the contrary, it is the disruption of the same by that which cannot be repressed or subsumed into a familiar category."[37] We also need to examine the more practical workings of tradition, especially when it names itself as a means of collecting—or subsuming—its texts.

A single detailed example will suffice here, the collection of essays edited by Paul Ruggiers in 1984, *Editing Chaucer: The Great Tradition.*[38] This volume offers testimony to the work of thirteen editors from Caxton to Robinson, each assessed in relation to one another, given credit for their innovations, or defended for their various deficiencies. Ruggiers's introduction summarizes the claims to fame of each of Chaucer's editors and traces both genealogical and canonical patterns among editors, picking out the heroes and dismissing the renegades. It is a series of glorious father figures and their sometimes less than distinguished offspring: as the first to print Chaucer, Caxton is the "father of the editing of Chaucer"; Thynne is the first to look for new manuscripts; Speght the first concerned with biography, and so on. Important, too, are its exclusions: Pynson and Stow are not real editors in the modern sense, while Urry is the worst. Furnivall is condemned as an enthusiastic *printer* of Chaucer's manuscripts and early editions, rather than being an editor as such.

Like Ruggiers, the contributors to this volume are as much concerned to define the tradition, to police its borders and patrol its territory, as they are to celebrate it: they write very much as modern professionals surveying their ancestral, mostly amateur predecessors. They also write as if the central debates on textual criticism are all but resolved. "Textual criticism of medieval English literature," Ruggiers writes, "is nearing *the end of* a long debate concerning the methodology or methodologies that may be employed in the editing of various kinds of medieval texts," while Root's *Troilus,* Robinson's entire canon, and Manly and Rickert's *Canterbury Tales* "mark *the end of* a long tradition of editing Chaucer" (my emphases).[39] This optimistic view is surely not unrelated to Ruggiers's position as general editor of the variorum edition of Chaucer, a project that is mentioned only briefly in this volume but that in effect makes it possible, since it marks the closure of this tradition, summarizing and encapsulating its various conclusions. But if that tradition *is* at an end, it does not follow that there now exists perfect consensus over how Chaucer should be edited. As we have already seen, in the fifteen or so years since Ruggiers edited this collection, there has been increasing dissatisfaction among contemporary Chaucerians with this very tradition and its most visible achievement in the standard modern editions of Chaucer.

Editing Chaucer also has an important humanizing function: in Ruggiers's words, "here we can pay tribute to the devotion, the practicality, the general good sense of those editors who have made their contributions to what we know today."[40] For example, George Reinecke explains the slow production of Robinson's famous edition partly in terms of the more leisurely, gentlemanly pace of scholarship in the early decades of the century, but also in terms of Robinson's character and his personal financial security. Comparing him with the more austere Kittredge, Reinecke comments: "He modeled himself less on Wotan and more on Geoffrey Chaucer. 'Robbie' or 'Uncle Fritz,' as he was called, was gregarious, decorously jolly, and avuncular. Short and solid of build, he enjoyed the atmosphere of Boston clubs and of resort hotels in summer, scholarly conversations with the learned and *thé-dansants* at the Copley with his nieces and their friends."[41]

Such eagerness to "model oneself on Chaucer," even bodily, is a recurrent theme among many of his commentators and editors. Reinecke's insistence on the *human* qualities of his subject—an odd mixture of the textual and the biographical—seems designed to counter the popular image of the editor, and perhaps especially the medievalist editor, as dry, scholarly, and ill at ease with any outside that field.

Editing Chaucer attempts to rationalize the variety of textual practices and the editorial uncertainties of Chaucer's representation and reproduction. The errors of the past can easily be assimilated as necessary steps in the formation of a single, canonical "Great Tradition," a phrase that seeks to glorify philological and textual inquiry, but that employs a metaphor that was long ago discredited in literary studies for its hegemonic linearity and exclusivity. Here, it has the effect of smoothing out the very real differences and contention among Chaucer's editors and the very different material and social contexts in which they worked. The concept of editorial tradition actually has the effect of insulating editorial history from critical theory: questions and issues that might seem to belong to literary criticism find little quarter in this collection, doing little to further the dialogue between those two fields. In this regard, the volume is typical of many celebrations of Chaucerian reception, insisting on continuity across a hotly contested field.

The idea of tradition remains very attractive, bridging the historical distance between medieval and modern: an effective cure for the alterity of the Middle Ages. To undermine the totalizing grandeur of a tradition in Chaucer studies, it will be necessary to reread some of these editions and commentaries rather more symptomatically, but also to interrogate the relationship between these two foundational but contradictory ideas in medieval studies: tradition and alterity.

Critical insistence on the difference between medieval and modern has often been diverted into an insistence on the irrelevance of the modern to the medieval. The habit of attributing authority and Otherness to the past has been crucial in the formation of medieval studies as a discipline and to the attempts of many medievalists to produce an objective authority in their own writing, freed from the distractions of modernity and postmodernity. In this style of historicism it is argued that the past is forever lost to us, that we can only gaze from an alien present and do our best to learn about that world. It is a version of the idealism that has dogged medieval studies, too ready to disallow political and modernist criticism as irrelevant and dispensable, too unwilling to consider its own speaking positions or its own methodologies. Or indeed, its own structures of authority.

Lee Patterson has shown how the imaginary unity of this self-contained, self-knowing, and inaccessible past has had formative implications for the institutional and pedagogical structures under which medievalists continue to labor. Patterson argues that "the sense of the Middle Ages as other confers upon the medievalist an unquestionably professional self-definition." By insisting on the special priority of philology and the associated sciences of paleography, manuscript study, and so forth, the medievalist is professionally prepared not by being educated but by being "trained," and the professional structure of medieval studies remains, as a consequence, remarkably hierarchical. Medieval studies is a "clerisy," and the more difficult it is to access its central mysteries, the more authority is invested in high priests.[42]

Patterson's characterization of the profession as a clerisy (especially in its formative decades at the beginning of this century) is telling, in both positive and negative ways. Positive in that he shows how hierarchic are the structures of medieval studies, but negative in that the very masculinity of a "clerisy," the relation between maleness and authority, goes unremarked and, thus, reinforced. Medieval studies authenticates itself as a mimetic discipline, whose principal business is to forget the present and reconstruct the past.

Louise O. Fradenburg challenges the force of this concept of alterity, through a feminism critical at every stage of the writing of literary history:

> The "past" continues to have authority for Chaucerians as that which knows itself fully and whose knowledge, though inaccessible, must be recovered. One of the most important theoretical contributions feminist theory can make to the project of historical understanding is analysis of the construction of authority in the practice and theory of historical knowledge. . . . From the standpoint of feminist theory, the notion that the Middle Ages was fully present to itself is as problematic as is the notion that we need to reconstruct such a fullness of self-understanding, or the notion—for that matter—that the "past" is indeed over, that "past" and "present" can be distinguished with absolute conviction.[43]

In another essay, Fradenburg shows how this insistence on the authority of the past is necessarily blind to social or political critique:

examining the critical reception of the anti-Semitic attitudes of the Prioress, she condemns those historicist studies which carefully explain that because anti-Semitism was part of the medieval orthodoxy of the saved and the damned, the Prioress can hardly be read as guilty by modern standards.[44] Fradenburg's objection is grounded in an ethical concern to develop what she describes as "a politically more compassionate medievalism." Her deconstruction of that opposition between past and present, as well as her critique of the past's ideal self-presence, is a liberating and enabling development for my own work, which situates itself as part of this project of reexamining "the construction of authority in the practice and theory of historical knowledge."

Christine Froula makes a similar point when defending the study of the canon against a gynocritical insistence that women's writing should replace the old canons. She argues that the basic structures, the economies of literary production, should be the object of examination. Since we cannot escape from reading what Froula calls the patriarchal archetext, we must continue to use canonical texts to interrogate and undo the cultural economy inscribed within them.[45] There must be a way of reading the archetext of Chaucer, his reception, and accounts of that reception in ways attentive to its rhythms and social meanings, but without necessarily replicating the structure of canonicity or the authority of a homogeneous past. Or, indeed, without obeying a knee-jerk response to the politics of Chaucer's life and works. Refusing to read the *Prioress's Tale* because we object to anti-Semitism or refusing to read Chaucer at all because we object to rape[46] or because we reject the canonical emphasis on white male representatives of the dominant culture does not take our understanding of these social forces or the nature of our own responses very far. On the surface, such moves might seem to confirm an enlightenment view of education and cultural progress, yet a consciousness that renders "Chaucer," or any text, unreadable is closer to repression than to either enlightenment or critique. Just as the methodologies of cultural studies focus on a wide range of social and cultural forms— not all of them socially edifying ones—so too there must be a place for the cultural analysis and critique of the historical forms of the past.

Given these pressures, it often seems as though the negotiations involved in reading canonical authors have become just about impossible. If we come to Chaucer inspired by the desire to hear the author's voice or the play of authorial voices—and both desires are an important fea-

ture of the canonical text and its pleasures, regardless of our profes-
sional skepticism—we must first encounter the readers of the past,
must negotiate the wealth of commentary, editorial tradition, and insti-
tutional mediation, as well as the various attempts by other readers to
hear, and sometimes speak, themselves in a Chaucerian voice. The long
history of Chaucer's reception is not merely an important archive. It is
an integral part of what we now call "the Chaucer effect"—our collective
and cumulative readings of his voice, style, and personality, and the cul-
tural formation and institutional force of "Chaucer."[47] Centuries of read-
ers have welcomed the feelings of empathy and identification conjured
up by inserting themselves into a tradition of Chaucerian reading, see-
ing themselves as Chaucer or as other readers and lovers of Chaucer.
But Chaucer scholars in a postmodern context tend to feel awkwardly
complicit with this tradition, anxiously desiring to effect a form of sepa-
ration with the Chaucerians of the past, while still maintaining a com-
plex form of relationship with "Chaucer." The relationship with other
Chaucerians is, if anything, even more fraught. Resisting identification
with the traditional image of the Chaucerian, they nevertheless depend
on other Chaucerians for an audience. Caught up in a competitive pro-
fessional environment, they embrace the idea of community.

VOICE AND COMMUNITY

The differences between the Chaucers discovered by his various readers
over the centuries can never be fully grounded in a historical point of
origin, since author and manuscripts are always already crisscrossed
with traces of other author functions. Nor can they be fully totalized by
any agency outside that history, by the critic, or by the literary historian.
The "Chaucer effect" is not the glorious culmination of continuous and
harmonious tradition; rather, it is a negatively structured phenomenon
produced by the changing and rival discourses of Chaucer criticism,
from which none of us is immune. It is preeminently an effect of voice,
an especially powerful concept when it comes to transcending the lin-
guistic difference that constantly threatens to alienate the modern
reader from the medieval poet. Articulated in the sixteenth century and
foregrounded in the eighteenth, Chaucer's linguistic inaccessibility
turns out, not surprisingly, to be an influential, if sometimes disabling,

determinant on subsequent criticism. But a more personal conception of poetic voice, implying the possibility of hearing Chaucer speak across the centuries and across different cultures, becomes an inclusive and enabling trope that allows us to contain and restrict difference, to foreclose the drift of meaning and significance across the centuries. If Chaucer can still "speak" to us, it means moreover that modernist and postmodernist criticism have not fractured his voice beyond recognition.

The question of voice has long dominated Chaucer criticism, though it takes many different forms, some more self-conscious than others. From the earliest scribal and editorial practices of "completing" unfinished or incomplete Canterbury tales or links to the more spiritual "infusion sweete" by which Spenser claims to inherit Chaucer's poetic spirit or to Dryden's appropriation of a "congenial soul," preprofessional Chaucerians, especially in the nineteenth century, find many ways of hearing and speaking in Chaucerian voices. And as a critical issue, the question of voice persists well into the twentieth century, in the "dramatic" readings of the Tales propounded by George Lyman Kittredge and R. M. Lumiansky and in E. T. Donaldson's dissection of the voices and personae that allow us to diagnose his irony.[48] Even H. Marshall Leicester's deconstructions of the illusion of voice testify to its continued appeal.[49] In more practical terms, the inculcation of a correct Chaucerian accent in the classroom has powerful ramifications for pedagogy and assessment.

The desire for direct communication with the poet is rarely expressed overtly in contemporary criticism. It is generally displaced onto the desire to become the best reader of the work or author in question. In this way a community of readers is formed through a doubled sense of rivalry and solidarity among the members of that community, sanctioning some and restricting other versions of Chaucerian voice. As Bourdieu comments, "No one has ever completely extracted all the implications of the fact that the writer, the artist, or even the scientist writes not only for a public, but for a public of equals who are also competitors. Few people depend, as much as artists and intellectuals do, for their self image upon the image others, and particularly other writers and artists, have of them."[50]

What we judge, still, when we judge the work of other Chaucerians is predominantly the persuasive force of their understanding of, their speaking with, Chaucer in ways that are sanctioned by the institution.

Or to put it another way, their performance of Chaucerianness. The ramifications can be immense and very direct, as the recent controversy over *Speculum's* reviewing practices implies.[51] In another instance, I once heard a senior medievalist on an appointment committee describe an applicant's postmodernist reading of *Sir Gawain and the Green Knight:* "It's very clever," she said, "but it's not the *Gawain* I know." Anecdotal evidence, admittedly, but no less revealing for its informality and its very material consequences. (Besides, as I argue throughout this book, it's in the marginal and the anecdotal that we can best examine the telling boundaries of professional and personal identity.) The younger scholar had been caught out in a kind of misrecognition of the medieval icon that might have been instrumental in the success or failure of a job application, in whether or not the candidate was welcomed into the academic community.[52]

In spite of, or perhaps because of, the great diversity in its practices, Chaucer studies often appeals to the idea of community as a means of linking different groups of readers over different centuries and countries by a shared love of the same poet, prized for his general humanity and humane wisdom, and also for his aesthetic value as canonical artist. The Chaucerian community typically models itself on the very diversity of character types on the Canterbury pilgrimage. Its disparate assembly of characters, occupations, class, and gender is frequently invoked as the sign of all that is most appealing and most general about Chaucer's writing, factors that link it to the modern critical enterprise. This particular pilgrimage also seems to reconcile, or at least to contain, both secular and spiritual concerns, and in this regard, too, it flatters its modern readers. Two examples will suffice.

The preeminent journal in the field and the showpiece of the New Chaucer Society, *Studies in the Age of Chaucer,* includes as its regular frontispiece a woodcut from Caxton's second edition of *The Canterbury Tales:* the pilgrims seated around a circular table, engaged in convivial social intercourse. As frontispiece, the woodcut has a double reference as both an image from Chaucer's history and a model for his present reception.

Or again, the editorial statement of *Exemplaria: A Journal of Theory in Medieval and Renaissance Studies* takes its motto from the narrator's account of the pilgrims' responses to the *Miller's Tale:* "'diverse folk diversely they seyde,' is the watchword, we think, of a vital and productive critical community." The community of medievalists and other scholars finds a guarantee of authenticity through its origins in Chaucer's own writing, another form of the invocation of Chaucerian voice.[53] We make ourselves part of a company of honorary Chaucerians, a welcoming group that is as tolerant of difference as it is united by attention to the work of one man. It is as if Chaucer had invited us to accompany the Canterbury pilgrims and join in that communal enterprise; indeed, as if criticism might legitimately compete with storytelling in the Host's competition. What better way to imply that Chaucer himself might have sanctioned our own critical and theoretical work, in all its diversity?

The idea of community is a complex and contradictory one, however. John Guillory, for example, criticizes the frequent invocation of community in contemporary debates about the literary canon, where it is marked by liberal assumptions about cultural unity or alternatively, by an uncritical, apolitical pluralism.[54] In his reading, the university is frequently misrecognized as a community by what he calls "the pedagogic imaginary" and its idealizing projections. It is better described as a form of "association," the more characteristic mode of modern and postmodern social organization.[55] There are great differences, after all, between the form of communal traveling represented by a medieval pilgrimage and an international group of scholars working in the same section of a highly abstracted discipline. Is the analogy really sustainable between, say, the rivalry of Miller and Reeve and the critical opposition of materialist and exegetical readings of Chaucer's poetry, or the professional competition among professors, lecturers, and students for the material and symbolic rewards of an academic career?

Writing more specifically of Chaucerian scholarship, Fradenburg argues that projecting a community of readers provides a subtle form of consolation for lost authorial presence: a form of criticism as melancholia. She suggests that "the seeking of community in the form of undifferentiated unions or of unions predicated on identity can never be anything other than a defense against loss."[56] Fradenburg introduces an important psychological dimension to the community's imaginings, which helps us to work our way through its contradictions.

More recently, James Simpson contends that the apparently liberal ideologies of textual or interpretive communities can sometimes be played out in rather more tyrannical form. Commenting on the work of Stanley Fish and Richard Rorty, he comments, "Fish and Rorty's textual communities are cozy and sensible places; the use of the word 'community' is itself designed, as it usually is, I think, to suggest their warmth subliminally."[57] By way of contrast, Simpson shows, in his reading of *The Legend of Good Women*, that Chaucer himself was fully aware how restrictive textual communities could be. Simpson is increasingly interested in reviving a version of intentionalism in our reading of Chaucer, but his implicit concern with the politics of this issue is germane to my own interests here.

When modern Chaucerians appeal to the ideal of a community, it is a complex act of cultural recuperation that may say as much about the desire to reach back into premodern or early modern social formations as any attempt to describe accurately the forms in which they actually correspond with or communicate with other Chaucerians, forms that are more often marked by competitiveness and rivalry or disagreement and misunderstanding.[58] Indeed, appeals to "community" may serve to disguise the very material differences between their own and the medieval poet's enterprise. Let us consider some of these appeals to Chaucerian community or union.

The most obvious form is the nostalgic projection that places Chaucer's modern readers in an intimate relationship with him, often a form of spiritual communion. Its dual historical origins are, first, the personal memories and recollections of Chaucer's friends and direct poetic successors in the fourteenth and fifteenth centuries. The invitation in *Troilus and Criseyde* to "moral Gower and philosophical Strode" to correct and, by implication, to supplement the text is taken up enthusiastically, if indirectly, by many Chaucerians. Second, the humanist practice of private, writerly communion with the writers of the past so favored by Petrarch and Machiavelli, among others, provides another powerful model for reading and writing. Its customary site is a private study or the reading of a specific book. Favored by poets, it also represents the secret desire of many critics to speak with and hear Chaucer directly; the desire, as Stephen Greenblatt famously describes it, to speak with the dead.[59] This has become a kind of unofficial, almost illicit pleasure, something we might invoke in the classroom or among our friends, but rarely in print.

More common is the projection of an affectionate community that accepts Chaucer's absence but substitutes for that absence with carefully fostered bonds between other members of that reading community, the other Chaucerians. The earliest example is the circulation of Chaucer manuscripts and printed texts among small circles of friends and intimates who consolidate their relationship with each other through their knowledge and "love" of Chaucer. This quickly extends to the possibility of imagining other, similar groups as the potential audience for published scholarship on Chaucer: a version of Benedict Anderson's "imagined community."

In his account of modern nationhood, Anderson stresses the role of print in enabling members of these communities to imagine one another in the absence of face-to-face communication: "in the minds of each lives the image of their communion."[60] This is, I suggest, the model of community that lies unconsciously behind much published Chaucerian discourse. From around the end of the sixteenth century, Chaucer's readers sense their increasing distance from the modes of direct communication and authorial presence enjoyed by Chaucer's own friends and first audiences. By way of compensation, writers and commentators on Chaucer are soon enabled to "imagine" their audience in Anderson's sense. Chaucer gradually becomes an author whose work is circulated in editions designed for an audience of strangers, but strangers who can be addressed as friends. Anderson links the development of the national community closely to the development of print capitalism in the sixteenth century. This is a powerful originary moment for the Chaucerian community, which, in its first manifestations, can also be seen as an instrumental form of imagining "Englishness." Chaucer is "made" as a modern author by one of the most important means—printing technology—by which the abstract community displaces the more intimate forms characteristic of feudal society.[61]

Work on Chaucer is still primarily addressed, not to a known audience of friends, but to an unknown, powerfully imagined audience of Chaucer readers and scholars who increasingly depend on each other to shore up their sense of professional identity in an academy under threat. In any given university department, after all, it will be unusual to find more than one "Chaucerian," while in my own country, Australia, the nearest might be hundreds of kilometers away.

This has been the dominant, unself-conscious mode of imagining the Chaucer community until quite recently. As the media of Chaucerian communication change, however, from books and journal articles to the more abstracted and interactive forms of the electronic conference, the Internet discussion group, and digitized hypertext, Chaucer studies are now disseminated in ways that make it harder to replicate the shared experience of reading the same books, producing a more dispersed sense of readership. Furthermore, there is now so much published on Chaucer that we can no longer assume we have all read the same, or each other's, criticism, and this is a potential source of considerable anxiety.

Since the 1980s, many Chaucerians have commented, sometimes with despair, on the increasing amount of Chaucer criticism being published. Typical is Florence Ridley, wondering why "the mountain of commentary" grows "alarmingly" larger every year.[62] A rather more apocalyptic vision is suggested by Leicester's summing up of the current state of Chaucer criticism in 1997. Early in this paper Leicester remarks, not entirely without hysteria, "We *know* we have more text than we can handle better than we did even a few years ago because our category system distinguishes and multiplies more *kinds* of texts, and, better or worse still, because more of us know more theory and know it better, we know that what we have more of isn't just quantity of text but the nature of text, even in little bits." He concludes the essay more positively with a self-correcting ethical imperative: "[M]y original formulation, 'confronting more text than you can handle,' is wrong, because, although you can't be *done* with text and textuality, the one thing you not only must but *can* do is handle it."[63] For others, the problem is not so much quantity but quality: reviewing a cluster of recent books on Chaucer, Peter Mack draws attention to the publishing imperatives of professionalism: "Everyone needs to write a 'major book,' and no one is willing to acknowledge how rare such books are or how long they take to write. It is irritating to have to struggle through inflated and rebarbative books in order to 'keep up' with an author who is so clear, so learned and experienced, and so adept at deflating the pretensions of the intellect."[64]

At the same time, the scholar who is purely a medievalist or a Chaucerian is less common: people who write on Chaucer are increasingly likely to be writing or teaching in other areas of literary or cultural studies as well. As a result, the community becomes dispersed, less concentrated, becomes, in fact, the form of association that Guillory describes. Simultaneously with this transformation in the media of Chaucerianism, the possibilities of easy identification with the medieval author recede.

Yet the long-established patterns of describing ourselves as "Chaucerians," as members of his community, are hard to relinquish, as is the pleasure we customarily find in our readings—and, importantly, our teaching—of Chaucerian texts that seem to produce that feeling of affinity, of love and knowledge of the poet. This is one of the governing contradictions we experience when we try to reconcile our relation to the tradition that grants us our professional identity with the social, cultural, and material challenges to that tradition we experience on a day-to-day basis. The skepticism we feel, however, does at least allow us to consider more critically some of the ideological work done through the assumption of community, however ironically or self-consciously it is invoked.

As a flattering image for a group of embattled professionals, the idea of a community is pleasantly inclusive, embracing difference and contention. Its ideological appeal is extensive, unlimited by gender, race, nationality, or colonialism; it implies a continuity that stretches into the notion of tradition we considered earlier, effacing its own historicity and the "loss" of which Fradenburg speaks. However, as Chaucerians are well aware, the medieval and early modern communities for which Chaucer wrote and in which he was read were far more exclusive, even elitist, while their critical enterprise in reading the poet's work was radically different from our own. Given the history of the Chaucerian community, it is hard to escape the idea that within the more inclusive communal image, there lurks a far more restricted kind of community, more like a "club" that polices entry on the basis of the applicant's likeness to Chaucer.

The invocation of community often glosses over the facts that the possibilities of identification with Chaucer and with other Chaucerians are deeply gendered and that the transmission of Chaucerian authority is generally patrilineal, while the most overt appeals to spiritual collaboration with the poet (those of Spenser and Dryden, for instance) are almost exclusively clerical and masculine. The ideology of authorial presence is structured around the direct transmission of poetic authority, intimate knowledge of Chaucer's personality, or the even more transcendent possibility of spiritual collaboration. But at a very important level, this transmission is limited to those who are already most like Chaucer in one of the primary cultural divisions, that of gender. In this model, the best reader of Chaucer really is the reader who is most like Chaucer, who identifies most strongly with him, both in terms of voice and, more specifically, in his sexual and social politics. The imagined community of Chaucerians depends heavily on the possibility of such communication and bonding, in forms that are most often expressed as imaginative empathy with Chaucer, but that often mask a more directly homosocial form of identification.[65]

CHAUCER'S FRIENDS: SCOGAN, BUKTON, AND OTHER "SOLID" MEN

We are friends, we react the same way to the matter of love.

R. T. LENAGHAN, "CHAUCER'S *ENVOY TO SCOGAN*"

We now turn to consider Chaucer from the perspective of the late twentieth century, a perspective that allows us to return to Chaucer himself, foregrounding some of the appeals to community in his writings. At the same time, we may offer some critical reflections on contemporary literary criticism as it inadvertently refigures the community of congenial souls for a new age.

While the pilgrim group of *The Canterbury Tales* is often figured as the ideal gender- and class-inclusive Chaucerian community, other Chaucerian texts provide less fictionalized images of an audience that is far more restricted. In the poems addressed to individuals, in particular, we are reminded that Chaucer speaks most familiarly to a male audience of friends and associates, men of social status similar to his own: the mobile middle classes of courtiers and civil servants. The most direct instances of these dynamics are found in some of Chaucer's "Shorter Poems." In these late poems, we find Chaucer confidently addressing particular individuals, providing us with less ambiguous evidence than many of his other works for his most immediate audience. These poems have been privileged as providing a kind of model situation for the reading of Chaucer, our best chance of hearing Chaucer's voice directly, and the fact that these poems are often densely worked and allusive in no way inhibits this reading. On the contrary, there seems to be a direct relation between the poems' difficulty and the pleasure taken by modern critics in describing them as some of Chaucer's most characteristic and most personal work. Lawrence Besserman finds the persona in the poem to Bukton quite close to "Chaucer the man,"[66] while in John Scattergood's formulation, "the more personal and philosophical" of the shorter poems "articulate, often in highly elaborate artistic form, those shared assumptions which separated off the court from what was outside it, refining ideas, feelings, and language, and playing with forms, genres and modes."[67]

Recent studies of Chaucer's audience agree that he wrote, most often, for this coterie audience, "a circle of social equals and near-equals," in the words of Paul Strohm.[68] This is not to deny Chaucer's contacts with members of the aristocracy or the royal court or the importance of his versatile fictions of courtly address in *Troilus and Criseyde* and other poems. In fact, Strohm stresses that "the membership of this group was in constant flux and . . . it played a variable role in his life." Still, he confirms his earlier thesis, which has gained general acceptance, that the main "point of attachment" for Chaucer was "a group of persons in social situations rather comparable to his own—knights and esquires of the household of Richard II or otherwise prominent in court circles (such as Clifford, Clanvowe, Vache, Scogan, and Bukton), together with a handful of lawyers, chancery figures, and other civil servants (including Gower, Strode, and in some qualified respects Usk and later Hoccleve)."[69]

Poems such as *Lenvoy de Chaucer a Scogan, Lenvoy de Chaucer a Bukton,* and *Truth,* with its envoi to Sir Philip de la Vache, seem to confirm that apart from the grander court occasions about which we can only speculate on the basis of his more extensive narrative fictions, Chaucer customarily read or presented his work to members of a group of male professionals whose mobile social background and unstable political prospects were similar to his own. Strohm comments: "Chaucer's realization of himself as a social being occurred primarily within the supple bounds of the king's affinity. Furthermore, the relatively free-wheeling social circumstances of the affinity appear to have encouraged horizontal ties based upon common interest, even at some expense to the vertical ties associated with more hierarchical formations."[70] In this early Chaucerian community, then, we find a challenge to the nostalgic projections of feudal society. The first Chaucerian community seems already to have more than a few traces of the "association," in David Wallace's sense, that is to become the dominant form of modernity.[71]

In recent decades, there has been a general critical agreement that these poems have a special significance for our understanding of Chaucer at his most intimate, or at least most personal. In R. T. Lenaghan's reading, "Bukton and Scogan were men whose standing and careers were like Chaucer's, and the envoys to them, full of ironic raillery, read like exchanges between equals," while the poem to Scogan "reminds [him] that he and Chaucer are friends, alike as literary men and civil servants—two styles of clerk. They are gentlemen. . . . The two poems, then, are joking exchanges between identifiable equals and serve in a sort of pitch pipe function."[72] If the poems function as bonding mecha-

nisms between Chaucer and his friends, many of his modern readers
are keen to wind themselves into the same environment, identifying
themselves with Bukton and Scogan, as Chaucer's best readers.

The variorum editors suggest that men like Bukton, Scogan, and
Vache "represent the most perceptive part of Chaucer's audience, men
whose station, experience, and education qualified them particularly to
understand Chaucerian irony and to appreciate the originality of *The
Canterbury Tales*."[73] In the same vein, John Ganim draws an interesting
contrast between Chaucer's audience and the more sophisticated liter-
ary and artistic culture of Boccaccio's Florence:

> A poet like Chaucer, then, could not count on the cultivated
> public that Boccaccio could claim, but had a more direct con-
> nection to a more popular and fluid literary tradition, and could,
> at the same time, count on *enough intelligent avant-garde readers
> connected with the court* to allow his experiments to succeed with
> those who would appreciate them, and yet not offend those who
> would not notice them. Hence the difference between the radi-
> cally relativist frame of the *Canterbury Tales* and the constant re-
> turn to patrician balance of the *Decameron*. (My emphasis)[74]

Dated around 1393, *Lenvoy de Chaucer a Scogan* complains in an
elaborate conceit that the recent rains are the tears of Venus, weeping in
distress that (Henry) Scogan has given up on Love at Michaelmas,
merely because his mistress ignored his sorrows. For Scogan's heresy,
Chaucer is afraid that Love will take vengeance "On alle hem that ben
hoor and rounde of shap, / That ben so lykly folk in love to spede / Than
shal we for oure labour han no mede." As in the preface to *Sir Thopas,*
and in *The House of Fame,* Chaucer refers to his own bodily plumpness;
in this case, he invites Scogan to participate in the joke. In the next
stanza, Chaucer develops a suggestive double entendre that is usually
interpreted to mean that he no longer writes love poetry to "spede" other
folk in their intrigues, that his "muse" of erotic art sleeps quietly:

> . . . in no rym, dowteles,
> Ne thynke I never of slep to wake my muse,
> That rusteth in my shethe stille in pees.
> While I was yong, I put hir forth in prees;

> But al shal passe that men prose or ryme;
> Take every man hys turn, as for his tyme.
>
> $(37-42)$[75]

But there is also a strong trace of sexual innuendo in these lines. "Shethe" is slang for "vagina," while the association of youth with sexual virility is hardly obscure.[76] Chaucer's "muse" is figured as a metaphorical penis, confirming the link between sexual activity and the writing of love poetry. The poem capitalizes on Chaucer's favorite narrative position, exploited in so many of his early poems as well as the *Troilus:* he is the poet who puts himself out of the sexual race, ostensibly to serve others, but with the important side effect, rarely noted by Chaucer's critics, that he need not compete and therefore will not fail. Sexual anxiety results in disengagement and in this case, the generalizing, rather unpleasant homosocial moral: "Take every man hys turn, as for his time," implying that heterosexual activity (and its object, the female body) is always available, but that men eventually grow out of it, in the same way that love poetry is traditionally seen as the province of the young.

P. M. Kean comments:

> We are *(if we can range ourselves for a moment with Chaucer's orig-inal audience)* at once lured into the comfortable position not only of appreciating our own quick awareness of the force of the conceit, but also our realization that its true significance lies in the inappropriateness of all this cosmic magnificence to Scogan's distressing tendency to "hop alwey behinde" in "the olde daunce," and even, it appears in the next stanza, to forswear it altogether. (My emphasis)[77]

Kean's remarks are absolutely typical of the reception of these poems, in their emphasis on the subtlety of response required and in the invitation to identify ourselves with Chaucer's real audience in a very flattering, even narcissistic manner.[78]

Again, in *Lenvoy de Chaucer a Bukton,* the subject is sexual relations and more precisely Bukton's uncertainty over whether or not to marry. Even if this uncertainty is part of the joke, in the face of Bukton's impending marriage, it is an important aspect of the rhetorical strategy by which Chaucer assumes his audience will share his anxiety about heterosexual relations. Interestingly, Chaucer both quotes from his own fictional creation ("though I highte to expresse / The sorwe and wo that is in mariage, / I dar not writen of it no wikkednesse") and then names her as a text, "The Wyf of Bathe I pray yow that ye rede / Of this matere." According to this text, marriage is a trap, and yet he counsels Bukton to marry. He concludes, "God graunte yow your lyf frely to lede. / In fredam; for ful hard is to be bonde." It is almost as if Chaucer sets the first precedents for quoting Chaucer, defining himself as author among his friends through his own poetry, both directly by quotation and indirectly by reference. "The Wyf of Bathe" is both text and woman to be exchanged among the male coterie, an exemplary instance of the "joly body" of the woman among men. Pearsall remarks astutely, "*The Envoy to Bukton* is not too genial, and its advice to Bukton to avoid the prison of marriage has a bitter edge: it would have given pleasure in an all-male company."[79] This is a less benign reading than that of George Kittredge: "The thing may well have been read at a farewell dinner, amidst the inextinguishable laughter of the blessed bachelors."[80] The variorum editors attempt to recuperate this more affectionate reading: "[O]ne would like to think his bride-to-be also, would have been capable of savoring the delicious irony of such a message on the announcement of their forthcoming marriage."[81] Perhaps this can be heard as an inclusive remark, alert to the possibility of a female audience: I read it, instead, as a denial of the homosocial structures that make the poem possible.

In both envois, the poet and his works have also become objects of exchange among his companions. The *Envoy to Scogan*, after all, includes an envoi proper, in which the poet commends himself to his friend "that knelest at the stremes hed / Of grace," asking for assistance with the king, while the Bukton poem self-consciously quotes "Chaucer." Chaucer is well on his way to becoming an author, once the specter of his death is prefigured in his senescent inability to write the love poetry of youth: he has already "died" that he may be quoted, may become an author. We will explore this phenomenon in more detail in chapter 2.

Both poems base their direct appeals to their readers on the grounds of a shared view of the problem of heterosexual relations. Chaucer's reading community is thus interpellated as homosocial (masculine and male-identified) by virtue of this shared anxiety. Even more dramatically, the rhetorical effect of these poems is mediated through the poetic personality Chaucer has already established for himself, a personality defined in large part by its attitude toward, and conspicuous failure in, heterosexual relations. In both envois, Chaucer either summons up this personality or quotes from poems already in circulation to thicken the narrative exchanges and to cement the social relations enacted by these poems of direct address. As Lenaghan comments, such friendships had the authoritative sanction of Cicero and Aristotle and performed an important social role: "Actual friendships, from the high dignified to the more unbuttoned, would have afforded relief to anyone intellectually hostile to, socially ineligible for, or just temporarily tired of the refined ideals of *love*" (original emphasis; Lenaghan is writing here only of male courtiers). Lenaghan compares the poetry of Deschamps: "[H]is sense of fellowship, almost like a schoolboy's, suggests the lively, sustaining satisfaction among companions."[82] This critical association of Chaucer's friendliness with schoolboy or college affinity will prove a remarkably persistent thread throughout the centuries of Chaucerian reception.[83] John Norton-Smith is also quoted by the variorum editors: "The love affair of Scogan is turned into a poetic equation for Scogan's friendship with Chaucer."[84] Problematic heterosexuality consistently finds consolation in congenial masculine friendships.

Finally, Strohm's remarks are representative of these poems' modern reception as privileged moments of direct Chaucerian communication:

> Whatever their ostensible subjects, these poems can also be appreciated as solidifications and celebrations of the relations that made them possible. As R. T. Lenaghan has said of "Scogan," "The statement of the poem is not, 'Renew my pension,' or 'Don't defy love'; rather, it is something closer to 'We are friends, we react the same way to [the] matter of love.'" Chaucer also, in my estimation, celebrates the high expectations he is able to entertain of these friends as addressees of his poems—expectations of their capacity for mixed perspectives and open forms, their ability to enjoy his abrupt shifts of direction and tone, their willingness to rethink and revise prior interpretations. One has in reading these poems a sense of symbiosis: a sense that Chaucer demands more of these friends and social equals than of his other possible audiences.[85]

The idea that this is a special audience, one that, in George Kane's view, had "grown in literary sophistication along with [Chaucer's] poetry,"[86] is frequently expressed, but it is less often acknowledged that modern readers themselves aspire to replicate this symbiotic relationship with the poet; to fill the shoes, as it were, of this best, most responsive audience. Kean's invitation, quoted earlier, that we should "range ourselves for a moment with Chaucer's original audience" is one example of such a wish. Less overtly, Strohm quotes with approval Lenaghan's "statement" of the poem ("We are friends, we react the same way to the matter of love"),[87] assuming with him that the poem can be made to speak—that *the good reader* can make the poem speak—in this more direct way. Lenaghan's statement has the attractive effect of bypassing the poem's knotty syntax in favor of a phatic affirmation of the bonds between poet and audience, giving the impression that he himself has "heard" this message from Chaucer.[88] The variorum editors also quote this homosocial summary of the poem.[89] How tempting it is for modern academic readers to identify with this original audience, to admire and imitate, in Strohm's words, their "capacity for mixed perspectives and open forms, their ability to enjoy his abrupt shifts of direction and tone, their willingness to rethink and revise prior interpretations."[90] Thus the modern Chaucerian community models itself on Chaucer's first community of readers, described in the most flattering terms.

Such acts of identification clearly have the potential to act as a covert form of exclusion. It can never be claimed openly that the best reader of Chaucer is someone as much like him, or his friends, as possible, since it is a crucial aspect of Chaucer's status as a canonical writer that his appeal be universal, that none be disenfranchised as an appreciative reader for reasons of class or race, let alone gender or sexuality. However, it can be insinuated through a generalized critical method that suggests that the best literary response is that which effaces most distance between author and reader, that the best reader is the one who can best speak in and hear a Chaucerian voice. Empirical facts never stand in the way of such appeals to literary fantasies. The fact that Chaucer's audience was predominantly male, for instance, is not supposed to inhibit modern Chaucerians from participating imaginatively in that primal scene of reception, any more than it has stood in the way of women readers like Kean from issuing such invitations.[91]

This recent emphasis on Chaucer's audience as a group of social equals replaces the earlier image of Chaucer as the highly favored poet in a sophisticated English court culture, an idea steadily debunked over the course of this century.[92] The new model relies heavily, to be sure, on documentary and sociological research, but it also seems to suit a more democratically oriented criticism, permitting easier forms of identification with Chaucer's original audience. Accordingly, we are invited to become Chaucer's friends, as we school ourselves to become his best readers.

Chaucer's friends also played an important role at an earlier stage of the poet's career. Modern accounts of the Cecily de Chaumpaigne case of 1380—in general or introductory accounts of Chaucer's life— often circle around the difficulty of interpreting the documents and the situation at the heart of this controversy. The question is often deemed too difficult to resolve, and commentators move quickly on to the case for the defense. Chaucer, they are happy to report, was able to call on a number of important men, his friends and associates, to defend his good name: Sir William de Beauchamp, chamberlain of the king; Sir John de Clanevowe; Sir William de Neville; Sir John Philipot, grocer and afterward mayor of London; and John Morel, a grocer and possibly Chaucer's neighbor.[93]

In fact, the concrete evidence of this list, its titles and short biographies, seems to provide welcome relief from the difficulties of the circumstances with Cecilia and the question over that phrase *de raptu meo*. Did Chaucer rape Cecily? What might be the implications if he did? What are the other possible interpretations of the phrase? Most accounts follow a very similar narrative. Typically, the scholar makes due acknowledgment of the difficulties in judging such a case but repeats the fact of Chaucer's legal innocence and supports it with the list of his friends and their high standing.[94] Kane cites the "standing" of the witnesses as "intended to imply that there was nothing to hide, nothing *deeply* discreditable in question" (my emphasis).[95] Brewer's conclusion in 1984 is also typical:

> All we can say is that whatever *tangled* story lies behind this *curious* document it impeded neither Chaucer's career nor the regard of his *friends*. The names of witnesses and *friends* of Chaucer appearing in the document are those of *distinguished* men. . . . These were all men of the "king's party" at court . . . and . . . give an *excellent* cross-section of the *friends* who made up Chaucer's more intimate circle of acquaintances—*solid* men, courtiers, merchants, men of *learning*, all closely associated. (My emphasis)[96]

At one semantic pole is the murky feminine world of sexuality; at the other, the clear, respectable, and public world of civic masculinity. Brewer modified his remarks when revising his introduction to Chaucer fourteen years later, but revealingly titled the new section, "Chaucer's Release from Accusation of Rape: His Friends" and makes a different kind of apology, concluding, "The incident may also suggest the powerful passions which surged within this remarkable man who seems normally to have maintained a genially self-deprecatory unaggressive appearance, and whose poetry, though often satirical, is so free from personal anger."[97] In thus accounting for sexual violence from a man "normally" so genial, Brewer claims the superior knowledge of an intimate friend, as well as normalizing a model of masculine passion and anger that must inevitably find release, *especially* when the man appears so gentle and passive. It is one of the most threatening passages in Chaucer criticism I have ever come across, and suggests an unusual, darker aspect to the "congeniality" so celebrated in Chaucer studies.[98]

In avoiding the implications of this troublesome document, moreover, it seems that modern Chaucerians are actually replicating a medieval response. Describing his recent discovery of a memorandum recording the release in the Court of King's Bench, dated three days after the better-known Chancery release, Christopher Cannon shows that Chaucer's contemporaries found the phrase *de raptu meo* "just as inflammatory . . . as it has seemed to its more modern readers." The word itself and any mention of rape have been "retracted" from the second memorandum. "In . . . carefully removing from its language any of the connotations that might attach to the noun *raptus* the memorandum acts as a ruler by which the boldness of that word can be measured."[99] As soon as three days after Chaucer is associated with sexual violence, the correction by a friendly clerk takes place.[100] The tradition of amicable or congenial "reading" and rewriting of Chaucer is a very long one indeed. Gavin Douglas famously described Chaucer as "evir . . . all womanis frend"; it seems that Chaucer has long had his own friends.[101]

We can nevertheless mark a kind of closure to this tradition. Cannon reports to Henry Ansgar Kelly that "many readers of his article have come to the mistaken conclusion that he has proved that Chaucer sexually violated Cecily Chaumpain. His actual conclusion is only that Chaumpain released Chaucer from a charge of sexual violation."[102] This trend to accuse Chaucer more directly of rape perhaps represents an attempt to break the magic of identification with Chaucer, but also signifies the persistent frustration with the unresolved ambiguity of the case. Kelly examines a number of similar cases of abduction and concludes by insisting on the opacity of legal documents when it comes to reconstructing the events that brought the litigants to court. "But whether the charge was meant seriously or fictitiously, whether it involved forced sex—in actuality or only as part of a conventional complaint—or only abduction (with or without an explicit or implicit charge of sexual violation) we must be on guard against concluding that she had proved it or could have proved it, or that it is likely to have been true."[103]

The notion of Chaucer's ideal readership, and the ideals of masculine friendship or affinity it implies, is particularly powerful because it resonates both with those who would reconstruct historically accurate reading practices and with those who would seek the transhistorical understanding of, even spiritual communication with, a dead author. To use a critical shorthand familiar to medievalists, I mean the "quarrel" between the Robertsonians and the Donaldsonians. A perspective drawn from feminist theory and gender politics helps us to break down the customary opposition between the historicists and the formalists, since both these approaches subtly appeal to ideal communities of readers who can be seen as masculine-identified, either by replicating a Chaucerian spirit or by insisting that his work be read through the clericist net.[104] Both, after all, encourage us to see the best reader as someone who "reacts the same way" as the author. The corollary argument is that if we do *not* react the same way as Chaucer, we cannot be the true inheritors of his spirit or members of that best, most sophisticated audience of his confreres, the "congenial souls" of the Chaucerian community.

For women readers, the implications of this pattern of identification are crucial, but they are not the only category of readers for whom becoming "Chaucerian" is far from straightforward. However, despite the many cogent challenges to canonical tradition, to the idea of transcendent authorial presence, to the hierarchies of scholarship and criticism, and to the dominance of imperialist, masculinist, heterosexist, and class-based pedagogies, despite many attempts from within and without to "reform" the Chaucerian community, Chaucer studies remain remarkably stable and unchanged. This is not to say that the content of Chaucer criticism has not undergone a profound revolution in the past fifteen or so years, but that the academic and pedagogical structures that sustain Chaucer studies have not been greatly disturbed by those broader movements. One way of focusing discussion around the dominant patterns of Chaucer studies and author studies is to ask whether it is possible to be a Chaucerian without sounding like Chaucer. But perhaps the question is even harder: Why do we want to be Chaucerians at all?

2

SIGNING GEOFFREY CHAUCER

MODELS OF AUTHORSHIP

When the Tapycer had finished his tale, the Haberdasher congratulated him on a worthy effort, and turning to the Host, asked who might be able to better such a wonderful story. Were not the guildsmen acquitting themselves excellently in the storytelling competition? The Host cast his eye over the company, and turned to the Pardoner. "Now, my friend, let us put aside our differences once more. For your fourth and final attempt, tell us something wonderful." "Certainly," replied the Pardoner. "I'll top you all with the tale of a woman who, like myself in a way, made her living by speaking in public, and how she lectured on Chaucer to students at a university in Australia. Her talks would often begin with a fascinating question . . ."

Where does Chaucer begin and end? In one sense, the difference between medieval poet and modern literary critic is stable and absolute: there is no danger of our mistaking one for the other, no likelihood that on the basis of my absurd opening, even without its prosaic anachronisms, I'd be suspected of having discovered and translated a new, complete text of Chaucer's *Canterbury Tales,* in which all the pilgrims tell four stories, as the Host says they must. We habitually regard the *Tales* as unfinished, but we also regard the body of Chaucerian works, the known textual corpus, as finite and closed. These works are closed to us, for example, in a way that inhibits the completions and supplements that proliferated so freely in the early centuries of Chaucer's reception. For all intents and purposes, it is as if the poet's works were signed with an authorial signature as binding and limiting as any invoked under modern copyright law, a signature that renders all other "Chaucerian" writing apocryphal. Everything outside those works—commentary, imitation, criticism of one kind or another—has become secondary, produced by an authorship of less intrinsic interest to Chaucerians than Chaucer's.

The distinction we ordinarily maintain between the medieval text and modern literary criticism has become so naturalized it seems absurd to draw attention to it. Our sense of the Chaucerian text as inviolate, immune from any such gratuitous supplements as my own, is a powerful instance of ontological alterity. Alterity is not simply an epistemological phenomenon, concerned with historical knowledge, though it is often discussed as if it were; it also governs the ontological status of the texts of the past. I have in mind their particular status as closed, finite works, sealed off as historical productions to which their modern readers respond, but do not contribute. That is, the modern commentator's text derives from a quite different order of being from the medieval commentator's or glossator's text. This difference has important material and social ramifications for the institutional distinctions we draw between poet and commentator, for our professional decorum as literary critics, and for the very style in which we write. Under the regime of modernism, the distinction between Chaucerian and non-Chaucerian writing is maintained as an absolute principle, already established as a quasi-scientific truth by the work of philology, before the tasks of criticism, evaluation, and interpretation can begin. Nevertheless, these processes are often circular: deciding which poems and which textual variants are truly Chaucerian necessarily involves evaluation, while in recent years, scribal work has come to be regarded as interesting in its own right as witness to the early reception of medieval literature, or indeed as properly *constituting* medieval writing, not just as a series of impure accretions.

Yet there is also a sense in which Chaucer studies naturalizes my ridiculous parody. Even in modern English prose, the simple facts of the storytelling competition, professional rivalry, and familiar characters are enough to identify this opening as some kind of Chaucerian reprise. It may not look very much like Chaucer, but it clearly belongs to the genre of pseudo-Chaucerian writing, whose long and complex history ranges from the earliest scribal and editorial additions through the additional tales and poems added to the sixteenth-century editions, the eighteenth-

century translations and modernizations, and the more indirect and dis-
placed forms of the modern era. Subsequent chapters will consider a
number of examples of this kind of writing, but I wanted to begin with
this more-than-usually fabricated fragment, to suggest how easy it is to
perform this genre, especially in this self-conscious, self-mocking form.

This kind of writing typically appears in the margins of academic
discourse. Modern Chaucerians often reserve an unofficial space in
prefaces and introductions for these informal, jovial invocations and im-
personations of Chaucer. Here, the authors and editors lower their pro-
fessional masks and speak more informally and casually, in holiday
mode. Similarly, when Chaucerians go to conferences, they can make
jokes about being like Chaucer, confident that the knowing community
of sophisticates will recognize the parameters of the joke. What we re-
press in our formal discourse returns to adorn its margins. But of course
the relationship is not this simple. Don't these fragments indicate a de-
sire to see Chaucer's text as in some sense incomplete or marked by a
more open form of writerly signature than the orthodox understanding
of his texts as closed to modern addition? In their desire to supplement
the Chaucerian text, these acts represent an affectionate refusal of alter-
ity, a refusal to accept the scientific, absolutist split between medieval
text and modern commentary.

For example, Julian Wasserman and Lois Roney open the preface to
their collection, *Sign, Sentence, Discourse,* with a familiar Chaucerian
phrase: "'The thanks so great, the page so short,' as Geoffrey might have
observed. Nevertheless, we wish to attempt to acknowledge some of the
many people who have helped us produce this volume." And here is
Priscilla Martin concluding the preface to her study, *Chaucer's Women,*
by acknowledging that the Wife of Bath has not remained confined to
one chapter, but has "argued her way" throughout the whole book. "In
this I am following my author," she concludes.[1]

Again, Wasserman and Robert Blanch write, in *Chaucer in the Eighties:*

> Whether the 1980s will be as kind to Chaucerians as the 1380s
> were to Chaucer remains to be seen. Whether our own re-
> thinking of our craft, its tools and its presumptions, will take us
> in new and radical directions or confirm the traditional values
> of our "ideal" we cannot as yet say. What we can say is that "di-
> verse scoles maken parfyt clerkes" and that the clerks of the

1980s speak diversely. We can also say, along with Robin the Miller, "God save al the rowte!"[2]

"Chaucerian" here patently means something like humanist diversity, tolerance of difference, as it does for the back-cover blurb of *Exemplaria,* discussed in chapter 1, where it signifies critical pluralism, interpretative rigor, and critical liveliness in medieval studies.

Derek Brewer refers directly to this convention in his preface to his revised *Introduction to Chaucer:*

> It has become something of a *topos* in the Preface to books like this on Chaucer to name a hundred or so persons to whom one is indebted. It is a useful device, cutting out a lot of potential reviewers and in a medieval way invoking a crowd of "compurgators" in one's own defence. . . . Like Chaucer himself, one hopes that "with this swerd shal I sleen envie" (*Astrolabe,* 64), and I would not wish to be guilty of ingratitude.[3]

Brewer's citation of this topos renders it more ironic and self-regarding than most instances, yet it evidently still has enough life to sustain its repetition.

It's very clear, though, that this is a game of the margins, that such easy identifications with the poet are abjured once the serious business of criticism begins. The delight in adapting Chaucer's words to suit one's own purposes or the flirtation with a Chaucerian identity, particularly the Chaucer of the *Canterbury Tales,* are signs of academic play, permissible—we will all understand this harmless pleasure—*outside* the "real" book. It is a form of discourse similarly found on Internet discussions: informal, collegial, and quite different from the published mode of Chaucerian discourse, where this form of prefatory play serves to point up by contrast the absolute seriousness of everything that follows.

Such prefaces are signs that the good scholar is able to step in and out of character; that he or she has a sense of humor, is a worthy member of the congenial community. They are signs, indeed, that academics have personalities, whose expression might otherwise be threatened by the professional decorum of scholarly discourse. These Chaucerian imitations, even in their customarily fractured and parodic forms, are perhaps the most distinctive discourse of the Chaucerian community. A non-Chaucerian readership, after all, would read my epigraph quite differently: worst of all, they might miss its irony and take my imitation seriously! Pseudo-Chaucerian writing reassures the reader that the critic can speak for Chaucer in all the varied and serious acts of criticism, interpretation, and commentary, without losing sight of the presiding personality that makes the whole enterprise possible.

This is not to say that such imitations are a necessary condition of being, or being regarded as a good Chaucerian: they will always represent just a fraction of the discourse on Chaucer. However, I think they are usefully symptomatic of the broader understanding of the critical project as imitation, as the detailed, empathetic response to authorial consciousness I outlined in chapter 1. What better way of indicating one's closeness to one's author than to speak in his voice? With this important acknowledgment: in comparison with the elevated spiritual distillation of Chaucer's voice claimed by Spenser or Dryden, these modern imitations are deliberately fragmented, partial, or parodic, as befits a professional decorum that, when pressed, would disclaim such identifications as merely personal, in contrast to the business of criticism proper.

The recognition of the canonical text is often structured by a comparable complex logic of supplement and completion. Regardless of the historical gap that separates it from the present, the Chaucerian text must be recognized as sufficiently closed, or complete, to license the description and representation of its primary features. In this way, we read the text as if it were effectively "signed," in the sense of closed and finished, by the author. On the other hand, six centuries of critical investment in the spaces around that authorial signature insist that it is, in an important ontological sense, incomplete, or at least open and receptive to the various hermeneutic wills of his readers. If the text were regarded as completely closed, entire unto itself, permanently self-sufficient, there would be no space for commentary, for criticism and interpretative debate, that is, for the critical industry that confirms the text's canonical status and that permits the accumulation of symbolic capital among its commentators.

The signature of the author is a crucial topic for reception studies, of course, but in the case of Chaucer, the complexities are compounded by the fact that "authorship" in the modern sense was only an emergent concept when Chaucer was writing and as the first phases of his written reception got under way. But as I suggested in my first chapter, Chaucer in many senses provides a model for the kind of authorship in English that later writers came to take for granted. Chaucer's authorship is thus intimately implicated with the historical development of that concept *and* its more recent dissolution under postmodernist and poststructuralist thought. It's not only the case that these critiques of authorship can help us read Chaucer; it is also the case, more unusually, that Chaucer's texts can help us read those critiques and the discourse they analyze.

The first section of this chapter sketches out the various historical and theoretical regimes of authorship and the signature that compete for our allegiance when we read the Chaucerian text. The second section will analyze those moments in Chaucer's text where the poet himself registers some kind of closure: the space of the signature, which seems to license the easiest forms of completion and supplement. The third section will zero in on the *Retraction*, that most emphatically closed text which modern criticism tends to rewrite as the most open. Throughout, my attention is directed less to the attributive or legalistic function of the signature, medieval or modern, than to the following question: What is the nature of the Chaucerian signature that seems to enable so many of his readers to sign themselves as "Chaucer," to countersign the works of the poet with their own Chaucerian writing?

WRITING CHAUCER'S AUTHORSHIP

> *A work of art, therefore, is a complete and* closed *form in its uniqueness as a balanced organic whole, while at the same time constituting an* open *product on account of its susceptibility to countless different interpretations which do not impinge on its unadulterable specificity. Hence, every reception of a work of art is both an* interpretation *and a* performance *of it, because in every reception the work takes on a fresh perspective for itself.*

UMBERTO ECO, THE OPEN WORK

Umberto Eco's familiar account of the simultaneously open and closed nature of the artwork can also be read as a useful account of the relations between the canonical text and its infinite richness. His metaphor of reading as performance also hints at the metaphysics of presence: performance permits a kind of impersonation of the author that in turn renders the artwork active again, as it "takes on a fresh perspective for itself." In Chaucer's case, generations of his readers have enacted the most delicate negotiations in making for themselves a space *around* Chaucer while at the same time keeping the space named "Chaucer" inviolate. They speak with, speak for, and speak over the voice of Chaucer as they perform his works, while continuing to cherish the fiction of that voice speaking directly into the present, performing itself, taking on its own "fresh perspectives."

But not all works combine openness and closed form in the same way. Eco draws a distinction between this general openness to interpretation and the more material openness of modernist "unfinished" musical compositions in which performers are given a range of choices in the execution of the score before them, choices concerned with the sequence of passages, duration or intensity of notes, and so forth. Eco contrasts this kind of open text with those produced by the medieval exegetical tradition, texts that posit multiple allegorical senses and whose literal surface thereby becomes an open invitation to interpretation. He quotes from Dante's famous letter to Can Grande in which he outlines the fourfold method for scriptural exegesis, but concludes by describing this kind of openness as strictly limited. While it offers a range of readerly choices, those choices are strictly circumscribed. "What in fact is made available is a range of rigidly preestablished and ordained interpretative solutions, and these never allow the reader to move outside the strict control of the author." For Eco, these two forms of openness, the traditional and the modernist, are distinguished by "a different vision of the world which lies under these different aesthetic experiences."[4]

These two extremes of textuality and the "visions" or aesthetic systems that underpin their production and reception provide two historical and conceptual poles between which it is now my task to place Chaucer's textuality and authorship, and our responses to them. The picture that emerges is a complex one, and I intend to complicate it further by qualifying Eco's characterization of medieval allegorical textuality.

In the traditional understanding of allegory, he is right; the biblical text in particular is open to a wide range of meanings that are nevertheless organized according to a prior understanding of divinely ordained truth and a systematic hermeneutics. A similar point is made by Jesse Gellrich, who argues *against* "that branch of scholarship that sees me-

dieval sign theory as inclining toward, if not prefiguring, modern con-
cerns with arbitrary signs, deferred meaning, postponed ends, and tex-
tual indeterminacy."[5] At the phenomenal, material level, however, of
textual reproduction and commentary, of *writing* (distinguished from
bookishness), the possibilities are far greater. This is certainly the im-
plication of the hierarchy defined by Bonaventura, where writerly func-
tions are distributed among the roles of author, commentator, compiler,
and copyist according to the decreasing degree of originality involved.[6]
This is a writerly system grounded in an ontological hierarchy that in-
sists on the absolute difference between the transcendental authorship
of the divine word and the partial, veiled understanding of its human
commentators. Within the limits of that finite realm of human under-
standing, however, a medieval text can always generate more textuality.
Texts can be lifted out of context and recombined with other texts, can
always accept an additional layer of glossing. Medieval writing need
never stop.[7] As Malcolm Parkes comments,

> A writer organized his work for publication, and if he did not
> do so then a scribe would, for inside many a scribe there lurked
> a compiler struggling to get out. The production of books be-
> came more sophisticated, and the increasing number of books
> and the increasing demand for readily accessible information
> led scholarly librarians to provide yet more bibliographical aids,
> in the form of tables of contents, and *tabulae;* for of the making
> of books there is no end.[8]

Gerald Bruns also describes the way in which texts from a manu-
script culture seem to "invite or require collaboration, amplification, em-
bellishment, illustration to disclose the hidden or the as-yet-unthought-
of." He links this closely with the material form of the manuscript text,
remarking, "[I]n a manuscript culture the text is not reducible to the let-
ter; that is, a text always contains more than it says, or more than what
its letters contain, which is why we are privileged to read between the
lines, and not to read between them only but to write between them as
well, because the text is simply not complete."[9]

It does not take much effort to translate this desire for textuality and
ways of organizing it into the contemporary vocabulary of search en-
gines and Internet access. This desire to "do" things with texts, even if

the core content of the *auctoritates* or sources remain stable, renders medieval textuality not so very different from the musical composition that depends on its performers to give it shape and form or, indeed (to preserve the textual analogy), from the infinite writerly spaces of hypertext and the World Wide Web, where the reader enters the text at the point of the keyboard, simultaneously reading, "writing," and performing the texts that appear on the screen in potentially endless variations. It is this material simultaneity of consumption and production of textuality that I argue medieval and postmodern textual practices have in common.[10] In neither dispensation are "reading" and "writing" so distinct from each other as they are in the case of the texts of modernity, where the reader more straightforwardly consumes an authorially sanctioned product.

At either end of the modern regime of authorship, then, which produces "closed" texts, we find medieval and postmodernist kinds of writing that are far more open. In contrast, the regime of modern "classic" authorship is not conducive to writing. In the most influential critique of modern authorship, Michel Foucault describes the author as "the principle of thrift in the proliferation of meaning," the "functional principle by which, in our culture, one limits, excludes, and chooses; in short, by which one impedes the free circulation, the free manipulation, the free composition, decomposition, and recomposition of fiction."[11] Foucault emphasizes fiction in his account, but we would do no violence to his theory to apply it to the proliferation of medieval textuality in the commentary tradition, a proliferation that is radically curtailed in the regime of authorship.[12]

Recent work in medieval studies has emphasized the distinctive forms of medieval writing and book production and their impact on medieval conceptions of writerly roles and textual production. The studies of Malcolm Parkes on medieval copying practices and of Alistair Minnis on the university commentary tradition are exemplary in this regard.[13] Their work pays attention to scribal incipits and explicits, to commentary-style introductions, to generic references and signals within the text, to the codicological semiotics of medieval book production, and to the active role of the scribe as compiler and anthologist to see what these factors reveal about medieval categories of reading and understanding. These researches make new sense, for example, of the Ellesmere manuscript's description of the *Canterbury Tales* as "compiled by Geffrey Chaucer."[14] Chaucer's texts were produced in a manuscript culture that is still wide open to glossing, extracting, compilation, and commentary.

While this writing culture seems deeply hierarchical in structure, with commentaries and texts deferring to a prior text, this hierarchy is never completely absolute. As Rita Copeland points out, many of these medieval commentary texts, like translations, actually work to displace the text they "serve."[15]

Curiously, some of the ultrahistoricist editorial and publishing proposals mentioned in the first chapter represent a recuperation of a more open textuality that affirms the affinity between medieval and postmodern forms. Following proposals that foreground all the variants and glosses, that open up the accustomed and neat order of tales and links, Chaucer's text would soon come to resemble the fragmented, multiple textual forms and artifacts we associate with postmodernism.

For all practical intents and purposes, though, Chaucer's texts are still read, normatively, as if they were closed, despite the practices of ventriloquism and imitation that adorn the margins of that normative discourse and with which I began this chapter. My chief concern here is the process by which the Chaucerian text *acquires* its alterity, its closure, and its authorial signature in a way that has been so complementary to modernism. The medium of print imposes a definitive form of closure upon medieval works, for example, as they are mechanically reproduced, incorporated into a system of simultaneous, multiple copies, and assimilated into a postmedieval textual climate that learns to privilege named authorship. Even so, determining the open or closed status of Chaucer's text is a complex issue. In the commonsense view, of course, it is closed, since it is marked by Chaucer's authorship *and no other*. Our historical understanding of medieval scholarship and paleography, however, encourages us to see it as open to the medieval writerly practices that characterize its production and first reception. According to the conventions of modern professional criticism, it is closed, to allow the business of commentary and interpretation to proceed. Yet in our informal expressions of affection for Chaucer, his text is still open, in that we still find it congenial to write or speak in Chaucer's voice, albeit with varying degrees of irony. To study these contradictory indications and their history is an important step in undermining the absolute alterity of the medieval text for modern readers and in stressing the historicity of the processes by which we now read Chaucer's texts.

It is time, then, to articulate the changing historical regimes and discourses of authorship that govern the production and the reception of Chaucer's texts before we consider the degree to which Chaucer conceptualized his own texts as open or closed. As I have suggested, however, reading and interpreting the evidence is far from straightforward, now that Chaucer has come to stand as the exemplary instance of a conception of authorship that is barely imaginable by him or his first readers. When we read Chaucer, we read through three sets of historical contexts, each with important ramifications for reading and interpretive practices. At the risk of oversimplifying, let me try to untangle their contradictory relations. For ease of reference, I will name them medieval, modern, and postmodern.

Medieval Paradigms of Authorship

The medieval context of authorship is perhaps the most complex and the one that bears the heaviest burden of methodological self-consciousness for medievalists. Most writing on Chaucer is at least minimally historicist, in that it sets out to identify the medieval understanding of secular writing and authorship in which Chaucer wrote. In the late fourteenth century, however, that understanding was in process of change: we can identify at least three competing models of authorship, or author roles, of relevance to Chaucer. Each can be identified with broader social movements in the transition from early to later medieval social forms. Adopting Raymond Williams's terminology, we can describe them as residual, dominant, and emergent discourses.[16] First, in decline as Chaucer starts to write in English, the socially oriented role of the *poet* performing before a group; second, the more individually oriented role of the *writer* working with the inherited textual tradition, the dominant mode of late medieval textuality; and third, Chaucer's anticipation of an emerging, modern understanding of the professional *author* setting the terms for his own posterity. Each model implies a different and incremental degree of textual closure.

Poet

The social functions of late medieval poetry have their origins in the traditional forms of oral culture, forms barely concerned with poetic personality or ownership of material, forms in which individuality is submerged into the broader, poetic function of transmitting tradition, of telling stories that derive their cultural authority precisely from their *not* being made up. Late-fourteenth-century poetry makes frequent, if ritualized, references to its oral heritage and, indeed, to the circumstances of its own performance in the highly socialized context of medieval court culture. The medieval poet who embraces this function presents himself less as an author and more as a narrator, a transmitter of oral tradition or of political truth, or as the teller of other people's tales. It is often the voice of moral authority, instructing and informing. But it is also the lyric or courtly voice that in its very anonymity or typicality affirms the strength of poetic convention: it is the voice of the many anonymous religious or erotic lyrics and also the perspective of many named authors. In such a context, there is little impediment to supplementation: an unfinished story needs to be completed and it matters little who undertakes the task. Individual voicing here is less important than the telling of the story, its antecedents or consequences. The image of the poet as storyteller and the narrative structures and terms of address associated with this mode persist long after the social dynamics that produce them have been transformed by textual and manuscript culture.

By the late fourteenth century, the role of the poet as entertainer had undergone a number of modifications. Richard Green describes the "shift in fashion from the old minstrel to the new household poet" in the fourteenth century, a shift defined by a "radical change in the relationship between the author and his audience." For Green, late medieval courtly society was "thoroughly conversant with the conventions binding the poet's imaginary world and confident in its role of literary arbiter." Poets performing in this context began to defer to the higher sensibilities of their audience in courtly conventions, for example, or in the "sense of obliqueness" that characterizes much of its love poetry.[17] Poetry, in this sense, participates in the elaborate games of the court, becoming a *social* act that defines new roles for both poet and audience in the transition from the traditional feudal court to the increasingly elaborate bureaucratic and civic administrative structures of the fourteenth century.

Another version of this social role is the narrator or author of the "public poetry," as Anne Middleton defines it, of the Ricardian period.[18] This is best described as an ethical role, a conflation of the traditional truth-telling role of the philosopher-poet of the *Secretum* tradition with the penitential voice associated with late medieval preaching, but combined with a greater sense of political urgency, often linked to political and ecclesiastical reform and freedom of expression.[19] It is a voice that invokes a common, or "middle," voice, the voice of the reasonable man, concerned with the common good.[20] It plays a relatively small part in Chaucer's development as a writer, being more fully exemplified in the writing of Usk, Gower, or Langland, but is certainly a discourse available to him. Judith Ferster reads Chaucer's *Tale of Melibee* as a tale about giving advice that in many respects deconstructs, with a "strong political valence," the ideology of giving advice.[21] If Chaucer does adopt this public voice, it is never in a straightforward way.

In neither of these later developments, however, does the author role exercise a much greater degree of propriety over the material of the telling. An incomplete, unfinished poem or manuscript can easily be completed, supplemented, translated, or annotated to make a fitting volume for courtly presentation or patronage.

Writer

Like much medieval textuality, Chaucer's writing represents the complex relations between oral and textual tradition, combining the twinned interpellations of the courtly or social group *hearing* his poetry with the individual *reading* a copy in manuscript and book form. This second context in which authorship evolves is that of the more textual, bookish culture deriving from medieval scholastic and textual tradition. Our understanding of this tradition and its late medieval vernacular manifestations was enlarged enormously with the publication of Minnis's *Medieval Theory of Authorship*. Minnis shows that the thirteenth century witnessed the development of a new kind of biblical exegesis, "in which the focus had shifted from the divine *auctor* to the human *auctor* of Scripture."[22] Minnis regards the analysis of biblical texts in academic prologues and commentaries, especially that deriving from the Aristotelian distinctions among the four causes of the text, as a species of literary criticism, whose idioms and author roles were often adopted by vernacular writers. He demonstrates how Chaucer adapts the idioms and vocabulary of the *compilator*, that "offshoot of scholastic literary discussion."[23] So Chaucer describes himself in the *Treatise on the Astrolabe* as a "lewd compilator," while the scribal explicit of the Ellesmere manuscript explains that the *Tales* were "compiled" by Geoffrey Chaucer.[24] Of particular interest is Minnis's discussion of the way Chaucer exploits the *compilator's* traditional fidelity to his written sources to defend the veracity of his reporting of the words of his fictional characters on the Canterbury pilgrimage. "In sum, it may be argued that Chaucer treats his fictional characters with the respect that the Latin compilers had reserved for their *auctors*. The 'lewd compilator' has become the compiler of the 'lewd.'"[25] Minnis concludes by contrasting Gower's interest in presenting himself as a modern author, remarking that "Chaucer was fond of assuming self-depreciating literary roles, and the role of compiler would have been particularly congenial to him."[26]

Related to the role of the *compilator* is the role of the vernacular translator, explicated in detail by Copeland, who shows how Gower and Chaucer in their translations both foreground the problem of historical difference and "the question of vernacularity itself" to "advance their own claims to displace their sources."[27] They thus invent a new kind of author role in English, using and adapting the vocabulary of the academic prologues.

In its writerly origins, this is an author role that positively encourages the kind of rewriting, annotation, and supplementation we associate with the fifteenth-century manuscript tradition. This is the context that actively facilitates the composition of "scribal" prologues and links found in many *Canterbury Tales* manuscripts, for instance, in that it foregrounds the supplementary nature of all writing and the openness of texts to recombination and to compilation in different contexts. This is also evident in the dispersal of tales and extracts from tales across a range of manuscript collections and anthologies after about 1450, often with specific aims and audiences in mind, or indeed, in the very distinctive ordering of tales in the Northumberland *Beryn* manuscript to be discussed in chapter 3.[28]

Author

The third medieval context in which "authorship" develops combines both textual and social contexts to create an emergent literary history into which poets can proleptically insert their own posterity and reputation as they anticipate their own reception, and to create, as well, an indissoluble link between text and person. Petrarch, more than Boccaccio, is the presiding spirit here, though Boccaccio is the more enabling model for a vernacular poetics. The minimal condition for this sense of authorship is the possibility that one's name might be linked to one's work, that one might be known *by* one's work. It was an international development that Chaucer was one of the first English poets to embrace, but one that his immediate successors readily took for granted as a speaking position.[29]

Seth Lerer argues persuasively that it is really only after Chaucer's death that this pattern becomes visible in Chaucer's work, as his poetic followers subject themselves to his authority, naming him "as author, as

'laureate,' and as 'father' of English poetry,"[30] using the terms and images of reader response embedded in his own poetry to position themselves as his infantilized, barely competent followers: "As children to the
father, apprentices to the master, or aspirants before the laureate, those
who would read and write after the poet share in the shadows of the secondary." We will return to this problem in the next section.

It is perhaps the greatest indication of the *Gawain*-poet's isolated
provinciality that the possibility of tying his own name securely to his
texts does not arise for him. Langland clearly struggles with the idea of
poetry as an occupation, but Chaucer and Gower are thoroughly interpellated by a patronage system that, if it never actually declares itself in
Chaucer's case as a system that will reward poetry (as opposed to other
forms of service), nevertheless encourages him to name himself in his
writings, to refer to his own works, while also joking modestly about his
own incompetence.

Even though this sense of authorship is "emergent," in Williams's
sense, in the late fourteenth century, it is important to qualify any implied sense of this kind of authorship as a necessary progression toward
the modern sense of authorship as a "real" against which the earlier medieval forms might be measured and found wanting.[31] Conversely, modern "authorship" can be seen as a kind of interruption to a much more
general sense of writing that early medieval and postmodernist texts
share. Gregory Stone interestingly warns against seeing the shift from
anonymity to named authorship as a cultural progression necessarily to
be embraced. He argues that "certain literary texts in the late Middle
Ages *already* ascribed such a negative valuation to this anticipated future
event, *already* saw the Renaissance as a *loss,* as the destruction of a philosophy of anonymity that had been one of the great positive gains of
medieval thinking. These texts have a presentiment of the idea of the Renaissance, and they do not like it."[32]

A simple diachrony is confounded, in any case, by the fact that these
three medieval senses of authorship in later medieval poetry depend on
each other and are rarely easily distinguished, one from another, by a distinctive voice or narratorial position. Questions of genre, for example, or
the dramatic contexts of performance on which all narrative fictions depend clearly cut across these traditions, while Chaucer, more than most
other poets, invokes them for the purposes of experimentation. As in so
many things, Chaucer is an exemplary embodiment of the transitions
and contradictions involved in late medieval understandings of author-

ship. At times, he embraces the role of translator, or "lewd compilator," or the avid reader of the romance tradition; at others, he projects an image of himself at the margins of courtly society; on other occasions, he writes himself into the world of literary fame, engaging in a more complex relationship with models such as Petrarch or Boccaccio, to place himself and his own writerly authority at center stage, to speak of his own career, and to list his own works. Considering the prehistory of the specific forms of authorship produced by print culture, Leah Marcus comments: "[W]e can find precursors in Petrarch's attempts to control the manuscript circulation of his materials, or even in the more equivocal and evanescent stabs at authorial presence made by Geoffrey Chaucer."[33]

This evanescence means that the sense of closure we sometimes find in Chaucer's works and in Chaucer's authorship is just as frequently lacking at moments where we would expect, or hope, to find it. In the next section, I will consider this space of the Chaucerian signature in more detail. In addition to these medieval paradigms, though, which we foreground when we self-consciously seek to historicize Chaucer's poetics, we also necessarily read his authorship through two other postmedieval paradigms: the "commonsense" modern conception of the text as bearer of authorial intention and propriety and the postmodern transfer of such intention onto the readerly activity that constructs the work.

Modern Paradigms of Authorship

The modern paradigm of authorship is most visible in its manifestations in literary history, where Chaucer is named in lists and canons and represented in courses and canons with writers from the centuries that followed the fourteenth. While the third late medieval paradigm sketched here represents the historical origins of this model in English literary history, its later manifestations are of a rather different order, even from the critical discourse of the sixteenth-century editions that I argue, in chapter 4, are so influential for modern Chaucer studies. This is the paradigm that sustains the institutional packaging and marketing of Chaucer, presenting his works before the modern reader as if Chaucer had tied his own name in the same relationship to his works as that of Austen, Blake, or Coleridge, or other writers established more securely in modern or more directly commercial systems of publishing and copyright.

This habit persists in many of our habitual practices in literary stud-ies. It still seems the most natural thing in the world to write sentences that start like this: "In the *Book of the Duchess,* Chaucer explores . . ." But such attributions of authorial expression, however formulaic, still speak to the model that sets the author at the intentional, sentient genesis of the work, the point to which all questions of interpretation and effect are to be referred.[34] This model is especially transparent in all those no-longer-fashionable readings of "Chaucer's personality" as deduced from his poetry, those biographical understandings of the disappointed love that colored his youth, of the deathbed fears that generated his uncon-scionable retractions, and so forth, even the long tradition of interest in Chaucerian biography itself. It is also present, though less obviously, in the persistent organization of medieval literary studies around its cen-tral authors. However skeptical of intentionalism are the readings pro-moted under the "Chaucerian" division of the MLA, for example, they are still predicated on the idea of the author as organizing principle. The complete lack of any comparable fourteenth-century interest in this as-pect of Chaucer's work—exemplified by the absence, in all those refer-ences to Chaucer's public and legal life in the *Life-Records,* to any aspect of his poetic career—throws the subsequent history of this development into sharper relief, reminding us of what we still take for granted in most of our critical paradigms.

It's also this modern emphasis on authorship that allows us to de-velop our elaborate theories of narrative voice and impersonation. Novel-istic readings of *Troilus and Criseyde* or *The Canterbury Tales* that depend on an omniscient author producing fully realized personae or psycho-logical characters who speak as if autobiographically derive from the as-sumption of modern authorship.[35] By the same token, the model of con-sciously ventriloquized voices works to thicken our sense of the author's presence in total control. Thomas J. Garbáty embraces the complexity of the "Chaucerian persona puzzle" in terms that, while no longer fash-ionable, nevertheless express concisely the trail of desire represented by the concept of authorial voice:

> The deeper satisfaction rests in the fact that this study of the narrator "Geffrey Chaucer" somehow increases our perception of the elusive personality of the poet and leads us into continual contact with the reality of the man, more intimately than would the study of his other themes or literary creations. Although the

persona puzzle will never be solved and no interpretation will ever be totally correct, every investigation is *to the good for it brings us into Chaucer's presence.* (My emphasis)[36]

By such quasi-ethical means has the modern paradigm of authorship and its capacity to mediate our historical and ontological distance from the author been naturalized in Chaucer studies. Its origins have been differently located in English, and attributed to different forms of technological or sociocultural change. For Walter Ong, the invention of print and the development of a print culture are instrumental in "a new sense of the ownership of words," and for Lucien Febvre and Henri-Jean Martin, the "profession of author" is born as a direct result of the advent of printing. For Richard Helgerson, though, the development of a self-defined "laureate" literary career, exploited by Spenser, Jonson, and Milton, marks the late sixteenth century as a period in which a new and decisive configuration of author functions was brought into existence in English literature. Leah Marcus dates the "installation of the poet's 'authentic' presence in the body of the book" to the 1630s and 1640s. For Simon During, following Foucault, authority in this sense is contingent on the development of copyright laws in the eighteenth century, when the authorial name signifies property. For others, a full-fledged system of authorship comes into place only with an increased interest in scholarly biography. Peggy Kamuf, for example, accepts Jacques Derrida's suggestion that Rousseau's is the first "modern signature" that "compels fascination for the living author or the life of the signatory. . . . The fascination that compulsively substitutes the narrative of a life for the disjunctions and disruptions of a work found its first or at least its most receptive repository in Rousseau himself."[37]

Whatever we take as the starting point of authorship (and I concede that each of the writers I've just cited is working from a slightly different perspective), the modern, "commonsense" understanding of authorship is customarily an amalgam of all these developments: literary, social, technological, and philosophical. But this understanding has come under sustained critique in literary studies over the past twenty or so years: contemporary suspicion of the institution of authorship and its insistence on intentionalist or expressive literary criticism also colors our reading of Chaucer. So this is the third, though less influential, framework through which we read the Chaucerian signature and Chaucerian authorship.

Postmodern Authorship

The postmodern critique of authorship takes shape in a framework of
suspicion, contesting the possibility of locating textual meaning or in-
tention in a transcendental authorial presence that must always precede
the text. Instead of being regarded as a necessary condition of writing,
authorship for Foucault becomes a historically contingent and finite *effect*
of critical discourse, aimed at organizing and hierarchizing literary pro-
duction. The impression, or effect, of authorship depends on the context
or contexts of reading and the dominant paradigms or ways of explain-
ing the fact of writing and the dynamics of reading. Indeed, for Derrida,
the name or the signature of the author always signifies the death of the
author, not just in the sense that Roland Barthes takes up (that the con-
cept of "author" is dead for hermeneutic purposes of recovering inten-
tion and therefore meaning); because the author's name can be cited out
of context, it therefore necessarily signals the author's death or, more gen-
erally, absence from the work.[38] The author effect, in this case the Chau-
cer effect, is what we find, or what we seem to *hear,* in the work.

This is the understanding implicit in David Lawton's reading of
Chaucer's narrative acts. Lawton works historically from the premise
that Chaucer's "textual rhetoric" is the first in English to foreground the
mutually informing relations of reader and writer:

> Chaucer's narratorial voice moves with increasing confidence
> in an ostensibly "oral" and self-consciously written medium. In
> the process, it loses authority and presence: the Chaucerian "I"
> is more self-effacement than self-projection. Its interaction, es-
> pecially in narratorial interjections, foregrounds the poet; but it
> also fictionalises him by embedding his voice in an avowedly
> fictional discourse. In deconstructionist parlance, it loses mean-
> ing and gains supplementarity. The narrator defers to writing
> so that the authorial "I" becomes a synecdoche of the book.[39]

H. Marshall Leicester's reading of the *Canterbury Tales,* emphasizing the
textual production of character and voice by and in each tale, also ex-
tends this insight.[40]

John Dagenais is critical of this trend among contemporary me-
dievalists to read medieval texts "like any other," in R. Howard Bloch's

phrase; that is, reading medieval texts as if they were indeed examples of Barthes's *texte,* the site of language's endless *jouissance.* Dagenais remarks, "It is in the thoroughly anthropomorphic idea that texts 'suggest' their own interpretive criteria that New Philology and related approaches get stuck in the web." For Dagenais, this "transfer" of *texte* to medieval textuality is problematic, partly because it conflicts with the "alterity" of the medieval that is otherwise insisted on by the New Philologists, or New Medievalists, and partly because there is nothing to stop the concept of *texte* from becoming, in the end, "as rigid and mechanical an abstraction as is the most Lachmannly restored medieval 'work'" and overdetermined by the ideologies of reading prevailing at the time of its conception and popularity.[41]

However, we can make a useful distinction between, on the one hand, the simple "application" of postmodernist textual theory to medieval or any other kind of literature and, on the other, the kind of study that draws attention to those phenomenal aspects of medieval texts shared with texts produced under a postmodernist regime. And if the only thing achieved by such a comparison is a sense of the historical contingency of "authorship" and the institutional forms it generates (the critical edition, the canon, the syllabus) or a heightened consciousness that modern authorship has both a historical inauguration and a historical closure, then this is still a substantial gain.

I sketch out these paradigms, familiar as they are, to remind us of the power of these formations, to insist that nothing is static in this issue; not the signature, not the concept of authorship, not the contextual frameworks through which they have been rewritten and read for us. Combining the historicist emphasis on context with a postmodern skepticism about the claims of "real" historicism to totalize our readings, moreover, permits the insight that the relations between author, text, and reader are historically variable: deeply influential in their cultural specificity at any one time, but mutable over the long term and offering a range of perspectives to the modern historian and theorist of reception. It's virtually impossible, now, to argue for a "pure" reading of the nature of Chaucer's authorship, either in his late-fourteenth-century context or in the subsequent phases of his reception, so deeply imbricated with each other are all the paradigms and subparadigms outlined here. It's here that I differ from Minnis, for example, who argues that much modern discussion of late medieval literature is insufficiently historicist, adopting concepts from modern literary theory, "which have no historical validity as far as medieval literature is concerned."[42] While not underestimating our lack of knowledge about medieval reading practices and the great achievements of Minnis himself in that research, I would still argue that medieval conceptions of authorship constitute only one of the several paradigms through which we *necessarily* read the Chaucerian text.

It's that combination of historicism and skepticism that I want to keep in the foreground, as I now return to the text, to pay detailed attention to Chaucer's representations of himself *as author.*

Does Chaucer Sign?

The evidence for the Chaucerian signature is not always self-explanatory or consistent, but these spaces in his text are crucial for the ways his readers come to represent his authorship, the ways in which they complete and supplement his texts, and the ways they voice their critiques of his writing. There are no surviving holographs of Chaucer's work, nor any manuscript that bears an authorial signature, while the attributive colophons that do survive are, or derive from, scribal or editorial explicits.[43] Nor does Chaucer embed the letters or syllables of his name in his poetry, in the kind of acrostic or anagrammatic signature so often employed by his medieval contemporaries[44] or by which he compliments John of Gaunt in the closing lines of *The Book of the Duchess.* Even more poignantly, it seems that no poetic manuscripts of his works survive from his lifetime, so the fantasy of turning the same pages Chaucer may have turned remains unfulfilled.

But as Middleton has shown with regard to *Piers Plowman,* there are many different ways of "signing" a medieval text apart from putting one's name at the end, and there are many different ways for such signatures to function as ascriptions.[45] We would be wrong to limit the notion of signature to the proper name "Geoffrey Chaucer" and the places where we might expect it to occur at the beginning and closing of his works. The forms of Chaucerian self-naming are many and varied, and while they are all mediated by variable and often ludic fictional contexts, they indicate Chaucer's changing relation to his work and the kind of authorship he increasingly claimed for himself.

Sheila Delany traces the gradual shift in balance between the functions of "the Chaucerian Narrator" as reader and then as writer, as he becomes increasingly conscious that he is writing for a public. The diegetic claims of the narration are her chief concern here: "what the work asks us to believe about its Narrator and the processes of its own poetic production."[46] In the dream visions, Chaucer immerses his narrator as a passive participant in the world of books and prior texts, where other characters, such as the Black Knight, are the true poets and makers. Even in *The House of Fame*, where the narrator is presented as a writer for the first time, "[t]he true centre of the poem is not yet the production of discourse but its reception." In *Troilus and Criseyde*, however, "Chaucer is able for the first time definitively to appropriate to his first-person Narrator the active authorial role, grasping the nettle to achieve the mature (although not necessarily unambiguous) voice that we recognise as the voice of the *Canterbury Tales*." Delany also points out that in tandem with this increasingly confident assertion of an authorial function goes an increased willingness for Chaucer to name himself *as* a writer, a process that begins with the (anonymous) listing of Chaucer's works in the *Legend of Good Women* and that finds fullest development in the naming of "Chaucer" as author of those works in the *Man of Law's Prologue*, using "the formal, dignified patronymic that will survive through history and set the poet apart from any other Geoffrey."[47]

That is, Delany tracks a shift from the second medieval context, which I described earlier, into the third. In her reading, Chaucer gradually becomes aware that his work will be linked to his own proper name, not simply to his text or the sources he translates or compiles: he comes to the realization that "his name . . . is going to have a function—the one, I suggest, that Michel Foucault has called an 'author-function.'"[48] Delany immediately acknowledges that this is only in a very premature, preliminary fashion, but argues persuasively that Chaucer was becoming conscious of the fact that his work was being commented on and received in different ways. For Chaucer, "it is an experience at once exhilarating and frightening," a consciousness as disturbing as Criseyde's vision of herself "frozen into a tradition 'rolled . . . on many a tongue.'"[49]

According to Tim Machan, this "strong self-consciousness about himself as a writer" in part leads writers such as Hoccleve and Lydgate to claim and identify Chaucer as an *auctor*.[50] In contrast, for Seth Lerer, Chaucer's confident self-presentations are tempered, as potential models for imitation, by the scenarios of reception that offer images of his readers as disabled, infantilized, as readers of imperfect understanding.

Both perspectives are valid, of course, since Chaucer's successors themselves experimented with a range of responses to Chaucer's authorship. But while Delany is right to trace this change in Chaucer's self-presentation across his career, it's worth remembering that this progression cannot be revealed *as* a progression until much later, once the modern study of Chaucer's canon has established the sequence of composition and revision of his work and allowed us to appreciate these changing modes. During Chaucer's own lifetime, and for his fifteenth-century readers, a range of narrative and preauthorial voices must have been available and audible in his work. "Chaucer" signifies simultaneously an *author*, a writing model worthy of imitation, but also a poet whose position as *compilator* of fictions can be inhabited and replicated with relatively little anxiety.

We can throw this question into sharper relief by comparing the signatures of Chaucer and Langland. Chaucer's signatures seem more equivocal than Langland's, less intense, and somehow less personal.

The most overt form of self-naming is the use of the proper name. Chaucer uses the two elements of his proper name only twice, and never together: the full name "Geoffrey Chaucer" appears nowhere in his works. The first occasion is the eagle's address to "Geffrey" in *The House of Fame* (line 729), some 170 or so lines after the earlier, more indirect hint, where the eagle "called me tho by my name" (line 558). This first naming chimes with the kind of fictional self-presentation characteristic of medieval poetry, especially where the narrative voice is a performing voice. For Middleton, this would be a straightforward example of open or referential self-naming, a mode that "requires little discussion." The reference to "Geffrey" seems to be of the same order as Thought's introduction of "Will" in *Piers Plowman*, a relatively direct form of signature, primarily attributive in function.[51]

A greater contrast emerges when we realize that Langland never uses his own family name, apart from occulted, anagrammatic references: "'I haue lyued in londe,'" quod I, 'my name is longe wille'" (B.15.151–53). In comparison, when the Man of Law names the poet "Chaucer" in the introduction to his tale, lamenting the difficulty of finding a story to tell that Chaucer has not already told (*Canterbury Tales*, II.47), the name registers quite differently. "Geffrey" invites the reader or listener to make a direct equation between the person narrating and the person who dreams the dream of Fame, affirming the fiction being performed, but "Chaucer" refers to an absent "author," known as a writer by his family name, whose works are circulating detached from his performing presence. One very material difference between the two poets is that Chaucer has other works to refer to: his works are studded with references to his other compositions, by name or by subject matter. Langland, in contrast, can't step outside his work in the same way; where Chaucer finishes or abandons his poems, Langland is perpetually revising, reliving, reworking the same one. He thus binds his name more closely to his single work, unable to mark his own absence from it, the absence on which modern authorship depends. In Chaucer's case, that authorship is additionally marked by a kind of historical association between the narratives and the narrators of the past:

> But nathelees, certayn,
> I kan right now no thrifty tale seyn
> That Chaucer, thogh he kan but lewedly
> On metres and on rymyng craftily,
> Hathe seyd hem in swich Englissh as he kan
> Of olde tyme, as knoweth many a man;
> And if he have noght seyd hem, leve brother,
> In o book, he hath seyd hem in another.
> For he hath toold of loveris up and doun
> Mo than Ovide made of mencioun
> In his Episteles, that been ful olde.
> What sholde I tellen hem, syn they been tolde?

$$(II.45-56)$$

The lawyer is reluctant to tell a story already told, but Chaucer has retold (admittedly in English) all of Ovid's stories and more, and has been telling them "of olde tyme" (for a long time). The word "olde" is used of both Chaucer and Ovid, a strategy linking the medieval with the classical poet and appropriating more than a little of Ovid's authority. As perhaps the first move toward the historical alterity of the poet in English, Chaucer places his "self," with Ovid, in the past. It is also a pairing that will be crucial for Chaucer's rehabilitation by humanist criticism in the sixteenth century.

Unlike the later verses in praise of Chaucer offered by Lydgate, Hoc-
cleve and others, Chaucer's learning, his eloquence, and his sugared
tongue play no part here. Instead, we find the modestly disparaging re-
marks about Chaucer's meters, the emphasis on his saying things in
English, and on the workmanlike nature of his enterprise. One book is
as good as another for finding stories of love by Chaucer, since he has
told so many.

The Man of Law's chief emphasis is on the inclusiveness of the
Chaucerian corpus, though he speaks as if Chaucer had written only sto-
ries of love. The vagaries and inaccuracies of his list of love stories are
well known: he omits the stories of Cleopatra and Philomela and in-
cludes others not recounted in the *Legend of Good Women*. Whatever the
reason for these discrepancies, so apparent to us with our superior cat-
alogs and bibliographies, the main effect of this catalog is the *inclusive-
ness* of Chaucer's "large volume" (line 60). This phrase also reminds us
of the material unity this work once enjoyed, instead of the divided state
in which we customarily now read the parallel texts of its prologue.

Langland, by contrast, can't refer to his work either by the names of
stories he recounts or by its own materiality, since he is bound always to
be speaking or writing within its own fictional frame. Middleton argues
that he developed a "signature system" as the A developed into the B and
C versions of *Piers Plowman,* that he built in so many references to his
name and his physical and social demeanor and drew such attention to
them as moments of authorial self-presentation that, eventually, even
the reader unfamiliar with any of these facts before reading the poem is
taught how to read them as internal signatures. These signatures are
tied to a distinctive physical and ethical presence. If the written signa-
ture is a quasi-legalistic guarantee of authorial ownership, it is also, as
Derrida implies, the sign of the author's absence and therefore death,
since it frees the work to travel and be replicated independently of the
author's presence. But when the author is physically present, reading
his work before an audience, his written signature, that formal guaran-
tee of the work, is not so relevant or important. The body of the poet per-
forms the same function, though more immediately, in linking the work
to the physical presence of the writer.[52]

In Middleton's reading, Langland's acts of self-naming are ethical
acts, intimately tied to the search for knowledge and the formation of
the reading and writing subject, a late-fourteenth-century "crisis of the
proper."[53] Chaucer, on the other hand, anticipates his own *absence* from

his writing and can easily envisage it circulating without him. Thus he anticipates a more modern modality of the signature, that is, standing for an "author" of a body of work, not just the work in question. His sense of a career, moreover, differs substantially from Langland's, where the narrator's progress is along spiritual and ethical trajectories, linked so firmly to the quest of Piers Plowman that the author was confused with his own character in the period of the poem's widest circulation.[54]

Chaucer certainly exploits the performative device of representing his own physical or social demeanor in his work. Having read all of Chaucer's works, we can put together a composite picture of his bodily signature, just as we can with Langland. And despite the fictional mediation of the particular narrative in question, the resulting composite picture is remarkably consistent. Chaucer only ever describes himself physically as heavy, "noyouse" for the eagle to carry (*The House of Fame*, line 574), or cuddly and rotund in the *Thopas* prologue: "This were a popet in an arm t'embrace / For any womman, smal and fair of face" (VII.701–2). He is the corporeal opposite of "Longe Wille." We might also speculate that a sluggish, passive, unthreatening "elvysh" body is more welcoming to subsequent criticism, a more likely point of focus for a congenial community of readers, than Will's lanky querulousness. Chaucer's social demeanor, in his various fictions of self-presentation, is far less threatening and more amenable. And if Chaucer often presents himself, in the opening of many early works, as a solitary, bookish figure, he always moves out from that solitude into the more heavily populated, even crowded world of dream or romance. And of course, his later narratorial self-presentations in *The Canterbury Tales* and elsewhere are far more social. The most telling indication of Chaucer's consciousness of his work's circulation is the throwaway remark in his *Envoy to Bukton*, where he implies that his friend is hesitant to marry: "The Wyf of Bathe I pray yow that ye rede." Here, Chaucer confidently assumes a knowing and willing readership for his poetry, as we saw in chapter 1. The short poem addressed to his scribe, Adam Scriveyn, is an oft-quoted instance of Chaucer's sense of himself as a writer, a master with someone else in his service, copying his works for a larger audience. This sense of Chaucer's own posterity is a more telling indication of his understanding of the regime of authorship than, say, Gower's "very elaborate and pompous" colophons, in Aage Brusendorff's phrase.[55] If Langland introduces a reference to writing poetry, on the other hand, it is to condemn it, as in the autobiographical addition to the C version, where he has Conscience berate him: "And thou medlest thee with makynges." Yet again, a comparison between the two poets marks out Chaucer's signatory modes as complex, but certainly allowing the possibility of his works circulating without him.

Chaucer signs in a number of different ways, inviting different kinds of responses to his work. However, there is one important moment in Chaucer's works that seems to offer a more definitive kind of closure: I write, of course, of the *Retraction*, and it is to this text that I now turn, to examine its claims to sign a work, the Works, and the Life of Chaucer.

CHAUCER'S LAST WORDS

"Heere taketh the makere of this book his leve." If the *Retraction*, following the *Parson's Tale* in all manuscripts that include the ending of that Tale, is generally taken to be Chaucerian, the status of its introductory rubric is harder to determine. Ironically, this incipit actually presages not the beginning, but the end of writing. It appears in fifteen manuscripts, including Ellesmere; a sixteenth "places the heading as if to indicate a subsection of the *Parson's Tale*," while four omit the heading.[56] The Hengwrt manuscript is incomplete at this point, since it lacks the conclusion of the *Parson's Tale*, though MS Hatton Donat I, copied from the same exemplar or one closely related to Hengwrt's, includes the *Retraction* with no heading at all.[57] According to Charles Owen, this represents the first stage of copying. BL, MS Harley 7334 is the first manuscript that includes the *Retraction*, introducing it with the heading *Preces de Chauceres*, while the four manuscripts of the *a* family complete at this point use the heading "Here taketh the Maker his leve." Finally, in Owen's reconstruction of this sequence, the words "of this book" are added, in the tradition represented by Ellesmere.[58] These tantalizing fragments, and their own historicity, sum up with remarkable prescience the issues of authorship and the signature at the end of the fourteenth century.

Describing the writer as "maker" implies an older minstrel-style model of the "finder" of material, though it might also refer to the more literal "making," that is, the writing, copying, or compiling of a book.[59] "Book" can also apply equally to the material object and the conceptual unity. The phrase "to take leave" implies the kind of authorial presence we associate with the poet performing his work in public, perhaps reading *from* the book, and about to depart our company. But we can also read this phrase as implying that the maker is taking leave from his own book.[60] This sense of the book circulating independently of the writer's presence seems to anticipate a more modern modality: the book compensating us for the absence of the author.

The sense of authorial presence in the *Retraction* is similarly complex. As a penitential act, the *retractatio* takes for granted the ethical responsibility of an author—whatever kind of writing or compiling is implied here—for the texts produced under that authority.[61] As a voice that seems progressively to take leave from the *Parson's Tale*, the *Canterbury Tales*, and seemingly from writing itself, the narrative also rings with closure and finality. It's a small step to seeing this as Chaucer's last word, his taking leave from life itself. But this is the poignant paradox: if we hear Chaucer finally stepping aside from his fictional voices to speak to us more directly, it is only to hear him, in this final moment, saying good-bye. The content of his adieu is equally unpalatable, since the speech-act in question, the retracting, or revoking, of all his most beloved works, is so uncongenial to modern Chaucer criticism. It's no wonder, then, that the critical reception of the *Retraction* for a long time was primarily one of disbelief, or at least of qualification.

This pattern began quite early, and dramatically, in the moves to reject all or part of the *Retraction* as inauthentic. Urry in 1721 links it to the *Plowman's Tale*, then regarded as authentically Chaucerian but unacceptable to earlier printers as dangerously anti-Catholic: "I fancy the Scriveners were prohibited transcribing it, and injoyn'd to subscribe an Instrument at the end of the Canterbury Tales, call'd his Retraction."[62]

More subtly, the *Retraction* has been explained away or bracketed off as a mystery, in moves that cast doubt on its authenticity without actually disproving it. Tyrwhitt confessed himself mystified by the text and could not give "any satisfactory account" of it, though he included it in his edition on the evidence of its strong manuscript attestation.[63] Tyrwhitt did speculate, though, that the problematic middle section might be either a scribal interpolation or the result of persuasion by "the Religious who attended him in his last illness, to revoke or retract, some of his works."[64] Ward was perhaps influenced by Thomas Gascoigne's famous theory of Chaucer's deathbed repentance,[65] though many modern commentators contend that Gascoigne's theory was itself based primarily on the evidence of the *Retraction*.[66]

For many, this skepticism about authorship extends backward into the *Parson's Tale*.[67] Modern readers are more willing to accept Chaucer's authorship of both texts, while many insist on the stylistic and penitential affinities between them. This affinity in turn can become the basis of an argument that this combination of texts was written earlier than other sections of the *Tales*,[68] or added by a compiler after Chaucer's death,[69] or intended as a work separate from the *Tales*,[70] or even that the middle section of the *Retraction*, naming Chaucer's works, represents a later interpolation into the *Parson's Tale*, either by Chaucer or a scribe, "in which material of urgent personal import is added."[71] Seeing the *Retraction* preeminently as a "natural" conclusion to the *Parson's Tale* also generates a number of subtle, "dualistic" readings of this part of the work, focusing on the transition from the various voices of the *Tale* to the *Retraction*, the shift from the world of fiction to that of history,[72] and the further shift from the poet's "quotidian reality to the ultimate reality of life after death with God."[73] Other readers stress the conventional force of the *Retraction* and the Augustinian literary and spiritual tradition it represents: as much a "review" as a "retracting" of prior works.[74]

The questions about the voicing of this text are similarly complex and laden with hermeneutic implications. While some readers find evidence of Chaucer's "genuine" repentance here, others insist on the force of generic conventions that produce the effect of penitence or argue for Chaucer's ironic deployment of those conventions. That the text seems to shift in its reference from the "litel tretys," probably the *Parson's Tale*, to the *Tales* as a whole or even Chaucer's life work is problematic. The referent for Chaucer's quotation from Saint Paul, "Al that is writen is writen for oure doctrine," is crucial here: as Douglas Wurtele remarks, "If this declaration is deemed to be made by Chaucer himself, then much advantage lies in referring 'litel tretys' to his whole work, for a comprehensively doctrinal intention and allegorical method can thereby be supported."[75]

Writers sensitive to the force of generic conventions tend to focus on Chaucer's own sensitivity to such conventions, suggesting that the penitential voice is produced by the requirements of the text that precedes it. Such a reading has the effect of undermining the force of the *Retraction* as a "proper" penitential speech-act. Commenting on Piero Boitani's attempt to discriminate between Chaucer's own voice and the persona of the Narrator at this point, for example, David Lawton remarks:

It would be fairer to say that Chaucer's prose voice returns in the Retracciouns; but for that, I cannot see—as with the *Troilus* epilogue—how they can be said any more or less genuinely in Chaucer's own voice than anything that has gone before. There is a decorum in the Retracciouns too: they are perfectly suited to the time of the work at which they appear, at the moment of the confession in Canterbury for which the Parson's Tale is the preparation.[76]

So also Derek Pearsall: "The Retraction . . . is Chaucer's own historical response to the call for penitence, and penitence now, which is the imperative logic of the closing paragraphs of the Parson's treatise."[77]

As a catalog of works, however, the *Retraction* constitutes virtually an ethical converse of the catalog in the *Legend of Good Women* or the prologue to the *Man of Law's Tale*. Here, the romances and songs in praise of love are rejected, where before they bore witness to the poet's credentials as a servant of love, proving that a poet's works can be summed up—canonized—in one fashion or another. Just as in the *Legend* catalog, Chaucer dismisses the "other besynesse": he is here similarly cavalier about the "many another book, if they were in my remembraunce." The *Retraction* draws attention to the selectivity, as it were, of the literary list or canon and its potential for mutation or rewriting according to different demands, different contexts, or different politics.

Derek Pearsall is the most recent writer to mount a serious challenge to the idea of the *Retraction* as Chaucer's last words, confirming Owen's view that the *Parson's Tale* and the *Retraction* represent an early ending to the *Tales*, written perhaps before Chaucer conceived the idea of a storytelling competition and a two-way pilgrimage.[78] Pearsall's alternative scenario for Chaucer's last year is a far more "agreeable" one: Chaucer, intending "to live forever," took out a fifty-three-year lease on a house in 1399 and started revising the *Canterbury Tales* "so that it could accommodate everything that he had no chance or intention of writing," as if warding off death by keeping closure of the *Tales* at bay.[79] He also imagines Chaucer spending his last days on the *Cook's Tale*, a rather more carnivalesque image than the penitential Chaucer evoked by the *Retraction*.

Pearsall's idea of the superseded ending will come, he thinks, "as something salutary in the way of a shock," given the way our editions of

Chaucer, early and modern, advertise the *Retraction* as so final a con-
clusion.[80] Yet as I have been suggesting, Chaucer's readers have for
many years now been qualifying or contesting this text in some way *as*
a conclusion. Consider the position of the *Retraction* in the typical mod-
ern sequence of his poems in a complete edition. Many editions, like the
Riverside, set the *Canterbury Tales* at the head of the volume, so that the
most canonical and the most final work appears at the front, followed by
all the other works in chronological order, followed by those of uncer-
tain authorship. This ordering has the effect of burying the *Retraction*,
or at least, obscuring any potential for this text to represent "Chaucer's
last words" in any easy spatial sense. In fact, it's often quite difficult to
find Chaucer's last words in the conventional ordering of his works.
Perhaps it could be argued that this burial of the *Retraction* is simply an
effect of the convention that opens the Works with the most famous
spring beginning (and follows its most wintry penitential conclusion
with another spring beginning in the *Book of the Duchess*). At the very
least, however, it compounds our unease at reading Chaucer's *Retraction*
as any kind of last word.

It is a deeply resistant text. Even though it signs the works by listing
them, naming them as books in the modern sense, even though it ex-
presses a "final" intention, and even though it seems to offer a Chauce-
rian voice speaking outside his fictions, it remains too problematic for
Chaucer's modern readers to accept it as a signature. As an act of sign-
ing, the *Retraction* seems to fulfill its formal requirements, naming the
works and acknowledging a degree of personal responsibility. Yet in
"making" this signature, Chaucer also unmakes—retracts—his works.
Moreover, in emphasizing the ethical converse of his earlier list, he ef-
fectively produces "two" Chaucers, opening up the possibility for selec-
tive variation in reading and in canon formation. He also repeats the
move made in the closing of *Troilus and Criseyde,* where he asks Gower
and Strode to "correct" his work. Thus the works are subjected to po-
tential correction, alteration, or rereading, a far more appealing possi-
bility for Chaucer's followers than to think of this retraction as the poet's
last words. This would have the rhetorical if not the practical effect of
ending criticism before it can begin.[81]

As we can see from this discussion, these "last words" are impossi-
bly mediated for us, by the scribal rubric, by the possible workings of an-
other "compiler" responsible for ordering the *Parson's Tale* and *Retraction*

last in the Canterbury sequence, by the penitential conventions and voice established by the *Parson's Tale,* by the literary and spiritual conventions of such acts of retraction, by the biographical narratives that circulate with Chaucer's texts, and by the traditions of editing that position this text in obscurity. In this they are only more dramatically typical of the problems of textual interpretation.

The problems in reading the *Retraction* show how deeply implicated are questions of reception and transmission with the earliest response to the text, how hard it is to draw that secure line between (authorial) text and (editorial and critical) commentary, and how difficult it is to read Chaucer's texts as completely closed. The degree to which they are read as open, however, is equally indeterminate and dependent on the various writing and critical practices that are responsible for transmitting the Chaucerian text. The question about Chaucer's signature can more usefully be phrased, then, not as a question about whether Chaucer signs, but as a question about how such a signature is found or read in his work. Reception becomes a structural as well as a hermeneutic issue: the very specific, indeterminate phenomenology of the medieval text throws up a distinct challenge to conventional models of reception and reception theory. We cannot easily use such models of readerly expectations and horizons, for example, since Chaucer's earliest readers, his scribes and editors, are in the most material way "producing" the text that is up for interpretation.

As we have seen, Chaucer experiments with a range of self-representations and models of authorship, not all of which are linked to his proper name. He "signs," that is, in a variety of ways, but none of them in the legalistic modality of the signature as it is understood by modernity, appearing only *outside* the work in order to guarantee the authenticity *of* the work. His citation, as we may more properly call it, of his own name in *The House of Fame* and the *Man of Law's Prologue* is too closely imbricated in the textual fictions at play in each poem to function, at the time of his writing, in this way. And yet later readers have no difficulty *finding* or reading Chaucer's signature, here or distributed more generally throughout his writing, as an effect of style and narrative voice.

We can adapt Jacques Derrida's theory of the signature to explain these dynamics. For Derrida, "the signature becomes effective—performed and performing—not at the moment it apparently takes place, but only later, when ears will have managed to receive the message. In some way the signature will take place on the addressee's side, that is, on the side of him or her whose ear will be keen enough to hear my name, for example, or to understand my signature, that with which I sign." In a characteristic undermining of the distinction between speech and writing, he links the signature of the author to the ear of the reader: it is the reader who hears, but who also countersigns, the text of the author, in part by hearing that text as having an author in the first place, but also by hearing that author in a particular way. And further: "[I]t is the ear of the other that signs. . . . Every text answers to this structure. It is the structure of textuality in general. A text is signed only much later by the other."[82] In foregrounding the role of the reader and the act of communication as a two-way process, Derrida reminds us to put our own habits of reading into the historical picture, in addition to examining the literary systems in which a text is produced and first received. We can say, then, that Chaucer is "signed," or countersigned, in different ways, by readers in different periods. The most obvious form of countersignature is the recognition of the proper name—Geoffrey Chaucer—as a signature. This becomes the organizing principle around which we learn to recognize what is "Chaucerian" about the writing that appears over that name, especially once we deploy the institutional machinery of authorship developed in the early modern period. Chaucer's citation of his own proper name can thus be read as a prefiguring of such countersignatures, enabling and in part recognizing what will be required for a signature, but still folding the name *into* the text, rather than attaching it externally.

The other way we countersign Chaucer, of course, is by hearing his narrative voices as expressions of, or subtended by, a controlling authorial consciousness. In this sense, the materiality of the signature is intimately related to the phenomenality of how that illusion of voice is produced. A. C. Spearing demonstrates how this works when he seeks to disrupt the conventional dualist stability between author and narrator, reminding us of the texts' origins in live performance:

> Much criticism has disregarded this mobility of the performing "I," the rapid movement among roles and the porosity of their borders, treating the first person legalistically and asking in effect, "Are you Geoffrey Chaucer?," "How do you know what you

tell me?," "Why should I believe what you say?" Such questions are still less appropriate when addressed not to a real performer but to the ghostly textual "I" that marks his final elusion, "'Tis here!" "'Tis here!" "'Tis gone!"[83]

Spearing tropes an uncanny dialogue—or interrogation—with Chaucer: a dramatic instantiation of modern projections onto the Chaucerian speaking voice and onto what the signature guarantees: control, authority, and self-knowledge. The desire to make Chaucer speak, to render our questions about authorship intelligible to him, is persistent and powerful, even when it is used to demonstrate the impossibility and inappropriateness of pinning Chaucer down to such dialogues.

In the next chapter, I will show how Chaucer's early imitators only gradually produce the effect of a Chaucerian signature; that is, they only gradually come to countersign Chaucer as author. Working within a textual tradition that encourages *compilatio*, the easy completion and supplementation of manuscript and of narrative, the early scribes and copyists only slowly come to see that "Chaucer" might function as a sign of closure, as well as an invitation to write more under that name.

3

WRITING CHAUCER

THE FIFTEENTH CENTURY

Whan Chauceres daysyes sprynge . . .

F. J. FURNIVALL, ED., *THE TALE OF BERYN*

There is no doubt that Chaucer's name signifies a powerful cultural effect in the early fifteenth century. He is early named as father or master, inspiring a range of poetic subjectivities among his followers and imitators. It is only later, and more gradually, that his name is countersigned in a way that constitutes "Chaucer" as the object of critical attention, as well as a model for poetic imitation. Yet both processes are inextricably tied to the manner in which his poetic texts acquire closure.

In the most sustained discussion of Chaucer's fifteenth-century legacy, Seth Lerer articulates a persistent pattern by which Chaucer's "sons" or "students" praise and imitate their father's or master's work in the same breath. Lerer explores the special "subjection" of Chaucer's followers to his poetic authority. It is, he argues, a laureate authority that poets such as Lydgate, Hawes, Hoccleve, and Clanvowe bestow on Chaucer, based partly on his style and their description of that style as "aureate," but partly also on a range of important social scenes in Chaucer's own writing. These are scenes where Chaucer "presents a class of readers and writers subjected to the abuse of their audience or subject to the authority of their sources."[1] Lerer is less concerned with the fifteenth-century English or Scottish poetics of imitation—"mere ventriloquism," he calls it—and rather with the "broader contours of . . . the 'literary system' for the age," invoking the formulation of Richard Helgerson.[2] In focusing on the conditions of patronage, on selected aspects of manuscript dissemination and scribal commentary, with a special emphasis on Caxton and John Shirley, Lerer considers the interventions of Chaucerians into the literary production of the fifteenth century.

For most of the poets Lerer discusses, the name of "Chaucer" signifies a stable entity, an iterable or imitable style, even if that style is characterized by irresolution and anonymity, as he argues in relation to Clanvowe's *Book of Cupid*.[3] His poets must negotiate a relationship with Chaucer as the poetic apogee from which they see themselves as falling away: a relationship of negativity that will be important for the poetic tradition in English and the genealogical structures its poets will embrace.

My own work is more concerned with the origins and development of literary criticism, especially insofar as this practice constructs a different kind of relationship with Chaucer and licenses different kinds of writing: commentary and criticism, at first in verse, and then in prose. Unlike poetic imitation or subjection, in Lerer's term, modern criticism depends on a relationship with the author that depends initially on distance, not intimacy or apprenticeship. The subjectivity of the critic is more self-consciously constructed than inherited, since it is built around the possibility of bridging the cultural and historical gaps between Chaucer's time and the present. This is the recuperative work of humanist criticism, which first develops its distinctive English form as a combination of devotion and labor in the sixteenth-century editions of Chaucer's works.

The origins of Chaucer criticism, however, clearly share a number of starting points and textual sites with the poetic tradition, and they are the subject of the present chapter, which will focus on the anonymous *Prologue* to *The Tale of Beryn* and Lydgate's *Preface* to his *Siege of Thebes*. These poetic texts represent symptomatic moments in the development of a critical tradition that will reach well beyond the fifteenth century's preoccupation with Chaucer's poetic inheritance.

There are three reasons why this should be so. First, these "supplementary" texts enjoy a close physical proximity, in their manuscript contexts, to the *Canterbury Tales*, and so constitute an important witness to the processes by which that text gradually acquires the closure and the countersignatures that modernity recognizes as "proper" to authorship. Second, and conversely, the subsequent reception of these texts allows us to explore the way that later Chaucerians—poets and critics, medieval and modern—come to negotiate those intriguing spaces around the edge of the Chaucerian text. Third, both these texts are fascinated by the possibility of further interaction with the congenial company of Canterbury pilgrims, a fantasy that I have suggested is a structural feature of Chaucerian critical reception. This social dynamic sets up an important contrast to the obsessions of the poetical tradition with individually competitive notions of paternity and inheritance.

Before we can talk about responses to "Chaucer," however, we need to look at responses to the text; in the earliest decades of the fifteenth century, this is still the primary ontological category. In those manuscripts that annotate, edit, supplement, and complete *The Canterbury Tales,* it is easy to see this text as still "open" in the sense described by Umberto Eco.[4] The scribes, editors, and compilers of these manuscripts find it relatively easy, even necessary, to write more of the *Canterbury Tales*—lines, links, prologues, glosses, conclusions—into its margins and the gaps around its incomplete segments. This textual porosity facilitates the more complex and extensive acts of narrative completion and supplementation in the same period: the writing of more Canterbury Tales. But it is only gradually that these acts come to seem like writing more of *Chaucer's* Canterbury Tales. That is, it is only gradually that Chaucer's fifteenth-century readers come to countersign his works *as* Chaucer's, that they find, read, or "hear," in Derrida's phrase, his works as if they were signed. And it is only then that they start to resemble the closed texts of modernity. Thus in the history of Chaucerian textuality and manuscript transmission we can track the transition from a more open medieval mode of textuality to a more closed modern form, where the lines demarcating "authorial" from "scribal" writing are etched in deeper and deeper.

It is a transition in the resonance of the proper name or names associated with a text, from a mode where any such name signified a rather impersonal, usually Latinate kind of authority, or the name of a main character, or even the main *idea* of a text, to a modern literary system that recognizes that name as a model for stylistic imitation in English, or as a privileged center of biographical and critical attention, or as a personality to be reconstructed from the surviving textual traces. The countersignature offered by the readers of an authored text distances the author, but simultaneously releases another kind of pleasure: the bridging of that distance through the discourses of affinity, expressing one's love for the author in knowledge of his life and works. In brief, then, I am concerned here with the transition from Chaucer as *auctor* to Chaucer as *author*.

CHAUCER'S AUCTORSHIP

If Chaucer is the first "author" in English literary tradition, the earliest responses to Chaucer, in the manuscripts of the late fourteenth and early fifteenth centuries, show little sign of such an awareness. Certainly the word *"auctor"* appears with consistent regularity in the margins of Chaucer manuscripts, against proverbs, sententiae, and so forth, but it draws attention to instances of narratorial *auctoritas,* rather than implying that Chaucer, as an English writer, has become an *auctor* worthy of commentary or a lecture series in a medieval university.[5] For such copyists, Chaucer is a repository of wisdom, at his most characteristically "authorial" when he voices the most "authoritative" sentiments. In contrast to the modern sense of authorship, "authoritative" in this context often means the most anonymous, the most culturally neutral pronouncements.

Let us return to the Ellesmere manuscript, the most "bookish" text of *The Canterbury Tales.* N. F. Blake reminds us that this manuscript has been favored as the basis for many modern editions on grounds of aesthetics rather than chronological priority: for its comparatively regular orthography and morphology, its coherent tale-order, and the obvious care taken in copying and illuminating this beautiful book.[6] Charles Owen comments, "Editorial preparation and control are everywhere apparent."[7] Ellesmere's very bookishness—its running titles, its obviously edited nature, the complexity of its rubrics, its scribal source annotations—make it an attractive, though in many views "deceptive" (the word is Owen's), source of authority for *The Canterbury Tales.*

Recent trends in textual criticism, however, have become suspicious of Ellesmere's very beauty, indicative of heavy-handed scribal and editorial imposition. In part through Blake's influence, critical attention has swung in favor of the Hengwrt manuscript as the best early text, and despite its incompleteness it was the choice of the variorum editors as the copy-text for most of the *Canterbury Tales.* Blake accounts for Ellesmere's popularity, in fact, on the grounds of its completeness: "[B]y using El the editor would need to make fewer emendations and editorial interventions in the text,"[8] while later commentators have discerned more subtle reasons for its popularity. Derek Pearsall comments:

> It is not surprising, in a way, that modern editors have been so impressed with Ellesmere, when the preoccupations of the Ellesmere reviser with neatness and regularity and consistency so much resemble their own. Yet clearly Ellesmere presents a text, not of what Chaucer wrote, but of what his editorial executors thought he should have written, or would have written if he had known as well as they did what he wished to write.[9]

In contrast, for Pearsall, Hengwrt is less attractive, less complete, and lacks illustrations, but remains "an early and uneditorialised manuscript of incontestably high quality, with excellent spelling, paragraphing and punctuation, a *mirror in which we may believe, without illusion, that we see Chaucer clearly*" (my emphasis: even the discourse of editorial theory is not immune from the metaphysics of presence).[10]

From a slightly different perspective than one concerned solely with authenticity, Tim Machan draws attention to the construction of the poet as author in Ellesmere, which "enunciates Chaucer's vernacular composition as uniquely worthy of the attention (and status) of the great."[11] In this dispensation, the Ellesmere manuscript becomes an important episode in the prehistory of literary canon formation.

If we are to find the beginnings of a modern sense of Chaucerian authorship, then, we might expect to find them in Ellesmere, which is generally agreed to be the earliest manuscript directed to public demand for a complete copy of Chaucer's text. Scholarship since the late 1970s has drawn attention to the layout and rubrication of manuscripts, their *ordinatio*, and their scribal additions and alterations as a preliminary form of criticism and response, and the Ellesmere text is a fruitful site of such inquiry.[12] Yet while this manuscript is beautifully illustrated and features running titles, annotations, and carefully ordered and planned divisions, there is no general incipit to the work, whose title does not appear until the final colophon. The pattern of marginal annotations, moreover, is surprisingly inconsistent, while the manuscript as a whole seems to fluctuate in its representations of Chaucer as either the *auctor* or the performer of the work.

The annotation *auctor,* for instance, appears with regularity only in *The Man of Law's Tale, The Merchant's Tale,* and *The Prioress's Tale.* The pattern here is quite consistent, at least, as the scribe marks instances of the rhetorical figure of the *apostrophe* or *exclamatio.* In the *Man of Law's Tale,* for instance, it appears opposite the following lines:

358 O Sowdanesse roote of iniquitee,

421 O sodeyn wo that evere art sucessour / To worldly blisse,

652 O queenes, lyvynge in prosperitee

771 O messager fulfild of dronkenesse, *and*

925 O foule lust of luxurie lo thyn ende.

It does not appear against all such addresses in this tale, but the same pattern is evident in the other two tales. That is, the annotation appears opposite lines that voice a distinctive ethical authority, or *auctoritas,* outside the principal narrative: *auctor* marks the exception, not the rule, in the performing narrative voice.

As a further indication that any "authorship" in this manuscript is primarily anonymous (a function of rhetoric, rather than personality or style), the margin opposite the mention of "Chaucer" in the introduction of the *Man of Law's Tale* is blank. There is no scribal or editorial consciousness, here, of the games his modern readers easily recognize Chaucer as playing with his own posterity and his rivalry with Gower. Our own interest in this moment is a good indication of the self-conscious games with authorship we tend to take for granted in postmodernism. If Chaucer does "sign" his text at this point, though, it is *not* countersigned by the Ellesmere editor: there is no recognition, here, of a system of literary authorship that could acknowledge the phenomenon of personality or the ironic performance of authorship.

The tale that is given the most elaborate treatment is, of course, *The Wife of Bath's Tale,* whose Latin glossator, in Susan Schibanoff's words, "supports and augments the construction of the text." Schibanoff draws an interesting contrast between Ellesmere and BL, MS Egerton 2864. Both sets of glosses were copied wholesale at one time, and both seem to be addressed to, and in part "about," the new, bookish reader of Chaucer, the reader who might be seated reading his or her own copy, as opposed to listening to a performance of the poem. Yet while the Egerton glossator struggles against the Wife of Bath, citing more and more glosses against women's drunkenness or against women's sovereignty in marriage, the Ellesmere glosses seem rather to support the Wife. Schibanoff also suggests that these glosses, if not *by* Chaucer himself, seem to represent a kind of "hoax": "pseudo-Chaucerian glosses, glosses meant to appear as authentic."[13] However, the distinction she draws between pseudoauthorial and scribal or editorial marginalia is hard to sustain in the absence of a signature to those glosses, which do not appear "authorial" in any sense except insofar as they do not argue with the Wife, as the Egerton glosses do. Schibanoff compares the authorial annotations in Boccaccio's *Decameron* and *Teseida*,[14] but there is an important further distinction to be made between these texts, where the annotations and rubrics appear consistently throughout the manuscripts, prefacing and effectively framing the works; and the Ellesmere's very selective, anonymous glossing, whereby only this tale and the *Merchant's Tale* are heavily glossed. Chaucer's *Tale of Melibee* and the *Parson's Tale* also receive heavy annotation, though mostly only to the extent that the names of the many textual authorities cited are rubricated in the margins.

The name "Chaucer" does figure in Ellesmere as the name of the *performer* of the *Tales,* however. When "Lenvoy de Chaucer" is introduced at the close of the *Clerk's Tale,* it introduces a direct address to the audience of "wedded m[e]n" and "noble wyves," which is separated, to a degree, from the preceding address to the "lordynges," drawing attention to Chaucer as performer of the Clerk's narrative. The Ellesmere incipits and explicits to the various exchanges between the Host and the narrator, moreover, use Chaucer's name at every stage. "Bihoold the murye Wordes of the Hoost to Chaucer," "Heere the Hoost stynteth Chaucer of his tale of Thopas," and so forth. When the famous picture of "Chaucer" appears in the margin opposite the beginning of *The Tale of Melibee,* pointing to his name in the rubric, the author is figured as the embodied, narrating presence who tells the tale on pilgrimage and who narrates the text to his audience or readers. This "most expressive portrait," in Pearsall's words,[15] shares a number of iconic features with the other portraits of the poet in the Harley 4866 manuscript of Hoccleve's *Regement of Princes,* whose verisimilitude is commended to its readers.

And yet the evidence of the running titles of *Thopas* and *Melibee,* on the other hand, affirms that "Chaucer" is seen here largely as a character in his own fiction, rather than as the author responsible for the entire work's conception. Most of the tales have the name of their teller as a running head, the same name that appears opposite the first line of each pilgrim's description in the prologue. The verso running head for *Thopas* and *Melibee* is "Chaucer," corresponding to the other running heads, *Knight*, *Miller*, and so forth. But the recto running head is first *Thopas*, then *Melibee*, an unprecedented identification of the tales by character, not teller. In other words, the Ellesmere editor and illustrator were quick to fill up the lack in their *ordinatio* that would be otherwise unable to label these two tales. "Chaucer" here names a character narrating two tales that need to be distinguished from each other, not an author. The copyist's priority throughout this manuscript is completeness, an insistence that every distinctive part of the text be named and described, either in the margins or in the running heads. The "Chaucer" signified here is closer to the first model of late medieval authorship I outlined in chapter 2: the poet visibly addressing his audience. The illustration of Chaucer similarly demonstrates the text's dependence on the poet's embodied, performing presence.

Similarly, at the close of the collection, the *Retraction* is introduced in a way that foregrounds the shift in speaking voice: the speech-act, "taking leve," is emphasized, rather than the act of authorial voicing or even the generic act of retracting, or narrative denial. The Ellesmere rubric, "Heere taketh the makere of this book his leue," is consistent with this manuscript's insistence on the completeness of its copy. It is a "book" the fact of whose complete bookishness is of higher priority than the person of the author. And of course, the final colophon—"Heere is ended the book of the tales of Caunterbury compiled by Geffrey Chaucer of whose soule Jhesu crist haue mercy. Amen."—stresses the book, the content, and the act of *compilation*, rather than authorship.[16]

Unlike the Hengwrt text, which was compiled hurriedly, leaving gaps for portions of text the editors hoped would come to hand later, the Ellesmere manuscript covers over and conceals, almost obsessively, any deficiencies in its copy. It is as "closed" and finished a manuscript as any from this early period in the *Tales'* transmission. These are the fullest acts of naming the poet, and, as I have shown, they are included principally to complete the *ordinatio:* there is little that is distinctive about the *author*ship of this text. For most of the text, Chaucer is primarily a narrative character within the poem, or a compiler of its contents, rather than an authority figure within it. To refer once more to Derrida's vocabulary, we can see that even the Ellesmere's *ordinatio* does not countersign

"Chaucer" as an author, does not attribute to him that proprietary right over the text we take for granted in a "modern" sense of authorship.

While I agree with Machan that this manuscript assimilates Chaucer into the rhetorical and authoritative structures of the *auctores,* the manuscript is more contradictory in its representations of Chaucer's authorship than this model implies. That is, the manuscript also presents Chaucer as the performative center of the *Tales* in a way that harks back to a model of vernacular poetry as public performance. Ellesmere barely presages Chaucer's subsequent importance as the point of inception for English poetry or as the object of critical commentary *in the vernacular.* This does not mean that later commentators can't look back at Ellesmere and find, as Pearsall and Blake remark, evidence of their own ideas of Chaucer as the preeminent medieval author in English,[17] but I would stress that this pleasing interpretation of Ellesmere has the effect of flattening the contrast between the medieval concept of *auctor* and the modern concept of *authorship,* absorbing the former into the latter.

By corollary, the favoring of Ellesmere over other less ornate and differently ordered manuscript collections of the *Tales* represents a kind of collective countersignature of Ellesmere as a manuscript, *as if it were* signed by Chaucer. This second-order countersignature can take dramatic form, such as the recent magnificent and expensive facsimile of the Ellesmere manuscript, even at the same time as textual scholarship recognizes its belated status in relation to the Hengwrt text.[18] Economic considerations also come into play; the concentration of capital in the United States and Japan, the main sponsors of the Ellesmere facsimile, is hard to replicate elsewhere. The National Library of Wales, the home of Hengwrt, it is not hard to believe, has fewer wealthy advocates, and we must be content with the Pilgrim Books black-and-white facsimile edited by Paul Ruggiers.[19] Before the Ellesmere facsimile was planned, Stephen Knight had already contrasted the national origins of Hengwrt and Ellesmere. Reviewing Blake's edition of *The Canterbury Tales,* he commented, "It is certainly easy to see why a British professor is charmed when Hengwrt, that battered Morris Minor among manuscripts, outperforms in its modest reliability the sumptuous Ellesmere, a true Californian Cadillac among medieval sources."[20] It is hard for Hengwrt not to be outshone by the glamorous Ellesmere facsimile: a visible sign of the attraction we feel and continue to generate toward these more ornate and seemingly more "knowing" manuscripts.

This brings us back to the issue considered in the previous chapter. We need to distinguish between closure in the epistemological sense and closure in the more material sense. *The Canterbury Tales* is unequivocally open at the time of Chaucer's death: incomplete, lacking order, and lacking the sacred attribution of authorship, even though the *name* of Chaucer was attached to it securely enough. If we are to examine the process by which the works of Chaucer gradually acquire greater degrees of both epistemological closure and symbolic capital, we need to consider a different kind of response in some of the manuscripts of the fifteenth century, in those which contain various attempts to complete or supplement *The Canterbury Tales*. If Ellesmere focuses on its *ordinatio* and its rubrics, other versions and responses are more concerned with establishing and expanding a sequence of tales and prologues or, indeed, with adding tales. These more self-conscious writerly responses to *The Canterbury Tales* gradually reveal a new development in "Chaucerianism," one that will prove surprisingly liberating for Chaucer's more modern readers.

WRITING CANTERBURY TALES
AFTER CHAUCER

The *General Prologue* of *The Canterbury Tales* seems to indicate a precise intention for structuring the work:

> . . . ech of yow, to shorte with oure weye,
> In this viage shal telle tales tweye
> To Caunterbury-ward, I mene it so,
> And homward he shal tellen othere two,
> Of aventures that whilom han bifalle.

(I.788–95)

A most ambitious plan, which seems to be almost immediately abandoned, or to belong to a different phase of composition from the rest of the fragments, for all other references to the tale-telling competition assume that each pilgrim will tell only one, or at most, two tales. But it is the Host, after all, who avows, "I mene it so," and as soon as due attention is paid to Chaucer's fictional characterizations, the failure to fulfill the narrative contract outlined here is easily displaced from Chaucer onto Harry Bailly, and the *Tales* read more comfortably as a witness to human, not Chaucerian, imperfection. With the benefit of hindsight, we can see the plan for the tale-telling contract as hopelessly optimistic. That hindsight, though, is one of the main objects of my attention, not least for the curious perfection it bestows on twenty complete and four unfinished or interrupted tales from thirty-odd pilgrims, three of whom are barely described or even mentioned in the *General Prologue*. If we now read Bailly's plan as marked by extravagant ambition, it's correspondingly impossible to imagine that Chaucer's Wife of Bath or the Pardoner should speak a second, third, and fourth time, or that his Tapycer should suddenly find a voice and a character and launch into narrative, except in the kind of pseudo-Chaucerian writing represented by my parody at the opening of chapter 2. With the benefit of this hindsight, knowing that the Pardoner speaks only once, for instance, helps us make our huge critical investment in his moral, rhetorical, and sexual bankruptcy, so that we regard the Host's insults as Chaucer's last, decisive word on the subject: thus, we countersign his characterization. Whenever we debate the suitability of tale to teller, too, our arguments rest heavily on the assumption that there is only the one occasion, in most cases, on which this relationship will be explored and tested and that the potential of characters to change and develop will be heavily restricted.

We turn now, however, to consider a phase in the reception of the *Canterbury Tales* before the text receives this collective countersignature, before the institutions of criticism start their work of restricting Chaucer under the regime of modern authorship, closing and sealing, once and for all, the book and the works of Chaucer. My emphasis falls on manuscript production, as the first material site for scribal and poetic response to the space around the Chaucerian text in the secondary stages of its textual transmission: that is, once the *Canterbury Tales* is recognized as a capacious story collection but before it is finally sealed off as *Chaucer's* story collection. I will also be suggesting in the next section that twentieth-century Chaucerians disclose a complex set of responses to these additional poems, ranging from scientific superiority to a barely repressed nostalgia for the relatively uninhibited ease with which these early writers and critics can "speak" and write in Chaucer's place and in Chaucer's voice.

John Bowers classifies the supplements to *The Canterbury Tales* into four types:

(1) The pilgrimage narrative was expanded to allow the pilgrims to reach Canterbury, then begin their return trip toward Southwark, in Lydgate's Prologue to the *Siege of Thebes* and in the anonymous Canterbury Interlude and Merchant's Tale of Beryn. (2) The intermediate frame-narrative was patched together with "spurious links" for tales lacking authentic prologues. (3) Tales without endings were provided with make-do conclusions, most fully in the version of The Cook's Tale printed here. And (4) a pilgrim who never told a tale, the Plowman, was given a chance to make his contribution.[21]

Bowers's vocabulary reveals a poignant sense of the deficiencies of the surviving text and the pathos of any attempt to amend those deficiencies. The Chaucerian text is described in negative terms that stress its need for supplementation: "to allow the pilgrims to reach Canterbury"; "tales lacking authentic prologues"; a pilgrim is "given a chance"; while the supplements themselves are "spurious" and "make-do."

The "scribal" links (John Bowers counts twenty-two such)[22] demonstrate the manner in which *The Canterbury Tales* are seen by their fifteenth-century copyists and editors as an open text, needing formal completion and extra prologues to introduce and arrange tales in the story collection. The two sequences printed by Bowers, from BL, MS Lansdowne 851 and from BL, MS Royal 18.C.ii, characteristically use the Host as the mediating figure, "tying together and unifying" the fragments left "maddeningly disconnected" by Chaucer.[23] By so thoroughly absorbing Chaucer's narrative structure and making frequent reference to the storytelling competition, these writers demonstrate minimal self-consciousness about writing Chaucer. Of all the various acts of writing *The Canterbury Tales*—whether we consider the glosses, the addition of extra tales, the extracting of separate tales for specialized anthologies, or the scribal or authorial revision of particular passages—these links demonstrate least concern for hermeneutics: their concerns are structural, to do with closing gaps in an incomplete text.

The two most extensive supplements from Bowers's first category embrace the idea of the text as an elastic story collection, but they are also inspired by the framing fiction of the pilgrimage and the possibility of developing the narrative and characterizations of the storytelling competition. Lydgate's *Siege of Thebes* and the *Tale of Beryn* are folded into the Canterbury sequence with elaborate prologues, both wildly dis-

proportionate to Chaucer's tale-link-tale sequences in their detailed so-
cial realism of pilgrimage and communal travel. Both also insist on clo-
sure of a kind, in their shared impulse to bring the journey to an end,
even if neither can actually complete the narrative and bring the pil-
grims back to London. Other possible sites for inquiry into the desire to
complete Chaucer's narrative are the various attempts to complete *The
Cook's Tale* or to substitute for it *The Tale of Gamelyn*, or the inclusion of
the *Plowman's Tale* in Christ Church, Oxford, MS 152 (listed by Bowers
as a separate category). These share a comparable interest in storytelling
and in seeing the *Tales* as a kind of narrative compendium, but little
interest in the pilgrimage frame and the possibilities it offers for narra-
tive closure.

The *Siege of Thebes* and *Beryn*, structurally similar inventions, written
around the same time, nevertheless disclose different understandings of
Chaucer's authorship and of their own. Lydgate, one of Chaucer's most
self-conscious poetic successors, adds an extra dimension by including
himself in place of the "Chaucerian" narrator, in effect introducing a
new character into the social dynamic, while the *Beryn* poet-narrator re-
mains anonymous and seems to efface as much difference as possible
between himself (as I suppose) and Chaucer.

The prologue to and *The Tale of Beryn* appear uniquely in the North-
umberland 455 manuscript of the *Canterbury Tales*, which dates from the
second half of the fifteenth century; that is, a relatively late copy. After
the *Canon's Yeoman's Tale*, with no further introduction, we simply turn
to the next leaf and read, from Bowers's lightly modernized edition:

When all this fressh feleship were com to Caunterbury,
As ye have herd tofore, with tales glad and mery,
Som of sotill centence, of vertu and of lore,
And som of other myrthes for hem that hold no store
Of wisdom, ne of holynes, ne of chivalry,
Nether of vertuouse matere, but to foly
Leyd wit and lustes all, to such japes
As Hurlewaynes meyné in every hegg that capes
Thurh unstabill mynde, ryght as the leves grene
Stonden ageyn the weder, ryght so by hem I mene.
Butt no more hereof nowe at this ilch tyme,
In saving of my centence my prolog and my ryme.

They toke hir in and logged hem at mydmorowe, I trowe,
Atte Cheker of the Hope that many a man doth knowe.
Hir Hoost of Southwork that with hem went, as ye have herd tofore,
That was rewler of hem al, of las and eke of more, . . .

(lines 1–16)

It is impossible to capture an innocent reading of these lines. Once
they have been categorized as apocryphal and supplementary, their dif-
ference from the rest of the *Canterbury Tales* is almost tangible, so over-
determined is our reading by our confident knowledge of Chaucer's
style, dialect, orthography, syntax, and speaking voice—his internal sty-
listic signature—let alone our familiarity with his characteristic begin-
nings. Yet the text reveals no sign of rhetorical anxiety about its inter-
vention. In particular, the first-person narrative is presented as a natural
continuation of the narrative position already established, suggesting
that if this position is stamped with any sense of Chaucerian personal-
ity, it can be easily overridden. It seems more likely, though, given the
presentation of the text and its reordering of its Canterbury material,
that no such sense was operative here, that the poet and/or the scribe
experienced no "anxiety," as we would call it, about interrupting or in-
habiting this text, which is not presented as in any way connected with
Chaucer. In fact, the narrative position gradually becomes more omnis-
cient over the course of the prologue, and its speaker less and less audi-
ble, reduced to what we might call a merely phatic or extradiegetic role
as storyteller, rather than the homo- or autodiegetic position adopted by
Chaucer in the *General Prologue*. Already in the extract quoted, for ex-
ample, it is clear that the narrator is not himself part of the Canterbury
company. This poet's response to Chaucer seems to have been primarily
stylistic and structural, a response to the idea of an anthology of stories
and a collection of pilgrim-characters, especially the Pardoner, the "mag-
nificent grotesque" who, in Bowers's words, "seems to have been the
one pilgrim who lingered most strongly in the memory of the fifteenth-
century audience."[24]

The prologue takes up the notion of the storytelling competition
structured around a two-way journey, to Canterbury and then back to
London. The poet exploits the pattern of alternating prologues and tales,
like so many of the early editors and scribes, and prefaces the *Tale of
Beryn*—told by the Merchant on the return journey—with an elaborate

"Canterbury Interlude" (the title is Bowers's), which seems designed to mirror Chaucer's "Southwark Prologue." It is an account of the after-noon on which the pilgrims arrive at Canterbury, where they perform various devotional and social rituals, before setting out on their return journey the next day. The Knight takes his son to view the battlements and fortifications of the city; the Pardoner and the Miller, with "other lewde sotes" (line 147), compete ineptly to identify the stained glass win-dows in the cathedral, from which they steal brooches and tokens; the Monk takes the Parson and the Friar off drinking with a brother monk in Canterbury; while the Wife of Bath and the Prioress stroll in the gar-den of the inn before enjoying a quiet glass of wine with their hostess in her parlor.

The prologue also features the Pardoner's unsuccessful and humil-iating attempt to make a tryst with Kit, the barmaid, inspiring Urry to title the work, "A Prologue of the Merry Adventure of the Pardoner with a Tapster at Canterbury." This fabliau-style adventure revolves around the price of a dinner, the duplicity of women, and a homosocial bond be-tween Kit's lover and the host of the inn at the expense of the Pardoner, presented here as the gullible outsider. The poet makes no reference to the Pardoner's effeminacy or possible homosexuality, and this remains one of the puzzles about the poem. Where most of the other characters are "well kept up," in Furnivall's words,[25] the character who is featured in most detail is the one who suffers the greatest sea change. Nor is there any mention of his corrupt ecclesiastical practices or drunkenness. It is hard not to see these changes as an ideological corrective to the dis-turbing ambiguity of the *General Prologue* description or the Pardoner's suggestive exchange with the Host at the conclusion of his tale.[26]

The tale given to the Merchant is a translation from the French *Béri-nus,* a merchant romance of travel, changing fortunes, and the bizarre legal practices found in other countries. It could well be read as a tale of orientalism, as Beryn, the young Roman, abandons his noble heritage and voyages into Alexandria to suffer the caprices of various trading cus-toms. Chaucer's name appears with no apparent irony in the ancient cripple named "Geffrey," who comes to the assistance of the hero in be-guiling the evil Steward who has threatened to confiscate the young man's profits.

In the Northumberland manuscript, this text appears with no scribal fanfare or introduction: this manuscript's *ordinatio* is antitheti-cal to that of Ellesmere, in that its rubrication, annotation, and visible ordering are minimal. Yet this does not mean the textual ordering is careless. Aside from the interpolated text, the Northumberland manuscript preserves a unique tale order. According to John Manly and Edith Rickert, this is largely due to "its having picked up the tales from at least three sources."[27] Like a number of other manuscripts, it lacked the conclusion of *The Summoner's Tale* at the time of copying that tale, but it was later found and copied in after the tale of Beryn. The order of the latter part of the manuscript is condemned by Manly and Rickert as "entirely irrational." In one respect, however, it makes perfect sense, since the *Tale of Sir Thopas* and the *Tale of Melibee* are separated by the interpolated text with the turnaround at Canterbury. The Thopas-Melibee link is missing, but the two tales told by the narrator are distributed evenly in the storytelling competition, one on the way down and one on the way back, just as the Merchant, in the new arrangement, tells the story of January and May on the way down and the story of Beryn on the way back to London. The conception of a pilgrimage narrative is clearly that of a two-way journey. The manuscript is incomplete, however, so we do not see what the scribal editor would have done at the beginning or end of the *Parson's Tale*.

This copy of the *Beryn* prologue and tale is certainly not the original (Bowers describes the Northumberland MS as a "mutilated descendant" of the first edition),[28] and its own exemplar seems to have been defective. We may speculate, though, that the distinguishing factor that eased the insertion of this tale and its accompanying prologue into the Northumberland manuscript was precisely that structural pattern. As Norman Blake has argued with respect to the fifteenth-century editorial reconstruction of the *Canterbury Tales*, the alternation of prologue and tale determined the ordering of the Hengwrt and Ellesmere manuscripts and also encouraged the scribal or editorial composition of missing links and prologues.[29] It is surely no coincidence, either, that the *Beryn* interlude appears directly after the *Canon's Yeoman's Tale*, Chaucer's own interruption, with narrative prologue, to his original plan.[30]

As the earlier quotation shows, the poet attempts to capture Chaucer's periodic and leisurely syntax; at the close of the prologue, the Host praises the beauty of the spring:

> "Now," quod the Hoost of Southwork, and to the feleshipp bent,
> "Who sawe ever so feir or so glad a day?
> And how sote this seson is entring into May!

. . . .

The thrusteles and the thrusshes in this glad mornyng,
The ruddok and the goldfynch, but the nyghtyngale
His amerous notes, lo, how he twyneth smale!
Lo, how the trees greneth that naked were and nothing
Barre this month afore, but now hir somer clothing.
Lo, how Nature maketh for hem everichone,
And as many as there been, he forgeteth noon.
Lo, howe the seson of the yere and Averell shoures
Doth the busshes burgyn out blosoms and floures!
Lo, the prymeroses, how fressh they been to seen!
And many other floures among the grases green,
Lo, howe they spryng and sprede of divers hewe!
Beholdeth and seeth both rede, white and blewe,
That lusty been and confortabill for mannes sighte,
For I sey for myselff it maketh my hert to lighte."

(lines 680–98)

Syntactically and astrologically straightforward in comparison, this passage nevertheless mirrors the famous spring opening to Chaucer's *General Prologue,* drawing on a number of familiar topoi to do so. At the end of the prologue, the Merchant similarly employs a Chaucerian modesty topos:

Ther shall no fawte be found in me; good will shal be my chaunce.
With this I be excused of my rudines,
Allthoughe I cannat peynt my tale but tell as it is,
Lepyng over no centence, as ferforth as I may,
But tell yewe the yolke and put the white a way.

(lines 728–32)

Like so many of the additional links and prologues, this passage is built around and confirms the Host's "will and ordinaunce," the narrative contract that sustains both the drama of the pilgrimage and the structure of the story anthology. There is little evidence here of the professional rivalry privileged by recent commentators or an older formation, the "marriage group."

Perhaps there is a sense of distance from Chaucer's conception at the point where the Host carefully eschews the use of lot to determine who will tell the next tale. He says it is perhaps unfair, the morning after the revels, to land on "som unlusty persone that were nat wele awaked, / Or semy-bousy over eve, and had i-song and craked / Somwhat over much" (lines 705–7). He concludes, "It were grete gentilnes to tell without lott" (line 716). At this point, the Pardoner is trying to keep a low profile after his night's adventures, which ended in savage beatings from both Kit's paramour and the Host of the Hoop and a night in the dog's kennel. In contrast to his proud departure from Southwark, he skulks under his hood, to conceal his cuts, bruises, and bites, trying to sing along with the others and so escape the Host's attention. In that sense, he is the obvious candidate for Fortune to call on for a story: perhaps the author implies he is more "gentil" than Chaucer in avoiding the vagaries of lot.

Direct references to the prologue are slight, and the poet makes no reference to Chaucer, either by name or indirectly as the original author. The "authorship" of the *Beryn* prologue is worn very lightly, if indeed authorship is an appropriate term for the narrator of a story who seeks, as far as possible, to efface the entry points and marks of his intervention, who assumes perfect continuity between his own text and the text he interrupts and disrupts.

On the surface, the prologue to John Lydgate's supplementary Canterbury tale shares a number of similarities with the *Beryn* prologue. It is similarly set in Canterbury, as the pilgrims regroup for the return voyage to London. Once more, the Host is firmly centered as master of ceremonies, the storytelling competition is the determining structure, the other pilgrims are mentioned in terms that recall (though less accurately) Chaucer's descriptions; and the interlude precedes a lengthy narrative, *The Siege of Thebes*.

And yet Lydgate's work appears to belong to quite a different order from the *Beryn*-poet's intervention, once we focus on authorship as our principal category, rather than the storytelling competition and the pilgrimage structure. Lydgate is engaged in an elaborate form of Chaucerian *imitatio*, responding to more than structure and style: the Canterbury pilgrimage provides him with the opportunity, quite simply, to step into Chaucer's shoes, and indeed his saddle, to "become" Chaucer himself. Lydgate does not simply invoke the same spring motifs as Chaucer and the *Beryn*-poet; he invokes *Chaucerian* spring motifs. Lydgate does not simply become another pilgrim-narrator; he becomes a *Chaucerian* pilgrim-narrator, describing, as if through some bizarre time warp, how he happened to be at Canterbury at the same time as Chaucer's pilgrims, twenty or so years after the poet's death. Less self-conscious than his modern commentators, Lydgate unabashedly puts himself where he wants to be as a reader of Chaucer, displacing him as poet-narrator at the diegetic center of the poem.

Many commentators have pointed out how Lydgate's prologue and tale both seem designed to out-Chaucer Chaucer. If Chaucer's twelve-line opening sentence to the *General Prologue* is propelled by a sequence of subordinate clauses and astrological time-settings, Lydgate's opening sentence seems to run for sixty-five lines, never sustains a principal clause, and mentions Phebus, Saturn, Lucina, Aurora, Jupiter, and Flora.[31] The tale itself is twice as long as *The Knight's Tale,* which it seems designed to complement, supplement, or even supplant, recounting the history of Thebes more or less up to the point at which the *Knight's Tale* begins.[32]

I want to focus, though, on those passages in the prologue that describe Lydgate himself and hint at his relationship to Chaucer, passages without parallel in the *Beryn* text. Part of the unwieldy first sentence is a passage of homage and praise to Chaucer, which is typical of fifteenth-century encomiums. Lydgate has mentioned a number of pilgrims, among them the Pardoner (whom he seems to have confused with the Summoner). We pick up the sentence midstream:

> Tellyng a tale to angre with the Frere,
> As opynly the storie can yow lere,
> Word for word with every circumstaunce,
> Echon y-write and put in remembraunce
> By hym that was, yif I shal not feyne,
> Floure of poetes thorghout al Breteyne,
> Which sothly hadde most of excellence
> In rethorike and in eloquence—
> Rede his making, who list the trouthe fynde!—
> Which never shal appallen in my mynde,
> But alwey fressh ben in my memoyre,
> To who be gove pris, honure, and gloyre
> Of wel seyinge, first in oure language,
> Chief registrer of this pilgrimage,
> Al that was tolde, forgeting noght at al

Feyned talis nor thing historial,
With many proverbe divers and unkouth,
Be rehersaile of his sugrid mouth,
Of eche thyng keping in substaunce
The sentence hool withoute variance,
Voyding the chaf, sothly for to seyn,
Enlumynyng the trewe piked greyn
Be crafty writinge of his sawes swete,
Fro the tyme that thei ded mete
First the pylgrimes, sothly everichon,
At the Tabbard assembled, on be on,
And fro Suthwerk, shortly forto saye,
To Canterbury ridyng on her weie,
Tellynge a tale, as I reherce can.

(lines 35–63)[33]

Lydgate's text is usually dated around 1420, that is, twenty years after Chaucer's death. Unlike the *Beryn* prologue, this text is supremely conscious of that fact, though Chaucer's name is not mentioned by Lydgate. He does use the phrase "Canterbury talys" at line 18, though it sounds almost aggressively like a generic reference to the *kind* of storytelling that takes place in springtime, rather than the title of the work into which the poet interposes himself. In the passage above, Lydgate establishes the terms of Chaucerian praise we will find throughout the century: the idea that Chaucer is supreme poet, skilled in rhetoric ("his sugrid mouth"), a linguistic innovator ("gloyre / Of wel seyinge, first in oure language"), and the one in whose works we find much of "sentence."

At the same time, the position from which Lydgate speaks reveals a degree of ambiguity in reference to Chaucer. It is surely significant that Lydgate does not name Chaucer in this prologue, just as Chaucer does not name Boccaccio, from whose *Il Filostrato* he translates and adapts much of his *Troilus and Criseyde*. The central line of the long passage cited here seems to be "Chief registrer of this pilgrimage" (line 48). The unnamed poet "registers," that is, records, the events of the pilgrimage, a word that emphasizes the poem's historical veracity and Chaucer's status as *compilator* of the pilgrimage.[34] Lydgate affirms that Chaucer's memory will never fade, though this in turn underlines Chaucer's death and absence from his own work.

Seeking to fill that absence, Lydgate describes himself in visual terms as Chaucer does not—dressed in sober habit of black and riding a slender palfrey—and makes the Host guess at his name in lines reminiscent of the Host's address to Chaucer's Monk (VII.1929–30):

> "Daun Pers,
> Daun Domynyk, Daun Godfrey or Clement,
> Ye be welcom newly into Kent,
> Thogh youre bridel have neither boos ne belle.
> Besechinge you that ye wil me telle
> First youre name, and of what contré—
> Withoute mor, shortly that ye be—
> That loke so pale, al devoyde of blood,
> Upon youre hede a wonder thred-bare hood,
> Wel araied for to ride late."
> I answerde my name was Lydgate,
> Monk of Bery, nygh fyfty yere of age—
> "Come to this toune to do my pilgrimage,
> As I haue hight. I ha therof no shame!"
>
> (lines 82–95)

Lydgate presents himself as pale and interesting, a shy though not totally reluctant participant who, like Chaucer in the *Thopas* prologue, needs to be drawn out by a sensitive Host. He has already told us he has visited the shrine of Saint Thomas to fulfill vows made when he was sick, proving his exemplary reading of the opening passage of the *General Prologue*. Now he stakes his claim to become the exemplary writer of the same text. Just as the *Beryn* prologue covers over the Pardoner's homosexuality with an ostensibly heterosexual misadventure, Lydgate's self-portrayal as a monk (lean and spiritual) is usually read as a strategically orthodox corrective to Chaucer's Monk, on his sleek and glossy horse, rung around with bells.[35] The Host goes on to give Lydgate a great deal of advice on the care of his body, but the real point here is that in line 92, "I answerde my name was Lydgate, / Monk of Bery, nygh fyfty yere of age." Lydgate names himself here without ambiguity or coding, in a literal manner quite unlike anything we have seen in Chaucer or Langland. He also ensures that the Host, as master of ceremonies, welcomes him into the company, sanctioning his participation.

The net effect of these differences is that Lydgate places himself firmly in the here and now, while Chaucer is effectively relegated to the vaguer realm of the literary past, an authoritative and influential figure, but a less personal shadow who can easily be replaced at the center of his own fiction. It is in this important respect that Lydgate's prologue differs most profoundly from the *Beryn* text. Like the *Beryn* author's, Lydgate's reprise of Chaucer's text is structural and stylistic, a response to the meter, the structure, and the narrative style of the *Canterbury Tales*, but it also approaches (cautiously, even grudgingly) a countersignature to the writer, Geoffrey Chaucer. In his consciousness that the text he supplements was in fact made by someone whose writing will always remind him of his name, by someone to whom he awards first place in English writing, by someone who wrote in a distinctive rhetorical style, Lydgate reveals a strong sense of Chaucer as an author, as someone who exists in a special proprietary, originary relationship to his text.

Lydgate's birth as a writerly reader (in this text, at least) comes about literally at the expense of the death of the author. Chaucer is not only dead, but markedly absent from his own work, since all the other Canterbury pilgrims, especially the Host, are pursuing their own fictional lives independently of the Chaucerian presence that first gave them "life." By occupying that autodiegetic position at the center of the narrative, Lydgate demonstrates that "Chaucer" has a different order of fictional existence. Lydgate does not actively seek to resurrect Chaucer from the dead, to "speak" to him across time and mortality. The predominant mode here is elegiac, in line with a great deal of fifteenth-century poetry. The structural possibility of recuperating Chaucer as a congenial soul is still some way away, a task to be performed by poets and critics experiencing a greater sense of cultural distance from Chaucer. Lydgate prefers to *inhabit* Chaucer's work by annexing his own narrative and displacing Chaucer's elusive ghost with his own firmly named and corporeal presence, not naming "My mayster Chaucer" until the very end of the epic narrative (*Siege of Thebes,* line 4501). Thus a degree of distance is marked out, but it is not the distance that will become a structural feature of literary criticism.

For the *Beryn* writer, narrative structure takes precedence over authorship as the point of entry to the *Canterbury Tales*. In this form of writing, or supplementation, the traces of authorial difference are obscured, and the manuscripts generally try to efface the nature of the intervention.

The name of the author, while it might be recognized, does not carry with it the burden of finite textual closure. This is true of the variant *Cook's Tale* of Bodley MS 686 and the *Plowman's Tale* of Christ Church Oxford MS 152, as it is of the shorter links. These texts regard the unfinished nature of the poem as unproblematic and see no closure attendant on the Chaucerian signature. Lydgate, however, is far more concerned with his own name and correspondingly more aware of Chaucer's. While he still regards the text of the *Canterbury Tales* as porous and susceptible to supplementation, Lydgate has only one model for literary authority in English. For Lydgate, Chaucerian authorship is a force to be reckoned with, though he has barely developed a conscious discourse in which to do so. We now turn to the critical history of Lydgate's partial countersignature and the late medieval and modern reception of these supplements.

READING THE SUPPLEMENTS

If we consider the manuscripts of the *Siege of Thebes*, we find a fascinatingly mixed picture of both Chaucer's and Lydgate's authorship. Of the twenty-one surviving manuscripts, three append the poem to copies of *The Canterbury Tales*. BL, MS Egerton 2864 (formerly Ingilby) reads, after the *Parson's Tale*, "Heer begynneth the laste tale of Cauntirbury talis tolde homward and maad by daun John Lidgate monk of Bury," with this colophon, "Heere endith the laste tale of Cauntirbury maad and told bi dan Johnn Lidgate mon[. . .]."[36] BL, MS Royal 18 D.II, the illuminated manuscript discussed in my introduction, does not include *The Canterbury Tales* but contextualizes Lydgate's poem with care: "In this preamble shortly is comprihendid A Mery conseyte of John Lydgate Monke of Bury declarynge how he aionyde þe sege of Thebes to the mery tallys of Caunterburye." And later, "Here begynneth The Segge of Thebes ful lamentably tolde by Johan Lidgate, monke of Bury, anneyynge [annexynge] it to þe tallys of Canterbury." These rubrics show how seriously the scribes took the internal signature of Lydgate in his prologue, and also how much more resonant is the signifier "Canterbury" than "Chaucer." The Royal manuscript is clearly fascinated by Lydgate's intervention: opposite line 70, where Lydgate demurs as to whether it is "Hap or Fortune . . . / That me byfil to entren into toun, / The holy seynt pleynly

to visite," the annotator adds, "How Daun John Lydgate enterd þe feli-
shipe of þe pilgremes in Caunterbury and of his discriptyon."

The patterns of annotation in several of these manuscripts also facil-
itate Lydgate's intervention. BL, MS Arundel 119 imitates the rubrication
of Ellesmere and other annotated manuscripts, recording in red ink the
names of the pilgrims mentioned by Lydgate: "The Cook the miller and
the reve" opposite line 28, "Lich as the Cook, the Millere and the Reve."
Opposite Lydgate's description of himself, the rubric reads "Discrybing
of the monk," and against the mention of his name, it reads "Lydgate
Monk of Bery." This manuscript is less coy, too, than Lydgate, in identi-
fying "hym that was, yif I shal not feyne, / Floure of poetes thorghout al
Bretayne" (lines 39-40) in the margin as "Chaucer." The Arundel man-
uscript is dated by Axel Erdmann and Eilert Ekwall as 1425–30.[37] An
early manuscript, it takes us one step further than Lydgate by citing
Chaucer as a *named* authority, in a different register altogether from the
anonymous *auctor* in the Ellesmere manuscript. Interestingly, this is not
one of the manuscripts that appends Lydgate's text to Chaucer's: it con-
tains only "the Destruction of Thebes," while the sole reference to the
original context of the work appears in the opening initial W, enclosing a
monk on horseback, dressed in black and wearing a wide-brimmed hat.

The manuscripts of Lydgate's poem that aren't *Canterbury Tales*
manuscripts sometimes group this poem with other works by Lydgate or
other works by Chaucer or, as in the case of BL, MS Addit. 18632, with
Hoccleve's *De regimine principium,* a poem by one of Chaucer's follow-
ers that contains, like Lydgate's prologue, praise of Chaucer. The manu-
scripts thus reveal a mixed response to Chaucer and Lydgate as authors,
with no clear picture emerging of the relationship between author and
text, or indeed between author and author, Chaucer and Lydgate.

These two continuations suffered very different fates in their early
history. The *Beryn* continuation survives in only one manuscript of *The
Canterbury Tales* and was not printed until John Urry included the work
in his edition of the *Tales* in 1721. Lydgate's text, on the other hand, ap-
pears in more than twenty manuscripts and a number of early printed
editions. Sometimes *The Siege of Thebes* is included as part of *The Can-
terbury Tales,* sometimes it appears independently of Chaucer's work,
and sometimes even independently of its own prologue, though it is in-
cluded in all sixteenth- and seventeenth-century editions of the *Tales*
after John Stow's 1561 edition.[38] F. J. Furnivall and W. G. Stone edited

the *Beryn* prologue and tale for the Chaucer Society in 1887, and this edition was reprinted for the Early English Text Society (EETS) in 1909.[39] The Lydgate text has a more complicated modern printed history. Erdmann brought out the first volume, the text, for the EETS in 1911, but left his student, Ekwall, to finish the second volume of introduction, notes, and glossary, not published until 1930. These remained the standard texts until John Bowers's 1992 edition of the *Beryn* texts and Lydgate's prologue.

The *Beryn* writer's work attracted less attention until the past ten or so years, presumably because it did not form part of a known writer's oeuvre. In contrast, Lydgate's Canterbury supplement, like his other "Chaucerian" writings, has been used as a measure of canonicity to confirm the superior position of Chaucer in the hierarchy of late medieval writers. In his attempts to outdo Chaucer, in style, in self-presentation, in syntax, in astrological reference, and in epic narration, Lydgate is generally seen to damn himself as a second-rate Chaucerian, unable to work his way out from under Chaucer's shadow, either despite or because of his great prolixity. Such assessments have the very pleasant effect of confirming the modern critic as the superior Chaucerian. Unable to write Chaucerian verse, we are still better able to judge what is Chaucerian than his closest imitator. What better way to demonstrate the superiority of one's own understanding of Chaucer than to assess, with the full weight of modern scholarly objectivity, the imperfect attempts of his first readers and critics to comprehend his greatness?

As I noted above, texts of both poems were available in modern editions by 1911. At first, both poems, particularly the *Beryn* prologue, were generally regarded as archaeological specimens, as inferior, marginal texts whose transparent realism might yet reveal something about fifteenth-century customs. For Furnivall, the *Beryn* prologue was "a piece of contemporary social history to be read and studied, whoever skips or skims the Tale."[40] For as long as the *Canterbury Tales* were regarded primarily as a realist drama of character, according to the influential readings of George Kittredge and R. M. Lumiansky, both supplementary tales and prologues were seen to be pursuing that "dramatic principle" (Lumiansky), to be similarly concerned with realism and thus reliable testimony to late medieval habits and social customs.[41]

As criticism of Chaucer began to examine the vexed question of the *Tales'* structure, critical discussion of these poems became predominantly idealist in nature, focusing on these works as "responses to

Chaucer," on the "idea" of the *Canterbury Tales* as evidence of fifteenth-century understandings of pilgrimage as a two-way journey, and on the characterizations of the pilgrims themselves, especially the Pardoner. Both prologues have often been "measured," even "graded," according to the degree of accuracy of their representations of Chaucer's characters and narrative plans.[42]

The year 1970 marks a distinctive rupture in the reception of these supplementary tales, however, for this year saw the publication of Derek Pearsall's substantial study of Lydgate.[43] A number of studies preceded him, but Pearsall's is remarkable for its lively sympathy with Lydgate, discussing his achievement as a fifteenth-century poet and the opprobrium customarily heaped on him by commentators from Skelton to Ritson.[44] In Pearsall's elegant and stylish treatment, Lydgate becomes an author worthy of serious interest, attempting, though not always succeeding, to outdo his master.[45] Pearsall does not take too literally Lydgate's praise of Chaucer as a reflection of his own practice. Describing Lydgate's opening sentence to his prologue, Pearsall comments:

> It is a particularly bad Lydgate sentence, but one can see that its badness is the result not of drivelling incompetence, but of lofty ambitions imperfectly fulfilled. This may not make it any easier to accept, but at least it clarifies the nature of Lydgate's relationship to Chaucer. It may be suggested that if Chaucer was the first to secure perfect control over long and complex poetic utterances, it is hardly surprising that his followers should sometimes have fallen short in their attempts to imitate him.[46]

In his later study of *The Canterbury Tales* Pearsall confirms his view that "fifteenth-century readers saw more in Chaucer than they were able to express in the current vocabulary of conventional eulogy."[47] He cites Lydgate's *Thebes* prologue, his *Mumming at Hertford,* and the *Beryn* prologue as evidence of fifteenth-century interest in Chaucer's humor and comic style; in particular, Lydgate's Canterbury link "shows the monk gambolling in elephantine playfulness after his master."[48] Yet there is no critical or poetic discourse available to Lydgate or his contemporaries in which to praise Chaucer's comic style.

A. C. Spearing explored this more indirect kind of response in his 1985 study, *Medieval to Renaissance in English Poetry.* In what was also one of the first sustained, self-conscious applications of modern "theory" to medieval English literature, Spearing's discussion of "The Chaucerian Tradition" takes up Harold Bloom's theory of poetic misprision or strong misreading, the idea that the "strong" poet finds a distinctive poetic voice by engaging agonistically with his strong predecessor, in a poetic version of the Oedipal struggle. Spearing questions Bloom's assumption that medieval poetry precedes "the giant age before the flood, before the anxiety of influence became central to poetic consciousness"[49] and reads Lydgate's *Siege of Thebes* as a Bloomian "tessera" or "completion" of the prior poet's poem. It's worth spelling out, though, that Spearing reads "completion" here rather more literally than Bloom, who follows Lacan's use of *tessera* to invoke a "token of recognition" from ancient mystery cults and the ritual by which fragments of a pottery vessel would be fitted together by the initiates. Bloom explains, "In this sense of a completing link, the *tessera* represents any later poet's attempt to persuade himself (and us) that the precursor's Word would be worn out if not redeemed as a newly fulfilled and enlarged Word of the ephebe."[50] The subtle and indirect relationship Bloom goes on to demonstrate between two poems by Whitman and Stevens bears little resemblance to the *literal* adding on of Lydgate's poem to Chaucer's. Spearing is on stronger ground when he suggests that this text

> "completes" Chaucer's first tale by recounting the earlier stages of the Theban legend, to which there are so many allusions in its predecessor, and . . . ends by taking us up to the beginning of *The Knight's Tale,* "as my mayster Chaucer list endite" (*Siege* 4501), with the appeal of the Theban widows to Theseus. In the two hundred or so lines of narrative from the assembly of the widows, whose "clothes blake" (*Siege* 4417) symmetrically match the teller's "cope of blak" (73) of the prologue, I count allusions to no fewer than thirty separate lines occurring in *The Knight's Tale* I 878-1010. Lydgate obviously had a manuscript of Chaucer's poem in front of him, and as he constructs a mosaic of his own from Chaucer's words and phrases his part of the Theban story merges into that of his master.[51]

The difficulty of untangling concrete from metaphorical accounts of writing is evident. Spearing begins with the Bloomian "tessera" but in the analysis above, this "mosaic" is actually far closer to the medieval writing practice of *compilatio* or *translatio* than to the unconscious relationships described by Bloom. Lydgate's "completion" of the *Canterbury Tales* owes a great deal, as Spearing implies, to the open conditions of manuscript production in the late medieval period. However, I should stress that I am less concerned here with Lydgate's method in creating his Chaucerian reprise than in the discourse in which he writes of Chaucer. Spearing here is describing *The Siege of Thebes* proper as a response to Chaucerian poetics, while my concern is primarily with the prologue and its recognition of Chaucer's authorship as an important step in the discourses of Chaucer criticism. Certainly Lydgate's modern commentators have become fascinated by Lydgate's relationship with Chaucer as prefiguring a kind of critical response. Discussing Lydgate's generally harsh treatment by later critics, for example, C. David Benson comments: "It might be even more appropriate for us to think of Lydgate not so much as a poet but as a critic. He often recognizes what Chaucer has done, even if he cannot do it himself. He would have been the appropriate first holder of a 'chair in Chaucer criticism.'"[52] Alain Renoir also finds an analogy with modern academic institutions, suggesting that Lydgate's *Siege of Thebes* "could . . . be regarded as the same sort of tribute to Chaucer which modern scholars are wont to pay to their retired or deceased elders in the form of a *Festschrift.*"[53]

Much recent criticism of these tales, however, focuses less on authorship and, in keeping with contemporary critical trends, contextualizes these works in their own right. Richard Green's study "Legal Satire in *The Tale of Beryn*"[54] shifts attention, as many have tried to do, from the prologue to the tale itself, while Peter Brown's study of the *Beryn* prologue suggests that the text was composed to assist in promoting the jubilee year of Saint Thomas's martyrdom in 1420, "written by a monk of Christ Church, who was probably a guardian of the shrine, to encourage visitors and gifts."[55] The poem is thus less a response to Chaucer than an occasional piece for which the *Canterbury Tales* was "a convenient, but by no means necessary, stimulus."[56] In Brown's reading, this would account for the special vilification and punishment of the Pardoner; of all the corrupt ecclesiastics, he is the one whose profession represented the greatest threat and competition to the prosperity of the saint's shrine: "The Pardoner as a travelling shrine, a purveyor of false relics and cash absolutions, is a threat to those who might consider themselves to be the guardians of true relics and the means of obtaining

legitimate forgiveness for sin."[57] Brown thus deflects attention away
from the poem as imitation and toward "the preoccupations of a Can-
terbury monk in 1420," a reading in harmony with Lerer's emphasis on
the social and historical contexts of fifteenth-century poetry. Both critics
consider the work of the "Chaucerian" poets as socially and culturally sit-
uated texts in their own right. Perhaps it's only now that contemporary
criticism has turned away from the ideals of sympathetic imitation and
empathy that we are released from obsessively tracing and retracing the
revoicing of Chaucer by his followers.

Such a release comes slowly, however. We have already seen how
contemporary Chaucerians toy with the idea of speaking in Chaucer's
voice, no matter how ironically they present this possibility to them-
selves. A number of twentieth-century writers have taken up the chal-
lenge in a more sustained way, and they are the subject of the final
section of this chapter.

"CANNE AUNGELS SYNGE IN ENGLYSSH?"

While modern criticism, in its most formal mode, analyzes the early
completions and supplements from a stance of objective assessment,
there is a strong strand of modern Chaucerianism that also seems at-
tracted to the possibility of writing Chaucer. I have in mind here not the
practices of translating and modernizing Chaucer, but a narrower, more
specifically modern tradition of writing Middle English, either speaking
as or speaking *to* Chaucer in his own language, to complete or, indeed,
to reply to his works in the mode of a conversation or dialogue. Unlike
the fifteenth-century continuations, these reprises fully acknowledge
Chaucer's signature as complete and marked by the modern regimes of
authorship. They are self-conscious tour de force performances of Mid-
dle English, written from a determinedly modern perspective. Unsur-
prisingly, they seem to circle around the same sites that enabled the
fifteenth-century writers: the incomplete, unfinished *Canterbury Tales*
with their cluster of congenial characters, whose narrative promise
seems to be always unfulfilled.

Of all modern Chaucer scholars, Frederick Furnivall, as we will see
in chapter 6, was the one who most loved to commune with Chaucer in
his voluble and eccentric prefaces. His editorial work "proper" was no
exception. When he edited *The Prologue and Tale of Beryn* for the EETS

in 1909, he took a very liberal hand, and constantly emended the meter and syntax of the poem, arguing that the MS is "often very faulty in metre, and is not a correct copy of the original poem."[58] He comments in general terms on these changes, addressing his own community of readers as equally competent and confident editors, prosodists, critics, and Chaucerians. Time and again he asks us to correct his corrections, to make more in the same vein, or indeed to cancel his additions. He tells us, "The proofs were read twice by me with the MS., and I believe the text is a faithful print of it, though unluckily, when editing it, I was affected for a time with the itch of padding out lines by needless little words in square brackets. The reader can easily leave them out in reading when he finds them unnecessary, or gratify his resentment at such impertinences by drawing a pen through them."[59]

Yet at a later stage, he adds a "Correction" at the end of the preface, suggesting precisely such a change (though it isn't clear if this is a proof-reading mistake or another emendation on metrical grounds, replacing *ageyn[se]* at line 2619 with *ageyn[es]*). "I leave each reader to supply, according to his taste, more insertions between brackets, to make all the lines of the Poem of normal length."[60] It seems as if he is asking us to put his emendations *sous rature,* as if they are both made and not made. It is a modern version of the Chaucerian stance of asking for correction and has the double effect of helping us to identify Chaucerianness as, indeed, asking for correction: a very enabling trope for literary criticism.

His most egregious breach of editorial decorum occurs when the manuscript seems to be missing a line, and Furnivall composes one of his own.

"Now," quod the hoost of Southwork, & to þe feleshipp bent,
"Who sawe evir so feir, or [evir] so glad a day?
And how sote this seson is, entring in to may,
[When Chauceres daysyes sprynge. Herke eek the fowles syngyng,]
The thrustelis & the thrusshis, in þis glad mornyng,
The ruddok & the Goldfynch; but þe Nyʒtyngale,
His amerous notis, lo, how he twynyth smale!"

(lines 680–86)

Furnivall's interpolation of this line, "When Chauceres daysyes sprynge. Herke eek the fowles syngyng," has the instant effect of removing the *Beryn* author's poetry one step further away from its original position, literally inscribed within the *Canterbury Tales,* and rendering it more marginal, more self-consciously distant and separate from Chaucer, as a "supplementary" tale. The added line also demonstrates Furnivall's own superior, if rather patronizing sense of what is "Chaucerian." Furnivall effectively countersigns the *Beryn* text, attributing to the anonymous author a very modern sense of distance between himself and Chaucer, making him mention the proper name in a way quite alien to his own project of writing a Canterbury tale that could be silently inserted into a manuscript. Furnivall also stamps his personality on the edition in a quasi-medieval fashion by providing marginal glosses, progressive running titles, and so forth. We will have occasion to consider his editorial decorum later on, but for now, let us be struck by Furnivall's struggle with the *Beryn* author for mastery, and for knowledge, of the Chaucerian signature, even in these tiny fragments.

Furnivall's advice might also have been behind F. J. Harvey Darton's version of tale order in his retelling of the tales in 1904. In this sequence, the *Parson's Tale* is followed by the *Beryn* prologue. Lydgate then joins the pilgrimage and narrates his own tale, which is then followed by the Merchant's second tale—*Beryn*.[61]

The more surprising form of modern Middle English, however, is the clever jeu d'esprit, rewriting Lydgate's continuation, or writing back to Chaucer. This form of writing is so marginal that to my knowledge, it has received no critical commentary.[62]

William Scott Durrant's play, *Chaucer Redivivus,* of 1912 can stand as an example of typical textual completion coupled with the poetic resurrection of Chaucer, a tradition that will be the subject of chapter 4. The "Foreword to the Action" presents Chaucer fantasizing about his return to the pilgrimage trail along the lines of the *Beryn* prologue: what had become of his creations after they had visited Becket's shrine? Then Chaucer enters.

> This is the place. There stant the little town
> Which that y-clepëd is Bob-up-and-down,
> Under the Blee, in Canterbury way . . .
> Methought, as newe in Paradise I lay,
> I heard a voice—"Chaucer, go back and see
> If thou canst find that merry companye
> That did to Canterbury onës ride. . . ."[63]

The play thus reenacts Lydgate's time warp: the pilgrims are sus-
pended at Canterbury, waiting to be revisited by a poet of sufficient genius,
or spirit, to give them new life. Durrant plays with a number of anachro-
nisms about the cars and bicycles Chaucer sees, but the narrative action,
"largely a cento of Chaucer's own lines," commences in earnest when
the Wife of Bath comes onstage and starts to court Chaucer in his own
words ("This were a poppet in an arm t'embrace / For any woman, smal
& fair of face"), encouraged from the sidelines by Harry Bailly. But Chau-
cer will remain faithful to his wife, and the play concludes as the Wife
and the Host, whose wife is now dead, agree to marry. Like the *Beryn*
prologue, *Chaucer Redivivus* seeks closure through normative heterosex-
uality and, like many Chaucerian revisitations, pictures Chaucer as a re-
alist, godlike novelist. So skillfully imagined and realized are his char-
acters, Durrant implies, that they easily take on a life of their own, like
toys in stories when children leave the room. In following the fortunes
of Chaucer's characters, the playlet also resonates generically with those
modern works that seek to continue the story of classic or popular nov-
els, such as Emma Tennant's *Pemberly* or Alexandra Ripley's *Scarlett*.

Less closely connected to *The Canterbury Tales,* Henry MacCracken's
The Answere of Adam, published in 1908, interestingly rehearses an al-
ternative position for writing Chaucerian Middle English.[64] This poem,
in rhyme royal, is written as the *apologia* of Adam Scriveyn, addressed
directly to Chaucer (The Scribe Writes Back?), in reply to the poet's com-
plaint about his careless copying. Adam explains to Chaucer that he was
hurrying to complete the copies of *Boece* and *Troilus* quickly to raise
money for the father of his girlfriend, Gretel. Peter was a Flemish trader,
innocently impoverished after the Uprising of 1381 ("tyl Richard putte
hem doun / And tauhte Wat to ben so despitous") and now imprisoned
for debt. Read in the light of complex modern theorizing about the sub-
jection of the copyist (Seth Lerer) and the textual "rape" he enacts (Carolyn
Dinshaw), this poem introduces a simple, material reality into the cir-
cumstances of textual production: texts are copied in exchange for
money, and the necessity of prompt financial return might affect the ac-
curacy of the copying. By writing faster, if more carelessly, Adam will
raise money to help Gretel's father and win the hand of the daughter.

MacCracken, the editor of Lydgate's works for the EETS, also intro-
duces his own Lydgatian moment, when the monk chances by Adam's
rooms, as a scribe lent to Adam by a senior monk from Bury, and sits

down to read the copy of the *Tales* under production. Visibly moved by the *Man of Law's Tale,* he asks aloud, "Canne aungels synge in Englyssh?"[65] Adam comments to Chaucer, "That day ye made a maker, as I hope." MacCracken dramatizes a moment of poetic origins, when Lydgate discovers the poetic possibilities of the English language.

The poem concludes with Adam informing Chaucer that he and Gretel are now married and warmly inviting him to dinner. Once again, a supplementary text introduces heterosexual closure into the scene of reception, rewriting, and recreation—a convivial scene of celebration around the marriage table. Writing in Chaucerian "Middle English," MacCracken establishes a position, that of the scribe, from which to speak to Chaucer, a position that has its origins in the Chaucerian criticism of the sixteenth century. Yet the poem also depends on the modern Chaucerian community of scholars for its readership, in its portrayal of Gower, Hoccleve, and Lydgate, and its various jokey references to the Chaucerian texts. The clever reader writes to Chaucer, but his scenes of intimate communication with the poet are equally firmly directed to the convivial academic Chaucerian community, bound by its love and knowledge of Chaucer's works.

One final example is worth a mention. As recently as 1985, John Gohorry published *A Letter from Lewis Chaucer to His Father Geoffrey Chaucer.*[66] Here, in another Middle English poem, Lewis narrates a terrifying, cosmological dream he had after reading the *Treatise on the Astrolabe,* in which he hears the music of the planets turn suddenly to discord: "a hideous huge wal of derknes swepte / From th'orisonte and put the sterres to flight." He is rescued, in his dream, by a beautiful maiden, Dame Sapience, who explains that once he has heard "the wild, fragmented clamoure of th'abysse," this cacophony can never be forgotten. She blesses him, and he awakes to a morning scene of birdsong, when "I shope me for to write, as I have done, / And ask a fadir's blessyng on his sone." Gohorry seeks to suggest in this poem "tragic personal reasons for the curtailment of Chaucer's project," seeming to imply that the child has had a vision of his own impending death.[67]

These modern reprises and direct addresses to Chaucer do not form a continuous tradition with the Canterbury supplements of Lydgate and the *Beryn* author, though it's possible that these poems were enabling models for the later versions of Middle English, appended to the Chaucerian oeuvre. For nineteenth- and twentieth-century readers, "Chaucer" signifies the signature of a finite body of works, so these are projects of imaginative reconstruction, clearly marked as separate, finite works in their own right. The Chaucer they conjure up is the Chaucer of traditional literary history, not a recently dead personal presence, whether that presence is seen as benign, in the case of the *Beryn*-poet, or more problematic, in the case of Lydgate. The making of that Chaucer, as the object of critical and editorial commentary, as opposed to poetic imitation, is the subject of the following chapter.

I want to close this section, and this chapter, with a passage from one of the most sophisticated and astute commentaries on Chaucer's fifteenth-century continuations that nevertheless enacts, albeit in miniature, a comparable attempt at narrative closure. John Bowers, remarking on the fact that the incomplete *Beryn* manuscript provides us "no end frame for the travel narrative" (it breaks off before the conclusion of *The Parson's Tale*), cannot resist the seductions of narrative and finishes the work of the Northumberland manuscript himself:

> Perhaps there once was a marvelously funny resolution to the story. Perhaps the wily Host found a way to render his verdict without offending his other twenty-nine paying customers, while his wife Godelief, wielding a medieval rolling pin, came elbowing her way to center stage. Or perhaps the Parson's long sermon had such a sobering influence on the pilgrims that they bypassed the Tabard and returned directly home filled with the piety and resolve described as appropriate by Christian Zacher.[68]

Bowers here writes alternative endings, bifurcating the narrative line and not making it clear whether these putative endings might originate from the *Beryn*-poet or Chaucer. It's the coy tone of Godelief's "medieval rolling pin" and his amplification of the Host's thumbnail sketch of her at the conclusion of the *Tale of Melibee* into a full-blown stereotype of the aggressive wife that betray Bowers's desire for a realist, comic narrative, his sense that the story can only be complete if we find out *what happened* to the characters introduced in the *General Prologue,* if our desire for a General Epilogue could ever be fulfilled. And once more, we notice the importance of marriage, or heterosexual relations, to the putative scene of closure. As he appears to realize, this scenario is not totally convincing, and Bowers rejects it for an alternative spiritual conclusion, unwittingly, perhaps, demonstrating the impossibility of tying all the threads with which Chaucer weaves into a single scene of ending.

In its throwaway quality, Bowers's ending is arguably only a more visible, more literal form of the completion and supplementation that structures all criticism. Similarly, Bradley Darjes and Thomas Rendall comment of the *Beryn* prologue, "Kitt, the Paramour, and the Hosteler, *would benefit from* at least some individualizing traits" (my emphasis).[69] These examples represent either the Chaucerian's desire to supplement the supplements or a displaced desire to improve Chaucer: if that desire seems beyond our reach, the work of his followers seems fair game. We could argue that all attempts to claim how Chaucer would or would not have finished the *Canterbury Tales* are not really all that different, in kind, from attempts to claim what the *Tales* mean. Similarly, the onus, or joy, of interpretation and "making" that modern editorial theory currently transfers to the reader is another form of invitation to write Chaucer. The reader now takes a more active role in sorting, reading, and in effect writing Canterbury tales from the same evidence that faced Chaucer's first editors and copyists.

So, although modern criticism distances itself from the projects of imitation or completion, there is still a persistent fascination with this pristine moment, the moment when Chaucer stops writing and when the process of rewriting commences. While this fascination currently takes the form of "scientific" examination of the remaining textual traces and manuscript forms, it seems to me also a more metaphysical fascination with nothing less than the origins of modern criticism, the moment when the readerly countersignature becomes possible and the moment when we find a voice in which to speak to or to speak of Chaucer. No wonder, then, that modern Chaucerians are so concerned to measure and chart the response of Chaucer's followers and imitators. While some attempts are made to consider these responses in their own sociocultural contexts, the general critical consensus is summed up aptly by Paul Strohm in his diagnosis of "the apparent inability of [Chaucer's] artistic legatees to claim more than a small portion of their inheritance."[70] This inability is most fortuitous for Chaucer's canonical status: its chief effect is to leave Chaucer isolated as the exceptional talent in early English writing.

4

LOVING CHAUCER IN THE

PRIVACY OF PRINT

THE SIXTEENTH CENTURY

And here I cannot forget to remember unto you those auncient learned men of our time in Cambridge, whose diligence in reading of his workes them selves, and commending them to others of the younger sorte, did first bring you and mee in love with him.

FRANCIS BEAUMONT, 1598

Lydgate's prologue to the *Siege of Thebes* carefully defines its own poetic trajectory from the margins of Chaucer's text into its own epic narrative. Of course, the idea of following in Chaucer's poetic footsteps does not depend on such physical proximity to Chaucer's texts or the idea of supplementing his works so literally. However, the twinned aspects of the *Tales'* incompleteness and the comic conversational style of the framing pilgrimage narrative seem to have facilitated the writing of more "Chaucer," from the rudimentary attempts to finish *The Cook's Tale* to added links and tales such as *Gamelyn* and *The Plowman's Tale* in the fifteenth century, right up to Spenser's more self-conscious supplement to the *Squire's Tale* in book 4 of the *Faerie Queene* and its more deliberate appropriation of a pseudomedieval voice.[1] It seems likely that the openness of the *Tales* comes to affect the openness of Chaucer's "Works" in this period: as if the idea of an incomplete story collection extended to the idea of an incomplete collection of works. Most of the early editors were under no illusion about the authorship of many of the poems added to the early collections and printed editions: "Chaucer's Works" served merely as a convenient umbrella term for works by him and works by other writers newly in print.[2]

And yet, as the courtly nature of most of these non-Chaucerian poems (more than forty-five) indicates, Chaucer's lyrical and romantic poetry and his poems of direct, courtly address were more popular than the sprawling comic narrative of Canterbury.[3] The dominant theme in these early printed collections is praise for Chaucer's elaborate, aureate rhetorical style, exemplified by the lyrics, *Troilus and Criseyde* and *The Legend of Good Women,* and for his learning, exemplified by the *Astrolabe* and the *Boece.* It's this mode of address to a relatively formal context of patronage and a restricted social circle that seems especially responsible for the levels of anxiety among Chaucer's followers that Lerer explores. That generic and stylistic preference also has the opposite effect, however, of accelerating the closure of the Chaucerian text and the recognition of the Chaucerian signature, since lyrics and ballads, especially those of personal address, are rarely incomplete.

But my concern is less with the inauguration of a Chaucerian poetic than with the growth of critical discourse on Chaucer and his poetry. Admittedly, for most of the fourteenth and fifteenth centuries this distinction is hard to draw, either in terms of the literary forms in which discussion or imitation of Chaucer takes place or in the social orientation of Chaucerian readers and writers: it is not until much later that poetry and criticism are distributed in the aesthetic hierarchy that privileges "primary" over "secondary" writing. Even leaving aside the Bloomian idea that all poetry itself constitutes a species of criticism, Chaucer's fifteenth-century poetic followers establish many of the influential terms and patterns of critical response to Chaucer.

Lois Ebin finds three discrete phases in Chaucer's reception through the fifteenth and sixteenth centuries. The first mode is eulogistic, focused around the moment and the fact of Chaucer's death, when the poets who follow him define their relation to Chaucer. The second commences around 1440, "after Lydgate has received considerable prominence," when Chaucer's name is no longer singled out so confidently from Gower's and Lydgate's as a poetic model. He is remembered, with them, for his role as one of the late medieval innovators of English poetry and for his enrichment of the language. By the early sixteenth century, however, Chaucer's language has come to be seen as obscure, requiring correction and modernization.[4] This third phase is crucial for the cultural

and linguistic distance his commentators are pleased to mark out be-
tween themselves and Chaucer and for the sense in which it enables the
work they need to do on his behalf. This is not to say that these two
modes do not continue to overlap: early criticism freely borrows terms,
voices, and images from Chaucer's poetic imitators.

Over the course of the fifteenth and sixteenth centuries, the critical
tradition gradually develops an independent course, becoming the dom-
inant mode of response to Chaucer and the predominant vehicle for the
voice of modernity in Chaucerian discourse. We can name three major
respects in which it differs from the work of those poets—chief among
them Lydgate, Henryson, Hoccleve, and Clanvowe, and later, Hawes,
Skelton, and Spenser—who take up a Chaucerian voice or stance. First,
and most obviously, criticism soon finds its most distinctive voice in
prose, not verse. Second, criticism has a strong sense of its own creative
work in actively bridging the cultural and chronological distance be-
tween Chaucer and its own present. That is, instead of embracing the
elegiac mode or the tropes of poetic paternity, apprenticeship and mas-
tery, or spiritual inheritance (modes that all stress continuity), early crit-
ics come to emphasize the discontinuity between themselves and
Chaucer, learning to value their own work in an ethically oriented char-
acterization of their labors in recovering and re-creating Chaucer from
the past, in bringing him forward into the present. A crucial part of this
process is the gradual closing of the Chaucerian text and the increasing
difficulty of "writing" Chaucer as directly and unabashedly as do the
poems discussed in chapter 3. Third, while the poetic tradition contin-
ues to naturalize the idea of an individualized inheritance, criticism de-
velops a strong sense of itself as a communal enterprise, as Chaucer's
readers share their knowledge and love of the poet with a community of
like-minded readers. Tied to each other by bonds of affinity, class, and
scholarship, they present themselves as similarly bound to Chaucer
through affection and duty. Their labors in reading and studying Chau-
cer become pleasurable, since they are generated by love. This chapter
will argue that such "love" comes to mark a special class, and gender, of
reader, as the community defines itself quite carefully around some un-
easy transitions from manuscript to print culture and from private to
public readerships.

These patterns emerge only slowly, of course: in its first stages, crit-
icism isn't named or defined as a special kind of activity. The second
feature of criticism just mentioned, the special sense of *distance* from

Chaucer, is first played out through Lydgate's mysterious time warp in the *Thebes* prologue, where that distance is emphasized by the chronology of his Prologue but transcended through the physical proximity of his work to the *Tales* and Lydgate's implicit claims to inherit Chaucer's poetic and narrative legacy. Not surprisingly, the physical site of the Chaucer manuscript is also the site of the first Chaucer criticism that is neither a narrative continuation nor a lyric imitation of Chaucer.

JOHN SHIRLEY

As copyist and collector of Chaucer's poetry, John Shirley uses the same manuscript space as the supplementary tale-tellers, though his concerns are quite different. Shirley evinces no anxiety about inheriting or replicating a Chaucerian style: his introductory notes and commendatory verses are written by a *reader*, a cataloger who wants to commend to his audience not his own poetry, but the works he has copied. Unlike the manuscripts commissioned by or prepared for the consideration of wealthy individuals or patrons, like the Campsall MS or the Corpus Christi *Troilus and Criseyde*, Shirley's compilations seem directed toward a multiple audience, a number of potential readers. Not a mass or a collective audience, of course, since only one copy will circulate at any time, but Shirley's prefaces reveal a conception of an audience quite unlike anything in earlier manuscripts of Chaucer's works.

Probably because Shirley's most fulsome praise is reserved for Lydgate, his comments on Chaucer are not really regarded as part of the "Chaucer tradition," while Eleanor Hammond influentially comments of Shirley's verses, "None of these bits has any literary value."[5] His work has traditionally been regarded of importance primarily for establishing the authorship of Chaucer's ballades and shorter poems; he preserves and titles, for example, the unique copy of *Chaucers Words unto Adam*.

Modern opinion is divided over whether Shirley was engaged in commercial or amateur enterprise as a bookseller or as a librarian.[6] In her recent and comprehensive study of Shirley, Margaret Connolly stresses that he was in general more interested in the work of living writers like Lydgate than in the antiquarian labors of collecting the poetry of the past, and it is certainly true that poems by Lydgate far outnumber poems by Chaucer in Shirley's manuscripts. Connolly also emphasizes those aspects of Shirley's secretarial career with the Beauchamp family that are generally neglected by literary historians, who have been principally concerned with Shirley's ascriptions of authorship or his activities in disseminating his texts. She traces the manuscripts associated with the Beauchamp family and argues that these contacts might have provided exemplars for many of his works.[7]

Seth Lerer similarly situates Shirley's compilations in a social context, implying the importance of Chaucer for Shirley as he establishes his own social role and his imaginative engagement with the poems he copies. He argues that Shirley's work reveals "the controlling idea of a lyric, public Chaucer," "a poet of political approval and personal request," an "amatory and epistolary Chaucer."[8] But instead of simply describing the terms in which Chaucer is represented by Shirley, according to the standard conventions of reception studies, Lerer examines the specific contexts into which a range of Shirley manuscripts are directed at different stages in the scribe's career. He reads their various fictions of address as important educative strategies by Shirley. If BL, MS Harley 7333 might be considered "a book of secular instruction" for the Austin canons at Leicester who commissioned it, then in contrast, Trinity College, Cambridge, MS R.3.20 is "a private assembly," in which the emphasis lies on the biographical contexts into which Shirley sets Chaucer's poems.[9] When discussing Shirley's two *Kalendars,* in BL, MSS Addit. 16165 and Addit. 29729 (Shirley's copy of his own prior collection), Lerer stresses Shirley's sense of himself as "scribe, traveler, and compiler, . . . as a kind of romance hero, reading and recording, setting in order the authors he transcribes. Much like the lover-narrators of the Lydgatean romances, Shirley is an anthologist of the imagination. Acts of travel dovetail with the processes of compilation."[10] Lerer's Shirley is a far more dynamic hero than the household secretary presented by Connolly.

In these *Kalendars,* Shirley interpellates an audience that is not exclusively aristocratic or courtly. His addresses to "dere sirs" or even "O ye my lordes" in Addit. 29729 are more general than specific or individualized and, indeed, seem to imply the circulation of these texts among a community in which Shirley feels himself to be a member. In Addit. 16165, he does submit himself, it is true, to the good opinion of those who will tolerate the "symplesse" of his own wit in compiling "þis litell booke. . . . To have þe more thank of youre grace," but he also insists he has had the book bound "þat boþe þe gret and þe comune / May

þer on looke and eke hit reede." The conclusion to this poem also sig-
nals his anticipated circulation of the book:

> And whane ye haue þis booke ouerlooked /
> þe right lynes / with þe crooked /
> And þe sentence / vnderstonden /
> With Inne youre mynde hit faste bounden
> Thankeþe þauctores þat þeos storyes
> Renoueld haue / to your memoryes /
> And þe wryter / for his distresse
> Which besechipe / youre gentylnese
> Þat ye send þis booke ageyne
> Hoome to *Shirley* / þat is right feyne
> If hit haþe beon / to yowe plesaunce /
> As in þe reedyng / of þe romaunce /
> And alle þat beon / in þis companye
> God sende hem Joye / of hir ladye
> And euery womman of hir loue
> Prey I to god þat sitteþe aboue /
>
> *Explicit*[11]

The *Kalendar* that prefaces the text in Addit. 29729 concludes in a
similar fashion, with the request for his readers to *return* the book, cor-
recting it where they find "fayllinge of þe scripture / of þe meter / or or-
tografyure." This request seems more social in orientation than the
"fashionable literary formulas"[12] of humility and apology: moreover, it's
not Shirley's *writing*, but his *copying* that is submitted to correction here.

These manuscripts certainly take for granted their circulation
among groups of readers, representing a distinct shift from the context
of a manuscript for the conspicuous consumption of a single individual,
family, or even religious community. Cheryl Greenberg comments:
"[Shirley's] manuscripts, as compilations mainly of the poetry of Chau-
cer and Lydgate, would have been of interest not only to the court and
aristocracy, but also to the upper bourgeoisie—the new readership with
more cultural ambition than financial means."[13] Indeed, A. S. G. Edwards
has argued that this was a deliberate strategy of Shirley's, to enhance
their commercial success.[14]

Connolly contends, however, that Shirley's prefaces ultimately "be-
tray a culture of service"—"the idiom of the old-fashioned oral house-

hold entertainer"—and insists that while Shirley's modes of address em-
brace both this feudal context and a more socially mixed audience, there
is no evidence that his books circulated more widely in his lifetime than
in household circles. These, if we include servants, would have provided
the "different social categories" embraced by the prologues.[15]

Even if we adopt Connolly's very literal reading of the evidence,
Shirley's assumption that there might be a broad community of readers
for these poems anticipates in manuscript form a collective or at least a
multiple readership that we have tended to associate with the medium
of print. Shirley's own forms of address equivocate between the rhetoric
of courtly patronage and the discourses of humility, on the one hand,
and a more widespread appeal, on the other, to "boþe þe gret and þe co-
mune." However, this is one of the last times a "common" readership
will be invoked in such a context for a long time. It took rather longer
for Chaucer's printers to appeal to such an audience.

WRITING CHAUCER IN PRINT

It is the familiar paradox of early print history: although the technolog-
ical innovations of printing would gradually bring about profound social
and cultural changes in communication, literacy, and the economy of
the written word, the products of the first presses bear little visible sign
of the changes they heralded. There was no immediate, radical shift in
the kind of work printed, and many printers sought to authenticate the
products of the new technology by making them look as much like man-
uscripts as possible. Accordingly, the typefaces and fonts of many of the
early editions imitate the scripts and letter forms used in their manu-
script exemplars. Overall, the *ordinatio* of these texts remained relatively
constant, and the early printed texts, like manuscripts, often lacked title
pages, contents tables, and so forth. Norman Blake reminds us, too, that
printed texts often featured illuminated initials, miniatures, and mar-
ginal decorations added by hand, while the first woodcuts were often im-
itations of manuscript illuminations.[16]

Chaucer editions are no exception to this general principle. Only
gradually are introductory materials such as title pages, prefaces, and
commendations introduced. Caxton's first editions, for example, had no
title page; this was an innovation introduced after his death by his suc-
cessor, Wynkyn de Worde, in the early 1490s. And it is only in Caxton's

second edition of *The Canterbury Tales*, produced in 1484, that he adds his famous preface, explaining his decision to print a new edition after the first had already been "sold to many and dyverse gentylmen." My interest in this often studied preface derives less from its critical content—its praise of Chaucer as "laureate poete"—than from its inaugural status as the discourse of an editor in English, just as my attention in this chapter moves away from the traditional emphasis on the changing portrayal of Chaucer by his editors or their methods of editing and selecting texts to be printed. Crucial here is the positioning of the editor in deferential relation to his readers:

> Of whome one gentylman cam to me and said that this book was not accordyng in many places unto the book that Gefferey Chaucer had made. To whom I answerd that I had made it accordyng to my copye, and by me was nothyng added ne mynusshyd. Thenne he sayd he knewe a book whyche hys fader had and moche lovyd that was very trewe and accordyng unto hys owen first book by hym made; and sayd more yf I wold enprynte it agayn, he wold gete me the same book for a copye, how be it he wyst wel that hys fader wold not gladly departe fro it. To whom I said in caas that he coude gete me such a book trewe and correcte, yet I wold ones endevoyre me to enprynte it agayn for to satysfye th'auctour, where as tofore by ygnouraunce I erryd in hurtyng and dyffamyng his book in dyverce places, in *settyng in somme thynges that he never sayd ne made and levyng out many thynges that he made whyche ben requysite to be sette in it. And thus we fyll at accord. And he ful gentylly gate of hys fader the said book and delyverd it to me.* (My emphasis)[17]

This revised edition is commended to the audience, not as better value for their money or as the latest innovation, but as the result of a carefully worded "accord" with this gentleman, respectful of the pure lineage of the text, now neither artificially augmented nor diminished, and respectful of the lineage of the book's ownership. Caxton agrees, before consulting this other manuscript, to correct his first edition. Noble genealogy sanctions textual genealogy, while the crucial connection between the two is love: love between father and son, and the father's love of his book. According to Lerer, this genealogy effaces Chaucer's own fatherhood and directs the text into the public marketplace.[18] The editor freely admits his own ignorance and error in his acts of damage and "defamation" of Chaucer, producing a judicious and flattering distinction between himself and his discriminating gentlemen readers. Whatever the nature of the "accord" that resulted in the second edition (did the gentleman offer some kind of publishing subvention?), we can be sure that Caxton was confident that there was sufficient commercial demand for it.

The editorial discourse that Caxton formulates here recognizes the authorial closure of the Chaucerian text to the extent that it is worth correcting a faulty manuscript. (In fact, Caxton still based his second edition on his first, rather than setting up a new edition from the new manuscript, though he did make a number of corrections beyond the removal of spurious lines and the addition of missing ones.) This does not mean that incomplete texts could not be completed by editorial intervention.

This is another important point of continuity between manuscript and early print practices. Chaucer's incomplete texts gave the earliest editors an opportunity to affirm their own authority in verse form, inhabiting that Chaucerian space at the close of the text just as his manuscript editors and scribes had done. Caxton's brief conclusion for *The House of Fame* is of this order. In his edition of 1484, he omits the final sixty-four lines of the poem, from line 2094 to the end: the chaotic flight of Fame's "tydynges," the pilgrims and couriers, and the rush to hear the "love-tydynges" and the "man of gret auctorite," and simply adds his own twelve-line conclusion. He picks up where a "lesyng and a sad soth sawe" are stuck in a window,[19] unable to go in or out:

> They were a chekked bothe two
> And neyther of hym myght out goo
> And wyth the noyse of them [t]wo   Caxton
> I sodeynly awoke anon tho
> And remembryd what I had seen
> And how hye and ferre I had been
> In my ghoost, and had grete wonder
> Of that the God of Thonder
> Had lete me knowen, and began to wryte
> Lyke as ye have herd me endyte;
> Wherfor to studye and rede alway
> I purpose to doo day by day.

Thus in dremyng and in game
Endeth thys lytyl *Book of Fame.*

Explicit[20]

Mimicking the return to books that marks the end of *The Parlement of Foules,* this conclusion imitates the voice of the Chaucerian narrator, the right-hand gloss seeming to legitimate, rather than qualifying, the supplement. The added verses are doubly appropriate for the editor, too, since this supplement stages his own coming to writing, as he "began to wryte / Lyke as ye have herd me endyte." Thus, the editor authorizes his own writing, underlining the similarities between what he writes now and what you have just been listening to. Adding his own signature in the margin makes it clear that he is not adding any spurious Chaucerian text, any "thynges that he never sayd ne made." And yet he also demonstrates his authority to edit and judge Chaucer on the basis of his being able to "write" Chaucer. (So attractive are these verses that when William Thynne prints *The House of Fame* from a more complete manuscript exemplar than Caxton, he still borrows these additional verses, though without the annotation "Caxton.")[21] Nicholas Haydock suggests, however, that "the excellent fit of the *Parliament*-inspired ending" should make us a little suspicious that Caxton might have deliberately omitted those last sixty-four lines to facilitate a neat conclusion and to avoid dealing with the troublesome "man of gret auctoritee." Haydock's thesis goes against the received wisdom that all of Chaucer's words were treasured, in the early editions, but it does have the attractive merit of imputing Caxton with a more active editorial role, concerned to produce ontological and narrative closure, as well as textual completion of the text at hand.[22]

In his prose conclusion, Caxton deflects attention away from his addition, displacing his own poetic achievement with a more scholarly discourse: "I fynde no more of this werke tofore-sayde, for as fer as I can understonde this noble man Gefferey Chaucer fynysshyd at the sayd conclyusion of the metyng of lesyng and sothsawe." After several lines in praise of Chaucer's wisdom and understanding, Caxton describes the enabling force of Chaucer's writing, "for of hym alle other have borowed syth and taken in alle theyr wel-sayeng and wrytyng." Once more, it is clear that for Caxton, Chaucer's works inaugurate a very *practical* tradition of writing. He then reverts, as it were, to the more traditional scribal form of the explicit and benediction, though not without the supplement of his own signature, ultimately drawing attention to his own role:

And I humbly beseche and praye you emonge your prayers to
remembre hys soule, on whyche and on alle Crysten soulis I
beseche Almyghty God to have mercy. Amen.
Emprynted by Wylliam Caxton.

In its consciousness of multiple reproduction, Caxton's imprint already
addresses a collective audience. Even though he does not characterize
the plural "you" of the final prayer in any specificity, it is quantitatively
and qualitatively different from Shirley's addresses to his audience.

Wynkyn de Worde's 1517 edition of *Troilus and Criseyde* is the most
dramatic instance of an editorial attempt to supplement Chaucer. Even
though this poem is as complete and finished as anything Chaucer
wrote, in glaring contrast to the patently incomplete *Canterbury Tales* or
The House of Fame, de Worde adds several stanzas that give the visual
impression of imitating Chaucer's rhyme royal, even though his lines
barely scan. After Chaucer's final stanza, of which I quote the last two
lines here, de Worde imposes his own emphatic ideological closure on
the poem.

So make vs Jhesu for thy mercy dygne
For loue of mayden and moder thyne benygne
Finis

The auctor
And here an ende of Troylys heuynesse
As touchynge Cresyde to hym ryght vnkynde
Falsly forsworne deflouryng his worthynes
For his treue loue she hath hym made blynde
Of feminine gendre the woman most vnkynde
Dyomede on here whele she hathe set on hye
The faythe of a woman by her now maye you se

Was not Arystotle for all his clergye
Vyrgyll the cunnynge deceyued also
By women inestymable for to here or se
Sampson the stronge with many a .M. mo
Brought into ruyne by woman mannes fo
There is no woman I thynke heuen vnder
That can be trewe and that is wondre

O parfyte Troylus good god be thy guyde
The most treuest louer that euer lady hadde
Now arte thou forsake of Cresyde at this tyde
Neuer to retourne who shall make the gladde
He that for vs dyed and soules from hell ladde
And borne of the vyrgyne to heuen thy soule brynge
And all that ben present at theyr latre endynge

A   M   E   N.

Thus endeth the treatyse of Troylus the heuy
By Geffraye Chaucer compyled and done
Ne prayenge the reders this mater not deny
Newly corrected in the cyte of London
In Flete Strete at the sygne of the sonne
Inprynted by me Wynkyn de Worde
The .M.CCCCC and xvii yere of oure lorde.[23]

The "AMEN" that appears in six manuscripts of the *Troilus* is thus de-
layed for three stanzas, while de Worde's final verse explicit, "Thus en-
deth the treatyse," encourages the illusion that he has added only one
stanza, not four. The heading "Auctor" also implies that the five books of
the poem have been narrated in a consistent fictional voice, which re-
quires a further authorial conclusion, one that will point to the misogy-
nist moral of the tale. It represents a reading of the poem completely
alien to the modern delight in Chaucerian ambiguity. The use of "auc-
tor" is reminiscent of the annotations in the Ellesmere manuscript,
whereby *auctor*ship remains a category less concerned with authenticity
than with authority and the "truth" of the proclamation or statement
made under such a rubric.[24]

De Worde does not hear the Chaucerian signature as a sign of an
authorship that might in any way inhibit his own potential to speak or
write Chaucerian. Accordingly, Criseyde is described as "vnkynde," "for-
sworne," and faithless, as "mannes fo." In his deliberate conflation of
Criseyde with the goddess Fortune ("Dyomede on here whele she hathe
set on hye") and in his invocation of the standard antifeminist exempla
of women's victims (Aristotle, Virgil, Sampson), de Worde effects a firm
ideological closure on the text, a closure he seems to have felt was lack-

ing in Chaucer's version of the story. He was not alone in this sentiment, of course: Henryson's *Testament of Cresseid* enacts a similar kind of supplement on a far more extensive scale, though one that depends less than de Worde's on its physical proximity to Chaucer's text. And dissatisfaction with Chaucer's narrative does not necessarily lead to supplementation: around 1630, it led to the censorship by Jonathon Sidnam, who modernized the first three books of the poem but refused to go any further in recounting "The wanton slipps of this deceitfull Dame."[25]

De Worde's supplementary text indicates dramatically that the question of a medieval text's closed or open state isn't simply an epistemological question: the ideological work done by any such supplement also needs to be taken into account. In this case, de Worde's stanzas have the potential to reread retrospectively the whole text of *Troilus and Criseyde* as if it expressed a totally fictionalized point of view, masking the true sentiments of its author, who now steps out to deliver a moral and warn his audience.

In his loving address to Troilus, "O parfyte Troylus," de Worde emphatically positions that audience as masculine, or at least, masculine-identified, in contrast to Chaucer's rhetorically similar address to his own mixed audience, "O yonge, fresshe folkes, he or she . . ." (V.1835). De Worde encourages an intimate identification with Troilus, using the difficulties of heterosexual relations—or more specifically, the duplicity of women—to narrow Chaucer's more inclusive address to his audience and to consolidate a homosocial bond between poet and reader. In this case, it is also a bond cemented by a spiritual dimension, as de Worde prays Jesus to bring Troilus's soul to heaven. The only solution, we may conclude, to the problem of faithless woman is refuge with the only acceptable female model, the Virgin.

Yet even though de Worde stakes his claim to this Chaucerian space at the end of this poem, his final stanza also makes a careful, technical distinction between Chaucer's work and his own labors. Chaucer is the learned *compiler* of the *treatyse;* de Worde is "corrector" (both textually and morally, it seems) and printer. This final verse uneasily combines the medieval scribal formula, *Explicit . . .,* with the more commercial discourse of advertising, commending the book for its textual accuracy, identifying the printer's name and workshop, and dating the edition, with a visual and typographic, if not metrical, recall of Chaucer's verse form. In a transitional step toward the editorial prefaces and introductions that the new medium of print gradually came to demand, many editors modified the scribal explicit in this way so as to commend themselves to their audience and to advertise their business. It was not before about 1530 that the material found in these colophons came to be routinely presented as part of the title page.[26]

As manuscript copying gradually gives way to print and as the printers and editors develop their own distinctive discourses of introduction and commentary, the text of Chaucer closes over. Sixteenth-century editors become less willing to rearrange the order of the tales in the Canterbury collection, for example, and the text and the ordering of Chaucer's other works become less fluid. At the same time, the question of Chaucer's authorship remains open to the point of elasticity: the sixteenth-century "Chaucer" is a very capacious entity. This expansion is tied to commercialism, of course. The printers needed to distinguish new editions from earlier imprints: works "never before imprinted," whether by Chaucer or not, added value to each new edition.

Similarly, the editors themselves gradually developed a sense of quasi-professional rivalry with each other, as they came to establish distinctively "editorial" voices and discourses, to authenticate their own work, and to authorize, as it were, the printing and, importantly, the reprinting of Chaucer. They learn to do this by authorizing their audience as an early version of a reading public, though in a way that preserves for as long as possible a sense of that public as an exclusive, gentlemanly society.

"My neere friends, who loved Chaucer, as he well deserveth"

The sixteenth-century editors of Chaucer gradually apply to "English Ovid" or "English Homer" the modes of humanist scholarship developed around classical Latin and Greek texts, especially in Italy.[27] For Chaucer to be worth printing and editing, he must be redeemed as a pseudoclassical writer, worthy of commentary and elucidation. This method is certainly related to the medieval Scholastic tradition, but its broader cultural agendas for the recuperation of classical and medieval texts are quite different. Chaucer's works become a productive site around which to explore the specifically English manifestations of linguistic mutability, a "source of authentic anxiety," in Thomas Greene's phrase, for most medieval and Renaissance writers.[28] At the same time, they evince great confidence that this very mutability has resulted in the refinement and adornment of the English language. Affirming their own linguistic and historical discontinuity from the medieval past permits his renaissance commentators to rescue Chaucer, as it were, from the period of cultural backwardness and ignorance that both necessitates and enables their own labors, to develop the discourses of linguistic and historical expertise by which to mediate between the medieval past and the modern present; and to explain the poet in authoritative terms to new generations of readers. By the end of the sixteenth century, a sophisticated editorial discourse foregrounds its labors in overcoming the otherness of Chaucer, surrounding his texts with more and more elaborate prefaces, commentaries, biographies, and glossaries. Chaucer is rendered emphatically "medieval," linguistically and culturally inaccessible except through the expert, modern mediation of his loving friends.

Where manuscripts are notoriously silent about their own textual antecedents, printed texts of the sixteenth century stage more complex relationships with their exemplars, their rivals, and their reading publics. These editors do not embrace any kind of professional or collective identity, though; they write as gentlemen amateurs, proud of their aristocratic patrons and concerned with scholarship rather than with profit. Interestingly, there is no name for this new, editorial author-role, as we recognize it: the word "edit" and its cognates are not used in the modern sense regularly before the eighteenth century. The famous "stigma" of print mitigates against the early development of a professional identity among editors,[29] who prefer to present themselves as authors being coaxed into print, reluctant to disseminate their amateur, antiquarian inquiries beyond their immediate circle. They write for a small, exclusive community of readers who share that circle's sensibilities, background, and, of course, gender, but the confidence of their discourse gives the impression that it is more broadly directed. These editions do not represent a straightforward instance of Anderson's "imagined community": print does not automatically or immediately guarantee an inclusive nation of readers.

As part of this self-presentation, the editors who follow Caxton and de Worde often make a point of carefully distinguishing themselves from the more menial laborers in the production of books, establishing a class-bound hierarchy around the mental and manual labors and the scholarly and the commercial interests involved in book production.[30] Before we consider the self-presentations of Chaucer's editors, it is worth briefly summarizing the conditions in which the fifteenth- and sixteenth-century editors were working and the discourses by which they represented themselves.

Caxton had combined the functions of editor, translator, bookseller, and printer, but these roles were soon to become more distinct. Caxton's successor, Wynkyn de Worde, was primarily a commercial printer, describing himself as a "citizen Stationer."[31] Unlike Caxton, de Worde was not a scholar or a translator and clearly had less interest in actively editing the works he printed. De Worde pursued Caxton's sense of a new mass market for printed books, introducing title pages and woodcut illustrations into most of his productions. One of his most telling moves was the physical shift in 1500 of the workshop from Westminster to Fleet Street, the location of the tanneries and the bookbinders. Away from the court environs and in the mercantile center of the capital, printing became much more closely linked with the bookselling trade. At the same time, the functions of printing and editing became more distinct from one another.[32] Russell Rutter is one commentator who expresses caution about the extent of Caxton's dependence on patronage and who rejects the customary opposition between Caxton and de Worde as oriented more to the court and to the city, respectively. Rutter's Caxton "saw that patrons could not support a trade in printed books, and he accordingly made strenuous and, we may assume, successful efforts to define a mass market for the volumes he produced."[33] Many of Caxton's references to various "gentlemen," in this reading, may well be generic fictions, rather than discreet compliments to publicity-shy individuals.

Not long after Caxton had first set up his press in Westminster, the English industry had to compete with foreign printers and booksellers, who had been specifically exempted under the Act of 1484 that regulated the trade of foreigners in England. This exemption was designed to encourage the growth of the English printing industry.[34] The act was not repealed until 1534, after bitter and sometimes violent altercations between local and foreign booksellers. Such legislation is a firm indication that printing was rapidly assimilated into the world of business and trade, far removed from the private, university, and monastic contexts in which manuscript reproduction had flourished.

At the time, these changes and developments went largely unnoticed in all but the commercial sphere, itself more concerned with the competition for market share than the implications for scholarship, the distribution of professional expertise, or indeed, the growth of nationalist Tudor and Stuart sentiment. As Lotte Hellinga points out, until the seventeenth century "early printing in England attracted scant attention and had only been mentioned in passing by the main chroniclers and historiographers."[35] We need to look forward, then, to get a sense of the issues surrounding print and its associated discourses.

Over the sixteenth and seventeenth centuries, we find a continuous jockeying for position among commercial and scholarly editors, printers, and booksellers. The one constant feature is the hierarchical distribution of roles and the pronounced distaste for the public, commercial aspect of book reproduction of those who saw themselves as separate from it. An important aspect of the distinction between the amateur and laureate poets of this period, according to Richard Helgerson, is that the amateurs, the aristocratic poets clustered around the court, avoided the print medium, while the laureates, those who embraced the public role of poetry, sought it out.[36] Chaucer's earliest editors, William Thynne and Thomas Speght, emphatically position themselves with the first group and draw attention away from any connections with print as an industrial or commercial activity. At the same time, printing was recognized as playing an important role within the humanist enterprise in making scholarship more widely available.

If we look ahead for a moment, the campaign of Richard Atkyns, in 1664, provides important evidence for the context in which Chaucer's editors had positioned themselves. In this year, Atkyns attempted to restore the monopoly of printing from the Stationers' Company to the Crown, in a pamphlet called *The Original and Growth of Printing: Collected Out of History, and the Records of the Kingdome. Wherein is also Demonstrated, That* PRINTING *appertaineth to the Prerogative Royal; and is a Flower of the Crown of England.*[37] Part of Atkyns's argument depends on refuting the claim made by John Stow that printing was first introduced in Germany in 1459 by "John Cuthenbergus," with a long delay before Caxton brought printing to England in 1471. The speciousness of Atkyns's reasoning is revealed in his apparent assumption that no advantage can derive from a mercantile enterprise, but only from the benefaction of public or royal patronage:

If this [Stow's claim] be true, there was as little Rarity as Expedition in obtaining it, the age of 12 years time having intervened, and so indeed it might be the Act of a Mercer rather than a more eminent Person: But when I consider what great advantage the Kingdome in general receives by it, I could not but think a Publique Person and a Publique Purse must needs be concerned in so publique a Good.

Atkyns propounds the theory that Thomas Bourchier, the archbishop of Canterbury, persuaded Henry VI to bring printing to England. In this narrative, Caxton and Robert Turnour were commissioned to seduce workers from Gutenberg's workshop to bring the secrets of printing to England and to set up a press at Oxford, at least ten years before printing was widely established in Europe. But in Atkyns's account, no sooner had printing been established, by this enlightened patronage, than the industry proliferated to dangerous degrees—the English being so proficient, numerous, and skillful as printers—spawning the ancillary trades of bookbinders, booksellers, and founders of letters, now incorporated as the company of stationers:

The Body forgot the Head, and by degrees (breaking the Reines of Government) they kickt against the Power that gave them Life. . . . Thus was this excellent and desirable ART, within less than one hundred years, so totally vitiated, that whereas they were before the King's Printers and Servants, they now grew so poor, so numerous, and contemptible, by being Concorporated, that they turn'd this famous ART into a Mechanical Trade for a Livelyhood.

For Atkyns, Art is exemplified by Music, which is exercised by princes themselves, whereas if an activity is performed to make profit, it is more truly called Mechanical. He argues that all the trades of which the Company of Stationers is composed are mechanical in this sense, and he makes a further hierarchical distinction between the more and the less commercial aspects of the trade, in a hierarchy that is distributed, metaphorically, along gendered lines:

Yet I cannot but side with the Printers thus far, as to Declare, That they, with the Founders of Letters, are the onely Instruments of absolute Necessity in this ART; whereas Booksellers might be supply'd out of the She-Shop keepers in Westminster Hall, if all the rest were higher promoted.

In fine, These Book-Sellers are the Drones that devour the Honey, made by the Laborious Printers.

He complains against the booksellers that they have taken the production and sale of books out of the king's direct patronage, where prices were more easily controlled, and out of the monastic realm of learning, into a more purely commercial sphere.

In praising print, Atkyns remarks that God reveals himself in his creation in manifold ways:

> But we of this Latter Age have all these so Lively represented to our View, by the benefit of Printing, as if we our selves were personally present: For Printing is of so Divine a Nature, that it makes a Thousand years but as yesterday, by Presenting to our View things done so long before; and so Spirituall withall, that it flyes into all parts of the world without Weariness. Finally, 'tis so great a Friend to the Schollar, that he may make himself Master of any Art or Science that hath been treated of for 2000 years before, in lesse than two years time.

This emphasis on the immediacy of print, its associations with learning, and its ability to efface time and distance from the past crystallizes familiar humanist attitudes to literary scholarship and reinforces Anderson's understanding of print technology as a crucial instrument in the imagining of people and things otherwise invisible or inaudible in the present.

Atkyns's pamphlet articulates hierarchies and issues that are already evident in sixteenth-century printing. Although the antiquarian movement of the sixteenth century is primarily concerned with historical rather than literary monuments,[38] Chaucer is a key figure, even here, for the recovery of the past. He is soon established as an important father for English history: a suitable object of veneration and recuperation for a nationalist humanism seeking to rival the Italian discovery of the Latinate past as an antecedent for its contemporary poetics. Chaucer's works also become an important object of scholarly, antiquarian researches that required comparatively little Latinate skill. Indeed, the first members of the Society of Antiquaries were "bound by an agreement to consult only English sources; Tate, in a discourse of 30 April 1600, declared that 'nothing be spoken but of this realme.'"[39] In this context, Chaucer's poetry becomes an exemplary site around which a gentlemanly English reading community can imagine itself.

In 1532, "The workes of Geffray Chaucer" were assembled by William Thynne, "the first comprehensive, single-volume collection of Chaucer's works, defining the form in which Chaucer was to be transmitted until the end of the 18th century."[40] Thynne was the first Chaucer editor who did not also print, or oversee the printing of, the text. He was a scholarly amateur and antiquarian, a member of the household of Henry VIII, "chefe clerke of your kechyn," as he is described in his dedicatory preface (actually written by Sir Brian Tuke).[41] "Thynne" here addresses the king, describing the comparisons he has made between "bokes of dyvers imprints" and condemning the "many errours, falsyties, and depravacions which evydently appered by the contrarietees and alteracions founde by collacion of the one with the other." Accordingly, he sought out other texts, lamenting the "neglygence of the people that have ben in this realme, who doutlesse were very remysse in the settyng forthe or avauncement" of both the historical and literary monuments of the past. Thynne's remarks seem to apply equally to Chaucer's medieval contemporaries, careless of the poet's posterity, and to Thynne's own predecessors: Caxton, de Worde, and Pynson. He describes his own activity as the recovery and restoration of Chaucer's texts according to truer copies and exemplars,[42] and he introduces his history of the English language and Chaucer's supremacy in that medium with a short humanist disquisition on the origins of language and the history of Greek, Latin, and other European languages.

Thynne's edition marks a crucial development in scholarly, or humanist, method and the textual recuperation of the medieval past. His own position is inspired by a nationalist desire to restore that past and to protect the literary heritage of England, strategically aligned here with its royal heritage, which in turn "protects" the editor as he ventures forth into the public world of print:

> I thought it in maner appertenant unto my dewtie / and that of
> very honesty and love to my country I ought no lesse to do /
> than to put my helpyng hade [sic] to the restauracion and bring-

ynge agayne to lyght of the said workes / after the trewe copies
and exemplaries aforesaid. . . .

So that under the shylde of your most royall protectyon and
defence it may go forthe in publyke / and prevayle over those
that wolde blemysshe / deface / and in many thynges clerely
abolyssh the laude / renoume / and glorie hertofore compared
/ and meritoriously adquired by dyvers princes / and other of
this said most noble yle / wherunto nat onely straungers under
pretexte of highe lernyng and knowlege of their malycious and
pervers myndes / but also some of your owne subjectes / blyn-
ded in foly and ignorance / do with great study contende.

Thynne follows his preface and its fulsome dedication with two tables of
contents, the first numbering the items and the second listing the folio
numbers of the first page of each item. Several dedicatory verses and bal-
lads follow, including one addressed to the king and the lords and
knights of the Order of the Garter. Thynne unequivocally seeks royal and
aristocratic patronage, less concerned with a reading "public" than to
solicit the good will of his potential benefactors and his own friends.
James Blodgett suggests, indeed, that with John Skelton, John Leland,
Sir Brian Tuke, and Thynne himself all at Henry's court for several years
after 1522, the court "in the 1520s and 1530s might even be considered
an unofficial center for Chaucer studies."[43] Consolidating this courtly
orientation, Thynne distances himself from the more mechanical activ-
ities associated with the printing and bookselling business; he mentions
his printer, Thomas Godfray, only in the brief colophon to the final
poem on the last leaf.

Thynne's edition, reprinted with variations in 1542 and 1545, was,
until John Urry's text of 1721, the model for all subsequent editions, in-
cluding various reprints, the greatly expanded edition prepared by John
Stow in 1561,[44] and the fuller and more fulsome edition of Thomas
Speght in 1598, revised in 1602 and used as the basis for additions and
revisions in 1687.[45] In Speght's edition, *The Workes of our Antient and
Learned English Poet, Geffrey Chaucer, newly Printed*, we witness one of the
most comprehensive, early affirmations of the editor's role as classical
scholar.[46] Through the classical portals framing the elegant title page, we
are confidently introduced into the world of humanist scholarship, with
an epigraph from Chaucer's *Parlement of Foules* balanced opposite one

from Ovid's *Metamorphoses*. In addition to some of Thynne's introductory material, Speght includes nearly thirty pages of prefatory letters, poems, summaries of all the works printed, and a *Life* of Chaucer, complete with an illustrated heraldic genealogy, framing a full-length picture of Chaucer and stressing his connections with the houses of Lancaster and Henry VII and with the de la Pole family, all surmounting a drawing of the elaborate tomb of Chaucer's son, Thomas.[47] His own personal connections with royalty and the aristocracy are thus enhanced in accordance with the vogue for heraldry and genealogical history.

As far as textual studies is concerned, attention is paid to the discovery of "new" Chaucerian works and the search for better manuscript sources, though the processes of discrimination among manuscripts remain casual rather than systematic. The texts themselves are introduced with elaborate prefaces and letters or verses of commendation or dedication.

Speght's scholarly agenda is clear: instead of blurring the distinction between poet and editor, his aim, like Thynne's, is to historicize Chaucer, to place him firmly in a medieval context, and to mark out the historical and cultural distance separating manuscript and print, and poet and editor. The editor's labors are archaeological, concerned to restore Chaucer's glories from historical obscurity and from the bunglers of the printing industry. One revealing indication of this historical difference is the typographical convention of printing Chaucer's poems in the black-letter fonts used by the earlier editions, but using a mixture of roman and italic faces for the "modern" commentary, inserting black letter again when quotations from Chaucer are embedded in the text.[48]

Speght writes out of love for Chaucer and for his own circle, in a mode he claims was initially intended for manuscript, not print circulation. Unlike William Thynne, who evinces only a little anxiety about the medium of print and its impact on his courtly orientation, Speght emphasizes his reluctance to go into print. He explains in his dedication, "To the Readers," that "I was requested by certaine Gentlemen my neere friends, who loved Chaucer, as he well deserveth," to repair Chaucer's memory. He had completed some of his research, "collecting" Chaucer's biography, correcting the copy from old manuscripts, summarizing each book, providing glosses and commentaries, and locating other previously unprinted works, "for those privat friends, so was it never my mind that it should be published," when it turned out that a new edition of Chaucer's works was in press, three parts already printed. His friends, as well as some "of the best in the Companie of Stationers hearing of these Collections, came unto me, and for better or worse would have something done in this Impression."[49] Speght positions himself carefully in a restricted, privileged social context: one of a company of friends united by love of Chaucer, and an amateur scholar who must be coaxed into publication under the dual auspices of his "privat friends" and the leading men of the Stationers' Company. That is, the amateur ventures into the commercial, professional world only under their assurances.

Wendy Wall demonstrates, however, that there was a counter-discourse, opposed to the aristocratic "hoarding" of learning, formulated in *Tottels Miscellany* in 1557, and taken up by a number of other writers. She quotes George Pettie, from 1581, who argues against the hypocrisy of devoting time to scholarship and learning, "only to devalue such learning disingenuously." Pettie insists on the nobility of learning: "You wyll be but *ungentle Gentlemen*, yf you be no Schollers."[50] Gestures of humility like Speght's need to be read in this context, too, as ritual expressions of modesty that probably belie a far more confident sense that publishing his research is precisely the gentlemanly thing to do. Because these tropes are predominantly associated with poetry, however, it may also be that Speght is assimilating his editorial function to this higher-status role.

Yet this "importunitie" of Speght's friends causes him to commit the fault of "publishing that which was never purposed nor perfected for open view," and he apologizes here, and at many other points, for the imperfections of the edition. Far from expressing reluctance to print, however, this regret voices reluctance to print before the work is perfect. It is a recurrent trope in editorial and critical discourse, a forerunner of modern academic disclaimers, and perhaps an echo of the proverb: *ars longa, vita brevis.*[51] This anxiety is repeated in Speght's gracious dedication to his patron, Sir Robert Cecil, where he attempts to shore up support for a second edition: "These collections and corrections upon Chaucer as they earnestly desire, so might they better have deserved acceptance at your honors hands, had they ben as fully perfected, as they have beene painefully gathered. But what is now wanting through lacke of time, may happily hereafter be supplied."

Although he condemns some of Thynne's conclusions and errors, Speght in his address "To the Readers" gladly echoes his complaints about the printers. *They* are concerned with publicity, where *his* interests are scholarly, his labors hard, and his motives a mixture of honor and love. He writes of the "pains" he has taken, in repairing damage caused by "injurie of time, ignorance of writers, and negligence of Printers." He asks us to accept his labors for Chaucer's sake, and after condemning all those who have neither wit nor learning, he flatteringly addresses a wiser and more appreciative readership, to whom he humbly commends himself: "And so making no doubt of the friendly acceptance of such as have taken pains in writing themselves, and hoping wel also of all others, that meane to employ any labour in reading, I commit our Poet to your favourable affection." Speght hereby assists in the formation of a new audience, a clubbish reading (and writing) community that mirrors the editor himself. So much so, that Speght concludes his edition on the final page of his "Annotations, with some corrections" with a most Chaucerian injunction to his readers to continue his own work of annotation, as well as a Latin epithet, to answer the lines from Ovid on the title page of the edition. Likening the general run of scribes and printers to Adam Scriveyn, Speght positions himself on Chaucer's side:

> These faults and many mo committed through the great negligence of Adam Scrivener, notwithstanding Chaucers great charge to the contrary, might have ben amended in the text itselfe, if time had served: Whereas now no more, than the Prologues only, are in that sort corrected: Which fell out so, because they were last printed. Sentences also, which are many and excellent in this Poet, might have ben noted in the margents with some marke, which now must be left to the search of the Reader: of whom we crave in Chaucers behalfe that, which Chaucer in the end of one of his books requesteth for himselfe,
>
> Qui legis, emendes autorem, non reprehendas.

FINIS

Speght finds yet another way to make this apology in the curious poem by "H.B.," "The Reader to Geffrey Chaucer," a dialogue in which Chaucer speaks from beyond the grave to commend the labors of the editor. Just as Speght invites the reader to correct the text, the reader is also given a position from which to speak intimately with "good Geffrey," in a conversation whose theme is the rescue of Chaucer from obscurity, indeed, from exile, by his loving friend, Speght.

The Reader to Geffrey Chaucer

Rea. Where hast thou dwelt, good Geffrey al this while,
Unknowne to us, save only by thy bookes?

Chau. In haulks, and hernes, God wot, and in exile,
Where none vouchsaft to yeeld me words or lookes:
Till one which saw me there, and knew my friends,
Did bring me forth: such grace sometimes God sends.

Rea. But who is he that hath thy books repar'd,
And added moe, whereby thou art more graced?

Chau. The selfe same man who hath no labor spar'd,
To helpe what time and writers had defaced:
And made old words, which were unknown of many,
So plaine, that now they may be known of any.

Rea. Well fare his heart: I love him for thy sake,
Who for thy sake hath taken all his pains.

Chau. Would God I knew some means amends to make,
That for his toile he might receive some gains.
But wot ye what? I know his kindnesse such,
That for my good he thinks no pains too much:
And more than that; if he had knowne in time,
He would have left no fault in prose nor rime.

In the last stanza, "Chaucer" raises the possibility of remuneration for his editor, but nips the idea in the bud. Speght's aims are too noble and altruistic to be repaid in monetary terms. Again, we find the insistent discourse of the scholarly amateur and a relationship between editor and author of amicable affinity, while the very form of the dialogue seems to facilitate the act of communication.[52] Author, editor, and reader are apparently bound together in ties of love and mutual obligation, of mutually flattering recognition and knowledge. This discourse "naturally" represses the exclusions of class, gender, and education that make such homosocial recognition possible.

An even more specifically gendered discourse of friendship is re-hearsed in the letter "to his very loving friend, T.S.," from Francis Beau-mont, who speaks of Chaucer's unique ability

> to possesse his Readers with a stronger imagination of seeing that done before their eyes, which they reade, than any other that ever writ in any tongue. And here I cannot forget to remember unto you those auncient learned men of our time in Cambridge, whose diligence in reading of his workes them selves, and com-mending them to others of the younger sorte, did first bring you and mee in love with him: and one of them at that time was and now is (as you knowe) one of the rarest Schollers of the world. The same may bee saide of that worthy man for learning, your good friend in Oxford, who with many other of like excel-lent judgement have ever had *Chaucer* in most high reputation.

"Chaucer" has become a mnemonic for friendship, for brotherly companionship in scholarship and patronage of "the younger sorte," and for a nostalgia for university days. In conjunction with Speght's ad-dress to his readers and with H. B.'s poem, it is clear that the "love" it is possible to feel for Chaucer is an important aspect of the bonds that link a company of gentlemen. These gentlemen are not only the source of Speght's own love and knowledge of Chaucer, but also the main audi-ence for the edition, a community of male readers. And if they are not all gentle by birth—Speght entered Peterhouse, Cambridge, in 1566 as a poor scholar, dependent on a scholarship and part-time work as a ser-vant of the college—they are soon wound into this genteel circle of like-minded readers. According to Pearsall, Speght's "good friend in Oxford" was Dr. Thomas Allen, fellow of Trinity College, "a renowned mathe-matician, philosopher, and antiquary," while Beaumont himself was later to become master of Charterhouse. Pearsall also reminds us that Edmund Spenser was a student at Pembroke College around this time, from 1569 to 1576.[53]

In *The Genius of Shakespeare*, Jonathan Bate cites the pair of plays known as *The Return from Parnassus*, produced by Cambridge students between 1599 and 1601. The plays vividly dramatize the popularity of Shakespeare, but they draw an interesting contrast between the two English authors when the character Gullio is asked to choose between

Ingenioso's imitations of Chaucer, Spenser, and Shakespeare. Bate comments, "The foolish Gullio's choice of Shakespeare above the venerable Chaucer and Spenser carries the clear implication that from the play's 'university' point of view the vogue for Shakespeare has grown severely out of proportion."[54] What is also intriguing is that Ingenioso does not quote but rather imitates the works of the three authors: it's the capacity to rewrite Chaucer here, as elsewhere, that marks him out as an author worthy of attention. In his introduction to these plays, J. B. Leishman quotes a letter by William Gager, defending the performance of such plays: "We . . . doe it . . . to practyse owre owne style eyther in prose or verse; to be well acquantyed with *Seneca* or *Plautus;* honestly to embolden owre plath; to trye their voyces and confirme their memoryes; to frame their speeche; to conforme them to convenient action; to trye what mettell is in evrye one, and of what disposition thay are of."[55] Ingenioso's imitations are clearly part of this humanist endeavor and indicate the ease and extent to which Chaucer and Spenser, at least, have been assimilated into these humanist models.

Speght's invitation to his readers and friends to correct his text was enthusiastically taken up by Francis Thynne, the son of William, who, in 1599, wrote Speght a letter, his *ANIMADVERSIONS uppon the Annotacions and Corrections of some imperfections of impressiones of Chaucers workes (sett downe before tyme, and now) reprinted in the yere of oure lorde 1598 sett down by Francis Thynne,* criticizing the edition for its errors and inaccuracies. The circumstances of this letter and its contents have been well studied;[56] let us focus, in the present context, on Thynne's assumptions about the nature of editing and the role of the critical reader. We note, first of all, that Thynne does not publish his critique, but sends it to Speght in manuscript form. That is, the community of readers is still, as Speght wished to see it, a private community, which has not yet found abstract expression in a public sphere in which textual and critical debate might be exchanged. Thynne assumes from the beginning that he, as commentator, and Speght, as editor, are engaged in the same enterprise and with the same motives:

> The Industrye and love (maister Speighte) which you have used, and beare, uppon and to our famous poete Geffrye Chaucer, deservethe bothe comendatione and furtherance: the one to recompense your travayle, the other to accomplyshe the duetye, which

we all beare (or at the leaste, yf we reverence lernynge or regarde
the honor of oure Countrye, sholde beare) to suche a singuler or-
namente of oure tonge as the woorkes of Chaucer are.[57]

Editing and commenting on Chaucer is hard work, but it is neces-
sary, gentlemanly labor that brings its own rewards: noblesse oblige.
Thynne reminds Speght that he had invited correction, and he describes
his own labors in terms similar to those in which he commends
Speght's. His discourse calls up the Horatian imperatives of pleasure
and instruction but also appeals to an affinity, or amity, between editor
and author, describing Speght's "Industrye and love" and for his own
part, the "duetye and love whiche I beare to Chaucer."[58]

Francis Thynne was an enthusiastic antiquarian and a "professional
scholar," in Pearsall's phrase.[59] He was a self-taught expert on alchemy
and heraldry whose achievements in this field were recognized only a
few years before his death, when he was made Lancaster Herald. Pearsall
summarizes his catalog of failures thus: "He published nothing of note,
and his whole life was a history of being put upon."[60] In this context we
may recall Thynne's unhappy marriage and his imprisonment for debt
at the hands of his wife's relations.[61] Furnivall prints several of his letters
from prison and two of his "Epigrams," one defining the best wives as
the dead ones and one a lament on the miseries of marriage. In his letter
to Speght, Thynne invokes two other, perhaps compensatory, bonds of
social obligation: the first, this emphasis on the "duty" owed Chaucer by
the company of those who love him and second, the emphasis on the
duty owed by a son to his father.

It is the Thynne family reputation that is at stake here. Even though
Francis Thynne was only two years old when his father died, he repeats
a conversation between Henry VIII, Cardinal Wolsey, and his father,
"beinge in great favore with his prince, (as manye yet lyvinge canne
testyfye)," about the inclusion of the controversial, because virulently
anti-Catholic, *Plowman's Tale* as one of the additional Canterbury Tales.
The whole letter is a defense of William Thynne's own "ernest desire
and love . . . to have Chaucers Woorkes rightlye to be published," and a
determined justification of all his editorial and textual decisions.[62]

Here is Thynne defending his father against the charges of Speght
and others of wronging Chaucer with an imperfect edition:

Wherefore, to stoppe that gappe, I will answere, that Chaucers woorkes have byn sithens printed twyce, yf not thrice, and therfore by oure carelesse (and for the most parte unlerned) printers of Englande, not so well performed as yt ought to bee: so that, of necessytye, bothe in matter, myter, and meaninge, yt must needs gather corruptione, passinge throughe so many handes, as the water dothe, the further yt runnethe from the pure founteyne.[63]

The ideological force of these polemics is blatant. Editing involves the restoration and purification of text that necessarily, over the course of time, becomes promiscuously involved with the lowly and dirty business of the printers. The textual tradition, like all patriarchal, genealogical traditions, is constantly threatened by uncertainty and faithlessness, in this instance, because it depends on a commercial trade. The work of the fathers—Father Chaucer, Father Thynne—must be protected and constantly policed. Embedded within this discourse is also a strong sense of the linguistic instability of the English language, which rendered Chaucer progressively more illegible to his sixteenth-century readers and the philological support offered by the editor increasingly necessary, increasingly elaborate.

By the end of this century, Chaucer's works have become almost unreadable without specialist expertise and assistance. Speght included a glossary explaining the "old and obscure" words in the text and a translation of his French phrases. This section of his edition was expanded in the revised version of 1602, adding some limited etymological information to the glossary, with a number of new entries and translations of Latin phrases. Editing has become a doubled act of veneration and alienation, since such apparatus inevitably has the effect of confirming the sense of historical distance between Chaucer and his modern readers. As Tim Machan comments, "like any glossary, Speght's efforts . . . simultaneously encourage a sense of modernity and stand as an index of the original work's alterity."[64]

A further effect of this perception of linguistic distance is gradually to make impossible the easy supplements and continuations of Chaucer's poems so popular in the manuscripts and early printed editions. It is no longer straightforward to inhabit the space at the end of Chaucer's poems, once an increased historical self-consciousness and this desire for scholarly objectivity intervene to produce an authoritative, editorial voice, emanating from a set of increasingly specialized functions. The implicit claim to familiar knowledge of Chaucer now takes the form of linguistic or historical expertise, rather than the ability to generate more Chaucerian verse.

This does not mean the editors no longer feel compelled to add completions to incomplete texts: as late as 1687, brief moralizing conclusions to the *Cook's Tale* and the *Squire's Tale* were appended to a reprint of Speght's edition.[65] Nor does it imply that they are not attracted to the possibility of the spiritual transmission of Chaucerian voice, but such possibilities will now be hinted at or described secondhand, rather than enacted directly. The desire to speak with Chaucer, or in his voice, is displaced onto the various discourses and voices that proliferate around the Chaucerian text, and perhaps this explains the ease with which other poems found their way, progressively, into the "Works" of Chaucer, sustained by the commercial pressures to include "new" material, "never before imprinted," in each successive edition. If an editor is to "become" Chaucer, to claim any kind of allegiance with him, this now takes place in the framing sections of the edition: the prefaces, dedicatory poems, and so forth, clearly signed with the name of the editor or other contributor. That is, the split between prose and poetry as vehicles for, respectively, criticism and "creative" or imaginative writing is not yet complete: editorial and critical discourse can still take poetic form. "The Reader to Geffrey Chaucer" is an instance of editorial self-promotion in verse that typifies these trends.

However, it's clear that the English poetic tradition of Lydgate, Hawes, Clanvowe, Hoccleve, and, most luminously, Spenser is increasingly regarded as separate from the editorial, critical strand, witnessed by Speght's approving summary of Spenser's dealings with Chaucer. Speght's remarks are spoken at some distance from the material he is discussing, in a careful tone of objective description (and careful attribution of his sources) that we would these days take for granted in academic criticism. The authoritative tone of this summary is as important to my argument as its emphasis on the relation of friendship between the two poets:

> In his Faerie Queene in his discourse of friendship, as thinking himselfe most worthy to be Chaucers friend, for his like natu-

rall disposition that Chaucer had, hee sheweth that none that
lived with him, nor none that came after him, durst presume to
revive Chaucers lost labours in that unperfite tale of the Squire,
but only himselfe: which he had not done, had he not felt (as
he saith) the infusion of Chaucers owne sweet spirit, surviving
within him.

Speght's emphasis on the "daring" of Spenser in continuing the
Squire's Tale can perhaps be read as a subtle critique of the earlier deco-
rum according to which such continuations were indeed acceptable,
while his emphasis on the theme of friendship chimes closely with his
own sense of his immediate audience.

Even so, as we saw so clearly in the Thynne-Speght-Thynne sequence,
the proper name of the editor now operates in a different social and
rhetorical sphere from that of the poet; editors define themselves in op-
position to other editors, rather than appealing only to dyadic, seemingly
organic relationships with the poets whose work they present. The nec-
essary converse of professional rivalry, moreover, is professional cooper-
ation, in the grace with which Speght seems to have accepted Thynne's
suggestions and criticisms. Rightly or wrongly, Speght incorporated
many of his proposals in his revised edition of 1602,[66] and even printed
Thynne's "poor poem" in praise of Chaucer.[67] This poem concludes with
a characteristic, though rather incoherent, emphasis on Chaucer's poetic
posterity:

> Then *Chaucer* live, for still thy verse shall live,
> T'unborne Poëts, which life and light will give.

The metaphors of spiritual poetic transmission are persistent and
powerful.

Another curious addition to the second edition is an anonymous
poem that seems to invoke a genealogical continuity between poet and
editor. Here, Speght is commended as "the child of *Chaucers* fruitfull
breine."[68] Yet the poem's insistence on "the learn'd praise-worthie peine"
and "The helpfull notes" of the edition reveal a strong consciousness of
the distinctive features of the editorial task. Dominant here is the idea of
the editor as historical scholar who can rescue the medieval poet from
obscurity.

> Vernishing his workes with life and grace,
> Which envious age would otherwise deface:
> Then be he lov'd and thanked for the same,
> Since in his love he hath reviv'd his name.

In spite of the historical and cultural distance on which the editorial task depends, the verse affirms the continuity provided by the affectionate bonds of affinity and the reciprocal love of poet and scholar, which can bridge the alterity of the medieval text and "revive" the medieval poet, bringing him into the present and into the presence of new readers.

FROM PRINT TO MANUSCRIPT

The technology of print did not transform literary or material culture overnight. The circulation of manuscripts was still an important aspect of sixteenth-century court culture, for example, an environment positively resistant to the medium of print. Many printed texts, like Speght's edition, are addressed to an audience imagined as if it were only slightly more extended than a group of friends presenting manuscripts to each other, the culturally privileged mode of textual transmission. Arthur Marotti and Wendy Wall both draw attention to *Tottels Miscellany* of courtly lyrics, first published in 1557, as, in Wall's phrase, "staging a collision between poetry in its social environment and in its typographical form."[69] She explains the significance of the anthology's frequent reference to the original occasion of these poems' composition and initial reception: *"Tottels* makes evident the existence of a real 'stigma' at mid-century simply by the fact that it discloses to the public the poems circulating privately that writers had chosen to keep from the realm of print. . . . For the courtier, print could damage rather than enhance social status."[70]

In the accounts of both scholars, poetry in print struggles to retain the epistolary function emphasized by Seth Lerer in his work on the courtly reception of Chaucer. Indeed, in *Courtly Letters in the Age of Henry VIII*, Lerer argues that Chaucer's *Troilus and Criseyde* provides a kind of model for courtly conduct and social and textual intercourse in Henry's court, though not as a manual for lovers. Rather, the figure of Pandarus as "teacher of the art of letter writing," and as voyeur, becomes an exemplar, "a generative figure . . . , embodying the complicated and ultimately self-baffled artfulness of courtly life."[71] In this sense, the courtly "Chaucer"—in manuscript form—signifies an elevated form of cultural capital: as Thomas Wilson remarked in 1553, "The fine Courtier wil talke nothyng but Chaucer."[72]

Chaucer's importance as an exemplar of courtliness is also sustained by implicit comparisons with the courtly Elizabethan poets, also starting to negotiate the transition to print. Speght's edition of Chaucer, for instance, appeared in the same year as the 1598 folio of Sir Philip Sidney's collected works published by William Ponsonby.[73] This was a comprehensive edition that, like other printings of Sidney's poems in the 1590s, went a long way to lessening the "stigma" of print, as part of a gradual shift in literary criticism to honoring or memorializing contemporary poets. Marotti also argues that the image of Sidney as "a national hero who was portrayed as a Protestant martyr" elevated the social standing of amorous sonnets and courtly verses over the 1590s, "helping to incorporate what had essentially been regarded as literary ephemera into the body of durable canonical texts."[74] If this is so, then Chaucer also benefits from this shift in sixteenth-century cultural attitudes. The synchronicity of Chaucer and Sidney becoming Authors, in a "comprehensive and monumentalizing edition that celebrated his or her total achievements," is suggestive. Marotti suggests that Speght's Chaucer is less significant than Ponsonby's Sidney, since the latter edition more radically implied the incorporation of other living or recently deceased writers into a printed, literary canon.[75] But Chaucer's sixteenth-century editions provided an authoritative model for this kind of canonization; the work of textual, biographical, and genealogical scholarship that surrounded the Chaucer editions set a pattern for and began to ease the assimilation of contemporary writers into a tradition of published English writing.

However, while Chaucer is gradually being disseminated to larger audiences, the imaginary scene of reading his work is consistently presented as intimate and exclusive, almost in spite of the new technology and its broader reach. We saw that Speght's prefatory discourse consistently foregrounded a private scene of reading and writing, describing his "neere" and "privat" friends as his ideal readers, while Francis Beaumont's letter "to his very loving friend, T.S.," nostalgically recalls the reading of Chaucer among their friends at Cambridge as an important site for personalizing Chaucer's readership. The discourse of friendship seems to preserve the reading of Chaucer for a small minority of special readers, while the text of "Chaucer" is exchanged among them as a token of social affinity and love.

The phrase "loving friend" has a wide range of applications, of course, in sixteenth-century discourse: it appears in a grant from Henry VIII of a number of oaks from Windsor Forest to "my loving frynde william Thynne."[76] And in John Stow's *Survey of London,* first published in 1598, Stow refers to Speght as his "loving friend Thomas Speight."[77] Speght's own preface to the *Nun's Priest's Tale* in his introduction emphasizes this theme: "the morall whereof is to embrace true friends, and to beware of flatterers."[78] But sixteenth-century friendship can also be coded erotically as well as ethically, as Jonathan Goldberg demonstrates.[79] Either way, this kind of personal friendship usually appeals to a relationship of likeness or similarity among men.

It's also a theme found in at least one documented case in the afterlife of Speght's edition. Gabriel Harvey purchased and dated his own copy of the first edition and annotated it with "handsomely penned appraisals of contemporary writers."[80] He also signed, below the "Finis" on the last page, "gabrielis harveii, et amicorum. 1598." According to Virginia Stern, this is a sign that he circulated this volume among his friends, "as was his practice with some of his books of general interest." Thus the printed book is used as if it were a manuscript. Describing the "avid" reception of Chaucer in the universities, J. A. W. Bennett described Harvey as being "in love," indeed "besotted," with Chaucer,[81] a comment that seems to find support in Harvey's annotations to Thomas Wilson's *Arte of Rhetorike* (1567) and his singling out of experts in the art of mirth: "The first, & last, Chaucer, & Sidney. Fine, & sweet men: almost like Tullie, & Cesar."[82] The rhetoric of literary adulation is almost indistinguishable here from that of friendship.

For Harvey, the circulation of manuscripts is also a sign of friendship. He writes to Spenser, after the latter had, unbeknownst to him, printed some of Harvey's compositions, just "fine and phantasticall toys": "You see nowe what homely and ridiculous stuffe I still send abroade amongste my frendes, accordinge to my wontid manners, rather desiringe continuance of entier frendshipp and ould acquayntaunce by familiar and good fellowlye writinge then affecting the commendation of an eloquente and oratorlike stile by over curious and statelye enditinge."[83]

The kind of friendship of which Speght, Harvey, and other sixteenth-century scholars speak, in imagining their own audiences, takes the form of a horizontally imagined community, but it also depends on a kind of vertically imagined communion with Chaucer himself, so important in Speght's edition. This vertically imagined relationship across time is often a kind of spiritual communion, a convivial, heavenly meeting. So when Harvey mourns the death of his own friend, George Gascoigne, in 1557, he includes in his verse tribute a series of quatrains telling of the Englishmen Gascoigne will meet in heaven: the poets and writers mentioned include Chaucer, Gower, Lydgate, Surrey, and More.[84]

Also worth mention in this context is the 1573 *Dialogue both pleasaunt and pietifull* between Medicus and Crispine, a pastoral vision of the nine Muses, with Homer, Hesiod, Ennius, Lucan, and others. Included near them are "old Morall Goore" and "Wittie Chaucer . . . in a chaire of gold covered with roses, writyng prose and rime, accompanied with the Spirites of many kynges, knightes, and faire ladies; whome he pleasauntly besprinkeled with the sweete water of the welle, consecrated with the Muses, ecleped Aganippe."[85] While Gower is depicted dispensing moral wisdom and while they both partake in the poets' symposium, Chaucer is shown sharing water from the muses' well with his audience: it's an emphatically social vision of Chaucer.

The heavenly symposium of poets is a common trope, of course, in subsequent versions and retellings of poetic history: a way of affirming continuity with the past and, indeed, often a way of inhabiting the Chaucerian position of sending out one's books to "kisse the steps" where the classical authors may pass. The writer who exploits this trope most extensively is John Dryden, the subject of the next chapter. Dryden is a "hinge" text for my own project in another sense, though, since his own discourse on Chaucer represents a different kind of trajectory and writerly subjectivity for the critic, one that modern Chaucerians are more comfortable in claiming as the origin of their own.

5

TRANSLATING CHAUCER

FOR MODERNITY

JOHN DRYDEN

Reading the sixteenth-century editions of Chaucer produces an uncanny sense of familiarity and unfamiliarity. In the format and *ordinatio* of these books, their structure of introduction, text, commentary, and glossary, we recognize the disposition and some of the content of modern editorial and critical material around the literary text. And yet current editorial and critical practice insists on a radical disjunction with the discourses represented in these old editions: according to the opposition I examined in chapter 1, they belong more to "reception" than to "criticism." Their voices, their implied audiences, and their presuppositions and assumptions bear little or no resemblance to those of contemporary scholarship. It's an even more uncanny experience reading the fulsome expressions of love for Chaucer in the writings of Beaumont and Harvey. Their writings declare so openly what we have taught ourselves to repress when *we* go into print: the love of Chaucer and his poetry that barely dares to speak its name in contemporary criticism, but that remains one of the reasons why we keep writing and thinking about his work. Nor can the various pleasures of reading Chaucer in pedagogic contexts be ignored. One final contradiction: we distance ourselves firmly from the imbrication of sixteenth-century scholarship in the world of patronage, but who among us can resist the desire to please our own reviewers and referees? We implicitly commend ourselves and our labors to their attention in all that we do.

This and the next two chapters are concerned with these and other contradictions in "modern" Chaucer scholarship. Given that the external form of the Chaucer edition or the genre of the critical essay on Chaucer does not undergo radical change from the seventeenth through the nineteenth or even into the twentieth century, what different kinds of relationships can we track between those genres, on the one hand, and the changing subject-position of the Chaucerian and the communities into which Chaucerian discourse is directed, on the other? What kinds of contradictions emerge from the changing contexts and conditions of criticism and those inherited forms? A dominant theme will be the continual return of the repressed: the way in which enthusiastic expressions of love for and identification with Chaucer keep returning, despite the best efforts of an urbane and professionalized criticism to rely on objective scholarship and considered judgment.

After the sixteenth-century editions have established the practices of humanist scholarship and recuperated Chaucer as the worthy object of nationalist attention, the next most influential formulation of a different kind of Chaucerian writing position is John Dryden's preface to his *Fables Ancient and Modern* of 1700. While it is certainly a preface *to* those translations, it's the first extensive discussion of Chaucer that does not introduce a collection or edition of Chaucer, so it offers a new kind of space in which to write about Chaucer, as well as an influential, individualized refiguration of the voice of critical judgment.[1]

In my opening chapter, I suggested that the various receptions of Chaucer needed to be read in relation to one another, not in simple diachronic sequence. Continuous chronology now gives way to a more symptomatic structure in the following chapters, a structure that increasingly reflects modern projections onto Chaucer's reception history. Dryden's preface comes under scrutiny in this chapter in part for the disjunctions he marks with his own predecessors, but in large part because of the position he holds in modern accounts of the history of Chaucer studies. It's widely accepted that Dryden inaugurates modern Chaucer criticism. How have we come to recognize this as the originary moment of our own labors?

Dryden's "Soul Congenial"

With the perfect arbitrariness of literary history, Dryden's *Fables Ancient and Modern* are poised at the middle point, chronologically speaking, of

Chaucerian reception. Published three hundred years after Chaucer's death and in the year of Dryden's own death, these translations and their preface chart an influential map for the reception of these two poets and for their relationship to one another. The historical accident by which both poets died in the final year of a century, three hundred years apart, has only enhanced the influence of Dryden's discussion of Chaucer on later writers, and has certainly contributed to the idea that literary history can be organized and written around neat historical periods. Rarely do literary history and historical chronology coincide so neatly, the "ages" of Chaucer and Dryden taking on a powerful symbolic resonance for any encyclopedic view of conventional literary history. Dryden himself formulates some of those parallels, describing Chaucer as his "Countryman, and Predecessor in the Laurel,"[2] supposing that Chaucer was "poet" to Edward III, to Richard II, and to Henry IV (1453, lines 355–57). He also adopts a number of Chaucerian stances, such as retracting his own "loose writings" and calling for correction.

More generally, Dryden's preface is an early and influential episode in the history of literary criticism, insofar as he improvises a distinctive writing voice that is at once personal and yet ostensibly detached. For example, one of his stated aims in translating selected works of Virgil, Homer, Ovid, Boccaccio, and Chaucer is to clarify the similarities between Ovid and Chaucer: "For by this Means both the Poets being set in the same Light, and dress'd in the same *English* Habit, Story to be compar'd with Story, a certain Judgment may be made betwixt them, by the Reader, without obtruding my Opinion on him" (1445, lines 46–49). Dryden claims merely to "present" these poetic texts to the reader, yet he has stripped them of their historical, linguistic, and cultural difference and assimilated them to English verse (and cultural) conventions— "dress'd in the same *English* Habit." Dryden here gives influential shape to a formalist aesthetic and influential voice to the critic's and the reader's "judgment."

For all his careless disregard of his own opinion, Dryden is continually drawing his own comparisons and similarities among the poets he considers. His own opinions are never far from the surface, and they are implicitly justified and sustained by his theory of poetic influence, the idea that poets beget and transmit their own linear traditions: "Milton was the Poetical Son of *Spencer*, and Mr. Waller of Fairfax; for we have our Lineal Descents and Clans, as well as other Families; Spencer more than once insinuates, that the Soul of Chaucer was transfus'd into his Body; and that he was begotten by him Two hundred years after his Decease. Milton has acknowledg'd to me, that Spencer was his Original" (1445, lines 32–37). In this passage, Dryden develops two mutually sustaining ideas that become fundamental to patriarchal literary tradition. His idea of lineal descent and the elite poetic family represents a benign notion of inheritance (in contrast to Harold Bloom's agonistic Oedipal poetics). Equally enabling is the idea that "father" and "son" in English poetry might be separated by as many generations as separate Spenser from Chaucer or Milton from Spenser. Should historical continuity fail, should another medieval period of scholarly neglect intervene, then the souls of older English poets might still be "transfus'd" into those of their spiritual descendants. This possibility of a transcendent connection guarantees poetic continuity: the perpetuation of the line in an elaborate metaphorical structure that takes for granted its parthenogenetic masculinity, and which also mitigates the dangers and risks of historical change. The male poet gives birth to his own poetry, certainly, but he also originates his own tradition, which can be perpetually renewed.

Dryden's poets aren't in competition or struggle with one another; nevertheless, the transmission of poetic authority brings its own privileges to those writing in the present, at the expense of older or earlier poets. Dryden invokes the same motif to license his improvements to Chaucer's poems in his translations:

> I have presum'd farther in some Places, and added somewhat of my own where I thought my Author was deficient, and had not given his Thoughts their true Lustre, for want of Words in the Beginning of our Language. And to this I was the more embolden'd, because (if I may be permitted to say it of my self) I found I had a Soul congenial to his, and that I had been conversant in the same Studies. Another Poet, in another Age, may take the same Liberty with my Writings; if at least they live long enough to deserve Correction. (1457, lines 521–29)

Dryden authorizes other poets to modernize his own writings, but it's an authorization that is grounded in the medieval tradition of asking for correction. It's a topos familiar to Dryden from the works of Chaucer and Boccaccio, and one that plays an important role in Chaucer's own editorial history. As a rhetorical trope, it partakes of the conventional modesty of the poet writing for patronage, but simultaneously implies the work's own future posterity. Dryden borrows Chaucer's petition, though not his words, to reinforce his claim to share a congenial soul. He also projects the similar "transfusion" of souls into the future, shoring up his own fame by challenging another poet to join this select group.

Now Dryden and Chaucer may share congenial souls, but Dryden is in a better position to give "true Lustre" to their shared poetic gift. From a bookish, continuous present, it's easy to claim an individualized affinity when one is about to rewrite the works of one's predecessor for modernity. The ritual gesture of humility here sounds more like defiance. It's an extremely powerful set of imagined relationships between readers and writers that will be crucial for the way modern Chaucerians imagine themselves into the presence of Chaucer, his books, and his other readers, at the same time as underlining the necessity of their own labors.

A good deal of this had become habitual with Dryden by 1700. As Earl Miner remarks of him, "He was perpetually discovering that his soul was like whatever poet of old he was engaged with,"[3] while Swift caricatured him in *The Battle of the Books* as, in Jennifer Brady's phrase, an "avid genealogist."[4] Dryden's claims to spiritual affiliation are usually read in terms of his nostalgia for the past and his affirmation of the continuity of father and son in poetic tradition. Even if we accept Bloom's original thesis that it is only after Shakespeare that the possibility of poetic intimidation arises, Dryden at least attributes a full measure of "authorship" to Chaucer. It is a measure of the degree to which Chaucer's authorship is now assured, or countersigned—Chaucer has become the poetic signatory to a body of works that attract critical commentary as well as poetic imitation—that Dryden speaks of him in precisely the same way as Homer, Virgil, Ovid, Boccaccio, even Dryden's own contemporaries. This is one of the reasons why Dryden is often heralded as the first modern Chaucerian critic: in addition to the urbane "objective" voice that prizes "judgment," he is the first to take Chaucer's authorship absolutely for granted as the starting point, not for biography or historical recovery per se, but for comparative, evaluative criticism. It is at the *expense* of Chaucer's medieval historicity, of course, and this is another reason for modern Chaucerians to be attentive to Dryden's discussion and its influence on twentieth-century formalisms and constructions of canonicity. Does elevating Chaucer into the canon of high literary cul-

ture in English lift him too far out of his medieval context? Does canon-
icity come at the expense of historicity?

Certainly, Dryden's understanding of poetic influence is relatively
benign.[5] And we will not be able to go much further in a Bloomian read-
ing of Dryden's relationship to Chaucer, as far as his poetry is concerned,
since the anxiety of influence—an *unconscious* struggle to surpass the
earlier poet—is hardly likely to reveal itself in translations and modern-
izations. Such an investigation, in any case, would be beyond the terms
of this study. We can, however, pay some attention to the critical model
Dryden is working with in his discussion of the medieval poet, since the
preface has been so very influential on subsequent Chaucer criticism.

It should come as no surprise that the "Lineal Descents and Clans"
of poets should mask greater rivalries and anxieties, even if Dryden is
not awed into negativity by Chaucer. The line of succession is not open
to everyone who would claim it, of course. Dryden is very clear that
poets are the only true legatees. For example, he gives himself license to
restore Chaucer's sense, which at times was "lost or mangled in the Er-
rors of the Press" (1457, line 530), and to correct Chaucer's meter and
his incomplete pentameters, at the expense of Thomas Speght, "he who
publish'd the last Edition of him; for he would make us believe the
Fault is in our Ears, and that there were really Ten Syllables in a Verse
where we find but Nine" (1453, lines 338–40). Dryden thus adopts and
elaborates the sixteenth-century writerly hierarchies, grouping the edi-
tor with the printer and downgrading both roles in comparison with all
three of Dryden's roles of poet, translator, and commentator: "But this
Opinion is not worth confuting; 'tis so gross and obvious an Errour." In
a textbook example of critical misprision, it is only the congenial poetic
soul who has a faultless ear for Chaucer's faulty metrics; while that con-
geniality is defined via a firm class hierarchy that privileges creativity
over scholarship and a relationship among soul mates over one between
professionals. Paul H. Fry makes the related point that Dryden is bound
to find Chaucer deficient in *some* respect: "otherwise there would be
nothing left to say for modernity, and in that case the reciprocity of
benefit between past and present souls, on the strength of which Dry-
den justifies his own election to the symposium of his 'Preface,' could
no longer be demonstrated."[6]

Dryden is equally insistent on the difficulties he has transcended in
communing with Chaucer, whom he infantilizes by associating him

with the youth of the English language: the medieval poet is "Father of English Poetry," but Dryden excuses some of his expressions and metrical forms, since Chaucer lived "in the Dawning of our Language" (1451, line 262). Or again, "We can only say, that he liv'd in the Infancy of our Poetry, and that nothing is brought to Perfection at the first. We must be Children before we grow Men" (1453, lines 347–50). If Chaucer is a poetic father figure, Dryden speedily disables him by associating him with linguistic infancy. It represents a dramatic reversal of Lerer's fifteenth-century poetic, in which Chaucer's poetic successors represent themselves as infantilized in comparison with their teacher and master.

Dryden's figurations of individual affinity with Chaucer thus play across a number of axes pointing in different directions: a continuous present that allows Dryden to share a soul with Chaucer but a sense of historical distance that necessitates his translation; Chaucer's paternity but the "infancy" of his language; Chaucer's past but Dryden's future; and individual affinity articulated against a rather vaguely defined sense of community. In the passages from Dryden already quoted, it is clear that the congenial soul is figured as much in horizontal, that is, brotherly, terms as in vertical, or fatherly, terms. Dryden shares not only a similar sensibility to Chaucer, but also, in a pleasant fantasy, shares a similar background and the same library. Importantly, his metaphysical magic turns out to have a strong social component. At two different points in the preface, Dryden also describes Boccaccio as another who, "living in the same Age with Chaucer, had the same Genius, and follow'd the same Studies," and also refined his mother tongue (1459, lines 601–2; see also 1446, lines 59–73). It is almost as if Dryden echoes Francis Beaumont's nostalgic Cambridge reminiscences, when he assumes that poetry derives from similar "Studies."

The model of the *congenial* soul, moreover, is a way of defusing Chaucer's influence, to appropriate him as a friend, not a rival. In the same way, Chaucer's envoy to *Troilus and Criseyde* positions his own book doing humble obeisance to the shades of Virgil, Ovid, Homer, Lucan, and Statius, but nevertheless enjoying their company, ascending the same staircase. Dryden invokes a spiritual company in the preface only in a displaced manner, using a trope we have already encountered. Here is Dryden praising Chaucer's naturalism: "I see . . . all the Pilgrims in the *Canterbury Tales,* their Humours, their Features, and the very Dress, as distinctly as if I had supp'd with them at the *Tabard* in *Southwark.*" Fry links this passage to Dryden's discussions of the temperaments of Shakespeare and Homer, and comments perceptively:

> In this convivial reaction Dryden finds a way of transcending time that resembles the First Circle of Dante or the symposium of the dead in other writers. . . . In seating himself at this banquet of souls, Dryden recoups whatever loss of pride he may feel as their translator. In the company of such writers, the excellence of whom his audience either knows or can be taught to perceive (to this latter end, he devotes most of his attention to Chaucer), Dryden can defy his petty detractors, again like Dante in the First Circle, as though he too were already canonized by posterity.[7]

Communing with Chaucer is soon transferred to a social occasion—drinking with Chaucer and his companions—as the trope of the heavenly symposium of poets descends to the more mundane world of everyday realism. One of the most important effects of this condensation is to smooth the path of access to that convivial feast to critics; that is, to attentive readers of Chaucer, as well as to poets. Fry is right to draw our attention to Dryden's literary antecedents in Dante's *Inferno*, but the material, social contexts for which Dryden is writing must also be considered. Dryden's vision of supping at the Tabard can also be read as an early vision of the coffee shop, a form of public sphere where ideas can be exchanged in an informal mode, where class (though not gender) differences can theoretically be transcended. In his discussion of this distinctively English form of the early public sphere in the early eighteenth century, Terry Eagleton describes a similar form of contradiction:

> *What* is spoken or written, within this rational space, pays due deference to the niceties of class and rank; but the speech act itself, the *énonciation* as opposed to the *énoncé*, figures in its very form an equality, autonomy and reciprocity at odds with its class-bound content. The very act of utterance discloses a quasi-transcendental community of subjects, a universal model of rational exchange, which threatens to contradict the hierarchies and exclusions of which it speaks.[8]

Similarly, Dryden's idea of sharing a "congenial soul" with Chaucer looks back, nostalgically, to a more elite model of paternity, but also forward, as it were, to a more democratic image of community: criticism as "rational exchange."

Dryden's Posterity

Chaucerians have been very ready to recognize Dryden's essay as a founding moment in modern Chaucerianism. His recognitions of Chaucer's realism, humor, sense of character, and humanity have been cited again and again.[9] John Burrow's remarks can stand as typical: "In Dryden's essay we see for the first time Chaucer's poetry submitted to the considered judgement of a man who is not predisposed only to praise it." And the "best criticism of Chaucer in the eighteenth century derives from Dryden."[10] Indeed, in its content, in its style, and in its distinctive critical voice, Dryden's preface seems to signal a decisive modernity in the history of Chaucerian response. And yet, as always, modernity is made through repressing its other, in this case the translations themselves. Chaucerians express little interest in Dryden's translations of *The Knight's Tale*, the *Nun's Priest's Tale*, the *Wife of Bath's Tale*, the description of the Parson, and the *Flower and Leaf* (printed as Chaucer's poem in Speght's edition). The hierarchies of criticism certainly give precedence to the preface over the translations, for modern Chaucerians, and effect a firm separation between them: the translations are discussed only as part of the history of reception, while the preface traverses both disciplines, both criticism and reception.[11]

The reasons for this are not hard to seek: the modern Chaucerian, learned in philology and history as disciplines of *recovery*, can hardly empathize with Dryden's sense that Chaucer so badly needs translation. Middle English is no barrier to the modern professional's path to Chaucer, though I will have occasion later in this book to consider the complex relations between philology and criticism. Dryden's claims that Chaucer *needs* translation are, of course, ontologically ambiguous, since in order to be *able* to translate him, he already presumes a full understanding of the original. It's possible that the reception of Dryden's translations has been colored by the work of his followers.

Dryden's translations are followed by many others in the eighteenth century, from poets keen to transform Chaucer's rude language into regular rhymes and iambic rhythms and feeling free to expand his lines at will. They rewrite and reorient Chaucer, transforming his voice into that of an urbane, often quite prolix satirist, concerned chiefly with "humour, sexuality, and interest in country folk and animals."[12] As Betsy Bowden notes in the introduction to her edition of these modernizations, they often refer either implicitly or explicitly to Dryden's theory of translation, expounded in his preface to Ovid's *Epistles*.[13] But they lean heavily on Dryden's and Pope's sense of Chaucer as a "rough diamond," rather than a ready-made congenial soul; they tend to go further than Dryden, too, in disparaging Chaucer. Caroline Spurgeon remarks on the popularity of the modernizations: "[M]ost of their admirers appear to think that the more they belittled the originals the greater was the honour which redounded to the modernizers."[14] She then quotes from Jabez Hughes's *Verses occasioned by reading Mr. Dryden's Fables:*

> Revolving Time had injur'd *Chaucer's* Name,
> And dimm'd the brilliant Lustre of his Fame;
> Deform'd his Language, and his Wit depress'd,
> His serious Sense oft sinking to a Jest;
> Almost a Stranger ev'n to *British* Eyes,
> We scarcely knew him in the rude Disguise:
> But cloath'd by Thee, the banish'd Bard appears
> In all his Glory, and new Honours wears.
> Thus *Ennius* was by *Virgil* chang'd of old;
> He found him Rubbish, and he left him Gold.

It was a hard line to maintain, that Chaucer was *worth* translating as well as so badly *needing* translation. Dryden's phrase, the "rough diamond," was the most eloquent way of getting around this difficulty. But Hughes's sentiments are common and go a long way to explaining the absence, through most of the eighteenth century, of the claims to affinity and congeniality made by Dryden. Injury, dimness, deformity, depression, estrangement, rudeness, banishment, and rubbish—these are hardly the qualities that would invite the eighteenth-century poet or scholar to congenial empathy with Chaucer. Chaucer must be dressed up in eighteenth-century costume—"cloath'd by Thee"—before he can be invited into the coffee shop. If this is an age when criticism first develops its distinctive modern form, it is developing as the response to *contemporary* writings. In order for his urbane wit and his very status as an author to be recognized, Chaucer must be reclothed in contemporary guise. Hughes of course echoes Dryden's phrase, dressing Ovid and Chaucer "in the same *English* Habit."

Such "dressing" could also take the form of a disguise. The signifiers "Chaucer" or "Canterbury Tales" often functioned as a convenient tag, through the seventeenth and eighteenth centuries, for further collections of poems or stories, often satirical or moralistic in intent, with little reference to Chaucer or medieval poetics. We could list the following: *Chaucers Ghoast; or, a Piece of Antiquity Containing Twelve Pleasant Fables of Ovid*, 1672; *Chaucer's Whims*, 1701; *Brown Bread and Honour, a tale. Moderniz'd from an ancient manuscript of Chaucer*, 1716; and "*Canterbury Tales*" by "John Chaucer, Junior" published in 1770.[15] None of these examples of pseudo-Chaucerian writing bears much relation to Chaucer's own writing, but must still color our sense of what "Chaucer" signifies in this period. William L. Alderson comments that through the many modernizations of his works, "Chaucer is brought into a title-page relationship with contemporary political satire."[16]

Even so, within the trajectory of criticism that takes us toward the end of the nineteenth century and Matthew Arnold, the terms of Dryden's preface are echoed again and again. Its discussion of Chaucer's language, his sensibility, his comprehensive interest in human nature, and his comic realism are all deeply influential on subsequent criticism. It becomes customary to speak of Chaucer's "genius," for example, and even Samuel Johnson, while disagreeing with Dryden's assessment of Chaucer's metrical originality, rehearses his description of Chaucer's genius and of Chaucerian poetry as "the infancy of our poetry."[17] Thomas Warton also writes of the "native genius" of the poet in his *History of English Poetry*, written in 1774.[18] This is the period when, according to Jonathan Bate, the category of "genius" was "invented in order to account for what was peculiar about Shakespeare."[19] In this usage, associated with a conception of the greatest poetry as bardic, "genius" implies a degree of artlessness, springing from a national culture in its infancy. Chaucer's genius, though less fully acknowledged than Shakespeare's at this formative stage in criticism, nevertheless seems to borrow some of its distinctive shape from the dramatist's.

Chaucer's natural or native genius is most clearly exemplified in the *General Prologue:* in terms that will become reminiscent of Shakespeare criticism, Dryden writes that here Chaucer "has taken into the compass of his *Canterbury Tales* the various manners and humours (as we now call them) of the whole English nation, in his age. Not a single character has escaped him." After praising the realism of their descriptions, the fitting-ness of their discourse and conversation, he remarks,

> here is God's Plenty. We have our Fore-fathers and Great Grand-dames all before us, as they were in *Chaucer's* Days; their general Characters are still remaining in Mankind, and even in *England*, though they are call'd by other Names than those of *Moncks*, and *Fryars*, and *Chanons*, and *Lady Abbesses*, and *Nuns;* For Mankind is ever the same, and nothing lost out of Nature, though everything is alter'd. (1455, lines 443–59)

The very fame of this passage is a clear indication of its perceived aptness as a characterization of what makes Chaucer both great and timeless. Chaucer's realism is linked with a national poetic ethos and a national character, and a simultaneous assertion of a constant humanism. It is a thread taken up and expounded by a number of Dryden's successors, to assert the distinctive continuity of the English character. Here is Thomas Warton, for example: "[H]is knowledge of the world availed him in a peculiar degree, and enabled him to give such an accurate picture of ancient manners as no contemporary nation has transmitted to posterity."[20]

William Blake also follows Dryden, though less nationalistically, in his *Descriptive Catalogue* of portraits:

> The characters of Chaucer's Pilgrims are the characters which compose all ages and nations: as one age falls, another rises, different to mortal sight, but to immortals only the same; for we see the same characters repeated again and again, in animals, vegetables, minerals, and in men; nothing new occurs in identical existence; Accident ever varies, Substance can never suffer change nor decay. . . . Of Chaucer's characters, as described in his *Canterbury Tales,* some of the names or titles are altered by time, but the characters themselves for ever remain unaltered, and consequently they are the physiognomies or lineaments of universal human life, beyond which Nature never steps. Names alter, things never alter.[21]

The constancy of human nature is, of course, the bridge between the present and the past that makes speaking with Chaucer possible in the first place: it is one of the founding premises of liberal humanism that facilitates the linguistic and cultural recuperation of the medieval poet.[22]

Academic Chaucerians have long recognized Dryden as the father of modern Chaucer criticism. An important form of misrecognition, however, troubles the line of simple inheritance, for we no longer claim so directly or so personally, in the fashion that underpins Dryden's criticism, to share a congenial soul with Chaucer. Similarly, while Dryden's digressive essayistic mode survives in some areas of modern criticism, it has no exact equivalent in the more specialized modes of Chaucerian scholarship. This is not a black-and-white opposition between amateur and professional modes, of course, because the professionals have not completely abandoned the traces of the more personal mode. Even so, if the model of the congenial soul has been, until recently, a structural condition of possibility for literary criticism, its most overt manifestations have been repressed from the decorum of the modern professional Chaucerian. We have already considered some aspects of that decorum: we turn now to consider its trajectory through the nineteenth century and into the twentieth.

6

READING CHAUCER

OUTSIDE THE ACADEMY

FURNIVALL, WOOLF, AND CHESTERTON

The modern recognition of Dryden's preface as an inaugural document
for Chaucer criticism depends on a number of factors in almost irre-
sistible combination. Dryden's appreciation of Chaucer's qualities as a
comic realist is given critical ballast by his own more serious act of in-
stalling Chaucer into a classical and European literary pantheon. More-
over, his ready identification with Chaucer along the individual trajec-
tory of spiritualized poetic affinity intersects satisfyingly with the more
convivial, inclusive model of the community of pilgrims. It has become
a most enabling combination for modern Chaucer studies, sustained by
Dryden's perceived influence on the development of literary studies
more generally.[1] Dryden's critical voice, his stance of balanced, reasoned
judgment, provides a flattering image for the professional critic looking
for a historical origin and tradition. Conversely, however, this recogni-
tion of Dryden's discursive and critical priority depends on effacing or
downplaying a number of important differences between our own prac-
tice and Dryden's.

These differences are obscured by the workings of the Chaucer tra-
dition, which throughout the twentieth century has specialized in an-
thologizing extracts of Chaucer criticism, removing them from their
original context, and setting them in linear, chronological sequence to
throw that tradition into sharper historical relief. Like other Chaucer
scholars, I depend on these anthologies, but it's worth recognizing their
necessary artificiality: the way in which these mesmerizing sequences

flatten the variety of genres and publishing contexts in which people write of Chaucer. Accordingly, fifteenth-century poetic responses segue into published commentaries, and eighteenth-century essays segue into articles published in professional journals. A very particular loss, for the concerns of *Congenial Souls,* is the distinction between work or writing on Chaucer directed to a restricted circle and that directed to a more general public sphere. This is a crucial distinction for early writers. Another factor virtually ignored by the anthologies is the pedagogical context in which most Chaucer criticism takes place in the twentieth century: histories of Chaucerian reception and of the changing images of Chaucer or critical fashions tend to follow the direction of the anthologies to focus on content at the expense of context.

Dryden's commentaries on Chaucer may seem to set the tone for modern Chaucer criticism, but he writes for a distinctive social and political context that bears little relationship to the contemporary academy. In 1958, E. M. W. Tillyard recognized the force of this difference. Writing a history of the English Tripos at Cambridge, he discusses some of the early English critics and remarks: "And I could remind the reader that Dryden, reputed father of English criticism proper, was a Cambridge man. But none of these had the least notion of English as an academic subject and thus cannot be called the patriarchs of English studies in any downright sense."[2] Tillyard is right: we would hardly describe Dryden as a "Chaucerian" in the same way as we might use this label to describe a Donaldson or Dinshaw. Such terminology belongs to a modern professional academic context, where special areas of expertise are recognized among a restricted cluster of institutional identities.

In this chapter and the next, I explore some of the contradictions in modern Chaucer criticism, especially in the relationships it articulates with its own history. The present chapter starts with the formation of "English studies" as an academic discipline, and the special case of Chaucer studies in that history. I'll be suggesting that modern professional Chaucerians line themselves up in a single, homogeneous tradition stretching back through Dryden to Speght, Spenser, and Lydgate only by radically misrepresenting their own enterprise and by repressing their own dependence on the conflicted institutional histories of English and medieval studies.

To do this, I turn my attention in this chapter away from the more or less continuous chronology of preceding chapters and toward a more disjunctive and selective history of literary studies, especially in England: the history of the discipline that recognizes Dryden as founder. This "turn" to the nineteenth century in this chapter must nevertheless seem dramatic. While Chaucer is certainly edited, translated, and modernized in the intervening period, I am particularly concerned now with the phenomenon by which professionally and pedagogically oriented literary studies shore up their own strength by forcing a split with a more specialized or amateur readership, a split whose origins we must seek in the nineteenth century and which is played out most dramatically in England. Chaucer studies plays a role in this history whose importance has not always been recognized. In the passionate and confused debates about what was proper to the academic study of English literature in the late nineteenth and early twentieth centuries, Chaucer often stands as a pivotal figure, or at least a pivotal marker of the difference between "Early English" and "English Literature." As the culminating point of "Early English," Chaucer is deeply associated with the philological study of medieval texts, but as the "father" of modern English literature, he stands at the head of the literary canon. The institutional histories of these two branches constitute a very complex pattern indeed.

The history, or the "rise," of English studies in nineteenth-century England is a narrative that has been told from many points of view in other contexts, with writers variously stressing the changes in critical fashion, in institutional formation, in the ideological functions attributed to literary studies, in the role of English in a national educational system, and so on. The general history of Chaucer criticism in the twentieth century is also reasonably familiar, I presume, to most of my readers. In this chapter, I want to examine the formation of the modern medievalist as a distinctive writing and speaking subject-position in an increasingly professional context. I will do this by a process of indirection, considering the Chaucerian writings of a number of figures whose relationship with the contemporary academy is at best vexed. I start with a figure who is absolutely central to nineteenth-century Chaucer scholarship, but whose legacy for modern Chaucerians is far more ambiguous and in some ways quite negative: Frederick James Furnivall.

Furnivall's career spans some of the profound changes and debates affecting the inception of modern (as opposed to classical) literary studies as an academic discipline at Oxford and Cambridge. Responses to Furnivall point up some of the most profound anxieties around those developments and his relationships with his contemporaries. Those differential relationships are crucial to this chapter. Constituting an extreme point of the patterns of identification with Chaucer I have been sketching in the last five chapters, Furnivall is the most extreme, most enthusiastic exponent of the discourses of affinity: the Chaucerians' Chaucerian. Furnivall is not part of any simple or continuous tradition with Dryden, yet he pushes Dryden's discourse of affinity to an extreme position, an extreme against which twentieth-century Chaucerians are careful to define themselves. The professional decorum that develops in his wake defines itself in partial sympathy with and in partial opposition to his own enthusiastic, and most Chaucerian voice. The chapter concludes with an exploration of what I argue becomes a cul-de-sac in Chaucer criticism: two early twentieth-century examples of "amateur" or "popular" Chaucerian commentary in the work of Virginia Woolf and G. K. Chesterton. Their writings both reveal, in different ways, some of the losses sustained by the development of a more "objective," professional critical mode.[3]

F. J. FURNIVALL AND THE WORKING MEN'S COLLEGE

By any account and from any perspective, Furnivall is a fascinating object of study. Of all the modern Chaucerians, he has attracted the most biographical attention, though this is largely because being Chaucerian was only one of his many occupations. Furnivall's prolific program of publishing and writing, his voluminous correspondence, his eccentricities, his unconventional personal life, and his impatient, conflictual personality have all been examined in detail; in the discussion that follows I will try to resist the temptation to revisit the most familiar aspects of his life and work. The lure of personality is remarkably strong, however, as the theme of my book suggests. My particular interest lies in the way Furnivall characterizes his own labors and models himself as a scholar: these are the aspects of his work that most fascinate his twentieth-century followers as they establish a professional discourse suitable for the institutionalization of literary studies. Furnivall's writings richly invoke the complex relations between individual personality and scholarly writing, and he seems at some times like one of the last great amateur scholars, associated with the traditions of gentlemanly leisure; at others, a tireless teacher and enthusiast for the education of working men and women. He prides himself on the "dryasdust" nature of his biographical, paleographical, and lexical work, but this scholarship is consistently put to the service of congenial communion with the writers of the past, particularly Chaucer.

Let us first consider how Furnivall is positioned institutionally. He was educated at University College, London, and at Trinity Hall, Cambridge, where he studied classics. He then entered the law, studying at Lincoln's Inn, and was called to the bar at Gray's Inn in 1849, but seems never to have been greatly engaged by his legal practice. His primary institutional affiliation was with the Working Men's College in London, founded by J. M. Ludlow and C. E. Maurice in 1854, where he taught English grammar and literature and where he spent much of his time organizing its social program.

Furnivall's lifelong commitment to the education of working men and, to a lesser degree, of women also took the form of many societies for the literary and historical study of favorite authors and special projects. The Early English Text Society, the New Shakspere Society (Furnivall insisted on this spelling), the Chaucer Society, the Browning Society, and the *Oxford English Dictionary* all serve as indications of his activity. His biographer William Benzie stresses that his early Christian piety became transformed, through his growing agnosticism, to the "fresh, optimistic, and compensatory energy" with which he devoted himself to the more secular cause of early English literature, with the clearly stated intention of revealing its comprehensive glories to the nation.[4] In Peter Faulkner's words, he became a "missionary for Early English,"[5] but it is important to stress that his mission was strongly conceived in nationalist and socialist, not religious, terms. His voluminous publications and his letters, his social and organizational drives bear strong witness to a passionate belief in what Chris Baldick calls the "social mission" of literary study and literary criticism: the liberal conviction, driven by a fervent secular nationalism, that education, literary education more particularly, can enhance the lives of its students.[6] One of the sustaining tenets of this nationalist agenda was that education would bring less privileged men and women into contact with the personalities and genius of past writers. In Benzie's phrasing, a liberal education "would stress social reconstruction and enrichment of personality through the study of English

literature, which [Furnivall] saw as the best means of establishing con-
nections with England's national heritage and contact with the great
minds of the past."[7]

Furnivall's many clubs and associations have been described as typ-
ical Victorian compensations for the loss of preindustrial social forms.
In Benzie's words, they were "social as well as literary 'institutions' and,
like his rowing clubs and student social outings and gatherings, repre-
sented a model community in miniature in which the keynote was com-
radeship and trust."[8] They seem to have been modeled on the working
men's associations sponsored by the Christian Socialists that had also
led to the founding of the Working Men's College.[9]

In the college, literature and language studies were promoted with
quite specific goals of social, national, and class cohesion in mind. Mau-
rice expressed the hope that "generous duties and common sympathies"
might help unite the classes.[10] This college, then, was distinguished from
the earlier mechanics' institutes, whose emphasis was technical and com-
mercial, rather than humanistic. Maurice shared with William Ruskin
and Matthew Arnold a belief in the redemptive power of literature and
art, while the college, like other institutions for the education of work-
ing men and women and the system of university extension lectures,
was an important ground for the mounting of arguments in favor of
literary study as a university discipline. Toward the end of his life, Fur-
nivall became one of the first vice presidents of the English Association,
founded in 1906, the organization that sponsored the famous Newbolt
Report on the teaching of English in 1921, which argued for the central-
ity of English literature at all levels of education in England.[11]

But the model of Maurice's college was a contradictory one, at least
where this relation to the universities was concerned. "College spirit"
was an important aspect of Maurice's vision for the College, and it re-
veals a nostalgic yearning for a university model that it is hard not to see,
ultimately, as elitist. And this is despite the fact that Maurice had been
expelled from King's College for his attempts to Christianize the social-
ist movement of association.[12] Looking back in 1904 to the founding of
the college fifty years earlier, G. M. Trevelyan describes a handful of the
early founders—Tom Hughes, Charles Kingsley, R. B. Litchfield, John
Westlake, and Furnivall, along with Maurice himself—as "the 'College
spirit' incarnate" and characterizes its heritage as "the air of friendship,
good-fellowship, equality, and common endeavour towards the things of

the mind, irrespective of any ulterior object, material, religious, or polit-ical. It is this that makes it so attractive to many Oxford and Cambridge men, and which renders the connection with the older Universities pe-culiarly easy and peculiarly desirable."[13] The optimistic view that "equal-ity" might be brought about by education is a crucial aspect of the liberal program that dominated many of these arguments in the second half of the nineteenth century. As we saw with Thomas Speght, Francis Beau-mont, and Gabriel Harvey, too, the university provides a model of genial companionship, equality, and study whose gender exclusiveness remains completely invisible to its participants.

In fact, Furnivall represents an important rupture into this cozy, brotherly image. The precise relations between scholarship or learning and the other aspects of "college spirit" actually became the subject of dispute and an eventual falling-out between Furnivall and Maurice. In Furnivall's words, as one of the "youngest unmarried members of the Council," it fell to him to organize the social life of the college: his row-ing and sculling clubs figure extensively in various reminiscences of Furnivall and the college, and need not be dwelt on here. Furnivall's in-terest in rowing does, however, highlight the force of the class system: the Working Men's College rowing club, even disguised as "The Mau-rice Club," was not recognized on the river and, like other working men's clubs, was not permitted to enter races with the other clubs, "a rule which justly raised the ire, and vexed the soul of Dr Furnivall."[14] But as Furnivall became less of a Christian and more of an agnostic, he came to diverge from Maurice on, for example, the appropriateness of Sunday outings, of dances, and of other entertainments in mixed com-pany.[15] In his history of the college, J. F. C. Harrison comments, "It says much for Maurice that he never attempted to drive Furnivall out, much as he was pained by his actions and speech; and it was the first big tri-umph of the College that it could continue to hold such diverse talents together."[16] One of the most important aspects of his fallout with Mau-rice, in addition to the question of whether women should be included in social activities, was over the degree of student representation on the college council.[17] Furnivall had become far more radical than Maurice as a proponent of socialist "association" and its concrete implications for college governance.

By the time the jubilee history of the college was being assem-bled in 1904, Furnivall's contribution was restricted to a seven-page

discussion of "The Social Life of the College," and even this is preceded
by an apologetic footnote from J. Llewelyn Davies, the editor of the his-
tory: "It will be seen that Dr. Furnivall, whose popularity amongst the
students will be easily understood, represents a line of action that was
out of harmony in some respects with Maurice's views and feelings."[18]
By this stage, it seems that Furnivall's personality has taken on a life of
its own: he writes in the same volume of "the pleasure I used to feel as
I walkt about the College rooms, and saw face after face light up as I
greeted its owner." In this short contribution to the history, he insists on
the pleasure and popularity of the controversial dances and Sunday
walks. In his final sentence he reveals something of his impatience with
Maurice and identifies unequivocally with the students in a communal
enterprise: "We studied and took exercise together, we were comrades
and friends, and helpt one another to live higher, happier, and healthier
lives, free from all stupid and narrow class humbug."[19]

In contrast to many of his contemporary medievalists who held pro-
fessional positions (Henry Bradshaw was fellow and dean of King's Col-
lege, Cambridge, and librarian at the University Library, for example,
while Walter Skeat took up the Elrington and Bosworth Chair of Anglo-
Saxon at Cambridge in 1878), Furnivall seems to belong in the tradition
of amateur scholarship. But he was not a landed or wealthy member of
that gentlemanly class. His father had been a doctor, and when the
banks in which his estate had been invested collapsed, Furnivall relied
on financial contributions from his friends until 1884, when he was
awarded a Civil List Pension of £150 by William Gladstone's govern-
ment. Benzie comments, "It has been suggested that £500 would be a
generous estimate of Furnivall's earnings during his long, industrious
career."[20] Even so, he was also generous in donating money, as well as
time, to his various societies, and in 1851 had sold his books to make a
donation of £100 to the strike fund of woodcutters.[21]

He vigorously disassociated himself from the aristocratic dilettante
who might make his research available only to a few subscribers, as we
will see shortly. Insistently democratic and liberal, he worked from the
optimistic assumption that given enough enthusiasm, anyone could
read, transcribe, and edit a medieval text. Far from being the pursuit of
the leisured classes or the preserve of the professional academic scholar
or librarian, medieval literature was the common inheritance of English
men and women, and participation in the promulgation and study of

that literature should be available to all. In contrast to most preceding writings on Chaucer, then, Furnivall's editions and notes were directed toward as wide and as inclusive an audience as possible. For the first time, if only temporarily, scholarly Chaucer studies took for granted an extensive public sphere.[22]

Furnivall is often characterized as an entrepreneur, or even a kind of scholarly bully, as he encouraged others into doing the work he saw as so important.[23] In 1865 he wrote to Henry Bradshaw at Cambridge: "The Warton note says there are 3 versions of P. Plowman. Why can't you lay hold of a young Kingsman & make him take up P.P. He could collate all the Cambridge texts at least. If any unoccupied man comes across me here, I shall try to set him on the London MSS."[24] K. M. Elisabeth Murray describes his editorial procedure in his work for the Early English Text Society:

He had a remarkable knowledge of the material and where it was to be found, and his practice was to get hold of the most accessible copy of the text and employ someone—often a clerk with no great expertise—to make a transcript. This was rushed into print and the proofs handed out to other scholars or clerks as available, to check with the various copies of the work. The official editor then cleared off the whole business of editing in the process of correcting the proofs, added a few notes and sometimes a glossary.[25]

Murray is writing a biography of her grandfather, James Murray, the editor of the *Oxford English Dictionary*. When she comes to Furnivall, her partiality to Murray is revealing: Furnivall is demonized as making unreasonable demands on the long-suffering lexicographer. This may make her account seem less reliable for my purposes, but it illustrates some of the contrasting terms by which the true scholar—Murray—is defined. Speaking of the 1870s and Furnivall's plans to interest Murray in becoming the editor of the great dictionary, she writes, "Furnivall, like a busy spider, was spinning the web in which to entrap him in the toils of the Dictionary." Elsewhere, she characterizes Furnivall as the antithesis of a scholar. Writing of the positive reception of Murray's well-received 1872 edition of *The Complaynt of Scotlande* (1549), she remarks, "His work was only what would be expected from an editor today, but

contrasted with Furnivall's frequent practice." Or writing of his corre-
spondence with Murray, "Letters from Furnivall flowed in at the rate of
several a week, sometimes two a day, all expecting James to respond with
an energy equal to his own. They read breathlessly, as though Furnivall
were catching a train rather than engaged on literary research."[26]

Murray defines the "proper" scholar in James Murray, against the
"improper" Furnivall. In the field of Chaucer studies Furnivall is re-
garded with more ambivalence: sometimes as a father figure to be em-
braced, sometimes as an embarrassing enthusiast; and more recently as
a proponent of middle-class British imperialism or rampant homo-
sociality. Before we turn to these contradictory readings, let us examine
Furnivall's Chaucerianness in more detail.

DOING HONOR TO CHAUCER

Furnivall brings the discourse of affinity in Chaucer studies to its great-
est rhetorical and imaginative heights: "To do honour to CHAUCER, and
to let the lovers and students of him see how far the best unprinted
Manuscripts of his works differ from the printed texts, this Society was
founded in 1868."[27] Furnivall's words situate the work of the Chaucer
Society in a decisive scholarly modernity, rejecting the early printed tra-
dition as flawed and invoking a quasi-scientific approach to the largely
unknown early manuscripts. The society's work will be enabling, free-
ing the lovers of Chaucer from the constraints of bad texts so that they
may see and communicate with the author more clearly. W. P. Ker wrote,
in his obituary of Furnivall, that he regarded unpublished manuscripts
of Old and Middle English as "souls in prison."[28] Furnivall insisted that
the manuscripts should be better known and read independently of the
editions by Tyrwhitt or Wright, and he printed as many as he could, but
the prefaces and footnotes to his editions for the Chaucer Society and
the Early English Text Society quickly became notorious for their casual
admissions of his own inadequacy and haste, for their chastising of the
more tardy editors whose work for the Early English Text Society had not
yet come to press, and for his impatient criticism of any who did not
share his own enthusiasms.[29] In his work on Chaucer, Furnivall often
borrowed Chaucerian verse to defend his position, as we saw in his edi-
tion of *The Tale of Beryn* in chapter 3. He is fond of asking for correction

for his texts, imitating Chaucer's stance at the close of *Troilus*, and of celebrating his own love of nature in terms that imitate the poet of the prologue to the *Legend of Good Women* as worshiper of the daisy. This daisy worship will become an easy target in later criticisms of this kind of Chaucerian identification.

Furnivall constantly appeals to the possibility of speaking face to face with Chaucer. Here is his introduction to Francis Tate's 1601 translation of Edward II's book of *Household and Wardrobe Ordinances,* the second volume of the *Life-Records of Chaucer.*

> The feeling which prompts folk to get at all the facts they can about the lives of men gone from them, whose works they love, seems to me natural and right. A few there are who profess to be above care for such details, and say they are satisfied to know a writer from his works alone. But the rest of us, as we delight to see, to know, our Tennyson, Ruskin, Huxley, of to-day, and get their looks, their tones, their little special ways, into our eyes and ears and hearts, to hear from an old schoolfellow or college friend, all their history, so we desire to realise to ourselves, so far as may be, the looks and life, the daily work and evening task, of the Chaucer, Shakspere, Milton, who've left us in the body, but are with us in the spirit, friends of our choicest hours, guides in our highest flights.[30]

The path of access to these "friends" is via detailed research into (and the imaginative reconstruction of) the social conditions of medieval life, a dimension sometimes ignored by the more common citation of such passages as signs of Furnivall's amusing eccentricity.

Importantly, in this passage, the familiar trope of spiritual communion with the dead once more undergoes a process of socialization. For Dryden, such communion had licensed his individual poetic development, with nodding references to the symposium of poets; for Furnivall, Chaucerian affinity is modeled both on the social forms of association and a kind of hero-worship of the poets: no detail is too trivial if it will help us know them better. At the most general level, of course, this seems more democratic and communal, but Furnivall's company of school and college friends is clearly also quite gender specific, as it was for the sixteenth century's imagining of friendship with Chaucer.

The discussion that follows speculates indulgently about Chaucer's boyhood and his career as a valet, as "a natty, handy lad, but full of quiet fun . . . well up in his classes, I'll be bound; the boy the father of the man in this, that he lovd his bookës well."[31] Furnivall's slip into Middle English is a typical marker, for him, of his own closeness to Chaucer. Indeed, it sometimes seems as if even the poetry itself might get in the way of knowing the author, and it's easy to imagine Furnivall's frustration with the complicated models of voicing and irony so beloved of modern Chaucer criticism. Benzie cites Furnivall's frustration with Browning's created characters, "whose necks I, for one, should continually like to wring, whose bodies I would fain kick out of the way, in order to get face to face with the poet himself, and hear his own voice speaking his own thoughts, man to man, soul to soul. Straight speaking, straight hitting, suit me best."[32]

Commenting on a passage in Edward IV's *Liber Niger* that describes the duties of the esquires to entertain lords, Furnivall once more blurs the distinction between his own voice and the text he cites: "That was what Chaucer could do, and did, I am persuaded. And I wish I'd been there to hear him talk Chronicles of kings and other pollicies [sic], to pipe and harp and sing, and to keep honest company with me, after his cunning. Well, wishing hurts nobody."[33] Here is the community of congenial souls in its most friendly incarnation. For Furnivall, the desire to speak with Chaucer, to speak in Chaucer's language, is always a desire to share in a friendly convivial company. A slightly later text, from 1904, provides graphic witness of this desire, though this time, instead of inserting Furnivall into Chaucer's world, it reverses the direction of the time travel. The Beinecke Manuscript and Rare Book Library at Yale holds a copy of *Tales of the Canterbury Pilgrims Retold from Chaucer and Others* by F. J. Harvey Darton, which includes an introduction from Furnivall. There is a pencil sketch on the flyleaf by the volume's illustrator, Hugh Thomson, that shows Darton and Furnivall smoking their pipes and seated either side of Chaucer. We could find no clearer illustration of the desire to bring Chaucer into the world of the editor, the timeless club of congenial souls. While translator, illustrator, and introducer all sign and date this flyleaf on three different days in October 1904, Chaucer's signature is conspicuously absent. As a ghostly presence, of course, Chaucer can appear anywhere, unconfined by time or space.

Pencil sketch by Hugh Thomson on flyleaf of *Tales of the Canterbury Pilgrims Retold from Chaucer and Others,* by F. J. Harvey Darton, showing Darton and Furnivall with Chaucer.

It is not just Chaucer, of course, for Furnivall. His preface to Kingsley's edition of Francis Thynne's *Animadversions* to Thomas Speght is typical of the inclusiveness of his vision. Here he mentions Thynne's own "love for Chaucer" and speculates that he "may have shaken hands with Shakspere, seen and heard him in his own plays; perhaps sighd at Spenser's death; and emptid a bottle with Marlowe." His own love of detail appears again: "I make no excuse for giving in full the details above as to William Thynne; for those who think them a bore, can skip them; and those who care for the old Chaucer-Editor as much as I do, will share the pleasure I had in going through his day's work and food with him."[34] He compares Shakespeare's use of Chaucer to Beethoven's of Mozart, then concludes: "In the bright air on this chalk down, memories of all four Masters come to me. The wild thyme under foot gives out its sweet scent, the tender gracefull harebell nods, the golden lady-slipper glows, the crimson ground-thistle gladdens in the sun, the fresh blue sky and fleecy clouds look down well pleasd. Would that Chaucer and Shakspere were here! Dated Riddlesdown, below Croydon, Sept. 5, 1874." This is typical of Furnivall's romantic image of Chaucer as a nature poet. Elsewhere he writes of the opening lines of the *General Prologue:* "Who can look at them now, who can read the oft-conned lines, without his heart opening, his hand stretching out, to greet the sunny soul that penned them?"[35]

But it is not all spiritual with him. Furnivall also borrows Johnson's stance as lexicographer—"harmless drudge"—most poignantly in the footnote that he adds to the preface just quoted, in the following summer: "And here I am, simmering in town, looking over Manuscripts and adding Francis-Thynne bits, this 16th of August, 1875! Why *will* men get up Early English Text and Chaucer Societies? What a bother they are! However, one has the Thames, and can get at the end of an oar again sometimes, to say nothing of eating one's dinner, and boiling one's kettle, on Kingston and Sunbury meadow banks."[36]

Setting his unpaid scholarly work in opposition to this more pastoral mode is a frequent motif with Furnivall. He is proud to characterize his work and that of his friends as hard drudgery that sometimes seems even to obscure, rather than clarify, the paths of access to the writers of the past:

And tho' this desire for knowledge of the outward life of our greatest men may in a few cases, with so-calld prosaic natures, seem to make them darken for themselves the genius of their hero, by the cloud of antiquarian dust they raise before him, yet you'll find, if you ask the grubbers themselves, that the cloud has not only for them its silver lining, but that they always feel the light and warmth of the Sun and its life-giving beams behind. And they may tell you, that the difference between you (the superior being) and them is simply this, that whereas they care weeks and months of *patient unpaid drudgery* [my emphasis] for the men they reverence, you care only to express your feeling about them in prettily-turned phrases in articles and Lectures, and *get well paid* [my emphasis] for doing it: "*You* give up your chance of guineas, or airing your feelings, to do a lot of distasteful work, for Chaucer or Shakspere? *You'd* see him damnd first!"[37]

This opposition between scholarship and criticism, along with the question of which discipline must take ontological priority over the other, has been a consistent theme in English literary and medieval studies.[38]

Furnivall's own position is more complex, however. Scholarly research into manuscripts, editions, and life records clearly takes precedence over criticism, when it manifests as belles lettres, or "airing your feelings" in "prettily-turned phrases." And yet he regarded his work as social history, rather than philology. "I never cared a bit for philology," he once remarked; "my chief aim has been throughout to illustrate the social condition of the English people in the past."[39] At one level, this fascination with the social condition of past lives looks like an anticipation of modern materialist criticism, but it is always framed by the imperatives of love, reverence, and spiritual affinity with the men themselves, the germinal idea behind the community of readers.

Moreover, it is not really literary criticism as such or the belletristic impulse that draws Furnivall's ire: his anger is more consistently directed against the idea that either scholarship *or* criticism should be the exclusive preserve of the leisured classes or indeed, the professional academic or librarian. In line with his socialist principles, Furnivall pays great attention to the means by which scholarly research and criticism are promulgated, to the institutions that publish and sustain such research. His position is rigorously egalitarian, supportive of the "ordinary student's" interest in and talent for medieval scholarship, even if that

ordinary student exists rather as an idealized entity than as a member of
a populous book-buying public. In 1886, in response to a complaint that
the Early English Text Society had wasted its energies in reprinting an
edition, Furnivall argues eloquently in defense of the society's publica-
tions as far cheaper and more useful than those put out by the "printing
clubs of exclusive constitution, such as the Roxburghe and Abbotsford,
or for private circulation only."[40] First he appeals to the "ordinary student
of Early English, whose spare minutes for Museum work (if he lives in
town) are few, and his guineas to buy texts with fewer: take the same
class of student in the country, where he can get at no library containing
the very scarce and dear publications of the private printing clubs." He
then considers the editors themselves: "If you had ever edited a book *you
care for* [my emphasis], but of which a printing club had only issued a
hundred copies, and given you *one* for yourself, as the Roxburghe did to
their best editor for his most celebrated book,—I assure you you would
not think it 'waste of power' to put the text you wanted or cared for
within the reach of 500 people, at the cost of from ten to twenty
shillings." This is followed by a jibe at Sir Frederic Madden and a sug-
gestion as to how he might be better employed producing cheap editions
of popular medieval texts than printing more obscure works for the Rox-
burghe Club. Furnivall concludes with this mission statement: "We want
to make 'household words' of the names of the early men and books we
delight in, and specially to print all they have written and contain about
Arthur. If our object could be made known to every Englishman who
cares for the due illustration of the formation of his own language and
the national mind, we feel that our Society would be enabled to do a
much needed and most useful work for the present age."[41]

The democracy of Furnivall's wish to make early English literature
available to all is surpassed only by his confidence that all such readers
might also be able to do the necessary editorial work themselves.[42] His
interpellation of a society of untrained amateurs—the "ordinary student
of Early English"—is an important aspect of his steadfast resistance to
the notion of scholarly expertise as the preserve of a specially trained
elite. Of course, the resistance could come from the other side, too: Elis-
abeth Murray quotes a letter from Walter Skeat to James Murray about
Furnivall: "[S]omehow, he isn't believed in at the Universities. . . it has
arisen from his odd prefaces, etc., & modes of expression."[43]

Since I am looking at Furnivall with an eye to the formation of the
modern academic, it is not inappropriate to jump, for a moment, to

1985, and a debate conducted in not dissimilar terms in the pages of the *London Review of Books* between Professors Graham Hough and Terence Hawkes, the general editor of the New Accents series, an enormously popular series of introductions to various aspects of literary theory in its heyday, the mid-1980s. Replying from Cardiff to Hough (at Cambridge), Hawkes defends "theoretical and analytic work, which costs little and concentrates on and uses only a few texts, [and] genuinely matches our resources." This is contrasted to the "broadly allusive, finely-tuned, widely-learned mode" espoused by Hough. Hawkes goes on to defend "theory" in terms that seem to echo both the early defense of English literature as a subject worthy of study and Furnivall's keen insistence that texts of early English writing should be cheaply accessible to all: "In short, it's one of the few games in town: 'paperback research,' you might say. Tell him that's not the only reason for engaging in it. Tell him it has its own integrity and our students find it fruitful. Tell him its existence in places like Cardiff might even be the price he and his pals have to pay for their quite different concerns elsewhere. Then tell him to piss off."[44] Hawkes's plain language sounds very much like Furnivall's, impatient with academic elites (be it Cambridge University or the exclusive printing clubs) and concerned for the general accessibility of learning. It might seem strange to us now that the proponents of "early English" and literary theory should form such an alliance, but the unlikeliness of this affinity indicates the complex history of literary studies in England and the sense in which this history needs to be read for its institutional, as well as its intellectual, narratives. Furnivall's version of medieval studies, at least, had a popular and radical edge that has been missing in many academic programs in the twentieth century.

"It's the nation that prints its MSS that can fight."

Furnivall's career and writings sit somewhat at odds with the customary narratives of the development of literary criticism in the late nineteenth century and the so-called rise of English studies in the early part of this century. If we try to place Furnivall in the arguments about the role of literary studies, we face a number of contradictions. He is only indirectly concerned with the struggle to institute English literature as a university discipline, yet his association with Maurice and the Working Men's

College places him at one of the germinal centers of the movement. As a Cambridge graduate, too, he is mentioned by Tillyard, with Skeat, Hales, and Ward, as one of the "patriarchs" of English literary study whose very existence became a form of pressure on Cambridge to admit English as an academic discipline.[45] Clearly, Furnivall shared with Maurice (the author of *The Friendship of Books*) the desire for friendly communion with dead authors and a belief in the salvific power of literature, but unlike his colleague, he was neither an educationalist nor a philosopher. His writings show little direct sign of Maurice's social mission of actively *uniting* the classes, though he certainly spent more time with the working-class men and women students of the college than did Maurice.

Maurice's liberal interest in education and literature as part of the national heritage and the power of the sympathetic imagination are more familiar to us from the work of Matthew Arnold and their institutionalized expression in the Newbolt Report of 1921, completed eleven years after Furnivall's death. This was the product of a committee chaired by Sir Henry Newbolt, appointed by the Board of Education, to investigate the teaching of English and to promote English literary studies, in the words of Brian Doyle, "as a cultural instrument of the nation-state."[46] The report is usually read as a central document in the history of literary studies and their relation to late-nineteenth- and early-twentieth-century English national and cultural policy.

Medieval literature is not foregrounded in the report; indeed, much to John Dover Wilson's dismay, the chapters on Old and Middle English were placed "in a sort of appendix to the volume."[47] Dover Wilson reports, indeed, that W. P. Ker of the University of London refused to cooperate with Newbolt and, when the report was finally published, responded by having it burned publicly in the courtyard of University College, presumably because the report argued against the necessity of comparative philology and the compulsory teaching of Anglo-Saxon, two of the prime supports of the academic teaching of early English.[48]

The committee was clearly concerned with the concept of Englishness and the role of literature in forming a national identity; the report expresses a good deal of nostalgia for the "organic community" of medieval and Elizabethan times (an idea that was to find fullest expression in Chaucerian criticism in the much later work of John Speirs). The spiritual value of "great" literary works is an important premise for the report: "[E]ven the teacher of English must bow before the experience of those great minds with which the works offer contact. This would allow a 'bond of sympathy' between members of society to be subjectively sealed."[49] English literature provides the "social glue" of ideology, through precisely such acts of empathetic identification as Furnivall's with Chaucer. However eccentric they seem, Furnivall's Chaucerian affinities may have given specific form to one of the most influential currents of thought about the role and uses of literature at this time. There is also at least one direct link: Caroline Spurgeon, one of Furnivall's protégés and admirers, and professor of English Literature at Bedford College at the University of London from 1913–29, was a member of the Newbolt Committee.

Newbolt himself published an independent appreciation of Chaucer in 1913, which celebrated the "curious" universalism of Chaucer's Englishness. Of the pilgrims, he comments:

> We are most of us, perhaps, more truly at home in their company than Chaucer himself was, for we are not troubled by his sense of isolation, that loneliness of the literary man among a throng of interests and forces which take so small account of him.
> . . . To an Englishman, Chaucer must always appear to be the most English of poets; for his diction, his metres, and his materials he may have drawn upon France and Italy, but the characters he creates and the standpoint from which he regards them are essentially our own.[50]

This naturalization of Chaucer's "Englishness" has been a persistent theme since Dryden, but Newbolt expresses a more romantic sense of the poet's isolation from the common run of humanity. The Newbolt Committee's main interest was of course with questions of pedagogy and criticism and the role of English literature in the national curriculum. For Furnivall, it was editing and publication that could best preserve the nation's identity. His own enthusiasm for his national heritage was further inspired by competitive rivalry with both Germanic philology, and its studies of English texts, and American scholarship, especially that of Francis Child, who at one time was projecting an edition of Chaucer.[51] It is a nationalist, not a professional, rivalry that makes extraordinarily direct connections between a publishing program and a position of national military strength. In 1870, Furnivall wrote to Henry Bradshaw:

"I think it's a *shame* for you to let Ten Brink come out with his *Studien* first—all honour to him for it, tho! You're not half such a patriot as the Germans are, or you'd never have allowed it. It's the nation that prints its MSS that can fight."[52] England's historical cultural capital can be converted into symbolic capital, in a way that becomes indicative of greater military force, through the work of medieval scholars in editing and publishing manuscripts. Furnivall's nationalism is expressed through the instrumentalist deployment of print in the Victorian public sphere. His idealization of medieval literature as a national heritage that must be available to all generated some other extraordinary comments and judgments, such as his unusual criteria for selecting his six texts for the parallel Chaucer series: three from private hands and three from public libraries, one each from London, Cambridge, and Oxford.

We can get a measure of the trend against which he was struggling when we realize how many important manuscripts were still kept in private collections in this period and how many of their aristocratic owners would not part with their manuscripts for copying.[53] Furnivall was not the only scholar to resent this: S. O. Halliwell complained in a letter to Furnivall about the owner of the York Miracle Plays, "the selfish locking up of which is truly deplorable."[54] Lord Bath, who withheld permission for Furnivall to quote from the Thynne family letter collection, may represent a throwback to the earlier aristocratic reluctance to enter the public sphere or, indeed, the practice of "hoarding" private treasures; another, slightly earlier, is the "one individual of literary eminence" who, when asked to contribute his translations of Chaucer to an edited collection, "boldly declared, that he still wished to keep Chaucer for himself and a few friends."[55] The extended public sphere so warmly embraced by Furnivall was the dominant mode of Victorian enterprise, but it was not the inevitable or the only sphere for the circulation of aesthetic or literary capital.

Nor was this aristocratic decorum the only front on which Furnivall encountered resistance to his publication program. Anticipating the conclusions of Elisabeth Murray, he increasingly defined himself in opposition to the professional scholars and librarians like James Murray and Henry Bradshaw, who worked in paid positions, in an intellectual environment Furnivall came to see as marked by frustrating caution and restraint. For many years, Furnivall wanted to make available a good, comprehensive edition of Chaucer's works, and to bring this about, he sought the cooperation of Henry Bradshaw. The two were quite different in situation and in temperament, and the arguments between them throw Furnivall's contributions to Chaucer scholarship into sharper relief. Both were editors of Chaucer, but all recent commentators insist upon an important distinction: Furnivall was a great *printer* of Chaucer, wanting to make the texts available with the urgency and enthusiasm that drove all his work. Bradshaw wanted to *edit* the works more fully and compare the manuscripts and print "good and pure texts" of the best writers.[56] He regarded the work of the EETS and the Chaucer Society with misgivings, accusing their work of "a remarkable absence of literary *editorial* power," with too much attention to marginalia, abbreviations, and so forth, "but not a feather's weight of care to the substance of the matter."[57] Wanting to proceed more slowly (Matthews describes him, indeed, as "dilatory"),[58] he wrote to Furnivall in 1868: "In plain words I cannot bear the thought of any publication *coming forth with authority*, when it is merely the result of a few hasty and crude speculations, which a little fair preliminary discussion would get rid of."[59]

To Furnivall, Bradshaw's caution seemed like selfish reluctance to make his work on Chaucer and other medieval texts and manuscripts more widely available, especially given the rich bibliographical and professional resources of the library. Frequently in his correspondence, he draws the contrast between Bradshaw, "in the Library all day" and "being a rich Fellow and despising poor devils like myself," as he urges him, many times, to print the results of his research.[60] He could also be warm in his admiration, however, and in his edition of *Beryn* described Bradshaw as having "a nose for missing MSS. like a bloodhound's for a fugitive."[61] At times, he confesses to provoking Bradshaw into print, so that "we outsiders'll all be deeply indebted to you." In another letter written the same year, Furnivall says, "As to contradicting me, nothing would please me better than to see you do it. I often print things to try & make you state your own case yourself." A few months later, he returns to the same theme, turning the accusation on Bradshaw more strongly:

It is of course impossible for you, who'd keep the existence of a unique English MS secret from me & many others for months to understand my view of the duty of knowers of such things to fix that knowledge in print at once, or to feel my belief that others have a right to share the pleasure I feel in learning such things. Could you do this, your reticence would be impossible to you. As to my palaver about working-men. When you've been among 'em, and tried to do as much for 'em, as I have, you may possibly change your note. A turn of such work for 15 years wouldn't hurt you as a change. But, answering sneers is not profitable work.[62]

In this exchange, Bradshaw complains about Furnivall's insistence on printing parallel editions of *Canterbury Tales* manuscripts, rather than Bradshaw's preferred option of "printing a manuscript as it stands, only with all the divisions and subdivisions marked," in line with his thesis that the tale order should be reorganized to fit the geography and topography of the pilgrims' route to Canterbury. Trying to resist Furnivall's haste, he says, "I did not see the object of printing merely to be penny-a-lined about."[63]

In reply, Furnivall takes up an urgent and familiar theme: "Talk of penny-a-lining as you choose, it enables one to interest a large circle of men not only in Chaucer but in other good men & good work. Had you just been willing to carry on a public with you in your work, it would have increased your usefulness & your power, & saved me & others a lot of trouble—There, that's over."[64] Bradshaw replied generously to Furnivall's "uncongenial blowing up." "My only fear is of boring people too much. As for the originality, I of course never laid claim or could to any *new facts*. My only point in my method, which I always insist on in anything in bibliography,—arrange your facts rigorously, and get them plainly before you, & let *them speak for themselves* which they will always do."[65]

This correspondence represents an exemplary moment in the development of professional decorum. Bradshaw's scholarly caution, his fear of boring people, and his resistance to commercial pressures are all familiar tropes of the modern academic, while Furnivall's enthusiasm and willingness to attract more and more people into the delights of Chaucer study clearly draw inspiration from the "missionary" work of the Working Men's College, especially where early English literature was concerned. Bradshaw's more decorous view that the "facts" can "speak for themselves" is also in direct opposition to Furnivall's own practice of speaking on behalf of Chaucer and other medieval writers. And though Bradshaw is a librarian rather than a literary critic, the contrast between the two is instructive for the development of the professional decorum of the medievalist, caught between enthusiasm and scholarship, between the work of philology and criticism.

For William Wimsatt and Cleanth Brooks, this apparent contradic-
tion between textual, philological, antiquarian research, on the one hand
and, on the other, the devotion to the poetic genius, and to the person-
ality, originality, and life of the poet is typical of "the peculiar tone of
19th century literary study, at least in England."[66] Some of the contradic-
tions in Furnivall's own practices can be clarified when set in the context
of the rapidly changing ideologies of English studies in the late nine-
teenth and early twentieth centuries. Yet many accounts of the struggles
at Oxford and Cambridge to found their English schools stress the con-
fusing nature of the debates, clouded by personalities and conflicting in-
terests. Baldick describes the situation at Oxford as "a confused
three-cornered fight with many overlapping positions."[67] Was English to
be allied with the philologists and Saxonists or with the classicists, or
was it to steer its own course and be damned as a lightweight, unexam-
inable subject fit only for women and tarred by its associations with the
working men's colleges, extension lectures, the movement for the edu-
cation of women, and the provision of the syllabus for the Civil Service
examinations?[68]

It is only recently that medieval studies has started tracing its own
institutional history, and it seems that there is at best only a partial fit be-
tween the history of "English" and the history of medieval studies. It's
arguable, though, that Chaucer is the historical fulcrum around which
many of the debates revolve. As the first "modern" writer, who also con-
stitutes one of the high points of the medieval syllabus, Chaucer strad-
dles the traditional divide between Language and Literature.[69] This divide
was one of the central points of contention at Oxford, where medieval
literature risked becoming swallowed up by philology.[70] Campaigning
for the formation of an English school at Oxford, but one based on the
classics and independent of the philologists and Saxonists, John Churton
Collins wrote, "[L]iterature must be rescued from its present degrading
vassalage to Philology." Otherwise, the Oxford graduate would know too
well "the barbarous and semi-barbarous experiments of the infancy of
civilization and . . . the niceties of the various Romance and Teutonic
dialects . . . would, indeed, have spent the three best years of his life in
mastering them."[71]

In this dispensation, "philology" signifies not simply the linguistic
skills involved in reading the Chaucerian text, but the whole range of
positivist disciplines set up as the necessary adjuncts to medieval litera-

ture—manuscript studies, medieval rhetoric, theology, history, and so forth. In its most severe form, it becomes the impossibility of medieval historicism, the requirement that its students absorb and master *all* the "background," the entire *Geistesgeschicht* of a period, *before* they pick up a literary text. In David Matthews's account, philology eased the path of English studies into acceptance at the universities, but quickly resulted in the marginalization of Middle English from the central, aesthetic business of literary study.[72]

In his admirable discussion of this aspect of early Chaucer criticism, Lee Patterson analyzes the uneasiness of medievalists such as R. K. Root, George Kittredge, and John Livingstone Lowes with the learning they deemed necessary to approach the medieval text. He describes Lowes's book on Chaucer, its first three lectures presenting detailed and scholarly accounts of the intellectual, biographical, and literary influences and contexts of Chaucer's writings and its second three lectures "that make virtually no reference to the preceding material at all." He concludes, "[H]istorical scholarship and literary understanding have here little to do with each other."[73] For Patterson, this is symptomatic of the crisis of literary historicism: it does not trust the products of its own scrupulous learning, preferring to rely on the intuitions of criticism to initiate and generate discussion of poetry. A comment from Lowes illustrates this early ambivalence among Chaucer's critics to the specter of medieval scholarship: "Learning could not live long in Chaucer's mind without assimilation to the temper of that bright spirit."[74] Clearly, "learning" must be subordinated to "spirit," whether of the poet or of the critic. Similarly, Leigh Hunt had commented on the Clerk, "Chaucer thought that good letters could bear a little banter, without losing their credit. All purely serious scholars in those times had a tendency to pedantry and formality. Chaucer only escaped it himself by dint of the gayer part of his genius."[75] In Furnivall's case, this contradiction inspires him to explore Chaucer's life and social conditions, but also fuels the desire to prove that Chaucer's genius was timeless and universal, rather than bound by those specific conditions. It is Chaucer's individualism and his almost Shakespearean genius, as we saw in the previous chapter, that most distinguish him from his contemporaries.

This is the recurrent theme of nearly all Chaucerian source study: identifying Chaucer's sources is the best way of measuring the contrast between the general run of medieval learning and Chaucer's genius. In fine, this was witnessed in the opposition between *The Tale of Sir Thopas* and the *Tale of Melibee*. Here the distinction between Chaucer's medieval learning and his comic genius seems at crisis point. For Ker, "the *Tale of Melibeus* is a thing incapable of life, under any process of interpretation, a lump of the most inert 'first matter' of medieval pedantry."[76] And on the same text: "Here again, though on a still larger scale, is the contradiction of the elements of the *House of Fame*, the discord between the outworn garment of the Middle Ages and the new web from which it is patched."[77] Only Chaucer's work evinced enough genius to transcend those limitations. Such comments have the effect of strengthening Chaucer's claims to stand at the origins of modern literature. If *Troilus and Criseyde* is lauded by Kittredge and others as the first novel in English, it is in the context of the suspicion that Chaucer otherwise belongs more to the past than to modernity. Chaucer can be redeemed for modern literature, though not all of Chaucer can be so redeemed. For Chaucer to be prized as a *literary* figure, some of his works must take second place. The *Tale of Melibee*, the *Parson's Tale*, and the *Treatise on the Astrolabe* are all regarded with some suspicion because they seem to embody, too purely, that weight of medieval learning which threatens to engulf the aesthetic and suck Chaucer back too deeply into the past.

In terms of scholarly practice and critical decorum, Bradshaw, Skeat, and the scholars discussed by Patterson, Matthews, and other historians of medieval studies clearly become the dominant models for later scholars and professional academics. Furnivall's own practices are now at best regarded with suspicion and at worst demonized, as we will see. Yet he was initially regarded as the Chaucerians' Chaucerian. Caroline Spurgeon describes the tradition of "Chaucer lovers and workers," "men who during these five hundred years have loved him and have been content to spend much time in the generally unremunerative labour of studying and editing his works, and in collecting information about him."[78] The historical roll call moves from Shirley, Caxton, and Thynne to Stowe, Speght, Urry, and Tyrwhitt, until we reach "one figure which stands out above the rest, one name and personality which older Chaucer students of to-day will not easily forget": Furnivall himself. Her final accolade echoes the themes Furnivall himself continually emphasizes:

> Somehow, one cannot help thinking that, of all the great and
> distinguished men who have so freely given of their time and

labour to our old poet, no one of them would have been more
congenial to Chaucer himself, with no one would he have talked
more readily or laughed more heartily than with this latter-day
"Clerk of Cauntebrigge" "that unto rowing haddè longe y-go,"
this happy octogenarian who almost to the end was young and
vigorous, who loved the river and the green fields, and youth
and good fellowship, and who

         . . . not for place or pay,
But all for the fame of the English wrought in the Eng-
lish way. (My emphasis)[79]

Spurgeon here is quoting a poem written by W. W. Skeat in honor of
Furnivall:

> A clerk ther was of Cauntebrigge also
> That unto rowing haddè long y-go.
> . . . .
> It was a joyè for to seen him rowè!
> Yit was him lever, in his shelves newè,
> Six oldè textès, clad in greenish hewè,
> Of Chaucer and his oldè poesyè
> . . . .
> Souning in Erly English was his spechè
> "And gladly wolde he lerne and gladly techè."[80]

    Furnivall's other friends and associates take up the same theme in
the volume of tributes compiled in his honor. Here is Alois Brandl:
"With Chaucer he literally lived on terms of personal friendship: Chau-
cer's character, indeed, was perhaps most closely analogous to his own."
J. J. Jusserand describes listening to "the voice of a man who had, it
seemed, personally known Chaucer."[81] Such remarks are early examples
of the trend for praising Chaucerians for their conscious or unconscious
similarity with Chaucer.

    Spurgeon was one of Furnivall's own protégés, and it is not surpris-
ing that she and the other contributors should borrow Furnivall's own
vocabulary of dutiful love for and enthusiastic identification with Chau-
cer. Clearly, Furnivall's self-identifications with Chaucer were an impor-
tant element of his own posterity among his friends and colleagues. Yet

not all honor him in the same way: the tone of James Murray's essay in this volume is distinctly cool.

Some modern scholars still embrace Furnivall as a model, however. Delivering the presidential lecture at the inaugural Congress of the New Chaucer Society in 1979, Derek Brewer encouraged members of the society to model themselves on Furnivall: "[W]e do well to honor in him the ideals which the New Chaucer Society would wish to follow." Brewer praises Talbot Donaldson, for example, as "that most Chaucerian figure." Describing Furnivall's internationalism and his interest in broader access to education, Brewer stresses his interest in women's concerns and suffrage, but reveals a rather old-fashioned sense of how exceptional this is:

> Furnivall was also true to his Shelleyan prototype in pressing for what I suppose we must now call Women's Lib. When he was eighty he was a vigorous supporter of women's suffrage, conceived in ardently idealistic Victorian terms. "Woman," he said in 1905, "is the beauty and glory of the world." . . . Being a sensible man, he liked women. The famous sculling club he later founded for working girls to enable them and eventually men to scull on the Thames on Sundays is the most famous if slightly comic example. At the A.B.C. tea-shop in New Oxford Street, where he did so much of his teaching, he was as charming to the waitresses as he was to lady scholars like Edith Rickert or Caroline Spurgeon. He treated everyone as equals, even women.[82]

In more formal accounts and studies of early medievalists, modern scholars are careful to define a greater distance between themselves and Furnivall. Introducing his discussion of Chaucer's "wonderfully complex, ironic, comic, serious vision," E. T. Donaldson describes that school of Chaucerian criticism, "now outmoded, that pictured a single Chaucer under the guise of a wide-eyed, jolly, rolypoly little man who, on fine Spring mornings, used to get up early, while the dew was still on the grass, and go look at daisies."[83] Here Donaldson distances himself from the enthusiasm of Furnivall in favor of a more reasoned, while still affectionate, mode.

Furnivall's energy, enthusiasm, and sheer productivity are often remarked on by his modern commentators, who seem, like Elisabeth

Murray, to take comfort in evidence of his sloppy scholarship, at the same time as giving him credit for his parallel-text editions of Chaucer's works.[84] Donald Baker considers his editorial and printing activities and accords him a founding role as an ethical model for modern Chaucer studies: "Whether we condescend in our own day of supersophisticated (perhaps too sophisticated) concepts of editing even to admit Furnivall into our ranks, he is the giant upon whose shoulders we all stand— enthusiastic, genial, enormously hard-working, quick to judgment and quick to admit error, encouraging all who followed and criticized and bettered his own work."[85] He concludes his discussion by comparing Furnivall with Chaucer, "that highly personal and curiously anonymous poet." More recently, Patterson links Furnivall's liberalism to that of Matthew Arnold but plays down his politics in favor of an emphasis on his hermeneutic assumptions.[86]

In contrast, Peter Faulkner throws a more political cast over Furnivall's writings in his study, emphasizing his ready indignation at class injustice and his interest in education: Furnivall "managed to retain for Medievalism, as it became incorporated into academic life and lost much of its political edge, . . . a generous concern for the lives of ordinary people."[87] David Matthews draws attention to Furnivall's desire to speak with Chaucer as a search for an ethical or moral guide, along the lines of Matthew Arnold's conception of literary studies, just as Baker invokes Furnivall as an ethical model in the passage I've quoted. In a more critical vein, Kathleen Biddick argues that Furnivall and the EETS, in particular, join "gender and imperialism to a traditional founding history of class and nationalism."[88] Similarly, Antonia Ward explores the possibility of reading Furnivall's desires for Chaucer and his desires for greater community among Chaucer's readers as expressions of homosociality, working *against* the interests of women.[89]

Furnivall's legacy remains quite tangible in modern Chaucer scholarship, particularly in the more informal margins of scholarship, as we have seen in previous chapters. The tradition of identifying enthusiastic teachers and readers of Chaucer with Chaucer himself seems to be inherited from Furnivall's own very fluid, informal sense of where Chaucer ended and he himself began. In 1934, John Livingston Lowes dedicated his own book on Chaucer to George Kittredge, "Myn owene mayster dere" (quoting Hoccleve's *De regimine principium*), and we saw earlier that Frederick Robinson "modelled himself" on Chaucer. As re-

cently as 1986, the trope of praising Chaucerians in Chaucerian terms—
often mediated through the figure of the Clerk, as in Skeat's poetic hom-
age to Furnivall—is still alive and kicking:

> *Chaucer in the Eighties* is the fourth collection of essays to honor
> Rossell Hope Robbins—"withouten oother honours in youth
> and age," as pilgrim Geoffrey might happily add. The following
> essays, taken from "Chaucer at Albany II," mark a milestone in
> Robbins' remarkable career—his retirement from active teach-
> ing at the State University of New York at Albany—although
> again our friend Geoffrey might with a wink note the difference
> between "worde and dede." True teachers, of course, never re-
> ally retire. They do perhaps pause to catch their breaths, but the
> urge to "profess" remains unabated.[90]

This citation is also intriguing for its resistance to the strict sense of
"professional" and for the idea that the true lover of literature is not re-
stricted to "mere" professionalism. For all his eccentricities and ex-
cesses, whether we choose to identify with him or not, Furnivall remains
an important figure in the Chaucerian critical landscape, because he
embodies so prolifically the idea of enthusiasm for Chaucer's life and
works: the critic as fan. In the context of the later nineteenth century,
when "English" was in process of formation as a privileged form of eth-
ical technology, grounded on its capacity to provide "closeness to life" for
the child or adult reader,[91] Chaucer and Furnivall were a potent mix. And
so of course, when modern Chaucerians react against this idea of liter-
ary studies, Furnivall is the most obvious, and easiest, target.

Chaucer studies after Furnivall were quickly assimilated into the ac-
ademic study of English literature, and while Chaucer continues to be
part of the mainstream of literary, poetic, and popular tradition, the pub-
lished discourse on his works is increasingly contained within the ter-
tiary education sector: the world of the professional Chaucerian. It's an
important part of this professionalism to distinguish itself from the
more enthusiastic, seemingly less disciplined writings of Furnivall and
many of his immediate contemporaries and successors. It was not an in-
stantaneous process, of course, and in the sections that follow, I want to
consider two writers on Chaucer—Virginia Woolf and G. K. Chesterton—
whose work found a wide readership at the time of publication, but who

are barely taken seriously these days as critical models. Their Chaucerian essays and books are nevertheless regarded as part of the reception of Chaucer, rather than part of the critical tradition.[92] This can tell us a great deal about that professional identity and its sense of its own mission.

VIRGINIA WOOLF: "WHEN WE SHUT CHAUCER, WE FEEL THAT WITHOUT A WORD BEING SAID THE CRITICISM IS COMPLETE."

For Virginia Woolf, the possibility of professional academic life and its accompanying scholarly decorum was a profoundly gendered question: her image of "Oxbridge" as a series of closed doors and interruptions to the meditation of the woman scholar in *A Room of One's Own* resonates powerfully through the twentieth century. The author of this essay and *Three Guineas* attacked the question of women's education and entry into professional life at precisely the period we are considering, though her discussions are rarely brought into consideration in either the standard histories or the more recent materialist accounts of the history of English studies; they remain relatively enclosed within the field of "Woolf studies." Her case is exceptional, as she is the first to admit, since she was inducted into the world of learning by her father, encouraged to learn Greek, and became, herself, a printer when the Hogarth Press was founded. Her discussion of Chaucer is included in the first series of *The Common Reader*, first published in 1925, and is written in a distinctive essayistic voice, addressed to the educated, general reader. Some such readers of Chaucer remain, of course, in the twenty-first century, though in radically diminished numbers: they rarely write or publish essays on Chaucer.

When I first turned to consider Woolf on Chaucer, I took the customary shortcut into the critical anthologies and reread the various extracts from the section on Chaucer from her essay, "The Pastons and Chaucer." In his *Critical Anthology*, J. A. Burrow cites the passage where Woolf characterizes Chaucer's love of detail and his immersion in the present: "Chaucer fixed his eyes upon the road before him, not upon the world to come. He was little given to abstract contemplation. He deprecated, with peculiar archness, any competition with the scholars and divines." For Woolf, then, like Lowes and like Ker, Chaucer and medieval "learning" sit awkwardly together, but there is a political cast to the comparison that follows, between two kinds of writers: "[T]here are the priests who take you by the hand and lead you straight up to the mystery; there are the laymen who imbed their doctrines in flesh and blood and make a complete model of the world without excluding the bad or laying stress upon the good." Woolf situates Wordsworth, Coleridge, and Shelley in the first camp, but Chaucer in the second, "who lets us go our ways doing the ordinary things with the ordinary people." Four years later, in *A Room of One's Own*, Woolf describes herself about to enter the library of the "Oxbridge" College, when "instantly there issued, like a guardian angel barring the way with a flutter of black gown instead of white wings, a deprecating, silvery, kindly gentleman, who regretted in a low voice as he waved me back that ladies are only admitted to the library if accompanied by a Fellow of the College or furnished with a letter of introduction."[93] The priestly figure who has power to show you the mystery directly also has the power to bar you from those mysteries, if you are a woman, and not a professional scholar.[94] By contrast, Woolf's Chaucer is far more approachable.

In a different collection, Sheila Sullivan quotes a longer section of Woolf's discussion of Chaucer. Woolf's final point in this context is that Chaucer almost resists criticism: "And so, when we shut Chaucer, we feel that without a word being said the criticism is complete; what we are saying, thinking, reading, doing, has been commented upon." No wonder Woolf has never been taken as a model for Chaucer criticism, since she practically renders it redundant! Chaucer's world is partly our daily world, but it is, more originally, "the world of poetry. Everything happens here more quickly and more intensely, and with better order than in life or in prose." Chaucer is hard to quote, since his writing is "very equal, very even-paced, very unmetaphorical."[95] The quality in his lines is hard to pin down, because it disappears when lines are quoted out of their original context.

> Thus the pleasure he gives us is different from the pleasure that other poets give us, because it is more closely connected with what we have ourselves felt or observed. Eating, drinking, and fine weather, the May, cocks and hens, millers, old peasant women, flowers—there is a special stimulus in seeing all these common things so arranged that they affect us as poetry affects

us, and are yet bright, sober, precise as we see them out of doors. There is a pungency in this unfigurative language; a stately and memorable beauty in the undraped sentences which follow each other like women so slightly veiled that you see the lines of their bodies as they go—[96]

And so on. We can see instantly why this form of criticism has spawned no followers. In part, Woolf's essay appeals to a very English ethos—Chaucer as the English writer for the English countryside—that would find only a rather specialized, nostalgic response in America and elsewhere. But, most important, Woolf is claiming Chaucer for a general, common readership that needs no scholarly or linguistic mediation: there is no sense here of Chaucer's philological otherness. Woolf speaks from and into a general reading position that seems inspired by Dryden and that has been superseded by an increasing professionalism and scholarship. Following Dryden, indeed, Woolf readily employs the trope of the symposium of poets, and writes in the essay "Reading" of "seeing" a company of male writers as she reads, including Chaucer.[97]

My discussion of Woolf is not meant to imply that as a woman, she was excluded from the field of Chaucer studies: obviously many women did pursue professional teaching careers and graduate degrees in the late nineteenth and early twentieth centuries.[98] My chief concern is rather with the modern reception of Woolf's Chaucerian writings, so when, after scouring the anthologies of Chaucer criticism, I turned to the complete essay in *The Common Reader,* I was surprised to realize that this discussion of Chaucer is very precisely framed. The Pastons appear in the title of the essay, of course, but like Burrow and Sullivan, I had been more interested in what Woolf had to say about Chaucer, and I assumed the essay's structure would be bifold. Taken as a whole, however, the essay is an exercise in comparative historicism of a kind that has only recently become fashionable in literary studies. The essay's triptych structure starts with an account of the first Sir John Paston, then shifts to his son, reading Chaucer in the library. After the discussion of Chaucer from which I have been quoting, Woolf then moves back to the son, trying to account for his failure to bury his father properly. The essay is now quite unfashionable in its imaginative re-creation of the fifteenth-century Norfolk family, and Woolf's desire to find out about the normal lives of medieval people is closer to the imagination of Furnivall. Yet the rigorous distinction between "literature" and "history" that crippled some later versions of medieval studies and set Chaucer as literature in opposition to the Paston letters as historical documents plays no part in Woolf's essay, which in fact seems to prefigure a more contemporary exchange between the two disciplines and the two kinds of textual evidence.

Woolf constructs a narrative fantasy around the delay by his son and his wife to build a permanent tomb for the first Sir John. His son is preoccupied by lawsuits and the court and by the civil wars, but "[t]hey were not quite so sure as the elder generation had been of the rights of man and of the dues of God, of the horrors of death, and of the importance of tombstones. Poor Margaret Paston scented the change and sought uneasily, with the pen which had marched so stiffly through so many pages, to lay bare the root of her troubles."⁹⁹ They were deeply in debt, but Sir John spent money on "clocks and trinkets" and on paying a clerk to copy the eleven volumes of books, including the works of Lydgate and Chaucer, "diffusing a strange air into the gaunt, comfortless house, inviting men to indolence and vanity, distracting their thoughts from business, and leading them not only to neglect their own profit but to think lightly of the sacred dues of the dead."

Woolf draws a picture of Sir John, lost in the works of Chaucer and the consolations of realism they offer, "instead of riding off on his horse to inspect his crops or bargain with his tenants": "Life was rough, cheerless, and disappointing. A whole year of days would pass fruitlessly in dreary business, like dashes of rain on the window-pane. There was no reason in it as there had been for his father. . . . But Lydgate's poems or Chaucer's, like a mirror in which figures move brightly, silently, and compactly, showed him the very skies, fields, and people whom he knew, but rounded and complete."¹⁰⁰

For Woolf, it is the Pastons' very matter-of-fact, unmetaphorical language, "far better fitted for narrative than for analysis," that reveals the origins of Chaucer's writerly power. This is in some ways a simple thesis, but one that is framed far more adventurously, representing a challenge to the author-based discipline of literary studies that would normally start with Chaucer, with at best a nodding reference to his historical contexts. And of course, this is how the essay has been read by the editors of Chaucer reception anthologies, who "naturally" pluck out the descriptions of Chaucer that focus on his own authorial voice and genius and thus present a more uniform version of Chaucerian reception than the actual evidence provides. As Susan Stanford Friedman puts it, "Woolf invades the house of Chaucer through the back door."¹⁰¹

For all the idealism and fantasy in Woolf's image of Chaucer, her essay shows a lively sense of the kind of cultural significance Chaucer might have had for his near contemporaries as they tried to make sense of the past. It is an early essay in cultural history: Woolf winds "fiction" and "historical documents" together in a way we tend to associate with the new historicists of the late 1980s and early 1990s. But Woolf's innovative, personalized method of reading and its generic orientation as "essay" or "opinion" have placed her work firmly in the tradition of reception and "opinion," rather than criticism.

Woolf has long been regarded as a woman writer of momentous importance for the twentieth century, the preeminent "mother to think back through" for feminist literary criticism.[102] Like "Chaucer," "Woolf" has become the object of her own professionalization, but in the field of feminist studies and women's writing, a field that in too many institutions is found at the opposite end of the corridor from Chaucer studies.

G. K. Chesterton: "Not books on Chaucer, but Chaucer"

G. K. Chesterton's *Chaucer* is a determinedly amateur's book, proud to disclaim any special expertise: "It describes only the effect of a particular poet on a particular person; but it also expresses a personal conviction that the poet could be an extremely popular poet; that is, could produce the same effect on many other normal or unpretentious persons. It makes no claim to specialism of any sort in the field of Chaucerian scholarship."[103] Chesterton's own "normal" responses are the base from which he can launch his attacks on the scholarly field. (It is an early version of the opposition between "common sense" and "theory" that was to characterize debate in literary studies in the 1970s and the 1980s.) While not citing their names or publications, he draws attention, for example, to the way that Chaucer has been treated:

> In short, there has been perceptible, in greater or less degree, an indescribable disposition to *patronize* Chaucer. Sometimes he is patted on the head like a child, because all our other poets are his children. Sometimes he is treated as the Oldest Inhabitant, partially demented and practically dead, because he was alive before anybody else in Europe to certain revolutions of the

European mind. Sometimes he is treated as entirely dead; a bag of dry bones to be dissected by antiquarians, interested only in matters of detail.[104]

Or again:

In one sense he is taken too seriously and in the other sense not seriously enough. But in both senses, almost as many men have lost themselves in Chaucer's mind as have lost themselves in Shakespeare's. But in the latter case they are like children wondering what their father means; in the former, like beaming uncles, wondering what the child means.[105]

The fact that Chesterton diagnoses these variations on the familial metaphors is a further indication of his distance from the general run of professional Chaucerians: he is also one of the first to observe the pattern of identifying with the poet, describing it as "losing one's mind" in the mind of the poet. It is only the independent analyst, from outside the fields of both Shakespeare and Chaucer studies, who can accurately diagnose the weaknesses of both groups. Of course, having adopted the stance of the amateur, general reader, disengaged from the business of serious scholarship, Chesterton is under no discursive obligation to provide *examples* of these critical tendencies. The Chaucerians, for example, he describes as "small and serious" in contrast to Chaucer, who is "large and humorous." Or, "A man might really learn more of the special spirit of Chaucer, by looking at daisies, than by reading a good many annotations by dons and doctors of literature."[106] His style throughout the book is that of the essayist giving himself license to make enormous generalizations to characterize Chaucer, his "age," and his poetry, as he writes for "fresh and casual readers" of Chaucer.[107] In this regard, it is a style of book that rapidly became unfashionable, and unreproducible, a book for which there is not really any longer a market. Like Woolf, Chesterton does his best to undermine the whole critical project: "[T]he book would have served its purpose if anyone had learned, even by getting as far as this page, that what matters is not books on Chaucer, but Chaucer."[108] It is rare to find such candid expressions of a view that may well be shared by many readers. John Burrow was right to remark in 1969: "In America, where so much of the best work on Chaucer has been done in recent years, the universities have a monopoly; and even in England non-academic writers do not often dare—or care—to follow in the footsteps of Dryden and Blake. G. K. Chesterton was the last notable exception."[109]

But if we look beyond Chesterton's antiacademic polemics, we find a strand of criticism in his work that in fact anticipates more modern preoccupations, just as Woolf's does. Chesterton's writing is far more quixotic, even whimsical, but his politics play an important role, not so much in the argument itself, but in his reasons for reading and writing about Chaucer in the first place, and in his generalized nostalgia for an orthodox religious past.[110] In his preface he admits that he sometimes seems to be writing more about modern politics than about medieval history. His justification? "[I]t is because we miss the point of the medieval history that we make a mess of the modern politics. I felt suddenly the fierce and glaring *relevancy* of all the walking social symbols of the Chaucerian scene to the dissolving views of our own social doubts and speculations today."[111] Chesterton's own politics are clearly conservative, yet he distances himself from the medievalism of Morris, Ruskin, and the Pre-Raphaelites, for example. He doesn't simply deplore the absence today of "the presence of the Guilds or the grades of Chivalry," but "the absence of any positive substitute for them."

In his rather disingenuous preface, Chesterton presents himself grappling with his discovery, after rereading and reconsidering his work, that Chaucer "came at the end of the medieval age and order," was indeed its "final fruit and inheritor." And while that order certainly included degrees of "fanaticism, ferocity, wild asceticism and the rest," Chaucer was far more "sane and cheerful and normal" than most of the later writers. From this derives the general thesis to be advanced in the book: "that, in spite of everything, there was a balanced philosophy in medieval times; and some very unbalanced philosophies in later times."[112] That is as bald and as unhelpful a statement as we get, but it does underline his sense that what he is doing is rather different from the general run of Chaucer criticism.

The prologue ends with an apology that seems to acknowledge the attractions of the Furnivallian mode: "I am sorry; I could easily have ended differently; it would be much more simple and sociable to treat Chaucer only as a charming companion and sit down with him at the Tabard without further questioning about whence he came. But something is due to conviction; my book was bound to make some attempt to explain Chaucer; and this is the only way I can explain him."[113]

Unlike many of Furnivall's later commentators and followers, Chesterton sees that the motif of the congenial soul can easily become apolitical, a fantasy of spiritual friendship that glosses over the more difficult question about what it means to read Chaucer in later centuries. For Chesterton, this kind of fantasy is set in direct opposition to a critical mode that would start from a reading of Chaucer and end with a theory, however general, about the nature of the world. In this respect, at the strategic level, Chesterton's writing seems to prefigure the more self-conscious political criticism of Marxist and materialist readers, seeking to make political sense of the literature of the past and its surprising fascination for modern readers. "May I be pardoned," he asks, "if I insert a sort of personal parenthesis here?" He goes on, rather less than coherently, to contrast the roles of revolutionaries and artists, working toward the key theme of the chapter, "The Greatness of Chaucer": "I have been mixed up more or less all my life in such mild revolutions as my country could provide; and have been rather more extreme, for instance, in my criticism of Capitalism than many who are accused of Communism. That, I think, is being a good citizen; but it is not being a great poet; and I should never set up to be a great poet on any ground, but least of all on that ground."[114]

The *content* of Chesterton's politics—a form of Catholic socialism—plays little part in contemporary literary studies: the last paragraph of his chapter defines Chaucer's "Greatness" as a grateful consciousness of the "light of the positive," or the "abyss of actuality," and the "primeval duty of Praise" that lies behind all true art. The final chapter, "The Moral of the Story," says little about Chaucer other than to define him as the "most human of human beings," the voice of a stable, centralized Catholicism.[115] And the book as a whole is essayistic, rambling, and personal, in opposition to the modern academic mode.[116] But Chesterton's so-called amateur mode reveals a level of political engagement that has until very recently been refined out of the professional discourse of Chaucer studies. He also finds a personal voice in which to speak of Chaucer without attempting to sound like Chaucer. Needless to say, when Burrow extracts from this chapter, "The Greatness of Chaucer," Chesterton's personal statements are left out.

When we reduce the history of Chaucer commentary to descriptive and evaluative accounts of his poetry, we not only insist on the split between the "reception" of the past and the "criticism" of the present; we also turn our backs on the rich social and political contexts in which Chaucer has been read. And in turn, we make it increasingly difficult to reintroduce those contexts into the current business of criticism, rendering our discussions liable to the charges of formalism and escapism that are so often leveled at literary and medieval studies.

This chapter has ranged both widely and narrowly in its coverage, discussing a range of critical styles, but focusing on English critics. By avoiding the standard trajectories by which we describe modern Chaucer criticism and by examining those Chaucerians whose influence on that criticism is at best mixed, if not repressed altogether, and whose work engages with Chaucer in both personal and political ways, I have aimed to set up a kind of counterpoint to the tradition that circumscribes most of our own work. I would not be understood as seeking a return to the impressionistic writings of Woolf or Chesterton, nor implying that they are the sole exponents of a more popular, though still privileged, Chaucerianism;[117] rather, I have sought to show that their more adventurous modes—like the rhetorical excesses of Furnivall—have been repressed by professional, academic Chaucer criticism, even when it seeks to examine its own history. What is at stake, in such reception histories, is the history of the self and its relation to the past, at least insofar as it intersects with the history of Chaucerianism in the decisions we make when we write about Chaucer. In the next chapter I examine the most self-conscious moment in that history: the reformation of Chaucerianism in the last quarter of the twentieth century.

7

REFORMING THE

CHAUCERIAN COMMUNITY

THE LATE TWENTIETH CENTURY

Throughout the twentieth century, Chaucer studies maintained their distinctive position on the cusp of medieval and literary studies within the institutions of higher learning. It has been a situation of considerable strength. As a canonical writer, Chaucer still appears regularly, if not universally, in the syllabus of tertiary, and sometimes secondary education, where his poetry is presented as an important foundational moment in English literary modernity. To the syllabus of medieval literature, on the other hand, Chaucer adds glamour and the symbolic capital associated with the canon of high culture to courses in medieval studies. With a foot in both camps, Chaucer studies also benefits from methodological developments in two, albeit increasingly divergent, disciplines. This is one explanation for the rich proliferation and variety of Chaucer criticism.

Neither of these formations—medieval or literary studies—enjoys the cultural prominence or institutional security it once did, though both fields have undergone substantial alteration over the past twenty years. Medieval studies is slowly being transformed by the critical methodologies now flourishing, but English literary studies was the sooner, and the more profoundly, revolutionized by these developments. Both fields are gradually redefining themselves once more, this time around the newer discipline of cultural studies. This chapter tracks some of the contradictory trajectories in Chaucer studies as Chaucerians negotiate the rapidly changing intellectual and institutional environments in which they practice their craft at the intersection of medieval, literary, and cultural studies. These negotiations have hardly been lacking in self-consciousness:

since the 1970s Chaucerians, along with other literary critics, have been talking and writing about what they do when they read Chaucer (though they have been less interested, perhaps, in the question of *why* they do that thing). Moreover, since the mid-1980s, the Chaucerian community has had to engage with some powerful attempts to reform that community from within: attempts to disrupt some of its cozier power structures and more authoritarian pedagogical practices, to undo its more overt ideological operations, to reread its history and its present, and to rethink dramatically the nature of our response both to Chaucer *and* to the Chaucerians who precede us.

Though it is sometimes misrecognized in this way, the revolution in critical theory and the transformation of literary studies mean more than simply reading Chaucerian works from different perspectives. One of the most consistent objects of critique is the customary identification and sympathy with the author that had previously been a feature of modern Chaucer criticism, as my previous chapters have shown; or indeed, the initial choice of Chaucer as subject matter, though such doubts tend to be expressed more vociferously from *outside* the field of Chaucer studies. In search of a new critical voice to match the innovations of their readings, the most radical Chaucer criticism of the 1980s and 1990s attacks the structures and hierarchies of medieval studies itself. This can have the effect of driving deep wedges into the congenial community of Chaucerians and their flattering image of themselves *as* a community, predicated on likeness with each other and with the genial fourteenth-century poet. At the same time, a more self-reflective move in medieval studies begins to examine some of the institutional and psychological dynamics of the discipline and the broader cultural patterns of which it forms a part.

But as I shall show in a later section of this chapter, there is a large portion of Chaucerian activity that barely acknowledges these reforming or analytical drives: the publications that induct students into the world of Chaucer and the Chaucerian community. In the majority of the large number of introductory guides to Chaucer still being written and published, the tasks of Chaucerian interpretation and study are presented as remarkably stable and homogeneous activities, untroubled by these critiques of the broader project of medieval studies or the implications of those critiques for the professional or preprofessional identity of the medievalist. And as far as that more professional, specialized discourse is concerned, it seems unable to chart a course between the sentimental and cozy identifications with Chaucer, on the one hand, and, on the other, the expression of an almost scientific detachment, as if embarrassed by any hint of the personal or the political in its own writing. Is there no other way to write about the authors of the past?

The first half of the twentieth century was a time of consolidation and gradual expansion in Chaucer studies: a period of massive scholarship in relation to his texts, sources, life records, and the elucidation of the historical contexts in which he wrote, and a period of the development of a distinctive pedagogical practice. As the century proceeds, Chaucer studies becomes thoroughly professionalized and institutionalized, especially in the United States, and the field of Chaucer criticism expands exponentially, sustained by the demands of curricula and the imperatives of publication. It's not my intention, however, to provide a historical narrative or a comprehensive account of these developments. My central focus remains the discursive voices of Chaucer criticism, particularly as they respond to the voices of their predecessors and competitors; as they construct different models of tradition, community, or rivalry; as they try out new models of hearing Chaucer's voice; and as they introduce students to Chaucer studies. As in previous chapters, I will focus on a series of texts that mark out moments of change or transition in Chaucer studies and, indeed, in the way we conceive of that discipline.

Accordingly, the first section examines some responses to the increasing amount of Chaucer criticism and the challenges posed by "theory" in the 1970s and early 1980s: how was the Chaucerian community affected by the innovations in critical theory of this period? The second section considers the earliest movements to "reform" Chaucer studies and the community of Chaucerians from within its own ranks, commencing in the mid-1980s with critical impulses drawn from Marxist and feminist criticism. The third section examines the aftereffects of these reforming and revolutionary impulses at the beginners' level: the student's guide to Chaucer. The fourth section seeks to articulate some of the contradictions facing the project of Chaucer studies and of writing about Chaucer in the future.

"NEW LITERARY THEORIZING . . . IS NOW ABOUT RIPE TO REACH CHAUCER."

Like many scholars in the field of literary studies, Chaucerians agonized over the revolutions in literary studies and literary theory that characterized the 1970s and 1980s. There is a belated quality about much of this writing, however, and it sometimes reads as if Chaucer studies were proud of being reluctant to embrace the possibilities raised by structural linguistics, political criticism of various kinds, psychoanalysis, reception theory, and other contenders in the dazzling smorgasbord laid out for the consumption of the adventurous critic. Medieval studies had already been split by its own distinctive theory wars in the fifties and sixties, in the struggle between American exegesis on the one hand and the English and American variations on formalist, Leavisite, and New Criticism on the other, so it was not as if Chaucerians had not already been forced to ask themselves quite self-conscious questions about what it was they did with medieval texts. The exegetical criticism propounded by D. W. Robertson was presented very much as a method based on certain and secure principles, with a surefire proof of hermeneutic success provided by Augustine himself: if the text was read in such a way as to promote the reign of *caritas,* the reading was the true one. In contrast, the humanist traditions of formalist and "New" Criticism, and other less programmatic versions of historicism, made it a virtue *not* to have a theory, naturalizing a number of empirical and personal approaches to Chaucer that were presented as both apolitical and liberal. Unable to compete methodologically, many of these critics abjured method altogether, even in responding to Robertson, Bernard Huppé, and their followers.[1] It's only more recently that Chaucerian commentators have analyzed this method more fully, critiquing the intellectual and political presuppositions of exegetical criticism. Non-American critics in particular have become ready to point out the competitive professional and academic pressures that generated such a satisfyingly positivist scholarly method.[2]

Patterson argues, however, that exegetics remains the "unfinished business" of medieval studies, that because it had the effect of polarizing its opposition in the 1960s, many of its powerful insights into medieval culture and reading practices have not been absorbed into mainstream medieval or Chaucer studies. Instead, they have been quarantined from those studies, in a field you either enter, to be absorbed by the method entirely, or do not broach at all, for fear of being labeled, and dismissed, as "Robertsonian."

It's a measure of this inability, on both "sides," to tackle properly the question of method that when, in the 1970s and 1980s, Chaucerians faced a potentially bewildering range of new critical theories, they seem to have collectively repressed this important division in their own history and presented, as it were, a united front, a tabula rasa, to the new challenge. Discussion proceeded as if *this* wave of theoretical and methodological possibilities were the first to be encountered. While they varied in their reactions from enthusiasm through caution to hostility, most Chaucerians, like many critics and literary historians in other fields, seem to have adopted the defensive position of respondent. What could the new theories do for Chaucer? Or, more negatively, what would they do *to* Chaucer? These seem to have been the dominant forms of inquiry. Many Chaucerians found themselves defending Chaucer against the onslaught, as it seemed, of theoretical approaches that seemed designed to defamiliarize his work, to make interpretation more difficult, if not altogether impossible. Despite the great differences in the varieties of Chaucer criticism up to the 1960s, it is fair to say that they were all predicated on a positivist hermeneutic. Whether the approach was grounded in empirical research or the less tangible expressions of finely tuned critical sensibility, it was still assumed that the critic could reveal the meaning of the text. Implicitly or explicitly, most critics claimed to understand what Chaucer was up to at any given point, *especially* if the text seemed to be constructed of layers of irony and complex speaking voices, as we saw with the poems to Scogan and Bukton discussed in chapter 1. It was only a short step from this assumption back to the cozy sense of familiarity and companionship with Chaucer that was the uneasy legacy of Frederick Furnivall and the nineteenth century. The institutional corollary of this hermeneutic confidence was the idea of the community of readers, each grappling with the complexities of Chaucer's work, but each striving toward a common goal of understanding.

It is true that a number of writers at this time were seeking to articulate a more complex dialectic between medieval and modern theory. This is the period when some of the most influential European theorists were looking to the Middle Ages for the prehistory of semiotics and philosophical nominalism (Umberto Eco); intertextuality, linguistic theory, and novelistic narrative (Julia Kristeva); alternative models of authorship and writing (Jacques Derrida); or of desire itself (Jacques Lacan). Conversely, many medievalists insisted from the beginning of this revolution in literary studies that medieval texts had their own distinctive contribution to make to the development of literary theory: for example, R. Howard Bloch, Kevin Brownlee, Sheila Delany, Roger Dragonetti, Peter Haidu, Hans-Robert Jauss, Alexandre Leupin, Stephen Nichols, Eugene Vance, and Paul Zumthor.

Few Chaucerians (or even Middle English specialists) can be counted among this group, however. It seems to have been harder for author-based disciplines to anticipate or chart this dramatic paradigm shift from author-based to text-based or problem-based studies, and harder for medieval English studies than medieval French or German studies to make the leap of faith, as it must have seemed, into "theory." In the late 1970s and 1980s, though, we see a number of important interventions that seek, either directly or indirectly, to transform Chaucer studies, reading his work through the new critical and theoretical paradigms formulated by scholars and theorists working in other fields, particularly in romantic literature.

It's important to see these moves in the context of a period of expansion within the tertiary education sector and in the related field of academic publishing, which began to capitalize on the huge market for theory, for introductory explanations of its arcane mysteries, and for detailed applications of its tenets ("approaches" was the favored term) to familiar texts. This is a period that sees the inauguration of a number of important series of books on canonical authors, and edited essay collections exploring new possibilities for an invigorated literary studies. These books show great confidence in the productive capacity of avant-garde theory to defamiliarize the works of the literary canon. These publication ventures are very much *of* the early 1980s, before worldwide recessions and the subsequent retreat into the economic rationalism and austerity that persisted well into the 1990s had shaken that heady period of economic growth and confident expansion. Most of these publications take for granted the value of literary studies, and the demand—both intellectual and material—of students and institutions for the kind of work they do. The more restrained nineties and the uncertainty of the new millennium have also made it hard to remember or recapture the fascination of the eighties with critical *play*. This emphasis on experimentation had an intellectual point of genesis in Derrida's "liberation" of the signifier from the signified and his intriguing articulations of the way language would not stay still, could not be contained either by its author's intentions or its own structures. We could also argue, though, that the extraordinary flourishing of interdisciplinary theoretical speculation and the publication programs that sustained it also found material support in the buoyant economic climate of expansion and risk-taking.

As a genre and as a publishing venture, the essay collection is particularly conducive to experimental forays into the newer critical modes and to reflective essays and commentaries in medieval studies. Even so, as late as 1987, Laurie Finke and Martin Shichtman remarked in the introduction to their important collection, *Medieval Texts and Contemporary Readers,* that medievalists thinking about "the implications of recent critical theory for their research . . . continue to encounter difficulty in finding forums that will allow for open communication both with more traditionally minded colleagues and with those whose interest in theory is well advanced."[3] Most of the journals that specialized in medieval studies were not overly welcoming to the newer modes: one of the most important moments in this revolution, by contrast, was the special medieval issue of *New Literary History* in 1979.

Chaucerian publishing in this period bears witness to the flourishing of literary studies and the expanded base of student and staff numbers rather than the expansion of literary theory into medieval studies. *Chaucer Review,* inaugurated in 1965, did eventually begin to publish "theoretical" essays on Chaucer, but without much fanfare or enthusiasm to signal any kind of break from their traditional emphasis on new critical and old scholarly readings. In the late 1970s the New Chaucer Society was formed, establishing the specialist journal *Studies in the Age of Chaucer* in 1979. This journal remains an important flagship for the society and witnesses to the strength of scholarship and criticism in this area. The late 1960s and 1970s also saw the publication of a number of "guides" to Chaucer studies: summaries of reception histories of individual works, collections of his reception history, and introductions to various contexts in which to read Chaucer. So the institutionalization of Chaucer studies as a distinctive section within literary and medieval studies (with the concomitant sense of a stronger professional identity for Chaucerians) is consolidated just in time to encounter the newer theoretical developments that were looming, as it seemed to many, over the horizon.

The exemplary encounter of Chaucer with theory is staged in a collection of papers deriving from the Second International Congress of the New Chaucer Society in 1980, a volume edited by Donald Rose under the auspicious title *New Perspectives in Chaucer Criticism.* I describe this encounter as exemplary because it embodies a number of contradictions in the response of the Chaucerian community, represented here by the society that sponsored the congress. Rose's introduction makes it clear that while the society and the contributors to the volume are celebrating the depth of current Chaucer studies, the members of the society in its early years had "expressed a growing concern about the multiple approaches found in Chaucer studies and voiced a need to recrystallize the historical and theoretical approaches to Chaucer criticism." Concerned about "a perceptible erosion of the more traditional approaches to scholarly appraisal of Chaucer," the writers of these essays "demonstrate a renewed commitment to *a kind of discourse about Chaucer which is learned and serious* and which makes this collection an important examination of major trends in Chaucer scholarship" (my emphasis: there will be no fashion victims here!).[4]

Rose's preface enacts a kind of discursive subterfuge. Using the vocabulary of innovation and theory, he actually argues for the strengthening of the status quo in criticism. Far from presenting an experimental foray into contemporary developments in literary criticism, these "new perspectives" are but sharpened versions of established modes of criticism and "appraisal." Rose also appropriates the buzzword of the 1980s—"theoretical"—only to link it to the historical approaches he sees as being under threat and needing "recrystallization." His admittedly brief preface makes no direct mention of the radical transformations taking place in other fields of literary studies and theory, but it's not difficult to read the vocabulary of "erosion," "renewed commitment," and "learned and serious" discourse as a veiled critique of contemporary theory as destructive, insincere, ignorant, and frivolous. Finally, his "new strategies for attacking" leads us to suspect an assault on a new target, whatever it might be, but in fact the target is simply the "ever present historical and theoretical problems of Chaucer scholarship." It's a fascinating example of the discourse of theory being used to shore up traditional modes. Chaucerians are reassured that the old problems will always be with them.

However, one group of essays in *New Perspectives* tells a rather different story. In addition to essays by a number of scholars on specific texts and problems in Chaucer, contributions by Morton W. Bloomfield, Florence Ridley, Alastair Minnis, Winthrop Wetherbee, and R. Allen Shoaf all examine the impact and potential of the new approaches to Chaucer. While voicing a number of reservations, these contributors are somewhat more sympathetic to and excited by these developments than Rose.

Even so, their writing maintains the conservative, liberal consumerist model that structures and organizes most Chaucerian responses to the new theories. By this I mean that the object of study—Chaucer's poetry—remains the absolute, stable given of criticism. What would vary would be the critical map used to chart that terrain or the critical perspective foregrounded by the reader. Faced with a range of newly theorized perspectives, all the Chaucerian need do is choose.

In the first essay of this group, Bloomfield cautiously surveys a range of new approaches, dividing them into those which are central and those which seem peripheral to traditional literary studies. His method is to survey these new disciplines (such as structuralism and semiotics) and disciplines newly applied to literature (such as speech-act theory and psychology) to examine their potential value for Chaucer studies. What value can these disciplines "add" to that text and its interpretation, since "new literary theorizing . . . is now about ripe to reach Chaucer"? This nice equivocation both ironizes the slowness of Chaucerians to take advantage of new methods while also implying that they were right to wait until the theories were fully developed. After all, Bloomfield "cannot in a short time turn out new articles on Chaucer in the new manner." Nor would we expect him to, of course, but this remark eloquently conveys both the excitement and the apprehension felt by so many literary practitioners in this period. Of all the methods and approaches he surveys, Bloomfield is most excited about structuralism and narratology: "All of Chaucer awaits structural analysis," he threatens.[5]

Bloomfield's essay is pluralistic and relatively open to the "new theorizing," even though the various scenarios he suggests would transform Chaucer studies in unpredictable ways. "We progress," he concedes, "through negations and dialectic."[6] But for all his liberalism, it's worth noting how restricted is his vision for Chaucer studies. In this essay, the category "literature" is still intact, for example, as is the assumption that Chaucer is the best place to test literary theory on medieval texts. Moreover, Bloomfield's panoply of theories is in fact quite narrow: Marxism and social history are dismissed with a brief mention, while feminist criticism, already starting to question the centrality of male writers and the invisibility of gender as an issue for most readers, remains itself invisible in this essay. The broader aims of literary criticism remain stable. "Our overall goal," he says, "is still the goal of Furnivall, Skeat, Kittredge, Manly: to recreate and undistance the past."[7] Thus are the Chaucerians' critical models set firmly before them: reassuringly, they will not need to reconceptualize their work, let alone their own personal relationship to it.

The structure of Bloomfield's response is typical of a great deal of literary criticism and pedagogy since that time: undergraduate and post-graduate students are made familiar with a range of theoretical approaches and encouraged to practice applying them to the text under discussion. In this way, literary studies becomes more self-conscious, but maintains its own internal structures of interpretation. It adds value to its canonical texts by demonstrating the complex range of possibilities in the act of reading, and since the 1980s it has expanded its power base by colonizing noncanonical texts and authors and subjecting them to the same treatment.

In the same collection, Alastair Minnis proposes a more cautious engagement with contemporary theory, arguing that we should defer our comparisons of late medieval and modern literary theory until we know more of the former. Minnis rejects much modern theory as instances of what Zumthor calls "blind modernism." Concluding, Minnis asks, "Do we drown in the impending 'new wave' of Chaucer criticism, or do we seize the driftwood offered by late-medieval literary theory?"[8] Minnis's apocalyptic tone is repeated in his magisterial *Medieval Theory of Authorship*, where he similarly insists on the power of late medieval theory to reveal medieval literature to us more fully: "The tacit assumption behind all these chapters is that medieval theory of authorship provides us moderns with a window on the medieval world of books. To our gaze this window may seem small and its glass unclear and distorting, but these, after all, are characteristic features of a medieval window, indications that it is genuine and historically right. Our standards must change if we are to appreciate what it has to offer."[9] There is little *jouissance* in this vision of medieval literature. And little compromise, either. Minnis takes for granted that it is we who must change, before the alterity of the medieval: students and scholars alike must subject themselves to the discipline of this small, distorting window.

As a self-conscious engagement with and response to "theory," the essays in *New Perspectives in Chaucer Criticism* represent a very conservative, if not embattled, response. United in the wariness of their response to new developments, these essayists, as Rose remarks, programmatically affirm the traditional strengths of Chaucer criticism: "the diagnostic analysis that has become the concern of the community of scholars in the New Chaucer Society."[10] This semiofficial statement neatly defines the predominant interest of Chaucer criticism in the

1980s, at the same time as it defines the community. To be concerned with diagnostic analysis (and *not*, for example, with political criticism) is to be a member of that community.

Chaucer studies survived the first wave of critical theory more or less intact, then, but at around the same time, more radical scholars such as David Aers, Janet Coleman, Sheila Delany, Terry Jones, and Stephen Knight were already experimenting with different kinds of hermeneutics, a more political criticism, and a less reverent attitude to the Chaucerian text or the Chaucerian tradition. The community of Chaucerians still proved remarkably accommodating to these changes, as we would expect of such a venerable collective. They would register division and contention far more powerfully, however, in the face of the more direct political critiques offered of the Chaucerian project in the mid-1980s from within their own ranks.

REFORMING THE CHAUCERIAN COMMUNITY: 1986 AND ALL THAT

The second wave of critical theory hit Chaucer studies as the tentative pluralism of the early eighties gave way to more vehement and more directed encounters with materialist and feminist criticism, particularly those arising out of resistance to Margaret Thatcher's Tory England in the 1980s. These projects represent the most dramatic challenge to traditional Chaucer studies, to its distinctive intellectual and institutional forms, and to the very idea of the Chaucerian community and the community's customary identifications with its genial author. Unlike linguistics, structuralism, or semiology (the critical practices that cast such a shadow over Donald Rose's volume), Marxism and feminism are already alert to the workings of institutions and their customary discourses and practices of inclusion and exclusion. From the mid-1980s to the early 1990s, these are the movements that most obviously inspire a series of attempts to reform, not just the *content* of Chaucer criticism, but its *voice* as well. Such attempts paid a new kind of attention to the structures of authority in the reception of Chaucer, and the way that authority is transmitted via pedagogical and other structures. It is a far more self-reflexive and at times even intemperate moment in Chaucer criticism.

The year 1986 saw the publication of two short introductions to Chaucer by British trained medievalists David Aers and Stephen Knight. Both books were part of two important English publishers' series, designed to articulate new sets of relationships between English literature and critical theory. Both writers also put into dramatic, sharpened practice ideas and theories of Chaucerian interpretation they had rehearsed either at greater length or more speculatively elsewhere.[11] Aers's *Chaucer* was part of Harvester's New Readings series, published by John Speirs, while Knight's *Geoffrey Chaucer* was one of the first volumes in Basil Blackwell's Re-Reading English series (1985–88), whose general editor was Terry Eagleton.

The two series express their aims in almost identical terms: to present original readings of canonical authors, readings that will be "responsive to new bearings which have recently emerged in literary analysis" (Harvester) or that will demonstrate the "value and usefulness" of "a striking proliferation of fresh methods and radical new approaches in literary theory and criticism" (Blackwell). These books are designed to introduce students to both literary theory and the important literary texts of the canon. The pedagogical aims in both cases are clearly expressed and reflect the importance in England of the A-level and elite university entrance examinations. Certainly this was an important aspect of their marketing strategies. Yet both also eschew the possibility of any kind of programmatic application of theory, warding off the charge of dogmatism. Here is the anonymous Harvester disclaimer:

> The series as a whole resists the adoption of general theoretical principles, in favour of the candid and original application of the critical and theoretical models found most appropriate to the survey of each individual author. The series resists the representation of any single either traditionally or radically dominant discourse, working rather with the complex of issues which emerge from a close and widely informed reading of the author in question in his or her social, political and historical context.[12]

This is the discourse of the restricted, candid pluralism that characterizes much of the work of the 1980s and early 1990s. Each series is seen as empowering the student, opening up a range of interpretative possibilities, and teaching them "theory" at the same time as introducing them to the work of major writers. The Harvester blurb claims a position of "resistance" to any single discourse, yet its preferred alternative, reading the author "in context," already makes it clear that individual authors aren't free, for example, to adopt formalist or psychological approaches. It's a discourse that claims to embrace the pluralism offered by "theory" in its broadest form, but which in fact presents a relatively stable kind of reading position. The Blackwell blurb promises to demonstrate the "insights of Marxism, feminism and deconstruction," though the latter is dismissed by both Aers and Knight, and only Knight declares any open Marxist allegiance. For both, feminism is in the background, an informing politics they neither transgress nor directly engage.

It's also clear that the new developments that these books aim to apply don't include the powerful challenges to the canon offered by feminist and multicultural theory. It's in this regard, as well as in their overall orientation toward a kind of cultural materialism, that both series reveal their Englishness: the debate over the canon has been argued more vehemently and for much longer in the United States, where the challenge of American and African-American literature forced a much earlier reconsideration of the traditional syllabus and its customary, taken-for-granted maleness and Eurocentrism. The writers discussed in both series are predominantly male and English.

The volumes by Aers and Knight are central to my study, as they constitute major documents in the radical interpellation of the English student of Chaucer in the late 1980s. They each adopt a breezy, fresh writing style, geared for the undergraduate audience (the keenest consumers of such books) and signaling their rupture from the dominant traditions they identify. Their style, and the cracking pace they are forced to set by their respective word limits, also force a radical break from the conventions of thoughtful meditation and detailed, reasoned debate. Thus their politics—in their rhetoric of address, as well as the content of their analysis—appear more forcefully than in their previous, more expansive books and articles. Their own intellectual trajectories vary, however. Aers was a doctoral student of Elizabeth Salter and Derek Pearsall, and he balances a materialist insistence on the force of medieval institutions with a sensitivity to Chaucer's poetics. Aers is also a Blake scholar, and there sometimes seems more than a hint of romanticism in his conception of the "creative imagination." At the time of writing

Chaucer, Aers was based at the University of East Anglia, but has since joined the migration of English academics to America, taking up a position at Duke University. Knight's first, most profound intellectual allegiance is to Raymond Williams and his Marxist analysis of the material forms of literary culture. At the time of writing *Geoffrey Chaucer,* Knight was working at the University of Sydney but was about to leave for the smaller, more progressive English Department at the University of Melbourne, where he took up the Robert Wallace Chair in 1987. He has since returned to the United Kingdom, to Cardiff University.

It is worth considering each volume in turn.

David Aers begins by drawing attention to the selectiveness that necessarily accompanies such a brief discussion of so prolific and so complex an author as Chaucer. Deciding to concentrate on a few major topics, society, religion, and marriage and sexual relations (in contrast to Knight, who works through Chaucer's major works on a chronological basis), he comments, "It is best to be as open as possible about this," and later in the introduction invokes Foucault and the need to avoid erasing signs of our own presence and informing ideologies when writing history or criticism. Aers's style is clear and fashionably self-reflexive, marked by the frequent use of ironic exclamation marks. It must be said, however, that he proceeds more by indirection than by direction in spelling out his own position. Quick to condemn the traditional practices of Chaucer studies, Aers does not really reveal his own method except by example. Rejecting the conservative, Robertsonian image of the Middle Ages as a period of homogeneous faith and social order, the book is admirably detailed (given its small scale, which nearly all its reviewers complained about) in its presentation of an alternative Middle Ages, one beset by social tension and religious dispute and critique. Yet Aers barely pauses to outline his own methodology. He is clear about rejecting a simple "background" approach to the historical and cultural contexts of literary texts, yet falls short of articulating an alternative explanation of the relations between literature and context. It sometimes seems that if we can but correct the dominant image of that context as heterogeneous and uncontentious, then all will fall into place.

Aers reworks some of the material from his earlier *Chaucer, Langland, and the Creative Imagination* to argue that Chaucer's poetry "dissolves" traditional ideologies and reveals an acute sense of the kinds of epistemological problems that beset the reader and writer of literature and literary criticism today.[13] Aers's Chaucer practices the art of engagement with contradictions and dialectic, dramatizing many of the tensions of medieval life. Chaucer is an active mediator of his intellectual and social contexts, and his texts are to be read as important interventions into some of the most important issues for both medieval *and* modern society.

In search of a new voice in which to speak of Chaucer, Aers finds his easiest target in exegetical criticism, defining himself in clear opposition to its allegorical certainties. Like many Chaucerians, Aers takes the *Nun's Priest's Tale* as his exemplary text, arguing in his first chapter that the "joke" here is "against those who feel the pressure to abstract" and "against those who in the light shed by this poem could find the claim that everything is written 'to our doctrine' anything other than a naive evasion of all the most fundamental problems in interpretation."[14] Chaucer cannily foresees the "readerly nostalgia for a stable, unquestionable authority" that would dominate twentieth-century readings of his work.

Aers's insistence that medieval religion is deeply imbricated in the medieval economy was a point well taken, even by his more critical reviewers. Similarly, when he sharply identifies the critical patterns that betray the affinities some medievalists feel with characters such as Theseus and Walter, this is a moment of profound importance in Chaucer criticism, articulating the vested moral and conservative interests of many critics and critical traditions, anticipating the later concerns of Carolyn Dinshaw, in particular. Once more, though, it is exegetical criticism Aers has most firmly in his sights: at times, his vocabulary seems barely under control, threatening to obscure the differences between the medieval religious practices he roundly condemns and those modern readers who invoke exegetical tradition. For Aers, they are all moralizing Christians, for whom his contempt is barely disguised. He uses the word "hymn" as if it were a neutral descriptor to characterize the discourse of exegesis (by which *The Knight's Tale* is made a "hymn in honour of Theseus and his values"); while the word "pious" and its derivatives are frequently used to describe Chaucer's allegorical readers.[15] It's hardly a balanced account, and here, as elsewhere in the book, Aers is restricted by space and forced into this kind of reductive shorthand to make a contentious point that probably won him few converts and may have simply mystified students unfamiliar with the Chaucer traditions of the 1950s and 1960s. Aers doesn't even name D. W. Robertson in this book, either in text or in bibliography: the student is left to guess the identity of the "pious critics" and to search around on her or his own to test whether Aers's generalizations are valid.

It's the apparent conflation of medieval and modern Christianity, though, that inspires the book's most shocking rhetoric. For example, the "externalisation and mechanisation of 'grace' [in the *Second Nun's Tale*] . . . is shown as part of an infantile fantasy. This bestows total power over a benevolent magic guaranteed to gratify the Christian's insatiable ego." Or again, *The Prioress's Tale* "reveals how such piety and the far from simple literary forms through which we encounter it block out all critical self-awareness encouraging grossly destructive models of 'love.'" Finally, when the *Parson's Tale* expounds the doctrine that sex between man and wife constitutes deadly sin if it is inspired "oonly by amorous love," Aers comments, "It is just here that the Christian ideology of sex joins hands with the most degenerate pornography to fragment the human person, to split off and debase sexual love."[16] In contrast to his own practice elsewhere, Aers here is decidedly *a*historical in his understanding of Christianity, sacrificing historical specificity and discrimination for the sake of provocative rhetorical effect.

These excesses aside, however, Aers nevertheless offers some of the most trenchant critiques of the dominant ideologies of medieval studies. In an article published in Australia a year later, Aers is even more pointed in his identification of the conservative, paternalistic traditions of much medieval scholarship, taking up Kenneth Burke's diagnosis of the shepherd as one who cares for "his" sheep, but who must also prepare them for slaughter. Aers goes on to contextualize and politicize his own situation, then at the University of East Anglia ("living, as I do, on board the USA's European nuclear aircraft carrier"), and his role as "a 'shepherd,' an intellectual and teacher paid to prepare sheep for the market (not *paid* to prepare them to resist)." Writing out of the heart of Margaret Thatcher's Britain, Aers writes with some urgency about the need to resist the "idealist and trans-historical universe of discourse" that represses or "forgets" the history of class conflict realized so dramatically by *Piers Plowman*, for example.[17] For Aers, such a "systematic education in amnesia" has affinities with what "current British Tory education policy might call a vocational and realistic education for life— and the market."[18] His *Chaucer* insists that medieval studies insert itself into the broader, more political context of radical critique. His targets are thus the more conservative forces within medieval studies, but also the right-wing climate of his own country and its interpellation of the student as "client" or "product."

Stephen Knight's book is substantially longer than Aers's, and this gives him the advantage of being able to pursue more detailed readings of the Chaucerian texts, without the necessity for the heavily coded critical shorthand that restricts Aers. Knight has the space to name and give examples from the various critical modes he identifies and, even more important, to describe the key methodological concepts at work in his own approach to Chaucer.

In contrast to Aers, who is decidedly cagey about naming and identifying his "opposition," Stephen Knight places his own sociohistorical work firmly in the context of Chaucer's reception, describing it candidly as the next stage in Chaucer's own complex historicity. He traces this trajectory twice: first to outline the reception of "Chaucer" himself, then of *Troilus and Criseyde.*

> A masterpiece of medieval courtesy, the first psychological novel, a classic account of earthly versus heavenly love—these are major receptions of *Troilus and Criseyde* and a history of cultural attitudes is inscribed in that succession. English renaissance writers like Sidney and Beaumont felt Chaucer provided an elegant and love-centred model that matched their own Italianate and emotive concerns. It was later critics, bringing bourgeois values of characterization, unitarian structure and worldly wisdom into culture, who elevated the novel-like elements of the poem. More recently a priestly caste of American professors has baptized the text in a shower of footnotes and pronounced it devout Christian allegory.[19]

Knight's earlier summary of Chaucerian reception describes the humanist, tolerant Chaucer as the predominant model of twentieth-century criticism, but comments that "the special social world of the academy" generates its own, "even more conservative versions," singling out the Chaucer of New Criticism, praised as the master of irony, "making wit and euphony a sufficient response to the world."[20] Like Aers, Knight identifies the exegetical school as distinctly American, and his criticisms of this school are similar to those mounted by Aers. For both critics, exegesis is as much concerned with the maintenance of structures of academic authority and mastery as it is with the historical reading of medieval texts.

Knight also briefly countenances the further perspective of postmodernism. Discussing his failure, or refusal, to deal with its textual strategies in any detail, he comments, "This limitation rises not from any revulsion from those methods, though at times they can become as self-assertive and reductive as any ironic individualist or awestruck allegorist."[21] Even so, postmodernism must resolve some major historical and theoretical problems before tackling the premodern era with the methods and strategies developed to date. Knight does not mention feminism as a distinctive critical methodology, though it's fair to say that like Aers, he absorbs some of the lessons of feminist reading practices; and one of his main themes— Chaucer's sense of the developing private sphere—has important implications for feminist criticism. But his first priority is a sociohistorical rereading, one that he presents as long overdue.

Knight tracks the changes in Chaucer's work and the poet's sense of his world as he grew older, not just succumbing to one literary influence after another, but as he moved from the courtly aristocratic setting that generated *The Book of the Duchess* into the more mercantile world of the Customs House, for example. The most typical of Knight's readings, and one that he himself foregrounds in his introduction, is his discussion of what he calls *The Book of Fame*. The surreal House of Rumour, situated beneath the House of Fame, is "made of wicker, sixty miles long, constantly spinning in the air, . . . full of noise and the activity of a working, marketing, chattering travelling humanity." For Knight, this is an imaginative re-creation of the medieval castle and its surrounding villagers:

> On that specific base Chaucer has *projected* in an extraordinary piece of analytic symbolism the actual situation of the late fourteenth century in England, when a market economy was developing through the peasant and urban structure that was formally tied to feudalism, when any serious thinker was aware of a socioeconomic movement contradicting the old order, and when there was a deepening sense that old authorities, such as those based on honour, were facing a crisis. *The Book of Fame,* seen in a sociohistorical way, is not a bungled or overambitious poetic exercise, as most critics have thought, still less a poem

about poetry, as is now a fashionable and escapist idea; it is a potent and searching *analysis* of the world so well known and so powerfully *realized* by Chaucer. (My emphasis)[22]

This passage is an intriguing instance of the inevitability of author-ial agency. Knight avoids the discourses of intentionalism or aesthet-ics—and of fashion!—as he resists attributing to Chaucer a prescient consciousness of future theorizing (the tendency of Aers's politics). At the same time, he needs to invent a different kind of vocabulary to de-scribe the complexity of Chaucer's sociohistorical "engagements." Knight's Chaucer, for all his dramatizations of sociohistorical tension, remains a conservative force, "neutralizing," for example, some of the Canterbury pilgrims' social, secular, and political concerns. Chaucer's "analyses," "realizations," and "projections" (to invoke Knight's own vo-cabulary, from this passage and elsewhere) necessarily imply a kind of dynamic, if depersonalized, agency in the writing of poetry.

Despite the reservations of many reviewers about the necessary generalizations in books so brief, nearly all agreed that both volumes represented an important challenge to traditional modes. Bernard O'Donoghue put it the most succinctly: these books "are a disturbing in-cursion into the calm territory of Chaucer criticism, ruled throughout this century by two very opposed dynasties, the breezy commonsensi-calists and the exegetes."[23]

Even those readers most sympathetic to Aers's and Knight's proj-ects, however, were conscious that this moment might represent a kind of last gasp for Chaucer or medieval studies. Here is John Simons in *Literature and History:* "Medieval literature has always been an embar-rassment to literary critics and since the demise of philology it has been increasingly marginalised. Before it disappears from our courses alto-gether two new books on Chaucer provide a timely reminder of its pres-ence and its potential. Whether they are buds on new shoots of growth or wreaths on a grave the next few years will tell."[24]

Sheila Delany also comments on the inclusion of Chaucer in both series in similar terms: this "should inject into the bloodstream of Chaucer studies the transfusion of critical controversy which keeps dead authors alive."[25] Her conclusion summarizes the differences between these two Marxist readings—Aers's Chaucer is a "likeable fellow indeed," a cryptoradical, while Knight's is "the finally conservative and orthodox Chaucer"—and regards this difference as "demonstrating the viability and the vitality of Chaucerian studies and of socially responsible scholarship." It's true that of all Chaucerians writing in the 1980s, Delany probably had most in common with Aers and Knight, and so is more likely to be sympathetic to their projects. But she is not without her criticisms, and she takes up the point with Knight that sociohistorical readings of medieval literature are not necessarily incompatible with studies that foreground poetics.

Many commentators, like Simons, were conscious of the publishers' imperatives that produce volumes and series like these, while Derek Pearsall takes pains to differentiate Aers's kind of criticism from the "familiar image of publishers scrambling to keep up and grab what's on this week's critical stall."[26] Knowing him well, he comments: "[A]s always, Mr Aers will stir up students and rile their teachers, which is, by and large, what he wants." Rather more acerbically, Tom Burton commented on the materialist imperatives of such enterprises, remarking that a number of the ideas in Aers's *Chaucer* were recycled from his *Chaucer, Langland, and the Creative Imagination:*

> [O]ne might applaud his cheek: in a capitalist society "al is for to selle," as Aers *keeps* telling us (five times in fifty-odd pages, . . .), and if a bloke can sell the same thing twice to two different publishers, bully for him! The social scientists get away with this sort of thing: why shouldn't we? Yet it sits ill with Aers's highly moral tone, and one cannot help thinking it behaviour more appropriate to Chaucer's Pardoner than to his Clerk.[27]

Burton does not explain *why* the Clerk's unworldliness should be the model for the Chaucerian critic: his comment represents the classic ad hominem critique of humanism against Marxist literary criticism that originates from the same academy, and that forms part of the same system of material and symbolic rewards as its own practices. Likening David Aers to the Pardoner is certainly an invocation of the Canterbury pilgrimage to describe modern Chaucer critics, but in contrast to most such idealizing analogies, Burton's antagonism is a rather more realistic deployment of professional rivalry.

As introductory volumes by eminent scholars, these volumes by Aers and Knight were reviewed thoughtfully but not extensively, and their impact seems to have been relatively restricted, especially in the United States: a combined result of their origins with British publishers, their status as undergraduate texts, and their overtly leftist orientation.

By contrast, the feminist project of reforming the Chaucerian community has had a far greater effect on that community and its customary attitudes toward both Chaucer and their readers. It has certainly been harder to contain or dismiss, even if the more overt signs of sexism have simply been edited out of Chaucer studies through political correctness and publication conventions, rather than through an active commitment to feminist reform. Feminist literary theory covers a far broader political spectrum from left to liberal than does materialist or Marxist criticism, so there was always greater potential for the cautious assimilation of aspects of feminism into mainstream Chaucer studies. It is always easier to be a little bit feminist than a little bit Marxist. Indeed, we might argue that Chaucer constitutes himself as a model for this strand within humanist thought. His famous interest in women characters naturalizes the voicing of such concerns among his modern readers, without necessarily committing them to anything more than sympathy with Criseyde, or fascination with the feisty Wife.

Far more powerfully, two books on Chaucer published in North America within four years of each other offered reasoned, full-length discussion of the gender politics not just of Chaucer's texts, but of the modern trends in Chaucer studies: Carolyn Dinshaw's *Chaucer's Sexual Poetics* (1989) and Elaine Tuttle Hansen's *Chaucer and the Fictions of Gender* (1992). It's in this second respect that these books differed from much of the feminist work on Chaucer already being published, by Delany, Susan Crane, Arlyn Diamond, Maureen Fries, Lisa Kiser, Jill Mann, and Priscilla Martin, among others. These scholars were already consciously mobilizing variants of feminist theory to write about the representations of women in Chaucer's poetry, and increasingly to study the gendered nature of Chaucer's poetics and his negotiations with the antifeminist and allegorical traditions. Of these, Delany and Diamond also wrote about Chaucer in studies or collections that ranged beyond the medieval to the modern, placing Chaucer studies in a broader institutional context.

Hansen and Dinshaw are often paired in modern discussions of Chaucer studies, in a way that sometimes has the effect of containing their critical or political impact. I focus here particularly on their broader concerns in reforming not just our processes of interpretation, but the very community of Chaucerians.

Dinshaw's book was the most wide-ranging and fully developed theory of Chaucerian "sexual poetics" to date, more expansive than the format of the introductory series permitted Aers and Knight to be. Her book was not intended as a students' introduction to Chaucer, but it has probably served that function for students already informed in feminist theory and wanting to test its implications when they come to read Chaucer.

Chaucer's Sexual Poetics is an intriguing attempt to bring together the undoubted importance of the exegetical tradition for Chaucer with a consciousness of broader social questions: she maintains, for example, that "literary activity as it is represented in Chaucer is always . . . a gendered activity; it is an activity that is represented in terms of relationships between people and that expresses larger principles of social organization and social power."[28] Dinshaw tackles the dominant traditions of Chaucerian exegesis and commentary head on. Her key text is the exposition by Jerome of Deuteronomy 21:10–13, in which the pagan text is figured as a captured woman who must be stripped, shaved, and cleansed before being married: that is, it must be domesticated and allegorized before it is fit for Christian consumption. In readings of the *Legend of Good Women,* the *Clerk's Tale,* the Wife of Bath, and the Pardoner, Dinshaw demonstrates the pervasiveness of this metaphor in Chaucer's poetics. Her method, then, is partially historicist, in the sense that Robertson's criticism is historicist, reading Chaucer firmly through medieval reading paradigms.

I say "partially," though, because in contrast to Robertson, Dinshaw is also concerned with the gendered implications for Western tradition of these ideas and their broader ramifications in other fields. In what represented a radical departure for Chaucer studies, Dinshaw also read Chaucer through the work of Lévi-Strauss on the exchange of women and Lacan on the fetish, though her take on these theorists is modulated by the critiques offered of their work by contemporary feminists, both French and American. We might argue, then, that her book attempts to "finish" some of the business of exegetics, in Lee Patterson's sense, renovating and politicizing some of its insights. Dinshaw's larger social and political principles remain relatively undeveloped, however, in favor of detailed readings of a selection of Chaucer's poems and the intellectual context within which he worked.

The main polemical force of the book, as far as her critique of the Chaucerian community is concerned, is found in the first chapter, in her discussion of *Troilus and Criseyde.* Here Dinshaw challenges the traditional opposition between the liberal humanist Donaldson and the stern

exegete Robertson, to show that these two "sons" in fact share compara-
ble readerly strategies for coping with Criseyde.

Each critic, I shall suggest, reads "like a man": each defines the
disruptive Other in, and of, the text as feminine and limits it,
turns away from it, in order to provide a single, univalent tex-
tual meaning fixed in a hierarchical structure. Each shaping the
course of Chaucer criticism, these major critical articulations by
Robertson and Donaldson thus perform "masculine" readings
(as Donaldson initially refers to his own) while each critic im-
plies that his reading is finally neuter and normative—"hu-
manistic" in Donaldson's case, "objective" in Robertson's.[29]

That Robertson's method should be characterized as concerned to
limit the text to a univalent meaning "fixed in a hierarchical structure"
should no longer surprise us: this accusation of totalization is one of the
more consistent burdens of the opposition to exegesis from the 1960s
to the 1990s. As we have seen, Aers and Knight also objected to its au-
thoritarian and moralizing mode. Dinshaw's analysis of the "culturally
pervasive, gendered understanding of [such] literary activity" is more
original, and points up how selective was the focus through which the
Marxist critics were working.

More startling to her readers, perhaps, was her invocation of the
idea that reading Chaucer might be a gendered activity, implicating
Donaldson as a kind of accomplice to Robertson in the patriarchal con-
tainment of the text. In spite of Donaldson's finely articulated sense of
the subtleties and complexities in *Troilus and Criseyde* and the love and
desire he expresses for Criseyde as an "emblem of . . . textual indeter-
minacy," Dinshaw comments, "I finally sense a desire for order, a desire
to control a threateningly uncontrollable libido, in Donaldson's analysis
not entirely unlike that in Robertson's."[30] She locates this desire in Don-
aldson's situating of himself, in company with Chaucer, outside the
poem: "Despite his claims of identification with the narrator and Troilus
as lovers of Criseyde, Donaldson is not, as they are, betrayed by the lady.
The critic can see farther than the limited narrator and Troilus, who
learn the hard way that Criseyde is a thing of this unstable world."[31]

For Dinshaw, Donaldson's invocation of the concept of the omni-
scient poet is the sign of the patriarchal literary project: "[W]ith its con-
cern to authorize, legitimate, and, finally, delimit meanings, the concept

of an author as all-controlling locus of meaning promotes patriarchal values of final authority, fidelity and legitimacy." This is what it means, then, to read "like a man" and to find femininity and femaleness characterized by instability and mutability. By contrast, in the *Clerk's Tale* and the Wife of Bath, Chaucer shows what it might be like to read "as a woman," while the Pardoner represents the breakdown of the traditionally stable opposition of text and reading.[32]

In its conceptual vocabulary and its fascination with the insights of anthropology and psychoanalysis, Dinshaw's book now reads very much as a product of 1980s feminism and its optimism that gender categories, practices and habits of reading and writing, for example, are "performed" and can thus be liberated from the categories of sex. She works from the idea of reading as constitutive of gender, employed by Peggy Kamuf and used most famously by Jonathan Culler and Mary Jacobus, among others. Reading "like a man" implies a hermeneutic positionality, rather than a biological or historical necessity; and herein lies the possibility for social reform and change.[33] If Pandarus reads "like" a man, for example, he is only acting, "and thereby opens up the suggestion that there are other ways to read *as* a man" (original emphasis). For Dinshaw, this prospect is "immensely liberating." It also allows her to recuperate Chaucer, much as David Aers does, for a modern readership.

Dinshaw was generally applauded for her work on Jerome's text, for the originality and insight of her readings and for the very fact of her text, as a sustained and original conjunction of Chaucer with feminist criticism. The reviews describe it as "dazzling," "intriguing, provoking, seductive,"[34] "highly readable and truly interesting," while Peter Allen typically writes of its "ease, clarity and flawless scholarship."[35]

Many reviewers pointed out, however, that Dinshaw's oppositions between male and female—or masculine and feminine—are remarkably stable and polarized, even stereotypical.[36] Certainly her understanding of gender difference is produced primarily through rhetorical rather than historical categories. Helen Cooper and Derek Pearsall both comment that Dinshaw is often, herself, tempted by the "totalizing meaning." Recall that key sentence condemning Donaldson as a totalizing reader: "I finally sense a desire for order."[37] Criticism ultimately comes down to the critic's sensibility, matched against another text, whether that text is a text of poetry or of criticism.

Pearsall also strikes a note of caution about a feminism that is tempted by the ad hominem identification of homology between two

radically different male critics: "Even that famous comparison of Robert-
son and Donaldson is in fact very suspect. The idea that the two great
dinosaurs of the fifties and sixties were on the same side was so delight-
ful that one was prepared to allow a few slipperinesses in the argument.
But truly, they are worlds apart. . . . There is a suspicion that Donaldson
has to be lumped with Robertson because he is a man and must be
shown to read like a man." Pearsall further objects to the "whimsical"
opening pages discussing Adam Scriveyn's "rape" of Chaucer's text,
where he accuses Dinshaw of bringing in history (the story of Cecily de
Chaumpaigne) when it suits the argument but ignoring it elsewhere:
"[I]f her book is designed to change the way people read, think, and act,
then there is no excusing the contempt for history that allows an allu-
sion to it, as here, to be simultaneously used and abused. If there is no
political context for the thesis, then I don't know what she is supposed
to be up to."[38] This is a problematic issue, of course: how can writing a
book about Chaucer, no matter how critical, be a political act? How *can*
we change the way people read, think, and act?

The most sustained and most critical review of *Chaucer's Sexual Po-
etics* came from Sheila Delany in *Women's Studies,* who asked a number
of searching questions about the kind of feminism that introduces an
essentialist polarity only to dispute it. Delany starts from a very different
kind of feminist base from that of Dinshaw, being more aligned with a
socialist feminism than the "metaphysical/romantic/essentialist trend"
in which she accurately situates Dinshaw. So one of her questions chal-
lenges the essentializing mode: "If either men or women can read or
write like either a man or a woman, what is the explanatory or illumi-
native power of this bipolar formula?"[39] Delany also took issue with Din-
shaw's easy invocation of Gayle Rubin, the implications of whose work
on Lacan and Lévi-Strauss she sees as being at odds with Dinshaw's
project. Delany was more familiar with the texts of feminist theory than
were most Chaucerians, and she is less excited about either the fact of
Dinshaw's book or its specific arguments. Remaining too confined to
Chaucer's own paradigms generates the risk of critics positioning them-
selves simplistically as either "for" or "against" women.

For my purposes, most interesting is Delany's confirmation to the
readers of *Women's Studies* that the persistence of "heterosexual erotic
imagery" remains "a truly irritating rhetorical feature in the talks and
writing of many senior male medievalists: the gratuitous elbow in the
ribs which not only perpetuates sexist stereotypes, but also effaces his-

tory and politics in implying that sex is always and eternally what we can all respond to."[40] This trend may have been written—or edited—out of most publications, but it's still a dominant pattern of thought among many influential medievalists.[41] Reforming the publications of the Chaucer community is one project; reforming the habits of centuries of patriarchal thought is rather harder.

Elaine Tuttle Hansen makes an insistent effort to do so, though— "to intervene in the ongoing critical enterprise of constructing in the name of Chaucer a literary father figure, like many fathers powerful and attractive by virtue of his distance and absence, a magisterial authorial self 'we' can know and trust."[42] Hansen's *Chaucer and the Fictions of Gender* (1992) remains one of the most detailed studies of modern Chaucer studies and its attempts to grapple with questions of gender. In a series of attentive readings of Chaucer's poetry and the work of his commentators, Hansen demonstrates the persistence of those critical habits of mind that license and encourage unconscious, gendered identifications with Chaucer, whereby the masculinity of the male reader is problematized, but ultimately affirmed at the expense of the unknowability and mystery of absent women. In contrast to Dinshaw, Hansen focuses on the constant threat of feminization experienced by Chaucer's narrators and Chaucer's readers. This feminization is carefully defined as a form of gender instability whose "risks and benefits" are for men only. In the history of Chaucer criticism that focuses on the representation of women in Chaucerian fiction, for example, Hansen hears "not a swelling chorus of female voices entering the text and speaking for and about themselves, but something of a monotone making known both feminine absence and masculine anxiety."[43]

Hansen's book appeared only four years later than Dinshaw's, but she writes more self-consciously out of a diverse feminist tradition. This is indicated in her opening gambit: a partial retraction of her own earlier feminist approach to Chaucer and his poetry. Instead of reading the *Legend of Good Women*, as she did in 1983, as an ironic critique of the antifeminist tradition, she now offers a reading that analyzes the potential "infectious" feminization of the male lovers in the stories, "because the rules of patriarchy are incompatible with the rules of love, and . . . men are caught in the consequent contradiction as they try to establish stable gender identity."[44] The poem of Chaucer's that is ostensibly most about women, that foregrounds the question of their representation, turns out to be as much, if not more, about men.

Hansen demonstrates the persistence of this question about men in modern Chaucer criticism. Sometimes this is done through carefully chosen epigraphs or citation from passing comments, sometimes through more systematic analysis. To argue from the criticism of Donaldson, she concedes, is "perhaps a cheap shot," though this emphasis is defended since his work is both typical and influential (Hansen makes no mention at this point of Dinshaw's critique, however).[45] Working with more recent critics, Hansen cautiously identifies a "post-feminist" strand in Chaucer criticism from the mid-1980s, a strand that seems to acknowledge a feminist critique but that also threatens to absorb it. Postfeminism often acknowledges gender difference, for example, but ends by affirming essentialist definitions of male and female and the relations between them.

Hansen draws attention to the persistence of this model of interpretation, "based on one falsely universal paradigm of heterosexual male response," citing as her examples of postfeminist response to Chaucer the writings of Lee Patterson and H. Marshall Leicester.[46]

Many reviewers commented on the surprising omission of the Pardoner from Hansen's study. Writing for the nonmedievalist *Journal of the History of Sexuality*, Marilynn Desmond also criticizes the book for its failure to engage with the "larger interdisciplinary debates within the study of sexuality."[47] Desmond also noted that Hansen worked more closely with other Chaucerian critics than with non-Chaucerian feminist theory, queer theory, or gender studies. This, of course, was not Hansen's project, but the comment indicates the perceived need, or demand, for such interventions in the future.

Among those responses from feminists broadly sympathetic to Hansen's project, there was much opposition to her implicitly poststructuralist critique of the possibility of Chaucer's speaking directly, of speaking to us. Hansen's stress on the strategic anxieties rehearsed by Chaucer's narrators and characters was felt most keenly by those liberal feminists who depend on recuperating some kind of humanism in Chaucer's poetics, located quite directly in the voice of the poet. Hansen's book articulated what was for many an unbearable possibility.

Kathryn Lynch comments that Hansen's working model of gender is more nihilistic than she acknowledges. If we do not speak, but are spoken through, then "the text dissolves into a web of strategies and positions lacking ultimate reference, which is largely how Hansen sees Chaucer's poetics."[48] Lynch is clearly rehearsing her own antagonism to the conclusions of Hansen's skeptical reading. She goes on to compare Hansen unfavorably to Jill Mann, who is more disposed to "take Chaucer at his word." The "payoff" here, for Lynch, is "an interpretation that permits Chaucer to speak *to* us, as men and women readers, not just *against* us; an interpretation that allows Chaucer's endorsement of patience, pity, and accommodation as genuine human ideals and not simply as strategies." Lynch here does not so much argue against Hansen as simply reject the central tenets of her book. Chaucer's "speaking" to "us" is not a payoff but a starting point of the kind of reading (i.e. Mann's) that Lynch would prefer, to ward off the losses that ensue from poststructuralism and to substitute a quietist Chaucer of "patience, pity, and accommodation." "Feminist" criticism here is diluted almost beyond recognition, conjuring up the fantasy of Chaucer speaking equally to men and women.

Jill Mann herself, in a brief review for *Medium Aevum,* is also more forgiving of Chaucer than is Hansen. If neither Criseyde nor the Wife is given an authentic feminine voice, this is not because Chaucer is concerned to silence that voice but rather that he as a matter of principle *refuses* to speak for women. In contrast, Mann implies, Hansen speaks in a critical monotone of the kind of which she accuses Chaucer.[49]

My very selective account of these movements to reform Chaucer studies concludes with a review of Hansen's book by David Wallace, a review that presents a rare moment of masculinity replying to feminist criticism in a way that is neither defensive nor patronizing. Wallace strategically inhabits the position of the masculine reader, while at the same time demonstrating that not all male readers read alike. He comments with approval on much of the detail of Hansen's readings and her insistence on "breaking up the happy marriage between masculine critics and masculine texts." He is even prepared to accept her parody of masculinity, in her account of book 3 of *Troilus,* "which reads like a running commentary on the state of the male member."[50] Considering the larger project of the book, Wallace also comments, "Hansen ends by answering the question that traditional male medievalists might be thinking but would not have the cheek to ask: why do feminists persist in reading Chaucer at all?" (In speaking for Hansen, Wallace both does and does not have the "cheek" to ask that question.) He quotes her "answer" with approval: "Feminist criticism of the canonical male author offers a place in which to examine the risks and benefits of critiquing hegemonic discourses and masterworks from a position of exclusion and to analyze the limits and powers of being constructed, as feminisms are constructed, in opposition to (rather than outside or beyond) the structures they seek to modify."[51]

Wallace has nothing to argue with here, but is surprised to find that this explanation comes at the end of nearly three hundred pages of close reading "that both challenges and extends the tradition of E. Talbot Donaldson."[52] Wallace thus implicitly feminizes Donaldson, contrasting this method to the more typically masculine pattern, which is "to abandon the poetic text entirely, disappear into some sort of archive, and emerge twenty pages later, sweaty and triumphant, with a new nugget of fact or a whole new social, political, or economic paradigm to fit the text into." If Dinshaw had aligned Donaldson with Robertson as two "manly" readers, Wallace tropes the strange configuration of critical affiliations further by aligning exegetical with political criticism, both engaged in this sweaty search of the archive or paradigm that will affirm the reader's mastery of the text. Given his account of Hansen's sexually charged humor in her discussion of the *Troilus,* Wallace's own suggestive vocabulary also demonstrates that he too can do what Hansen does, this time at the expense of his male colleagues. He reads, we might say, "like a feminist." Like a number of other reviewers, Wallace also comments on Hansen's failure to engage with female critics in much detail, demonstrating his own knowledge of recent feminist work on Chaucer. He thus recuperates an interesting version of masculinity in Chaucer studies. It is perilously close to the postfeminism that Hansen identified in Patterson and Leicester, but can best be read, I think, as a kind of postmasculinism that is actually more responsive to Hansen's critiques of Chaucer studies than are several of the feminist reviewers I discussed earlier.

While Wallace's review of Hansen is exceptional in its willingness to engage with the broadest implications and questions in Hansen's text, it's fair to say that in the last ten or so years, Chaucer criticism has been transformed in its ready accommodation of a wide range of theoretical and methodological approaches. The books I have considered in this section represent only a small sample of the work in Chaucer studies produced over the period spanned by their publication. Yet they represent the most considered attacks on many of the conventional subject positions of Chaucer studies and the cozy bonds that hold the masculinized imaginary community of readers together. Their impact, particularly the work of Dinshaw and Hansen, has been profound. Some of the most recent feminist books on Chaucer, for example, take for granted the homosociality of his work,[53] or the idea that Chaucer's texts enact their own distinctive dialectic between sex and gender or between politics and poetics.[54] The work of Aers and Knight is frequently acknowledged in, if not directly assimilated into, Chaucer studies, while other theoretical possibilities and methodologies are frequently exercised over the field, from various forms of historicism and gender studies to reinventions of poststructuralism and queer theory.

If we turn our attention, though, to the implied readerships of these reforming books, another interesting divide emerges. The two English scholars write directly for a student market. When they affirm Chaucer's importance, they focus on the sense in which his work engages with medieval ideologies, not simply on his aesthetic greatness. Hansen and Dinshaw, however, write almost exclusively about past and present scholars and critics of Chaucer. Addressing the scholarly community at its highest levels, their work is directed as much to the professors who taught them, and to their colleagues, as to their students. Advanced students devour these books: the students in my own department are ravenous for feminist and "theoretical" medieval studies. But they are not and do not pretend to be books for the beginning Chaucerian. We turn now to what is arguably the most influential discourse on Chaucer: the discourse of the students' guides and introductory texts.

Becoming a Chaucerian

As I have been arguing throughout this book, the Chaucerian community is able to withstand a great deal of difference and a great deal of criticism from within and among its own ranks. This is a function of all canonical author studies: canonicity is affirmed, indeed produced, by the proliferation of multiple readings, endless variations on those readings, and vehement dissent from those readings, all circulating within the same restricted institutional ambit. Few Chaucerians in the eighties or nineties went so far as to challenge the centrality of Chaucer or Chaucer studies or their intrinsic value. It's only a minority voice within feminist Chaucer studies that is prepared even to raise this issue.

Moreover, in spite of widespread apprehension about the future and the fate of Chaucer studies, the "business" of Chaucer studies goes on.

Student numbers may be falling; Chaucer and medieval studies may no longer be compulsory where they once were; but a good many institutions of Chaucer studies, such as the New Chaucer Society, the Chaucerian division of the MLA, or the study of Chaucer at A level, are still flourishing. Large numbers of introductory guides to Chaucer are still being commissioned by publishers optimistic of healthy sales and undaunted by competition from their many rivals.

This distinctive form of Chaucerian discourse deserves attention: in this period of "crisis," at the end of the Chaucer tradition, how is the Chaucerian student interpellated by the community of scholars? And how do these introductions register the concepts, and the work, of reform?

The general introductory monograph on the canonical author has a long and distinguished history: A. W. Ward published his *Chaucer* with Macmillan in 1888, while we have already considered Chesterton's *Chaucer* in chapter 6. Lee Patterson in *Negotiating the Past* also describes a number of important instances from the early part of the century. The second era is represented by books by, among others, John Speirs, John Norton-Smith, George Kane, and Derek Brewer, whose *Introduction to Chaucer*, first published in 1984 (and originating in revisions of Brewer's own *Chaucer* [1953] and *Chaucer in His Time* [1963]), has recently been revised to provide what is puzzlingly described as "a controversial and modern re-statement of some of the traditional views on Chaucer."[55] Clearly, "controversial" remains a strong selling point, while it is also clear that there is an important student market for more introductory material than lecturers and professors can easily provide.

Between 1987 and 1998, Macmillan published no fewer than four such books on Chaucer, across four series: The Critics Debate (Alcuin Blamires, *The Canterbury Tales*, 1987), How to Study Literature (Rob Pope, *How to Study Chaucer*, 1988), Macmillan Writers in Their Time (Janette Dillon, *Geoffrey Chaucer*, 1993), and Analysing Texts (Gail Ashton, *Chaucer: The Canterbury Tales*, 1998). Each series does slightly different work, but this variety testifies to a healthy market for this kind of publication, as well as the publisher's desire for comprehensiveness and inclusiveness in each series. Like the Harvester and Blackwell series already discussed, these are organized around the canonical British writers, reflecting the syllabus for literary study at A-level and university entrance exams, whose most typical assignment is to print an extract from the *Tales* and ask the student to generate a commentary on that passage and the work as a whole. If we consider the whole spectrum of these general introductions to Chaucer or the *Canterbury Tales*, the repetition of background information, if not critical opinion, across these four volumes is simply staggering. When we include the productions of other publishers, the repetition is multiplied: a good indication of the market's perceived need to spread its product across a wide field.

It's true that this genre is more typical of publishers in the United Kingdom than in the United States: the British upper secondary syllabus and the tertiary entrance exams provide a consistent and ready market for these volumes. The closest American comparison is the Twayne's Masterworks series, which produced David Williams's *The Canterbury Tales: A Literary Pilgrimage* (1987), or Continuum's series called Literature and Life: British Writers, in which Velma Bourgeois Richmond's *Geoffrey Chaucer* appeared in 1992. American college students seem to demand a different kind of introduction to Chaucer: the distinctively American elementary genre is that of the "Notes," represented most famously, perhaps, by Cliffs Notes, though other series are also available. Chaucer has always been represented in this kind of publication, which tends to focus on summaries and a kind of formalist criticism, giving "background" information where explanation might otherwise be difficult, but also demonstrating, quite practically, the kind of writing on Chaucer that might be rewarded in a competitive assessment system.

My focus falls principally on the first kind of volume—the preeminently English kind, since they are the ones we might more reasonably expect to engage with contemporary critical issues. In addition to the volumes already mentioned and the books by Aers, Knight, and Mann for Harvester and Blackwell, we should also include Anne Rooney's *Geoffrey Chaucer: A Guide through the Critical Maze* (in Bristol Press's State of the Art Series, 1989); Steve Ellis, *Geoffrey Chaucer* (in Northcote House's Writers and their Work, 1996); S. H. Rigby's *Chaucer in Context: Society, Allegory, and Gender* (Manchester Medieval Series, 1996); and Peter Brown's *Chaucer at Work: The Making of the Canterbury Tales* (Longman, 1994), which, while not part of a series, is clearly pitched at the same level, including lots of introductory and background material and questions to generate class discussion.

Considering the sheer numbers of these publications (eleven in twelve years in the United Kingdom alone), we might wonder about the economics of the venture—and this is without including the many anthologies of recent Chaucer criticism, designed to keep the modern student well informed, or the many annotated and introductory texts of

Chaucer's works designed for the undergraduate user. A quick search through www.amazon.com, for example, reveals many such titles in print. In 1999, of the 740-odd items responding to a "Chaucer" title search (compared with more than 6,000 on Shakespeare but only 400 on Spenser), more than half, on a rough count, were nonscholarly publications: introductions, translations, modernizations, or notes. Commenting on the proliferation of editions of Shakespeare over a comparable period, Gary Taylor draws attention to the surprising capacity of the market to bear this amount of repetition. He implies that proliferating editions actually generate the desire for more editions:

> The editing of Shakespeare is a small but paradigmatic example of the economics of culture, which depends upon the manufacture of desire. People do not need editions of Shakespeare in the way they need, for instance, food, shelter, clothing, health, self-defense, or even sex; consequently, the demand must be created in order to be satisfied. Just as a bestseller is a book you read because everyone is reading it, so a classic is a book you read because everyone has read it—a book you edit because everyone is editing and has edited it.[56]

A classic, we might correspondingly argue, is also a work you write a student guide to because everyone is writing a student guide to it.

Chaucer studies thrives at this elementary level, then, but these books rarely take up the challenge represented by the theoretical and political work of Chaucer studies in the mid-1980s. It's also clear that the vogue for uncompromisingly materialist readings of canonical texts has been short-lived: Aers's and Knight's books appear all the more remarkable from a new millennial perspective. All the titles mentioned represent a withdrawing from those heady days to a more circumspect and far less engaged view of criticism. A shift of a different order is also evident in these books. The straightforward notion of the "introduction" to Chaucer's writing has gradually been supplemented, though not totally displaced, by introductions to the modern critical debates around Chaucer's writing. These are presented as nonpartisan inductions into criticism and the historical patterns of reading Chaucer. Chaucer criticism—right, left, uncommitted—has become commodified: an object of study to be mastered, though not necessarily practiced, let alone engaged with politically.

In this sense, the very weight of Chaucer criticism almost mitigates against the student. As a number of authors point out, medieval studies and Chaucer criticism do not easily fit into the boxes made customary by the proliferation of introductory guides to literary theory in the 1980s: formalist, structuralist, Marxist, feminist, poststructuralist, psychoanalytic.[57] In their desire to chart an accurate map of this terrain, moreover, some of the guides to criticism become almost numbingly detailed in their conscientious summarizing of modern scholarly views on, say, the kind of consolation offered in or by *The Book of the Duchess*. "Criticism" here is not a reading strategy that can be learned and applied to different texts, when its force is so often diluted across a range of opinions about what individual texts mean. It's hard to imagine the new student making much of these summaries: one suspects that after reading a "guide through the critical maze" (Rooney) or an account of the "critics' debate" (Blamires), they may feel there is very little left, themselves, to say. Blamires, it is true, does try to sketch out a broader critical map and briefly describes Marxist or structuralist thought (though in terms that direct the student to Terry Eagleton's *Literary Theory: An Introduction* [1983], rather than original works of theory themselves).

Moreover, it's surprising how many of these books resist labeling their own approach. Alcuin Blamires insists that his appraisal of the *Canterbury Tales* is "not a specimen of any clear-cut 'X' or 'Y' sectarian approach. It is best characterised through a process of partial elimination, which leaves room for a broadly based (but not infinitely elastic) reading, and thereby acknowledges the unsectarian multifaceted quality of Chaucer's writing."[58] Here is Chaucer the liberal, defined, quite precisely, in *opposition* to literary theory, characterized narrowly here as programmatic hermeneutics.[59]

The majority of these introductions to Chaucer, if they are prepared to spell out their approach, will make it as general and safe as possible: the need to read Chaucer's works in their medieval English and European context. But instead of problematizing this approach or taking on board the challenges mounted against it in contemporary Chaucerian criticism and, indeed, in the debates around the new historicism, it's clear in most instances that the aim is rather more old-fashioned: to induct the student into the medieval world. They often proceed by discounting "modern" responses, acknowledging the presuppositions the student might bring to the text only in order to correct them. This is the most obvious, direct way in which the student is taught to be Chaucerian.

In his relatively early (1987) volume on the *Canterbury Tales* for the Twayne's Masterstudies series, the most conservative of all those I'm discussing here, David Williams stresses the importance of the audience's good intentions in understanding the work. "At that point, we see that the motive and understanding—the two meanings of *entencioun*—are the same for both, and that audience and author merge."[60] Subtitled "A Literary Pilgrimage," this book works to correct any modernizing impulses. For example, in discussing Theseus's marriage to Ypolita, Williams remarks, "The conventional use in the Middle Ages of female to represent appetite and male to represent reason was intended as an analysis of the human psyche, not as sociology or sexism." Thus reassured, "the Canterbury audience has had set for it a *proper and orthodox* philosophical structure to follow in their tales" (my emphasis). The politics of gender and class here are deeply hegemonic: the "impertinent" Franklin "loathes" himself as a representative of the nouveau riche, while in the *Wife of Bath's Tale* "the author herself is the rapist knight," in that she imposes her will and her desires over her five husbands (Jankyn's violence to her notwithstanding) and insists on her own interpretation of Scripture.[61]

Williams's book is the most egregious instance of the "guide" to Chaucer leading the student reader firmly down the quietist path of critical response to Chaucer. Overall, his book stresses the changing dynamics of authorship and audience in the *Tales* (storytellers become audience, audience members become storyteller), but the end result is a greater intimacy with this "world master" through the familiar metaphysics of presence: "Chaucer reminds us frequently in one way or another that, like him, we are not really on the road to Canterbury but listening to a poem or sitting alone somewhere, reading the text. This increases our intimacy with him, because Chaucer, too, sat alone somewhere and wrote the text, and he later stood somewhere and read it aloud." The persistence of this trope of solitary identification over the centuries is remarkable, an intimacy embracing both the site of composition and the site of public performance. Williams closes with an equally persistent gambit, quoting "Chaucer's own last words" to affirm authorial intention as the "mature theoretical basis of his art": "'All that is writen is writen for oure doctrine,' and, says Geoffrey Chaucer, with finality, 'that is myn entent.'"[62] The circle is firmly closed.

Less dramatic, but just as powerful, is Anne Rooney's conclusion about *The Canterbury Tales:* "Finally, the completeness or integrity of the

work is so uncertain, its proper order and form so precarious and elu-
sive, that critical analysis must remain contingent, conjectural and, ide-
ally, humble. This is a state of affairs which I feel Chaucer—with his
interest in the contingency of all knowledge and the elusiveness of
truth—would have liked."[63] As we saw in earlier chapters, it's an impor-
tant trope for modern criticism to assure itself that Chaucer would have
approved, or been pleased by, what we do.

More recently, Peter Brown, in *Chaucer at Work* (1994), is conscious
of the number of beginners' guides to Chaucer but argues that they
rarely open up the best place for a student reader: "[I]n their drive to be
authoritative, and bolstered by the publisher's blurbs, the books leave
precious little room for the learning experience of the stumbling student,
in spite of their well intentioned gestures in that direction."[64] Brown
cites the Penguin Masterstudies series as an example of annotated texts
that provide essential background information but that risk making stu-
dents too dependent on the introductory guide for explication. On the
other hand, the suggestive, more open-ended criticism, represented for
Brown by Piero Boitani and Jill Mann's *Cambridge Chaucer Companion*
or Helen Cooper's *The Canterbury Tales* in the Oxford Guides to Chaucer
series, tends to leave the student unable to pursue the implications of
these more elaborate readings. For Brown, it's important that students be
enabled to "duplicate the processes whereby respected scholars and crit-
ics themselves reach their wise conclusions."

After this refreshing concern for the process by which the student
"becomes" the critic, Brown shifts gear into a consideration of the "kind
of literary guide or companion with which Chaucer was familiar, and to
the kind of guide which he favoured within his own compositions."
Seeking for a model for the "feelings of hesitancy, tentativeness and
doubt" that beset the student of Chaucer, Brown finds them, reassur-
ingly, in Chaucer himself, in the "logic of emotion" demonstrated by
Geffrey in response to the Eagle in *The House of Fame* or in the Miller's
insistence on capping the *Knight's Tale*. By approaching the *Tales* through
Chaucer's sources and contexts, *Chaucer at Work* aims to introduce stu-
dents to the medieval process of composition through sources and prior
texts. Avoiding the authoritative structures of the "clerisy" of which Pat-
terson speaks, Brown reinstitutes the traditional humanist fiction of
identifying with the author, and the author at his desk, reading like a
critic. At the same time, modern questions of political theory and radi-
cal critique are simply evaded: the student working through Brown's

book might be on the first step to becoming a "respected scholar and critic," but he or she will not learn how to be an interrogative scholar and critic.

These books tend to interpellate their student readers into a world that no longer has much currency. They teach students, well enough, how to become "Chaucerians," but with little reference to the other things they will also need to become—from the statistically almost negligible fraction who will become full-fledged professional Chaucerians, to the slightly larger but still small percentage who will make literature, reading, and writing their profession, to the vast majority who will make only the most indirect use of their studies.

Most of these volumes are unabashed in their pedagogical orientation and the disciplinary and aesthetic training they offer. In the most recent book to be considered here, Gail Ashton remarks on her first page, "My hope is that in reading this book you too will come to an enthusiastic understanding of why Chaucer might merit the adjective 'great.'"[65] This is a very conditional invitation into the Chaucerian community: "you too" can enter, on the basis of such an "enthusiastic understanding" of Chaucer's canonical merit. Or again, what is taken for granted in Anne Rooney's questions as she opens her discussion of *Troilus and Criseyde?* "Does the poem celebrate love, or condemn secular, sexual passion? Should we approve of some, or all, or none of the characters?"[66]

These very restrictive ethics of reading are best represented by Rob Pope's volume for the How to Study Literature series. Here, the author's casual, chatty tone obscures and evades the institutional demands that structure and determine his approach. "We start together from scratch," he democratically reassures the reader on the first page, yet his first question, "Who (or what) is 'Chaucer'?" is answered in such a way as to leave no doubt that the structures of pedagogical authority are well and truly in place. In fact, we learn that "Chaucer" is constituted by four things: Chaucer the man, Chaucer the works, Chaucer the narrator, and Chaucer the exam.[67] Ultimately, this book is designed as a guide to mastering the latter Chaucer. The constraints on the student reader, constantly reminded of this teleology, are very powerful, and as the volume proceeds, the difficulties of "Chaucer" are carefully processed into marketable, that is, examinable discourse.

Pope's book is in fact a very practical introduction to reading Chaucer's language, but as a reflection of the British higher education system, it's striking for its conservatism. The whole book stresses "contrast and tension" as a way of both reading *and writing* about Chaucer; the aesthetic principles of New Criticism still have an enormous impact on Chaucerian pedagogy. In the introductory chapter, Pope observes that "all experienced exam-setters know that there are just *three or four basic questions* on any author."[68] The implications for modern pedagogy, if this is true, are damning indeed, since they imply a system of critical attitudes and structures that hasn't changed for more than sixty years. And in fact, it's no surprise that these three or four questions turn out to be simply variants of the *one* question: "How does Chaucer produce a sense of variety and complexity in his work?" The remainder of the book will be dedicated to applying this question to particular texts and to showing readers "how to go about forming a 'varied and complex' response of their own."[69] This may be the kind of guide students need to pass their A levels, but it will give them little indication of the critical world and its history. It's true that "varied and complex" might cover a range of theoretical approaches, but it's clearly implicit in Pope's readings that he is inducting students into the ethical world of Leavisite criticism, obviously still dominant in the English examination system.[70]

Some of the more recent volumes present a more subtle interpellation of the Chaucerian student. I would single out Janette Dillon, who employs the metaphor of "dialogue with the past"; Steve Ellis, who starts with the disjunction between the professional and the popular Chaucer; and S. H. Rigby, who writes as a historian and is less weighed down, it seems, by the weight of the Chaucerian critical tradition.[71]

At the other end of the spectrum of introductions to Chaucer studies are the cheap "notes" series that characterize American publication at this level. They are distinguished by their format, their price, and the stability of their contents. In contrast to most other areas of scholarly endeavor, they take for granted that bodies of critical knowledge remain relatively stable: these volumes are printed and reprinted without variation.

Cliffs Notes are one of the most well known of these series: in fact, they attribute their success to the fact that this is *all* they publish. In 1985, Clifton Hillegras, the founder of Cliffs Notes, was honored by the Newcomen Society of Lincoln, Nebraska, where the company is still based. In accepting the award, Hillegras recounted the history of the series and his commercial precepts. It is primarily a story of how his business grew (he mentions, for example, that his printer, Boomer's, has printed more than fifty million volumes since 1958), but it also features some of his reflections on literature and the demand his series fills. Hillegras comments:

> Cliffs Notes contain nothing that cannot be found by research-
> ing a number of volumes at the library, but we provide the stu-
> dent with a concise source under one cover. We offer the stu-
> dent a distillation of that information, in addition to the unique
> and priceless knowledge that comes from teaching in the class-
> room, furnished by the teachers who write the Notes. We have
> always used the best minds we could find in order to promote
> learning. . . . There should be no monopoly on information, nor
> on the motivation to learn. Our aim has always been to create a
> new sense of confidence and excitement about reading.[72]

Cliffs Notes play no major role in disseminating critical theory or the history of critical traditions, but Hillegras's comments do shed some light on the proliferation of such books. Ever since the company was es-tablished in 1958, the growth of sales was phenomenal until it "paused" between 1965 and 1970, then declined until 1975, when sales leveled be-fore picking up again in 1978 and steadily increasing ever since. For Hil-legras, there is a direct correlation in this pattern with the "prevailing standards of education." In the 1960s, education began to "falter," as students demanded radical changes and more "relevance" in their edu-cation. Students insisted on grading themselves or enrolling in pass/fail courses, with the result that everyone got A's. "It was not until teachers once again took charge of the classrooms, in the mid-1970s, that our sales began to increase once more. From 1980 until the present, sales have grown steadily—parallel to the academic excellence that was lost in the mid-1960s and finally restored to the classroom."[73] It's an interest-ing perspective from an unabashedly commercial context: the period we see as the growth of radical criticism is perceived as the restoration of teacherly order and authority and an increased competitiveness among students, willing to buy such study guides as will help them compete against their peers. Hillegras's comments force us to recognize that the "community" of which we so like to speak is founded, absolutely and at all levels, on competitiveness rather than cooperation. It almost seems like bad taste, too, to mention that far more copies of Cliffs Notes and similar texts will be bought and read by college and university students than most of our scholarly theorizing put together. These more commercial texts can be read, perhaps, as the popular culture of Chaucer studies, as opposed to the high culture of avant-garde theory and more specialist studies.

Similarly, we might observe that "hearing" Chaucer speak—the imaginative fiction on which I've been arguing Chaucer studies depends, whether this is acknowledged or not—is a learned activity. Chaucer criticism is built on this transcendence, and it is supported by an enormous publishing and educational industry. In the same way, when Tim Machan discusses the economics of publishing Chaucerian and Middle English texts, he admits that anthologies are the cheapest way to keep this material in circulation, but laments that these are the texts that most distort, since they modernize and extract.[74]

We could conclude, then, by suggesting that Chaucer studies has done its best to expel the popular Chaucer from consideration, only to find it reentering through these satellite Chaucerian publications. The academic sector does its best to ignore the more populous segments of the discipline: its students, eagerly buying and reading books that many university libraries don't hold. Once more, the community of students and scholars working together turns out to be a fiction that is only part of the story.

CONCLUDING QUESTIONS

What can it mean, then, to read Chaucer at the beginning of the twenty-first century? What kind of social and intellectual acts are performed by writing about Chaucer? Or indeed, to turn the question onto my own project, by writing about Chaucerians? As I have been arguing throughout this book, the Chaucerian community is able to withstand a great deal of difference and a great deal of criticism from within and among its own ranks. This book is positioned firmly within the discourses and traditions of Chaucer studies, though I have no doubt that it has offended and frustrated many readers, unaccustomed, perhaps, to having their throwaway, prefatory remarks analyzed in more detail than their interpretive or methodological strategies, or "frustrated" because my refusal to offer a reading of a single Chaucerian poem seems in contradiction with the whole purpose of writing about Chaucer. What kind of Chaucerian doesn't interpret Chaucer's poetry?

By way of response, I contend that it's impossible to separate the reading of Chaucer from the reading of Chaucerian discourse; that when we read Chaucer's poetry, we are necessarily reading through the conventions and traditions of editorial presentation, of criticism and commentary, and of the highly socialized models of reading communities, clustered around the familiar presence of a beloved author. An attentiveness to the formal and informal voices of Chaucer criticism and their various imagined forms of community and identification should become an important part of Chaucer studies, as we attempt to rethink our relation to the canonical authors of the past, in a future that is skeptical of the seeming ease of those relationships.

The significance of this apparently marginal aspect of criticism—its voice and its rhetoric—can be traced along three paths. The first leads back into the past, in an unapologetic insistence on the significance of the origins of Chaucer studies and literary studies in the humanist criticism of the fifteenth and sixteenth centuries. As I argued in chapter 4, at the same time that Chaucer becomes the object of scholarly work, he is distanced from its present, necessitating a range of identifications and imaginative leaps to bridge that distance, producing patterns that are replicated and normalized in most other fields of literary studies. In its attempts to make sense of the medieval past, we could argue that English literary criticism is thus a species of medievalism. This would signify a radical dialogic integration of two disciplines customarily kept far apart.

Second, the voices of Chaucer critics are not really marginal to their concerns, as the reforming critics of the 1980s are at pains to show. The style of Chaucer critics, their various attempts to get close to Chaucer or to distance themselves from him, to set up hierarchies of formality and informality in the degrees of identification they will permit in different contexts—these are all intrinsic to the functions of criticism and the definition of what it is to *be* Chaucerian, or rather, to *perform* Chaucerianness in any given social and historical context. As well as seeking to analyze those voices and the discourses of affinity through which they speak, I have also sought to examine the reception of those voices, as Chaucerians over the centuries rehearse their own history, setting up their own relations of difference and similarity with the Chaucerians of the past.

Third, in drawing attention to the performance of Chaucerian readers as Chaucerian writers, I hope I have shown that being a Chaucerian is not simply a professional activity, though it has become predominantly so. It is also a social act, and not just in the pleasant image of the

Chaucerian pilgrimage that adorns our conferences and published productions and that informs our sense of professional identity. It is also, more actively, a form of writing and publishing with important implications for both the present and future of literary studies and, more politically, the profession's relationship with its own future, in the embattled postgraduate cohorts who must now be asking, Why study Chaucer? Or medieval literature? Or literature at all? These questions are also asked by professional academics, responding to an environment of economic rationalism or an intellectual and pedagogical institution that often favors contemporary forms of writing and other more popular media as the object of analysis. A number of medievalists have also begun to engage with the problem of the meaningfulness of literary or medieval studies where questions of social equity and access to the plentiful resources most of us enjoy remain unresolved, and mostly, indeed, unasked. These are not always questions to be answered from within the academy, but as a way of starting to think about their implications I have found it important to think about *how* we write about Chaucer and the ways the traditions and practices of author studies, exemplified in Chaucer, have been able to withstand considerable criticism to date.

For example, it's perhaps surprising that the formal autobiographical voice is rarely invoked by Chaucer scholars. A trope popularized by feminist criticism—where it aims to break down the apparent neutrality of masculinist authority—and by new historicist criticism—where it is used to demonstrate the imbrication of the scholar with his or her knowledge of the material studied—it's not an established part of Chaucerian or medievalist discourse. The asides and prefaces I've considered here, because they are so marginalized, do not fall into the same category as the serious annexing of personal reflections on the nature of being a Chaucerian. How odd it would seem, for example, if I began to meditate on the strangeness of writing about Chaucer in a house on the banks of the Merri Creek, where the Wurundjeri people told stories about the Sacred Kingfisher, thousands of years before the English came to Australia. The colonialists described it as *terra nullius* in order to appropriate its bushland and forests for grazing pastures and to dig up its rich mineral deposits, enacting the politically sanctioned dispossession and cultural and physical genocide on which the economy that employs me depends. What sorts of uses of the past are enacted here, in my choice to write about Chaucer and medieval England in such a setting?

That we *don't* write in this way is a clear indication of how professional decorum works to rule out such meditations and questions as irrelevant and subjective. Why would a Chaucerian possibly be interested in asking or answering such questions? Besides, we might argue that Chaucer himself already anticipates that autobiographical turn. When he sets up the disjunction between his daily work and his nightly fantasies in *The House of Fame* or when, as a love poet, he interposes his own inadequacies, Chaucer has already established the parameters of personal interventions into serious discourse, leaving his modern critics to imitate such moments only in weak imitations that often verge on parody and that appear only on the margins of their critical discourse.

And as for the question of how we should write Chaucer criticism? It was never my intention to rank or to evaluate the critical work whose voices I have analyzed, although I would not shy away from the sympathy with the more politicized versions of Chaucer criticism that my readers will have discerned. The patterns of Chaucer studies, of medieval studies, of author-based studies are broader and more deeply entrenched than any single reading of Chaucer's works can effect on its own. However, although my book has been concerned primarily with reception, I see it as contiguous with studies that pursue an interest in the social work represented in and performed by Chaucer's own poetry and its interventions into the society and life of fourteenth-century England. Drawing these connections can help us think more carefully about the nature of what we do when we write about Chaucer from the very different perspective of the twenty-first century; can help us to construct complex and thoughtfully self-reflexive models of our dealings with the past.

Those dealings will always be contradictory. As long as the traditions of humanist scholarship and literary criticism persist, we will always want to hear Chaucer's voice, in some form or some level or another, will always find some way of expressing our pleasure in the literature of the past and the contact it seems to offer with the people who lived there. I think this is a structural feature of literary studies and their origins in author-based criticism. The desire to "know" Chaucer isn't reducible to a simplistic intentionalism or a retreat to a "commonsense" view, but taps into the communicative function of all writing and, perhaps especially, self-conscious writing like Chaucer's. But as long as we continue to reflect on that wish, we will always want to problematize that possibility of communication. This is how it is possible to mark the closure of a tradition but not end the study of Chaucer. The easy identifications with Chaucer as a clubbish congenial soul belong to an important era that is all but over; this doesn't mean that temptation doesn't haunt current practice or that future criticism won't find some other way of hearing, and responding to, the voices that play across Chaucer's poetry.

Some recent discussions of medieval studies seem to me to accept too quickly that our subject is by definition of less "relevance" than more practical social work or other fields of intellectual inquiry. On the contrary, I argue that medieval studies—defined as the attempt to understand other cultures and the prehistory of our own—can address some of the most profound issues in what is sometimes described as a global economy or global culture. Chaucer studies still has the capacity to be an exemplary topic in our meditations on similarity and difference with other cultures, on the uses we make of the past, and on the models and images we construct to describe what we do. An attentiveness to the voices we use in which to speak Chaucer and the way we establish relationships with each other seems to me a good place for medievalists to begin.

NOTES

Introduction

1. John M. Bowers, ed., *The Canterbury Tales: Fifteenth-Century Continuations and Additions* (Kalamazoo, Mich.: Medieval Institute Publications, 1992).

2. My use of this phrase derives, of course, from Pierre Bourdieu, particularly his *Education, Society and Culture*, trans. Richard Nice (London: Sage, 1977); *Distinction: A Social Critique of the Judgement of Taste*, trans. Richard Nice (Cambridge, Mass.: Harvard University Press, 1984); and "The Market of Symbolic Goods," *Poetics* 14 (1985): 13–44. For a clarification of "symbolic capital" in response to some of his commentators, see Pierre Bourdieu, *In Other Words: Essays Towards a Reflexive Sociology*, trans. Matthew Adamson (Cambridge: Polity Press, 1990), 111–12. Bourdieu has been influentially mediated for literary studies through John Guillory's important study, *Cultural Capital: The Problem of Literary Canon Formation* (Chicago: University of Chicago Press, 1993).

3. James Kinsley, ed., *The Poems of John Dryden*, 4 vols. (Oxford: Clarendon Press, 1958), 4:1457.

4. See also Jacqueline Cerquiglini-Toulet's discussion of readerly affinities in *The Color of Melancholy: The Uses of Books in the Fourteenth Century*, trans. Lydia G. Cochrane (Baltimore, Md.: Johns Hopkins University Press, 1997), 141.

5. Beryl Rowland, introducing *Chaucer and Middle English Studies in Honour of Rossell Hope Robbins* (London: Allen and Unwin, 1974), 9.

6. My use of the term "homosocial" throughout this book, while obviously indebted to Eve Kosofsky Sedgwick's work, is rather more general and metaphorical than the instances in the mid-eighteenth- to mid-nineteenth-century novels she discusses in *Between Men: English Literature and Male Homosocial Desire* (New York: Columbia University Press, 1985, rev. 1992). Like many other scholars, I have drawn on her application of this sociological term to think about the particular forms of desire expressed or displaced in activities like male bonding, about vigorous assertions of masculinity, or, in the present study, about identifications with a male heterosexual author.

7. Hunt's annotated copy of *The Poetical Works of Geoffrey Chaucer*, ed. Robert Bell (London: Parker, 1854), is in the British Library.

8. Peter J. Curwen, *The UK Publishing Industry* (Oxford: Pergamon Press, 1981), 75–76.

1. Speaking for Chaucer

1. Charles Muscatine, "What Amounteth Al This Wit? Chaucer and Scholarship," presidential address 1980, *SAC* 3 (1981): 9.

2. Larry D. Benson, ed., *The Learned and the Lewed: Studies in Chaucer and Medieval Literature* (Cambridge, Mass.: Harvard University Press, 1974), vii.

3. Anthony Easthope, "The Subject of Literary and the Subject of Cultural Studies," in *Theory/Pedagogy/Politics: Texts for Change*, ed. Donald Morton and Mas'ud Zavarzedeh (Chicago: Chicago University Press, 1991), 36.

4. See also Anthony Easthope, *Literary into Cultural Studies* (London: Routledge, 1991).

5. See, however, John Guillory's critique of this development, in *Cultural Capital: The Problem of Literary Canon Formation* (Chicago: University of Chicago Press, 1993), 10.

6. Seth Lerer, *Chaucer and His Readers: Imagining the Author in Late-Medieval England* (Princeton, N.J.: Princeton University Press, 1993).

7. For A. C. Spearing, even if we no longer regard Chaucer as the father of English poetry, he is still "the father of English literary history." Spearing, *Medieval to Renaissance in English Poetry* (Cambridge: Cambridge University Press, 1985), 34.

8. Renee Swanson, "The Living Dead: What the Dickens Are College Students Reading?" *Policy Review* 67 (1994): 72–73. Swanson concludes that classic texts remain popular because "they seem to be eternally relevant," but quotes the editor of Cliffs Notes, Gary Carey, predicting that the "new multicultural titles" will soon displace many of these classic texts. The Cliffs Notes catalog for 1998 confirmed his prediction: the volume on the *Canterbury Tales* had slipped out of the top ten but remained in the next most popular grouping.

9. According to seventeenth-century tradition, Spenser had expressed a wish to be buried next to Chaucer (as noted in the 1679 imprint of his *Works*). See also Derek Pearsall, "Chaucer's Tomb: The Politics of Reburial," *Medium Aevum* 64 (1995): 51–73; and Joseph A. Dane, *Who Is Buried in Chaucer's Tomb? Studies in the Reception of Chaucer's Book* (East Lansing: Michigan State University Press, 1998).

10. Charles Muscatine, *The Book of Chaucer: An Account of the Publication of Geoffrey Chaucer's Works from the Fifteenth Century to Modern Times* (San Francisco: Book Club of California, 1963), 45.

11. Richard Beadle, "Turning the Pages," *TLS* 19 April 1996, no. 4855, 33.

12. Compare Peter Conrad, *To Be Continued: Four Stories and Their Survival* (Oxford: Clarendon Press, 1995), and Steve Ellis, *Chaucer at Large: The Poet in the Modern Imagination* (Minneapolis: University of Minnesota Press, 2000).

13. Bruce Mansfield and Mark Hutchinson, *Liberality of Opportunity: A History of Macquarie University, 1964–1989* (Sydney: Macquarie University, in association with Hale and Iremonger, 1992), 58. The Web site of Macquarie University edits the description of the Clerk, breaking the last line in two to give the motto greater prominence. The temptation to write more Chaucer here was also irresistible, as the final instruction shows: "*And gladly returne* to Macquarie University Home Page" (http://www.mq.edu.au/PubRel/about/lighthou.html#name).

14. Robert Longsworth, "Chaucer's Clerk as Teacher," in *The Learned and the Lewed*, ed. Benson, 61.

15. Mansfield and Hutchison, *Liberality of Opportunity*, 58.

16. The university also formulated a traditional blazon: "The arms of the University shall be on a field vert, the Macquarie lighthouse tower, masoned proper, in chief the star Sirius, or. Motto: And gladly teche." The Lord Lyon King of Arms in Edinburgh, Sir Thomas Innes of Learney, was not impressed with the specificity of the Sydney landmark when the university sought to register its arms: "Where people ask us to include a representation of this or that building, or even send us a photograph asking us to reproduce their beloved dog, we have to point out that this would not be regarded as efficient or satisfactory heraldry" (ibid., 58). This contemptuous response from the heart of empire is a

good indication of the complex negotiations faced by postcolonial nations seeking to articulate a sophisticated relationship with tradition. As the final blazon shows, the university went ahead with the Macquarie lighthouse anyway.

17. Gayatri Spivak, "The Making of Americans, the Teaching of English, and the Future of Culture Studies," *NLH* 21 (1990): 785.

18. The MLA bibliography reveals only a slight reduction in the number of items published in the last decade, proportionate to the reduction of Shakespeare studies after the boom period of academic expansion in the 1980s.

19. See, for example, Sheila Delany, "Geographies of Love: Orientalism in Chaucer's *Legend of Good Women*," *Chaucer Yearbook* 1 (1992): 1–32; and Susan Schibanoff, "Worlds Apart: Orientalism, Antifeminism, and Heresy in Chaucer's *Man of Law's Tale*," *Exemplaria* 8 (1996): 56–96. For a response to Spivak, see Jenna Mead, "The Anti-Imperial Approaches to Chaucer (Are There Those?): An Essay in Identifying Strategies," *Southern Review* 27 (1994): 403–17. See also the collection edited by Jeffrey Jerome Cohen, *The Postcolonial Middle Ages* (New York: St. Martin's Press, 2000).

20. See Florence Ridley's "Introduction: The Challenge of Teaching *The Canterbury Tales*," in *Approaches to Teaching Chaucer's Canterbury Tales*, ed. Florence H. Ridley (New York: MLA, 1980), xi.

21. Peter Mack, "The Scholars' Tales," *TLS*, 5 April 1996, no. 4853, 23.

22. Ellis, *Chaucer at Large*.

23. Harold Bloom, ed., *Modern Critical Views: Geoffrey Chaucer* (New York: Chelsea House, 1985), 1. See also his more extensive discussion of the Wife of Bath and the Pardoner in *The Western Canon: The Books and School of the Ages* (New York: Harcourt Brace, 1994), 105–7.

24. Patt Morrison, Paul Houston, and Michael Ross, "Chaucer on the Potomac," *Los Angeles Times*, 19, 20, and 21 January 1993.

25. Bourdieu, "The Market of Symbolic Goods," *Poetics* 14 (1985): 13–17.

26. Tim William Machan, *Textual Criticism and Middle English Texts* (Charlottesville: University Press of Virginia, 1994), 189.

27. Derek Pearsall, *The Canterbury Tales* (London: Allen and Unwin, 1985), 23. Twelve years later, Pearsall comments that no publisher has taken up this suggestion, in "Preempting Closure in *The Canterbury Tales*: Old Endings, New Beginnings," in *Essays on Ricardian Literature in Honour of J. A. Burrow*, ed. A. J. Minnis, Charlotte C. Morse, and Thorlac Turville-Petre (Oxford: Clarendon Press, 1997), 31.

28. Russell Alan Potter, "Political Chaucer: The Deployment of the Chaucer Canon, 1390–1990" (Ph.D. diss., Brown University, 1991), 153.

29. Ralph Hanna III, "Presenting Chaucer as Author," in *Medieval Literature: Texts and Interpretation*, ed. Tim William Machan (Binghamton, N.Y.: Medieval and Renaissance Texts and Studies 79, 1991), 19. See also Machan, *Textual Criticism*, 79–80; John Dagenais's comments about the "limited usefulness" of published editions, in contrast to his own practice of using manuscript readings, in *The Ethics of Reading in Manuscript Culture: Glossing the "Libro de Buen Amor"* (Princeton, N.J.: Princeton University Press, 1994), 216; and, with reference to Renaissance literature, Leah S. Marcus, *Unediting the Renaissance: Shakespeare, Marlowe, Milton* (London: Routledge, 1996).

30. Helen Cooper, "Averting Chaucer's Prophecies: Miswriting, Mismetering, and

Misunderstanding," in *A Guide to Editing Middle English*, ed. Vincent P. McCarren and Douglas Moffatt (Ann Arbor: University of Michigan Press, 1998), 92.

31. Peter Robinson, ed., *The Wife of Bath's Prologue on CD-ROM* (Cambridge: Cambridge University Press, 1996).

32. Compare D. C. Greetham, "Editorial and Critical Theory: From Modernism to Postmodernism," in *Palimpsest: Editorial Theory in the Humanities*, ed. George Bornstein and Ralph G. Williams (Ann Arbor: University of Michigan Press, 1993), 17. Greetham remarks that most literary critics simply ignore the textual apparatus of scholarly editions.

33. Tony Durham, "Traces on Vellum Offer Clues to the Definitive Chaucerian Text," *THES*, 12 June 1998, 31.

34. Examples are B. A. Windeatt's four-column edition of *Troilus and Criseyde: A New Edition of "The Book of Troilus"* (London: Longman, 1984) and the variorum editions, with three or four tiers of text and commentary. Helen Cooper commends Helen Phillips's edition of *The Book of the Duchess*, which signals the "major changes of textual affiliation between Fairfax 16 and Thynne . . . so that students cannot help but learn that texts are made and not found" ("Averting Chaucer's Prophecies," 91).

35. Caroline Spurgeon, ed., *Five Hundred Years of Chaucer Criticism and Allusion, 1357–1900*, 3 vols. (London: Cambridge University Press, 1925); J. A. Burrow, ed., *Geoffrey Chaucer: A Critical Anthology* (Harmondsworth: Penguin, 1969); Derek Brewer, ed., *Chaucer: The Critical Heritage*, 2 vols. (London: Routledge and Kegan Paul, 1978). See also Jackson Campbell Boswell and Sylvia Wallace Holton, "References to Chaucer's Literary Reputation," *Chaucer Review* 31 (1997): 291–316, and their announcement of their larger project of updating Spurgeon for the period covered by the short-title catalog.

36. Betsy Bowden describes the evolutionary approach of Caroline Spurgeon, who organizes five hundred years of Chaucer criticism and allusion into six stages "that culminate, like civilization itself for her compatriots, in late nineteenth-century Britain," in Bowden, ed., *Eighteenth-Century Modernizations from "The Canterbury Tales"* (Rochester: Brewer, 1991), xi.

37. Gerald L. Bruns, "What Is Tradition?" *New Literary History* 22 (1991): 8.

38. Paul Ruggiers, ed., *Editing Chaucer: The Great Tradition* (Norman, Okla.: Pilgrim Books, 1984).

39. Ibid., 1.

40. Ibid., 2.

41. George Reinecke, "F.N. Robinson," in *Editing Chaucer*, ed. Ruggiers, 232.

42. Lee Patterson, *Literary Practice and Social Change in Britain, 1380–1530* (Berkeley: University of California Press, 1990), 3. Comparable critiques of French medieval tradition are found in R. Howard Bloch and Stephen G. Nichols, eds., *Medievalism and the Modernist Temper* (Baltimore, Md.: Johns Hopkins University Press, 1996), and in William D. Paden, ed., *The Future of the Middle Ages: Medieval Literature in the 1990s* (Gainesville: University Press of Florida, 1994).

43. Louise O. Fradenburg, "'Voice Memorial': Loss and Reparation in Chaucer's Poetry," *Exemplaria* 2 (1990): 92. See also her more recent essay, "'So That We May Speak of Them': Enjoying the Middle Ages," *NLH* 28 (1997): 205–30.

44. Fradenburg, "Criticism, Anti-Semitism, and the *Prioress's Tale*," *Exemplaria* 1 (1989): 69–115.

45. Christine Froula, "When Eve Reads Milton: Undoing the Canonical Economy," in *Canons*, ed. Robert von Hallberg (Chicago: University of Chicago Press, 1984), 164.

46. This idea was mooted, however informally, at the New Chaucer Society congress in Dublin, 1994.

47. Shakespeare has been examined as this kind of cultural product; for example, by Terence Hawkes, *That Shakespeherian Rag: Essays on a Critical Process* (London: Methuen, 1986); Gary Taylor, *Reinventing Shakespeare: A Cultural History from the Restoration to the Present* (London: Hogarth Press, 1990); and Jonathan Bate, *The Genius of Shakespeare* (London: Picador, 1997).

48. George Lyman Kittredge, *Chaucer and His Poetry* (Cambridge, Mass.: Harvard University Press, 1915); R. M. Lumiansky, *Of Sondry Folk: The Dramatic Principle in "The Canterbury Tales"* (Austin: University of Texas Press, 1955); E. T. Donaldson, *Speaking of Chaucer* (London: Athlone Press, 1970).

49. H. Marshall Leicester, *The Disenchanted Self: Representing the Subject in the Canterbury Tales* (Berkeley: University of California Press, 1990).

50. Bourdieu, "The Market of Symbolic Goods," 18–19.

51. For an account of this debate, conducted on the Medieval Feminist Listserve and at the 1998 MLA conference, see Charlotte Allen, "Dark Ages," *Lingua Franca* 9, no. 2 (1999): 11–12.

52. Sheila Delany analyzes the strictures of Larry D. Benson against those "punsters" who delight in identifying Chaucer's puns as an example of the way the profession polices itself, in "an exhortation to professional censorship." Delany, "Anatomy of the Resisting Reader: Some Implications of Resistance to Sexual Wordplay in Medieval Literature," *Exemplaria* 4 (1992): 17.

53. The editors chose not to quote from the more homosocially resonant passage in *The Merchant's Tale*, where Januarie's more specifically male friends advise him about marriage—"Diverse men diversely hym tolde / Of mariage manye ensamples olde"—and where "altercacioun" and "stryf" result between Placebo and Justinus.

54. Guillory, *Cultural Capital*, 27.

55. Guillory draws on Ferdinand Tönnies's distinction between *Gemeinschaft* and *Gesellschaft* (ibid., 34–35). It is worth distinguishing "association" here from what David Wallace calls an "associational ideology" in the *Canterbury Tales* and fourteenth-century England, more generally. This ideology is akin to that of republican Florence, and it finds its fullest social form in medieval England in the guilds. Wallace, *Chaucerian Polity: Absolutist Lineages and Associational Forms in England and Italy* (Stanford, Calif.: Stanford University Press, 1997), 2–4. In contrast, Guillory's sense of "association" moves away from "community": he reminds us that literary culture and universities aren't really organized around consensus, though that is the common view: rather, they are complex social and institutional sites of hierarchies "in which the position and privilege of judgment are objects of competitive struggles" (50).

56. Fradenburg, "'Voice Memorial,'" 93.

57. James Simpson, "Ethics and Interpretation: Reading Wills in Chaucer's *Legend of Good Women*," *SAC* 20 (1998): 74.

58. In a rare public example, Florence Ridley candidly describes her concern at being unable to recognize the Pardoner in a portly ceramic figurine crafted by Robert Welker.

Ridley quickly moves to show how such diversity of interpretation is a testament to Chaucer's intriguing open-endedness, but the anecdote reveals how little consensus there can be between two modern professional Chaucerians on something seemingly as basic as what the Pardoner looks like. Ridley, "Questions without Answers—Yet or Ever? New Critical Modes and Chaucer," *Chaucer Review* 16 (1981): 103.

59. Stephen Greenblatt, *Shakespearean Negotiations: The Circulation of Social Energy in Renaissance England* (Berkeley: University of California Press, 1988), 1.

60. Benedict Anderson, *Imagined Communities: Reflections on the Origin and Spread of Nationalism* (1983; rev. ed., London: Verso, 1991), 6.

61. Here I draw on Paul James's coining of this phrase in *Nation Formation: Towards a Theory of Abstract Community* (London: Sage, 1996).

62. Ridley, "Questions without Answers," 103. See also Steve Ellis's summary of "The Chaucer Business" in his *Geoffrey Chaucer* (Plymouth: Northcote House, 1996), 1–5.

63. H. Marshall Leicester's paper was first presented at the New Chaucer Society Congress in 1996 and subsequently published, with annotations, as "Chaucer Criticism in 1996," *Envoi* 6 (1997): 1–14 (quotations at 5–6, 14).

64. Mack, "The Scholars' Tales," 23.

65. Elaine Tuttle Hansen diagnoses the masculinism of much mainstream Chaucer criticism in *Chaucer and the Fictions of Gender*, but focuses on the feminization of the Chaucerian critic in the twentieth century. See chapter 7 in this volume.

66. Lawrence Besserman also describes the poem as "more than just a witty antifeminist ballade," in "Chaucer's *Envoy to Bukton* and 'Truth' in Biblical Interpretation: Some Medieval and Modern Contexts," *NLH* 22 (1991): 177.

67. V. J. Scattergood, in *Oxford Guides to Chaucer: The Shorter Poems*, ed. A. J. Minnis, with V. J. Scattergood and J. J. Smith (Oxford: Clarendon Press, 1995), 457.

68. Paul Strohm, *Social Chaucer* (Cambridge, Mass.: Harvard University Press, 1989), 50.

69. Strohm, "Chaucer's Fifteenth-Century Audience and the Narrowing of the 'Chaucer Tradition,'" *SAC* 4 (1982): 6. See also Strohm, "Chaucer's Audience," *Literature and History* 5 (1977): 26–41; Alfred David, *The Strumpet Muse: Art and Morals in Chaucer's Poetry* (Bloomington: Indiana University Press, 1976); and Anne Middleton, "Chaucer's 'New Men' and the Good of Literature in the *Canterbury Tales*," in *Literature and Society: Selected Papers from the English Institute, 1978*, ed. Edward W. Said (Baltimore, Md.: Johns Hopkins University Press, 1980), 15–56.

70. Strohm, *Social Chaucer*, 46.

71. See Wallace, *Chaucerian Polity*.

72. R. T. Lenaghan, "Chaucer's Circle of Gentlemen and Clerks," *Chaucer Review* 18 (1983): 157.

73. George B. Pace and Alfred David, eds., *The Minor Poems*, vol. 5, variorum edition (Norman: University of Oklahoma Press, 1982), 141.

74. John M. Ganim, "Chaucer, Boccaccio, and the Anxiety of Popularity," *Assays* 4 (1987): 58.

75. All quotations from Chaucer, unless otherwise specified, are taken from Larry D. Benson, gen. ed., *The Riverside Chaucer* (Oxford: Oxford University Press, 1988).

76. See Jane Chance, "Chaucerian Irony in the Verse Epistles 'Wordes unto Adam,'

'Lenvoy a Scogan,' and 'Lenvoy a Bukton,'" *PLL* 21 (1985): 122. The *MED* also lists a figurative sense of *shethen,* viz. "to copulate."

77. P. M. Kean, *Chaucer and the Making of English Poetry,* 2 vols. (London: Routledge and Kegan Paul, 1972), 1:34.

78. See also Derek Pearsall, *The Life of Geoffrey Chaucer: A Critical Biography* (Oxford: Blackwell, 1992), 183–84.

79. Ibid., 184.

80. Kittredge, *Chaucer and His Poetry,* 34.

81. Pace and David, eds., *The Minor Poems,* 141.

82. R.T. Lenaghan, "Chaucer's *Envoy to Scogan:* The Uses of Literary Conventions," *Chaucer Review* 10 (1975): 48, 59.

83. See also Velma Bourgeois Richmond: "[T]he shifts are so quick and contradictory, and the tone playful, so that only a sense of verbal and mental facility and good will seem clear. . . . Like any friend, Chaucer comments about his friend's possible marriage, but does not offer a simple judgment." Richmond, *Geoffrey Chaucer* (New York: Continuum, 1992), 195.

84. Pace and David, eds., *The Minor Poems,* 150. The quotation is from John Norton-Smith, *Geoffrey Chaucer* (London: Routledge, 1974), 219.

85. Strohm, *Social Chaucer,* 75.

86. George Kane, *Chaucer* (Oxford: Oxford University Press, 1984), 286 n. 34.

87. Lenaghan, "Chaucer's *Envoy to Scogan,*" 57.

88. Besserman also resorts to paraphrase to make Chaucer speak in this poem, in "Chaucer's Envoy to Bukton," 191–92.

89. Pace and David, eds., *The Minor Poems,* 140–41.

90. In a much earlier essay, Strohm even contrasts the "Scogans and Buktons" against the more "wrongheaded" readers John Shirley and John of Angoulême in the fifteenth century. Paul Strohm, "Jean of Angoulême: A Fifteenth Century Reader of Chaucer," *NM* 72 (1971): 69–72. He cites Alfred David's identification of the less imaginative readers, represented in Chaucer's fictions by the Man of Law, the Eagle, and the God of Love, in "The Man of Law vs. Chaucer: A Case in Poetics," *PMLA* 82 (1967): 219. Strohm elsewhere contrasts the worst writings of Hoccleve and Lydgate, unable to find "a congenial audience," in "Chaucer's Fifteenth-Century Audience," 17.

91. Alastair Minnis observes, however, that the widespread acceptance of Richard Green's view that women were underrepresented in Chaucer's audiences seems to have had the effect of "discourag[ing] discussion (particularly among male critics) of the female audience which may plausibly be allowed to Chaucer." Minnis, ed., *The Shorter Poems,* 25.

92. Ibid., 12–13.

93. The documents are printed in *Chaucer Life-Records,* ed. Martin M. Crow and Clair C. Olson, from materials compiled by John M. Manly and Edith Rickert with the assistance of Lilian J. Redstone and others (Oxford: Clarendon Press, 1966), 343–47.

94. Christopher Cannon also comments that many writers typically avoid the mention of rape and draw attention instead, through a variety of euphemisms, to the oddity of the situation. Cannon, "*Raptus* in the Chaumpaigne Release and a Newly Discovered Document Concerning the Life of Geoffrey Chaucer," *Speculum* 68 (1993): 92–93.

95. Kane, *Chaucer,* 69.

96. Derek Brewer, *An Introduction to Chaucer* (London: Longman, 1984), 68. Richmond also comments, "Chaucer's legal innocence is a matter of record, and those who gave witness were of high standing." Richmond, *Geoffrey Chaucer,* 18. Minnis is more circumspect: "What is perfectly clear is the high rank of Chaucer's witnesses. . . . Chaucer's eminent social standing and his enjoyment of considerable political power are manifest." Minnis, ed., *The Shorter Poems,* 10.

97. Derek Brewer, *A New Introduction to Chaucer,* 2nd ed. (London: Longman, 1998), 118.

98. Carolyn Dinshaw draws a relationship between Chaucer's representations of rape and the fiction of the rivalry between Chaucer and Gower: "[A]t the moment when these men seem most explicitly preoccupied with each other, they are most fundamentally misogynist." Dinshaw demonstrates how rivalry (and masculine violence) combine to expunge the feminine, in much the same way, I suggest, that the feminine is expunged from the poems under discussion here. Dinshaw, "Rivalry, Rape and Manhood: Gower and Chaucer," in *Chaucer and Gower: Difference, Mutuality, Exchange,* ed. R. F. Yeager (Victoria: University of Victoria, 1991), 134.

99. Cannon, "*Raptus* and the Chaumpaigne Release," 94.

100. Cannon speculates about the "coercion, persuasion, or some more complicated manipulation in the court of the king" (ibid., 94) that resulted in this retraction, but the document sheds no light on the process. See also Monica Brzezinski Potkay and Regula Meyer Evitt, *Minding the Body: Women and Literature in the Middle Ages, 800–1500* (London: Twayne, 1997), 139 ff., especially their comparison between this rewriting of rape as felony and the verbal echoes of the release with the final moments of the *Wife of Bath's Tale* (164–65.)

101. From the prologue to Douglas's translation in 1513 of Virgil's *Aeneid,* cited in Burrow, *Geoffrey Chaucer: A Critical Anthology,* 47.

102. Henry Ansgar Kelly, "Meaning and Uses of *Raptus* in Chaucer's Time," *SAC* 20 (1998): 101.

103. Ibid., 147.

104. I intend here a less specific comparison than that offered by Carolyn Dinshaw, *Chaucer's Sexual Poetics* (Madison: University of Wisconsin Press, 1989).

2. Signing Geoffrey Chaucer

1. Julian N. Wasserman and Lois Roney, eds., *Sign, Sentence, Discourse: Language in Medieval Thought and Literature* (Syracuse, N.Y.: Syracuse University Press, 1989), xv; Priscilla Martin, *Chaucer's Women: Nuns, Wives, and Amazons* (Houndmills: Macmillan, 1990), xv.

2. Julian N. Wasserman and Robert J. Blanch, eds., *Chaucer in the Eighties* (Syracuse, N.Y.: Syracuse University Press, 1986), xix–xx.

3. D. S. Brewer, *A New Introduction to Chaucer,* 2nd ed. (London: Longman, 1998), xii. In a footnote Brewer refers the reader to his discussion of the *raptus* accusation at p. 119 and the defense offered by Chaucer's friends, considered in chapter 1 in this volume.

4. Umberto Eco, *The Open Work,* trans. Anna Cancogni, intro. David Robey (Cambridge, Mass.: Harvard University Press, 1989), 6, 7.

5. Jesse Gellrich, *The Idea of the Book in the Middle Ages: Language Theory, Mythology, and Fiction* (Ithaca, N.Y.: Cornell University Press, 1985), 22. For Gellrich, the overarching medieval Text of culture remains firmly logocentric, even if specific medieval fictions such as Dante's or Chaucer's explore the "destabilization" of signification (23–24).

6. I draw on the discussion of M. B. Parkes in "The Influence of the Concepts of *Ordinatio* and *Compilatio* on the Development of the Book," in *Medieval Learning and Literature: Essays Presented to Richard William Hunt*, ed. J. J. G. Alexander and M. T. Gibson (Oxford: Oxford University Press, 1976), 127ff.

7. This sense of "writing" differs from Gellrich's metaphorical sense of writing, or *écriture*, as participating in mythology: I have in mind the far more material practices by which texts are produced. Parkes describes, for instance, the manner in which some fourteenth-century readers and librarians came to expect the features of *ordinatio* in the texts they read—chapter divisions, running titles, paragraphs marks—and freely added them to manuscripts where they were lacking (ibid., 135–36).

8. Ibid., 139.

9. Gerald Bruns, *Inventions: Writing, Textuality, and Understanding in Literary History* (New Haven, Conn.: Yale University Press, 1980), 56–57.

10. Michael Camille offers the most subtle account of the differences and similarities between medieval and postmodern textuality in "Sensations of the Page: Imaging Technologies and Medieval Illuminated Manuscripts," in *The Iconic Page in Manuscript, Print, and Digital Culture*, ed. George Bornstein and Theresa Tinkle (Ann Arbor: University of Michigan Press, 1998), 33–54. And in the same volume, see also Theresa Tinkle, "The Wife of Bath's Textual/Sexual Lives," 55–88.

11. Michel Foucault, "What Is an Author?" in *The Foucault Reader*, ed. Paul Rabinow (Harmondsworth: Penguin Books, 1984), 118–19.

12. In his reading of Spenser's texual structures, Jonathan Goldberg draws a similar comparison between the readerly text, "enslaved to sequence," and the writerly text, "produced by writerly reading [which] is open, endless and reversible." Goldberg, *Endlesse Worke: Spenser and the Structures of Discourse* (Baltimore, Md.: Johns Hopkins University Press, 1981), 10–11.

13. Parkes, "The Influence of the Concepts of *Ordinatio* and *Compilatio*," and, with A. I. Doyle, "The Production of Copies of the *Canterbury Tales* and the *Confessio Amantis* in the Early Fifteenth Century," in *Medieval Scribes, Manuscripts, and Libraries: Essays Presented to N. R. Ker*, ed. M. B. Parkes and A. G. Watson (London: Scolar Press, 1978), 163–210; A. J. Minnis, *Medieval Theory of Authorship: Scholastic Literary Attitudes in the Later Middle Ages* (London: Scolar Press, 1984).

14. See Minnis's discussion of Chaucer as "'rehearsing' compiler" in *The Canterbury Tales*, in *Medieval Theory of Authorship*, 198–209.

15. Rita Copeland, *Rhetoric, Hermeneutics, and Translation in the Middle Ages: Academic Traditions and Vernacular Texts* (Cambridge: Cambridge University Press, 1991), 3; see also 65. Jeffrey T. Schnapp describes the commentary tradition in Derridean terms that resemble many accounts of modern criticism. "Commentary is . . . a discourse concerned with cultural memory, monumentality, and, ultimately, mourning. It erects a modern edifice around the predecessor text in what amounts to an elegiac gesture that at once commemorates, recalls, reactivates the dead primary text and monumentalizes it, distances and

frames it, engulfs it and introjects it, ultimately displacing and erasing it in the act of con-
secration. It builds a funerary monument that entombs the very thing it claims to resur-
rect." Schnapp, "A Commentary on Commentary in Boccaccio," *SAQ* 91 (1992): 815–16.

16. Raymond Williams, *Marxism and Literature* (Oxford: Oxford University Press,
1977), 121–27.

17. Richard Green, *Poets and Princepleasers: Literature and the English Court in the Late
Middle Ages* (Toronto: University of Toronto Press, 1980), 110–12.

18. Anne Middleton, "The Idea of Public Poetry in the Reign of Richard II," *Speculum*
53 (1978): 94–114. See also Middleton's "Chaucer's 'New Men' and the Good of Literature
in the *Canterbury Tales*," in *Literature and Society: Selected Papers from the English Institute,
1978*, ed. Edward W. Said (Baltimore, Md.: Johns Hopkins University Press, 1980), 15–56.

19. For the *Secretum Secretorum* tradition, see Green, *Poets and Princepleasers*, 140ff.
See also David Lawton, *Chaucer's Narrators* (Woodbridge: Brewer, 1985), 13.

20. Middleton, "The Idea of Public Poetry," 94.

21. Judith Ferster, *Fictions of Advice: The Literature and Politics of Counsel in Late Me-
dieval England* (Philadelphia: University of Pennsylvania Press, 1996), 106–7.

22. Minnis, *Medieval Theory of Authorship*, 5.

23. Ibid., 191ff. See Chaucer, *Treatise on the Astrolabe*, prologue, line 61. According to
Parkes, it was Vincent of Beauvais who "elevated *compilatio* into a literary form which
served as a vehicle for others." Parkes, "The Influence of the Concepts of *Ordinatio* and
Compilatio," 128.

24. Paul Strohm similarly cites Jean of Angoulême's manuscript of the *Canterbury Tales*,
which refers to Chaucer in the heading to the *Man of Law's Tale:* "sequntur verba Galfridi
Chauncers compilatoris libri," in "Jean of Angoulême: A Fifteenth Century Reader of
Chaucer," *NM* 72 (1971): 70.

25. Minnis, *Medieval Theory of Authorship*, 203. Cf. Parkes, "The Influence of the Con-
cepts of *Ordinatio* and *Compilatio*," 30–31.

26. Minnis, *Medieval Theory of Authorship*, 209.

27. Copeland, *Rhetoric, Hermeneutics, and Translation*, 180, 184.

28. For a list of these extracts and a description of their manuscripts, see M. C. Sey-
mour, *A Catalogue of Chaucer Manuscripts* (Aldershot: Scolar Press; Brookfield: Ashgate,
1997), 1:131–54. For more detailed discussion, see Paul Strohm, "Jean of Angoulême";
B. A. Windeatt, "The Scribes as Chaucer's Early Critics," *SAC* 1 (1979): 119–41; N. F. Blake,
The Textual Tradition of the Canterbury Tales (London: Arnold, 1985); Seth Lerer, "Rewriting
Chaucer: Two Fifteenth-Century Readings of the Canterbury Tales," *Viator* 19 (1988):
311–26; and Derek Pearsall, "Text, Textual Criticism, and Fifteenth-Century Manuscript
Production," in *Fifteenth-Century Studies: Recent Essays*, ed. Robert F. Yeager (Hamden:
Archon, 1984), 121–36. See also David Lorenzo Boyd, "Compilation as Commentary:
Controlling Chaucer's *Parliament of Fowls*," *SAQ* 91 (1992): 945–64. Boyd examines three
different manuscripts of the *Parliament*, each of which foregrounds a different reading of
the poem.

29. For the most trenchant account of Chaucer's relation to this tradition, see David
Wallace, *Chaucerian Polity: Absolutist Lineages and Associational Forms in England and Italy*
(Stanford, Calif.: Stanford University Press, 1997), in particular, chap. 10. Michael Hanly

has described the "international network of literary exchange" in which Chaucer was a participant, especially Philippe de Mézières's Order of the Passion. Hanly, "Courtiers and Poets: An International System of Literary Exchange in Late Fourteenth-Century Italy, France, and England," *Speculum* 28 (1997): 305–32.

30. Seth Lerer, *Chaucer and His Readers: Imagining the Author in Late-Medieval England* (Princeton, N.J.: Princeton University Press, 1993), 3–4.

31. In this regard, I'm sympathetic to the critiques by David Aers and Lee Patterson of Renaissance theorists of "the subject" who posit a formless, premodern self in opposition to the self-determining, interiorized subject of the sixteenth century. See in particular David Aers, "A Whisper in the Ear of Early Modernists; or, Reflections of Literary Critics Writing 'The History of the Subject,'" in *Culture and History, 1350–1600: Essays on English Communities, Identities, and Writing*, ed. Aers (Detroit, Mich.: Wayne State University Press, 1992), 177–202; and Lee Patterson, "On the Margin: Postmodernism, Ironic History, and Medieval Studies," *Speculum* 65 (1990): 87–108.

32. Gregory Stone, *The Death of the Troubadour: The Late Medieval Resistance to the Renaissance* (Philadelphia: University of Pennsylvania Press, 1994), 3. See also Middleton, "The Idea of Public Poetry," 25.

33. Marcus, *Unediting the Renaissance*, 192.

34. James Simpson foregrounds the naturalness of this habit, "confessing" to this "sin of intentionalism" in teaching and writing like this about Chaucer, in the face of critiques by Robert Jordan, David Lawton, and H. Marshall Leicester of the idea of the "unified narratorial agent" behind Chaucer's ironically realized narrators, in "*Ut Pictura Poesis:* A Critique of Robert Jordan's *Chaucer and the Shape of Creation,*" in *Interpretation: Medieval and Modern, The J. A. W. Bennett Memorial Lectures, Eighth Series*, ed. Piero Boitani and Anna Torti (Cambridge: Brewer, 1993), 167–68; see also Tim Machan, "Middle English Text Production and Modern Textual Criticism," in *Crux and Controversy in Middle English Textual Criticism*, ed. A. J. Minnis and Charlotte Brewer (Cambridge: Brewer, 1992), 3.

35. Compare Lawton, *Chaucer's Narrators*, 1–8.

36. Thomas J. Garbáty, "The Degradation of Chaucer's 'Geffrey,'" *PMLA* 89 (1974): 97.

37. Walter J. Ong, *Orality and Literacy: The Technologizing of the Word* (London: Methuen, 1982), 6; Lucien Febvre and Henri-Jean Martin, *The Coming of the Book: The Impact of Printing, 1450–1800*, trans. David Gerard ([1958] London: Verso, 1990), 159; Richard Helgerson, *Self-Crowned Laureates: Spenser, Jonson, Milton, and the Literary System* (Berkeley: University of California Press, 1983), 3; Marcus, *Unediting the Renaissance*, 192; Simon During, *Foucault and Literature: Towards a Genealogy of Writing* (London: Routledge, 1993), 124; Peggy Kamuf, *Signature Pieces: On the Institution of Authorship* (Ithaca, N.Y.: Cornell University Press, 1988), 25.

38. Jacques Derrida, *Of Grammatology*, trans. Gayatri Chakravorty Spivak (Baltimore, Md.: Johns Hopkins University Press, 1976); Roland Barthes, "The Death of the Author," in *Image-Music-Text*, trans. Stephen Heath (Glasgow: Fontana/Collins, 1977), 142–48.

39. Lawton, *Chaucer's Narrators*, xiv.

40. H. Marshall Leicester, *The Disenchanted Self: Representing the Subject in the Canterbury Tales* (Berkeley: University of California Press, 1990). See also Robert Jordan, *Chaucer's Poetics and the Modern Reader* (Berkeley: University of California Press, 1987), and "Lost in

the Funhouse of Fame: Chaucer and Postmodernism," *Chaucer Review* 18 (1983): 100–15.

41. Dagenais, *The Ethics of Reading in Manuscript Culture: Glossing the "Libro de Buen Amor"* (Princeton, N.J.: Princeton University Press, 1994), 13.

42. Minnis, *Medieval Theory of Authorship*, 1.

43. This is certainly the conclusion of John M. Manly and Edith Rickert in their study of the *Tales* manuscripts, *The Text of the Canterbury Tales Studied on the Basis of All Known Manuscripts*, 8 vols. (Chicago: University of Chicago Press, 1967), 2:41, 475, 488ff; 3:528. It is summarized with support from Charles A. Owen Jr., in *The Manuscripts of the Canterbury Tales* (Cambridge: Brewer, 1991), 6. So also Seymour, *A Catalogue of Chaucer Manuscripts*, 2:1.

44. There are some examples but they are ambivalent at best: the "Tregentil . . . Chaucer" appended to *Troilus and Criseyde* and the Rawlinson Poet. MS 163 copy of "To Rosemounde," or the thesis put forward by Dolores Frese that with the initial "Ge" for "Geffrey", "the name *CHAUnteCleER* engenders the epithet '(ge)ntele Chaucer.'" Frese, *"The Nun's Priest's Tale:* Chaucer's Identified Master Piece," *Chaucer Review* 16 (1982): 330–43.

45. Anne Middleton, "William Langland's 'Kynde Name': Authorial Signature and Social Identity in Late Fourteenth-Century England," in *Literary Practice and Social Change in Britain, 1380–1530,* ed. Lee Patterson (Berkeley: University of California Press, 1990), 15–82.

46. Sheila Delany, *The Naked Text: Chaucer's Legend of Good Women* (Berkeley: University of California Press, 1994), 14.

47. Ibid., 25, 30, 33.

48. Ibid., 32.

49. Ibid.

50. Machan, *Textual Criticism*, 113.

51. Middleton, "William Langland's 'Kynde Name,'" 31.

52. Once more, we find Chaucer in a transitional period, however. Compare the fascinating study by Lois Bragg, "Chaucer's Monogram and the 'Hoccleve Portrait' Tradition," *Word and Image* 12 (1996): 127–42. Bragg reads the portrait of Chaucer in Hoccleve's *Regiment of Princes* as "embedding the finger-alphabet monogram GC in the figure's two hands: the 'pointing' right hand forms a *G* and the left, holding a rosary, a *C*" (127). Bragg plays down the degree of verisimilitude in this portrait, which she dates precisely to the watershed years (1410–16) "between the age when verisimilar portraiture was unimaginable and unknown and the age of its vogue" (129). It is a remarkable account of the body literally "signing" itself.

53. Middleton, "William Langland's 'Kynde Name,'" 18. See further Burt Kimmelman's important study, *The Poetics of Authorship in the Later Middle Ages: The Emergence of the Modern Literary Persona* (New York: Peter Lang, 1996).

54. Middleton, "William Langland's 'Kynde Name,'" 16.

55. Aage Brusendorff, *The Chaucer Tradition* (1925; reprint, Oxford: Clarendon Press, 1967), 48.

56. Helen Cooper, *The Canterbury Tales*, Oxford Guides to Chaucer, 2nd ed. (Oxford: Oxford University Press, 1996), 411.

57. Charles A. Owen Jr., "What the Manuscripts Tell Us about the Parson's Tale," *Medium Aevum* 63 (1994): 239–49.

58. Ibid., 243–44.

59. J. A. Burrow, *Medieval Writers and Their Work: Middle English Literature and Its*

Background, 1100–1500 (Oxford: Oxford University Press, 1982), 29–30.

60. For David Lawton, this is the compiler's acknowledgment of "Chaucer's premature departure from the work," as he assembled fragment I in its final place, in "Chaucer's Two Ways: The Pilgrimage Frame of *The Canterbury Tales*," *SAC* 9 (1987): 3–40.

61. In Minnis's reading of this passage, "the 'shield and defence' of the compiler has slipped, and *for once* we see Chaucer as a writer who holds himself morally responsible for his writings." Minnis, *Medieval Theory of Authorship*, 208 (my emphasis).

62. Quoted in William L. Alderson, "John Urry," in *Editing Chaucer: The Great Tradition*, ed. Paul G. Ruggiers (Norman, Okla.: Pilgrim Books, 1984), 107. Alderson remarks that the author of this note may well have been Timothy Thomas, who completed the edition after Urry's death.

63. B. A. Windeatt, "Thomas Tyrwhitt," in *Editing Chaucer*, ed. Ruggiers, 120.

64. Thomas Tyrwhitt, ed., *The Canterbury Tales of Chaucer*, 5 vols. (London: Payne, 1775–78), iii, 311. So, also, A. W. Ward, *Chaucer* (London: Macmillan, 1888; reprint, 1909), 142.

65. Derek Pearsall, *The Life of Geoffrey Chaucer: A Critical Biography* (Oxford: Blackwell, 1992), 275–76. See also Douglas Wurtele, "The Penitence of Geoffrey Chaucer," *Viator* 11 (1980): 335–59.

66. For more sympathetic readings of the plausibility of Gascoigne's narrative, see James Dean, "Chaucer's Repentance: A Likely Story," *Chaucer Review* 24 (1989): 64–76, and Melissa Furrow, "The Author and Damnation: Chaucer, Writing, and Penitence," *Forum for Modern Language Studies* 33 (1997): 245–57.

67. See Lee W. Patterson's account of this skepticism in "The 'Parson's Tale' and the Quitting of the 'Canterbury Tales,'" *Traditio* 34 (1978): 331–32.

68. Charles A. Owen Jr., *Pilgrimage and Story-telling in "The Canterbury Tales": The Dialect of "Ernest" and "Game"* (Norman: University of Oklahoma Press, 1977); Minnis, *Medieval Theory of Authorship*, 207–10.

69. Lawton, "Chaucer's Two Ways," 13ff.

70. Owen, "What the Manuscripts Tell Us." Míceál Vaughan similarly suggests that the *Parson's Tale* might have been composed as a text independent of the *Tales*. Vaughan, "Creating Comfortable Boundaries: Scribes, Editors, and the Invention of the Parson's Tale," in *Re-writing Chaucer: Culture, Authority, and the Idea of the Authentic Text, 1400–1602*, ed. Thomas A. Prendergast and Barbara Kline (Columbus: Ohio State University Press, 1999), 45–90.

71. Wurtele, "The Penitence of Geoffrey Chaucer," 342.

72. Lawton, "Chaucer's Two Ways," 14.

73. Gale Schricker, "On the Relation of Fact and Fiction in Chaucer's Poetic Endings," *PQ* 60 (1981): 13–27.

74. Rosemarie Potz McGerr provides the fullest analysis of the relationship between Chaucer's Retractions and Augustine's *Retractationes*, in *Chaucer's Open Books: Resistance to Closure in Medieval Discourse* (Gainesville: University Press of Florida, 1998), 131–46. See also Olive Sayce, "Chaucer's Retractions," *Medium Aevum* 40 (1971): 230–48; Wurtele, "The Penitence of Geoffrey Chaucer"; and Robert Boenig, *Chaucer and the Mystics: The Canterbury Tales and the Genre of Devotional Prose* (Lewisburg, Pa.: Bucknell University Press; London: Associated University Presses, 1995), 169–73.

75. Wurtele, "The Penitence of Geoffrey Chaucer," 340–41.

76. Lawton, *Chaucer's Narrators*, 101.

77. Pearsall, *The Life of Geoffrey Chaucer*, 269.

78. See Charles A. Owen Jr., "The *Canterbury Tales*: Beginnings (3) and Endings (2+1)," *Chaucer Yearbook* 1 (1992): 189–212. Pearsall agrees that the *General Prologue*, written relatively late, is still the likeliest site for "extensive revising activity." Owen and Pearsall both stress the influence of the Ellesmere manuscript's ordering of the tales, particularly on our sense of the *Retractions* as final. See Derek Pearsall, "Pre-empting Closure in 'The Canterbury Tales': Old Endings, New Beginnings," in *Essays on Ricardian Literature in Honour of J. A. Burrow*, ed. A. J. Minnis, Charlotte C. Morse, and Thorlac Turville-Petre (Oxford: Clarendon Press, 1997), 34.

79. Pearsall, "Pre-empting Closure," 35–36.

80. Ibid., 37.

81. Melissa Furrow, for example, dares us "to take his fears [of damnation] seriously and resolve never to read or teach his better poems again" ("The Author and Damnation," 254).

82. Jacques Derrida, "Roundtable on Autobiography," in *The Ear of the Other: Otobiography, Transference, Translation*, ed. Christie V. McDonald, trans. Peggy Kamuf (New York: Schocken Books, 1985), 50, 51.

83. A. C. Spearing, "A Ricardian 'I': The Narrator of 'Troilus and Criseyde,'" in *Essays on Ricardian Literature*, ed. Minnis et al., 19.

3. Writing Chaucer

1. Seth Lerer, *Chaucer and His Readers: Imagining the Author in Late-Medieval England* (Princeton, N.J.: Princeton University Press, 1993), 3.

2. Ibid., 4.

3. Ibid., 81.

4. Eco, *Open Work*, 6, 7.

5. There is more than a degree of circularity about these terms: an *auctor* becomes an *auctor* by producing *auctoritates*, while *auctoritates* are the expressions of *auctores*. In Minnis's influential formulation, "an *auctoritas* was a quotation or an extract from the work of an *auctor*." A. J. Minnis, *Medieval Theory of Authorship: Scholastic Literary Attitudes in the Later Middle Ages* (London: Scolar Press, 1984), 10. Tim William Machan remarks that the word *auctor* by definition virtually excludes vernacular writers, in "Middle English Text Production and Modern Textual Criticism," in *Crux and Controversy in Middle English Textual Criticism*, ed. A. J. Minnis and Charlotte Brewer (Cambridge: Brewer, 1992), 4.

6. N. F. Blake, *The Textual Tradition of the Canterbury Tales* (London: Edward Arnold, 1985), 24–43.

7. Charles A. Owen Jr., *The Manuscripts of the Canterbury Tales* (Cambridge: Brewer, 1991), 13.

8. Blake, *The Textual Tradition*, 15. As Blake remarks, however, completeness does not necessarily imply authenticity.

9. Derek Pearsall, *The Canterbury Tales* (London: Allen and Unwin, 1985), 11.

10. Ibid., 12.

11. Tim Machan, *Textual Criticism and Middle English Texts* (Charlottesville: University Press of Virginia, 1994), 87.

12. This work proceeds from the influential article by Malcolm Parkes, "The Influence of the Concepts of *Ordinatio* and *Compilatio* on the Development of the Book," in *Medieval Learning and Literature: Essays Presented to Richard William Hunt,* ed. J. J. G. Alexander and M. T. Gibson (Oxford: Oxford University Press, 1976), 115–45.

13. Susan Schibanoff, "The New Reader and Female Textuality in Two Early Commentaries on Chaucer," *SAC* 10 (1988): 90, 76, 92.

14. For Jeffrey Schnapp, however, the introductory sonnets, rubrications, glosses, and commentaries in the *Teseida* are always written "as if composed by someone other than the poet." Schnapp, "A Commentary on Commentary in Boccaccio," *SAQ* 91 (1992): 826.

15. Derek Pearsall, *The Life of Geoffrey Chaucer: A Critical Biography* (London: Blackwell, 1992), 285.

16. As Paul Strohm comments, *compilator* has a lower status than *auctor* or even *maker:* "[A]nyone calling Chaucer *compilator* probably valued him more for his organizational abilities than his originality; more as anthologist than as poet." Strohm, "Jean of Angoulême: A Fifteenth Century Reader of Chaucer," *NM* 72 (1971): 71.

17. See also Tim Machan, *Textual Criticism,* 91–92.

18. Daniel Woodward and Martin Stevens, eds., *The Canterbury Tales by Geoffrey Chaucer: The New Ellesmere Chaucer Facsimile (of Huntington Library MS EL 26 C9)* (Tokyo: Yushodo; San Marino, Calif.: Huntington Library Press, 1995).

19. Paul G. Ruggiers, ed., *The Canterbury Tales, by Geoffrey Chaucer, A Facsimile and Transcription of the Hengrwt Manuscript, with Variants from the Ellesmere Manuscript,* with introductions by Donald C. Baker, A. I. Doyle, and M. B. Parkes (Norman, Okla.: Pilgrim Books, 1979).

20. Stephen Knight, *"The Canterbury Tales* by Geoffrey Chaucer, Edited from the Hengwrt Manuscript by N. F. Blake," *Parergon* 31 (1981): 35.

21. John M. Bowers, ed., *The Canterbury Tales: Fifteenth-Century Continuations and Additions* (TEAMS, Kalamazoo, Mich.: Medieval Institute Publications, 1992), 1–2. M. C. Seymour classifies the additions rather differently, grouping *Beryn* with the *Plowman's Tale* and *Gamelyn,* in *A Catalogue of Chaucer Manuscripts* (Aldershot: Scolar Press; Brookfield, Vt.: Ashgate, 1997), 2:22.

22. Bowers, ed., *The Canterbury Tales,* 41. This category of "spurious links" could itself be supplemented if we were to adopt Norman Blake's view that the Hengwrt manuscript preserves the only authentic Chaucerian text. Accordingly we would include the so-called "Epilogue to the Man of Law's Tale," "The Merchant's Prologue," and, of course, the entire "Canon's Yeoman's Prologue and Tale," which would necessitate a fifth category, for a pilgrim who was not part of the original group but who joined the company and told a tale.

23. Ibid., 42.

24. Ibid., 55.

25. F. J. Furnivall and W. G. Stone, eds., *The Tale of Beryn, with a Prologue of the Merry Adventure of the Pardoner with a Tapster at Canterbury,* Chaucer Society (London: Trübner, 1887), vi. For a summary of responses to the *Beryn*-poet's Pardoner, and a revisionary reading that stresses the ways in which the *Beryn* text closes down the ambiguities of the Pardoner, "wimping" his character, see Glending Olson, "The Misreadings of the *Beryn* Prologue," *Mediaevalia: A Journal of Medieval Studies* 17 (1994 for 1991): 211.

26. Betsy Bowden is most unsympathetic to this corrective tendency, describing the "silly heterosexual Pardoner," in *Chaucer Aloud: The Varieties of Textual Interpretation* (Philadelphia: University of Pennsylvania Press, 1987), 23.

27. John M. Manly and Edith Rickert, *The Text of the Canterbury Tales Studied on the Basis of All Known Manuscripts* (Chicago: University of Chicago Press, 1967), 1:389.

28. John M. Bowers, "*The Tale of Beryn* and *The Siege of Thebes*: Alternative Ideas of *The Canterbury Tales*," *SAC* 7 (1985): 33. Seymour describes it as "an anomalous textual composite" in *A Catalogue*, 2:38.

29. Blake, *The Textual Tradition*, 81–82.

30. See also A. C. Spearing, *Medieval to Renaissance in English Poetry* (Cambridge: Cambridge University Press, 1985), 67.

31. Ibid., 71.

32. For further discussion of the *Siege* itself in comparison with the *Knight's Tale,* see Spearing's discussion; also Alain Renoir, *The Poetry of John Lydgate* (London: Routledge and Kegan Paul, 1967), 110ff.

33. The text is taken from Bowers's edition.

34. *MED register(e)*, n., (b) "a recorder, historian." Also *register(e)*, n., "a record keeper, recorder."

35. See John M. Bowers, "Controversy and Criticism: Lydgate's *Thebes* and the Prologue to *Beryn*," *Chaucer Yearbook* 5 (1998): 92–95.

36. The manuscript is damaged at this point.

37. Axel Erdmann and Eilert Ekwall, eds., *Lydgate's Siege of Thebes*, 2 vols., EETS 108, 125 (London: Kegan Paul, Trench, Trübner, 1911; Oxford University Press, 1930), 2:38. Its marginal annotations are repeated with some precision in Wynkyn de Worde's edition of c.1498.

38. Rosamund Allen, "*The Siege of Thebes*: Lydgate's Canterbury Tale," in *Chaucer and Fifteenth-Century Poetry,* ed. Julia Boffey and Janet Cowen (London: King's College, London, Centre for Late Antique and Medieval Studies, 1991), 131.

39. For a detailed account of this text's history, see Peter Brown, "Journey's End: The Prologue to *The Tale of Beryn*," in *Chaucer and Fifteenth-Century Poetry,* ed. Boffey and Cowen, 143–47.

40. Furnivall and Stone, eds., *The Tale of Beryn,* viii.

41. George Lyman Kittredge, *Chaucer and His Poetry* (Cambridge, Mass.: Harvard University Press, 1963); R. M. Lumiansky, *Of Sondry Folk: The Dramatic Principle in the Canterbury Tales* (Austin: University of Texas Press, 1955).

42. See E. J. Bashe, "The Prologue of *The Tale of Beryn*," *PQ* 12 (1933): 1–16; and Karen Winstead, "The *Beryn*-Writer as a Reader of Chaucer," *Chaucer Review* 22 (1988): 225–33, who concludes the work is "on the whole Chaucerian in both spirit and accomplishment" (225). Bradley Darjes and Thomas Rendall commend the work as a subtle narrative that pursues a number of structural, generic, and stylistic aspects of Chaucer's work, in "A Fabliau in the *Prologue to the Tale of Beryn*," *Mediaeval Studies* 47 (1985): 416–31. For the most sustained discussion of both poems with reference to fifteenth-century ideas of

pilgrimage travel, see John Bowers, "*The Tale of Beryn.*" An important exception to the tradition of evaluation and comparison is Stephen Kohl, "Chaucer's Pilgrims in Fifteenth-Century Literature," *Fifteenth-Century Studies* 7 (1982): 221–36. In a move away from the field of poetics, Kohl seeks to evaluate the changing cultural context that produced the two Canterbury prologues, arguing that both poems "share the conviction that the cultural norms of the Middle Ages no longer regulate the actual practice of their age" (234).

43. Derek Pearsall, *John Lydgate* (London: Routledge and Kegan Paul, 1970).

44. Walter F. Schirmer, *John Lydgate: A Study of the Culture of the Fifteenth Century*, trans. Ann E. Keep (1952; London: Methuen, 1961); Renoir, *The Poetry of John Lydgate*.

45. Pearsall, *John Lydgate*, 54–55.

46. Ibid., 59.

47. Pearsall, *The Canterbury Tales*, 300.

48. Ibid., 300.

49. Harold Bloom, *The Anxiety of Influence* (New York: Oxford University Press, 1973), 5.

50. Ibid., 14, 67.

51. Spearing, *Medieval to Renaissance*, 68.

52. C. David Benson, "Critic and Poet: What Lydgate and Henryson Did to Chaucer's *Troilus and Criseyde*," *MLQ* 53 (1992): 26.

53. Renoir, *The Poetry of John Lydgate*, 114.

54. Richard Firth Green, "Legal Satire in *The Tale of Beryn*," *SAC* 11 (1989): 43–62.

55. Brown, "Journey's End," 153.

56. Ibid., 156.

57. Ibid., 157.

58. Furnivall and Stone, eds., *The Tale of Beryn*, xi.

59. Ibid., xi.

60. Ibid., xii.

61. F. J. Harvey Darton, *Tales of the Canterbury Pilgrims Retold from Chaucer and Others*, with introduction by F. J. Furnivall and illustrations by Hugh Thomson (London: Wells Gardner, Darton, 1904).

62. Steve Ellis has recently turned attention to some of these more popular versions of Chaucer, in *Chaucer at Large: The Poet in the Modern Imagination* (Minneapolis: University of Minnesota Press, 2000). Most of the examples I consider here are not directed to that popular sphere: they are texts for relatively restricted academic or poetic consumption and are all distinguished by their attempts to replicate a version of Middle English. In the present context, though, Ellis does discuss a series of "verse pastiches" published in *Punch* by G. H. Vallins commencing in 1944, presenting a series of representative English figures in pseudo-Chaucerian verse (63–64).

63. William Scott Durrant, *Chaucer Redivivus: A Playlet for the Open Air or Hall* (London: Allen, 1912).

64. Henry Noble MacCracken, *The Answere of Adam* (Oxford: Horace Hart, Printer to the University, 1908).

65. "Wyld Tom Hoccleve" also appears and, unusually calm ("ne nothing rechelees ne ryotous"), sits quietly to read the story of Arcite and Theseus "Tyl that his yen popped from hys heed!"

66. John Gohorry, *A Letter from Lewis Chaucer to His Father Geoffrey Chaucer* (Salisbury: Perdix, 1985). This was published in a limited edition, and I consulted the copy in the British Library.

67. Gohorry says he takes up Kittredge's suggestion that the Lewis to whom Chaucer's *Treatise* is addressed died in 1391 and that this might explain why Chaucer never finished the work.

68. Bowers, *"The Tale of Beryn,"* 36.

69. Darjes and Rendall, "A Fabliau," 418. This remark seems in curious contradiction to their later claim that in its "greater depth of characterization" the *Beryn* author's achievement is "most impressive" 419; cf. also 427.

70. Paul Strohm, "Chaucer's Fifteenth-Century Audience and the Narrowing of the 'Chaucer Tradition,'" *SAC* 4 (1982): 5. See also Peter Brown, "Journey's End," 166.

4. Loving Chaucer in the Privacy of Print

1. We could also add John Lane's 1616 Spenserian "Continuation" of the *Squire's Tale,* in BL, MS Douce 170 (and its revision in MS Ashmole 53), edited by Furnivall for the Chaucer Society in 1887. Lane's conclusion strikes a most un-Spenserian note: "Lastlie, yee woold afoord his gentile squire, / if he call at your house, a cupp of beer."

2. W. W. Skeat, *Chaucerian and Other Pieces* (Oxford: Clarendon Press, 1897), ix.

3. See Lois B. Ebin, *Illuminator, Makar, Vates: Visions of Poetry in the Fifteenth Century* (Lincoln: University of Nebraska Press, 1988), 9.

4. Ibid., 6–7.

5. Eleanor Hammond, "John Shirley: Two Versified Tables of Contents," in her *English Verse between Chaucer and Surrey* (New York: Octagon Books, 1927), 193.

6. For a comprehensive summary of opinion, see Margaret Connolly, *John Shirley: Book Production and the Noble Household in Fifteenth-Century England* (Aldershot: Ashgate, 1998), 2–4.

7. Ibid., 114–16, 191.

8. Seth Lerer, *Chaucer and His Readers: Imagining the Author in Late-Medieval England* (Princeton, N.J.: Princeton University Press, 1993), 119, 122.

9. Ibid., 125–28.

10. Ibid., 130.

11. The text is taken from Hammond, "John Shirley," 196.

12. N. F. Blake, *Caxton and His World* (London: Deutsch, 1969), 18.

13. Cheryl Greenberg, "John Shirley and the English Book Trade," *Library,* Sixth Series 4 (1982): 379.

14. A. S. G. Edwards, "John Shirley and the Emulation of Court Culture," in *The Court and Cultural Diversity: Selected Papers from the Eighth Triennial Congress of the International Courtly Literature Society,* ed. Evelyn Mullally and John Thompson (Cambridge: Brewer, 1997), 309–17.

15. Connolly, *John Shirley,* 193–94.

16. N. F. Blake, "Manuscript to Print," in *Book Production and Publishing in Britain 1375–1475,* ed. Jeremy Griffiths and Derek Pearsall (Cambridge: Cambridge University

Press, 1989), 404–6.

17. All quotations from Caxton are from N. F. Blake's slightly modernized edition, *Caxton's Own Prose* (London: Deutsch, 1973); this extract from 62.

18. See Lerer, *Chaucer and His Readers*, 166–67.

19. Caxton's own text here reads, "A lesynge and a soth sayd sawe": as N. F. Blake remarks, Caxton was not so concerned with accuracy that he corrected his compositor's work, even at this crucial juncture, in "Caxton and Chaucer," *Leeds Studies in English*, n.s. 1 (1967): 25.

20. Blake, ed., *Caxton's Own Prose*, 102.

21. *Riverside Chaucer*, textual note, 1143; J. A. Burrow, "Poems without Endings," *SAC* 13 (1991): 23.

22. Nicholas Haydock, "Remaking Chaucer: Influence and Interpretation in Late Medieval Literature" (Ph.D. diss., University of Iowa, 1994), 101–5.

23. The text is a slightly modernized version of my transcription of the Huntington Library copy. See also C. David Benson and David Rollman, "Wynkyn de Worde and the Ending of Chaucer's *Troilus and Criseyde*," *MP* 78 (1981): 275–77.

24. Compare the similar though less programmatic verse conclusions de Worde added to his *Scala perfectionis* and *De proprietatibus rerum*, reproduced in facsimile in James Moran, *Wynkyn de Worde: Father of Fleet Street* (London: Wynkyn de Worde Society, 1960), opp. pp. 17 and 24.

25. Herbert G. Wright, ed., *A Seventeenth-Century Modernisation of the First Three Books of Chaucer's "Troilus and Criseyde"* (Bern: Francke Verlag, 1960), 86.

26. H. S. Bennett, *English Books and Readers, 1475–1557, Being a Study in the History of the Book Trade from Caxton to the Incorporation of the Stationers' Company* (Cambridge: Cambridge University Press, 1952), 212.

27. See in particular Tim Machan's emphatic account of the "immanence" of textual criticism in the humanist project, with special reference to Middle English and the subsquent conventions of editing Chaucer, in *Textual Criticism and Middle English Texts* (Charlottesville: University of Virginia Press, 1994), esp. 14–19.

28. Thomas Greene, *The Light in Troy: Imitation and Discovery in Renaissance Poetry* (New Haven: Yale University Press, 1982), 6. See also Alice Miskimin, *The Renaissance Chaucer* (New Haven, Conn.: Yale University Press, 1975), 12–13, 26–28.

29. The phrase comes from J. W. Saunders, "The Stigma of Print: A Note on the Social Bases of Tudor Poetry," *Essays in Criticism* 1 (1951): 139–64. The concept is updated, politicized and gendered by Wendy Wall, *The Imprint of Gender: Authorship and Publication in the English Renaissance* (Ithaca, N.Y.: Cornell University Press, 1993), 1–3.

30. It became customary for authors, too, to rage against the inaccuracy of the printers; for examples, see Bennett, *English Books*, 218–23. Compare also Brian Richardson, *Print Culture in Renaissance Italy: The Editor and the Vernacular Text, 1470–1600* (Cambridge: Cambridge University Press, 1994), 11–12.

31. Frank Arthur Mumby, *Publishing and Bookselling: A History from the Earliest Times to the Present Day with a Bibliography by W. H. Peet* (London: Jonathan Cape, 1930), 48.

32. Russell Rutter, "William Caxton and Literary Patronage," *Studies in Philology* 84 (1987): 440–70.

33. Ibid., 470.

34. Mumby, *Publishing and Bookselling*, 49–52; Bennett, *English Books*, 30–32; Moran, *Wynkyn de Worde*, 30.

35. Lotte Hellinga, *Caxton in Focus: The Beginning of Printing in England* (London: British Library, 1982), 21.

36. Richard Helgerson, *Self-Crowned Laureates: Spenser, Johnson, Milton, and the Literary System* (Berkeley: University of California Press, 1983), 29, 37–38.

37. The pamphlet was printed in London by John Streater, "for the Author," in 1664.

38. Harrison Ross Steeves, *Learned Societies and English Literary Scholarship in Great Britain and the United States* (1913; reprint, New York: AMS Press, 1970), 7.

39. In Joan Evans, *A History of the Society of Antiquaries* (Oxford: Oxford University Press for the Society of Antiquaries, 1956), 11.

40. A. S. G. Edwards, "Chaucer from Manuscript to Print: The Social Text and the Critical Text (Geoffrey Chaucer)," *Mosaic* 28 (1995): 3–4.

41. Furnivall quotes the letter from Henry Bradshaw recording this discovery in Tuke's hand in the copy of Thynne's edition at Clare Hall, Cambridge: "This preface I sir Bryan Tuke wrot at the request of Mr Clarke of the Kechyn then being / tarying for the tyde at Grenewich." G. H. Kingsley, ed., *Animadversions vppon the Annotacions and Corrections of some imperfections of impressiones of Chaucers workes (sett downe before tyme, and now) reprinted in the yere of our lorde 1598*, rev. F. J. Furnivall (London: EETS, 1865; rev. 1875), xxvi. R. F. Yeager remarks that if this preface had to be composed in such haste that Thynne entrusted it to Tuke, he yet made no effort to correct its ascription in the second edition in 1542. "From this it is simplest and doubtless most nearly correct to assume that strict accuracy about who wrote the Preface did not seem a problem for Thynne—and if not in his own case, would it have seemed so for Thynne in the case of Chaucer?" Yeager, "Literary Theory at the Close of the Middle Ages: William Caxton and William Thynne," *SAC* 6 (1984): 158–59.

42. James E. Blodgett, "William Thynne," in *Editing Chaucer*, ed. Paul G. Ruggiers (Norman, Okla.: Pilgrim Books, 1984), 36, 41–47.

43. Ibid., 38–39. Blodgett also traces a possible connection between Thynne and Thomas Berthelet, the king's printer from 1530 to 1547 (40).

44. These additions are famously condemned by Thomas Tyrwhitt, for whom "[i]t would be a waste of time to sift accurately the heap of rubbish, which was added, by John Stowe, to the Edition of 1561," in *The Canterbury Tales of Chaucer*, 5 vols (London: Payne, 1775–78), 5: xxii–xxiii. While most of Stow's additions are courtly in orientation, the Chaucer canon was also expanded in the direction of Protestant polemic, witnessed by the addition of the *Plowman's Tale* in 1542 and *Jack Upland* in 1602. For Machan, the early modern Chaucer is recuperated "both as a courtier and as a prophet of the Reformation" (*Textual Criticism*, 88).

45. Derek Brewer, ed., *Geoffrey Chaucer, The Works, 1532 (Facsimile, with Supplementary Material from the Editions of 1542, 1561, 1598, and 1602* (London: Scolar Press, 1969; reprint, 1974, 1976), "Introduction" (pages are not numbered). There were three imprints of the first edition, for George Bishop, Bonham Norton, and T. Wight.

46. See Machan, *Textual Criticism*, 43, 89–90.

47. See Derek Pearsall, *The Life of Geoffrey Chaucer: A Critical Biography* (Oxford:

Blackwell, 1992), 295.

48. See Tim William Machan, "Kynaston's Troilus, Textual Criticism, and the Renaissance Reading of Chaucer," *Exemplaria* 5 (1993): 176–77; see also Machan, *Textual Criticism*, 44–48.

49. Pearsall identifies the men from the company as George Bishop and Bonham Norton, in "Thomas Speght," in *Editing Chaucer*, ed. Ruggiers, 73.

50. Wall, *The Imprint of Gender*, 24–28.

51. Compare Bennett, *English Books*, 55–56.

52. "Peter Burke has recently made a cogent case [in an unpublished paper] for the Renaissance dialogue as a favorite form of printed discourse during the period because of its replication of oral setting for readers who had not yet adjusted to the seeming anonymity and silence of print." Leah Marcus, *Unediting the Renaissance: Shakespeare, Marlowe, Milton* (London: Routledge, 1996), 199.

53. Pearsall, "Thomas Speght," 71–73, 73 n. 6, 82.

54. Jonathan Bate, *The Genius of Shakespeare* (London: Picador, 1997), 22–23. See also J. B. Leishman, ed., *The Three Parnassus Plays* (London: Nicholson and Watson, 1949), 54–55.

55. Leishman, ed., *The Three Parnassus Plays*, 35.

56. Furnivall, in his revisions to Kingsley's edition; Pearsall, in "Thomas Speght," 83–90.

57. Kingsley, ed., *Animadversions*, 4.

58. Ibid., 4–5.

59. Pearsall, "Thomas Speght," 84.

60. Ibid., 84.

61. Kingsley, ed., *Animadversions*, xlviii–lvi.

62. Ibid., 10, 6.

63. Ibid., 5–6.

64. Machan, *Textual Criticism*, 42.

65. This edition is accompanied by a brief preface by "J. H." (John Harefinch), who describes how he has been "greatly sollicited by many Learned and Worthy Gentlemen" to reprint Chaucer.

66. Pearsall, "Thomas Speght," 87.

67. Kingsley, ed., *Animadversions*, cvi.

68. Ibid., cvii.

69. Arthur F. Marotti, *Manuscript, Print, and the English Renaissance Lyric* (Ithaca, N.Y.: Cornell University Press, 1995); Wall, *The Imprint of Gender*, 25. Marotti remarks that Tottel's printed collection is comparable to John Shirley's collections (18 n. 53).

70. Wall, *The Imprint of Gender*, 26.

71. Seth Lerer, *Courtly Letters in the Age of Henry VIII: Literary Culture and the Arts of Deceit* (Cambridge: Cambridge University Press, 1997), 6–7.

72. Miskimin, *The Renaissance Chaucer*, 232.

73. See Marotti, *Manuscript, Print, and the English Renaissance Lyric*, 229–36.

74. Ibid., 229.

75. Ibid., 236.

76. Kingsley, ed., *Animadversions*, xxvii. For the intellectual and literary contexts of friendship in this period, see Reginald Hyatte, *The Arts of Friendship: The Idealization of Friendship in Medieval and Early Renaissance Literature* (Leiden: Brill, 1994).

77. Anne Hudson, "John Stow," in *Editing Chaucer*, ed. Ruggiers, 56.

78. Pearsall, "Thomas Speght," 76.

79. Jonathan Goldberg, *Sodometries: Renaissance Texts, Modern Sexualities* (Stanford, Calif.: Stanford University Press, 1992), 66–71.

80. Virginia F. Stern, *Gabriel Harvey: His Life, Marginalia, and Library* (Oxford: Clarendon Press, 1979), 125.

81. J. A. W. Bennett, *Chaucer at Oxford and Cambridge* (Oxford: Oxford University Press, 1974), 10 n. 1.

82. Quoted in Stern, *Gabriel Harvey*, 160.

83. Alexander B. Grosart, ed. *The Works of Gabriel Harvey* (1884), 2nd ed., 3 vols. (New York: AMS Press, 1966), 1:119. For an elegant discussion of the relations between Harvey and Spenser implied by *The Shepheardes Calendar* and the friendship of Colin and Hobbinol, see Goldberg, *Sodometries*, 71–81.

84. Stern, *Gabriel Harvey*, 33.

85. *Dialogue both pleasaunt and pietifull, wherein is a godlie regiment against the Fever Pestilence &c.* (London, 1573). Extracted in Rev. Henry J. Todd, ed., *Illustrations of the Lives and Writings of Gower and Chaucer Collected from Authentick Documents* (London: F. C. and J. Rivington, T. Payne, Cadell and Davies and R. H. Evans, 1810), xxix–xxx.

5. Translating Chaucer for Modernity

1. In this latter regard Dryden's voice is far more distinctive and influential than that of Richard Brathwaite, for example, in his *Comment upon the Two Tales of our Ancient, Renowned, and Ever-Living Poet Sir Jeffray Chaucer* (London: Godbid, 1665).

2. All quotations from Dryden are taken from *The Poems of John Dryden*, ed. James Kinsley, 4 vols. (Oxford: Clarendon Press, 1958); this quotation from 1445, line 50.

3. Earl Miner, "Introduction: Borrowed Plumage, Varied Umbrage," in *Literary Transmission and Authority: Dryden and Other Writers*, ed. Miner (Cambridge: Cambridge University Press, 1993), 4.

4. Jennifer Brady, "Dryden and Negotiations of Succession," in *Literary Transmission and Authority*, ed. Miner, 28–33.

5. Compare Brady: "[Dryden] persists in regarding his influential fathers as allies and mentors" (ibid., 33).

6. Paul H. Fry, *The Reach of Criticism: Method and Perception in Literary Theory* (New Haven, Conn.: Yale University Press, 1983), 122.

7. Ibid., 114.

8. Terry Eagleton, *The Function of Criticism: From the Spectator to Post-Structuralism* (London: Verso, 1984), 14–15.

9. See D. S. Brewer, *Chaucer, The Critical Heritage* (London: Routledge, 1978), 1:160.

10. J. A. Burrow, ed., *Geoffrey Chaucer: A Critical Anthology* (Harmondsworth: Penguin Books, 1969), 36–37.

11. I discuss the relations between the preface and the translations in "Singing Clearly: Chaucer, Dryden, and a Rooster's Discourse," *Exemplaria* 5 (1993): 365–86.

12. Betsy Bowden, ed., *Eighteenth-Century Modernizations from "The Canterbury Tales"* (Rochester: Brewer, 1991), xv.

13. Ibid., xiii.

14. Caroline Spurgeon, ed., *Five Hundred Years of Chaucer Criticism and Allusion, 1357–1900* (London: Cambridge University Press, 1925), 1:xliv.

15. *Chaucers Ghoast; or, a Piece of Antiquity Containing Twelve Pleasant Fables of Ovid Penn'd after the Ancient Manner of Writing in England* (London: T. Ratcliff and N. Thompson for Richard Mills, 1672); *Chaucer's Whims: Being Some Select Fables and Tales in Verse, Very Applicable to the Present Times* (London: Printed by D. Edwards, 1701); "Geoffrey Chaucer," *Brown Bread and Honour, a Tale. Moderniz'd from an ancient manuscript of Chaucer* (London: Printed by John Morphew, 1716); and "John Chaucer, Jr," *Canterbury Tales: Composed for the Entertainment of All Ingenious Young Men and Maids* (London, 1770).

16. William T. Alderson and Arnold C. Henderson, *Chaucer and Augustan Scholarship* (Berkeley: University of California Press, 1970), 88. Tim Machan comments, similarly, of an earlier period, that between 1558 and 1625, thirteen plays based on Chaucer's works were composed. Machan, *Textual Criticism and Middle English Texts* (Charlottesville: University Press of Virginia, 1994), 41.

17. Burrow, ed. *Geoffrey Chaucer*, 74.

18. Ibid., 75–76.

19. Jonathan Bate, *The Genius of Shakespeare* (London: Picador, 1997), 162–63.

20. Burrow, ed., *Geoffrey Chaucer*, 76.

21. From *A Descriptive Catalogue of Pictures, Poetical and Historical Inventions, Painted by William Blake* (1809), in *Geoffrey Chaucer*, ed. Burrow, 77.

22. Derek Pearsall tracks the trajectory of this theme from Dryden through the 1950s in "Chaucer's Poetry and Its Modern Commentators: The Necessity of History," in *Medieval Literature: Criticism, Ideology, and History*, ed. David Aers (Brighton: Harvester, 1986), 132–34.

6. Reading Chaucer outside the Academy

1. As recently as 1997, Jonathan Bate affirms Dryden's "twin roles as father of both English literary criticism and English heroic verse." Bate, *The Genius of Shakespeare* (London: Picador, 1997), 173.

2. E. M. W. Tillyard, *The Muse Unchained: An Intimate Account of the Revolution in English Studies at Cambridge* (London: Baves and Baves, 1958), 22.

3. Steve Ellis emphasizes the "Englishness" of the Chaucer discussed by both Woolf and Chesterton in *Chaucer at Large: The Poet in the Modern Imagination* (Minneapolis: University of Minnesota Press, 2000).

4. William Benzie, *Dr F. J. Furnivall: A Victorian Scholar Adventurer* (Norman: Pilgrim Books, 1983), 22.

5. Peter Faulkner, "'The Paths of Virtue and Early English': F. J. Furnivall and Victorian Medievalism," in *From Medieval to Medievalism*, ed. John Simons (London: Macmillan, 1992), 145.

6. Chris Baldick stresses the importance to this movement of Matthew Arnold's understanding of education as a civilizing agent and the special role of literary criticism in developing a sympathetic understanding in *The Social Mission of English Criticism, 1848–1932* (Oxford: Clarendon Press, 1987), 34–43.

7. Benzie, *Dr F. J. Furnivall*, 7. See also Faulkner, "The Paths of Virtue," 147.

8. Benzie, *Dr F. J. Furnivall*, 26. In his obituary of Furnivall, W. P. Ker draws attention to his first publication, in 1850, of a pamphlet entitled "Association a Necessary Part of Christianity." "Obituary: F. J. Furnivall," in *Proceedings of the British Academy, 1909–10* (London: Oxford University Press, 1910), 375.

9. On the associations, see J. F. C. Harrison, *A History of the Working Men's College, 1854–1954* (London: Routledge and Kegan Paul, 1954), 10–14; and for a brief discussion of the European socialist and communist concepts of "association," see Renate Haas, "V. A. Huber's Characterization of F. J. Furnivall," *Studies in Medievalism* 4 (1992): 217–18.

10. Quoted in Baldick, *The Social Mission of English Criticism*, 63.

11. See Baldick, *Social Mission*, and Terry Eagleton, *Literary Theory: An Introduction* (Oxford: Blackwell, 1983), 27–29. Carey Kaplan and Ellen Cronan Rose discuss the 1945 Report of the Harvard Committee, *General Education in a Free Society*, prepared in part by I. A. Richards, in similar terms, in *The Canon and the Common Reader* (Knoxville: University of Tennessee Press, 1990), 54–55.

12. Haas, "V. A. Huber's Characterisation of F. J. Furnivall," 217–18. The fact of Maurice's expulsion is either omitted or discreetly veiled in most accounts of his work.

13. G. M. Trevelyan, "The Older Universities," in *The Working Men's College, 1854–1904: Records of Its History and Its Work for Fifty Years*, by Members of the College, ed. Rev. J. Llewelyn Davies (London: Macmillan, 1904), 188–89.

14. R. H. Marks, "The College Clubs," in *The Working Men's College*, ed. Davies, 220. Benzie's comment is typically less political: "The ideals of comradeship, freedom, equality, and healthy exercise which he sometimes failed to inculcate in the lecture room he applied in a more practical way in educational excursions to the countryside, rowing on the river, playing cricket, dancing, singing and picnicking" (*Dr F. J. Furnivall*, 54).

15. Harrison, *A History of the Working Men's College*, 39.

16. Ibid., 39.

17. Ibid., 91–92.

18. Davies, ed., *The Working Men's College*, 54.

19. Ibid., 60.

20. Around this time he also began to receive a small income as "trustee of one of the family estates." Benzie, *Dr F. J. Furnivall*, 32 n. 70.

21. Ibid., 33.

22. David Matthews points out that while texts of Chaucer were widely available before the work of Furnivall and the Chaucer Society, they were not scholarly productions. Moreover, "the very familiarity and popularity of Chaucer as an author, before the founding of the Chaucer Society, had actually hindered scholarly endeavor," in "Speaking to Chaucer: The Poet and the Nineteenth-Century Academy," *Studies in Medievalism* 9 (1999 [for 1997]): 10. In *The Making of Middle English, 1765–1910* (Minneapolis: University of Minnesota Press, 1999), Matthews argues that while Furnivall was instrumental in creating Middle English as an academic subject of study, in part through the publications of the

Early English Text Society and in part through integrating the study of Chaucer with Middle English, he also unwittingly oversaw the displacement of interest away from private individuals onto university institutions (160–61, 172).

23. A. S. G. Edwards describes his "positive genius for talent-spotting." Edwards, "Walter Skeat," in *Editing Chaucer: The Great Tradition*, ed. Paul Ruggiers (Norman, Okla.: Pilgrim Books, 1984), 172.

24. Furnivall to Bradshaw, 12 May 1865, CUL, Addit. MS 2591, no. 250.

25. K. M. Elisabeth Murray, *Caught in the Web of Words: James A. H. Murray and the Oxford English Dictionary*, with a preface by R. W. Burchfield (Oxford: Oxford University Press, 1979), 91.

26. Ibid., 100, 92, 93.

27. This statement of the Chaucerian Society's aims appeared in most of its publications. Furnivall continued: "There were then, and are still, many questions of metre, pronunciation, orthography, and etymology yet to be settled, for which more prints of Manuscripts are wanted; and it is hardly too much to say that every line of Chaucer contains points that need reconsideration." The idea of Chaucer lovers appears again in Furnivall's dedication of his edition of Harley MS 7334: "To the Lovers of Chaucer, Past, Present and to Come." *The Harleian MS 7334 of Chaucer's Canterbury Tales*, edited by Frederick J. Furnivall (London: Chaucer Society, Trübner, 1885), iv.

28. W. P. Ker, "Obituary: F. J. Furnivall," 375.

29. Murray, *Caught in the Web of Words*, 90.

30. F. J. Furnivall, ed., *King Edward II's Household and Wardrobe Ordinances* (London: Chaucer Society, 1876), v. In a similar vein, Matthews also quotes Furnivall's commentary on the Hoccleve portrait in support of his argument that Furnivall (and to a lesser degree Skeat) looked to Chaucer as a kind of ethical guide: "One feels one would like to go to such a man when one was in trouble, and hear his wise and gentle speech" (*The Making of Middle English*, 180). This accounts for Furnivall's defensiveness at the suggestion (merely implicit in a remark of Bradshaw's) that *Troilus* might have been written as a defense of John of Gaunt's relationship with Katharine Swynford. "I should like to kick Chaucer if he wrote *Troilus* for such a purpose. He can't have done it" (ibid.).

31. Furnivall, ed., *Household and Wardrobe Ordinances*, v. The account of Chaucer as valet inspires a story of uncertain resonance about a friend of Furnivall's who, being sent with a valet to Oxford, took a while to discover his valet's "calling in life," which turned out to be to "bring him clean boots and straps and brush his clothes" (ix). After this discovery, both the young man and the valet were happy. The story seems at odds with Furnivall's dismissal, nearly thirty years later, of "all stupid and narrow class humbug."

32. Benzie, in *Dr. F. J. Furnivall*, citing *Browning Society Papers*, no. 1 (1881): 139 n. 70.

33. Furnivall, ed., *Household and Wardrobe Ordinances*, xiv.

34. G. H. Kingsley, ed., *Animadversions uppon the Annotacions and Corrections of some imperfections of impressiones of Chaucers workes*, rev. F. J. Furnivall (London: EETS, 1865; rev. 1975), cxv, cxvi.

35. F. J. Furnivall, "Recent Work at Chaucer," *Macmillan's Magazine*, March 1873, 27, 383–93; quoted in D. S. Brewer, ed., *Chaucer: The Critical Heritage* (London: Routledge and Kegan Paul, 1978), 2:175.

36. Kingsley, ed., *Animadversions*, cxvii.

37. He adds a footnote: "My Dryasdust friend uses strong language occasionally. How far it is justified in this case, let the absence of monographs on the thousand and one points still needing elucidation in both poets, witness." Furnivall, ed., *Household and Wardrobe Ordinances*, v–vi. Certainly Furnivall's eccentric prefatory style did not go unremarked; see the unsigned review of Furnivall's *Education in Early England, Some Notes used as Forewords to a Collection of Treatises on "Manners and Meals in Olden Times,"* for the EETS, in *The Athenæum*, 26 October 1867, no. 2087, 532–33.

38. Compare John Simons's introduction to his collection, *From Medieval to Medievalism* (London: Macmillan, 1992), 1–3.

39. Benzie, *Dr F. J. Furnivall*, 7.

40. F. J. Furnivall, "The Early English Text Society," *Athenæum*, 28 January 1886, no. 1944, 128. See also Matthews, *The Making of Middle English*, 85ff., 104–5.

41. Furnivall, "The Early English Text Society," 128.

42. There was, of course, much resistance to this idea: Madden was scathing about the carelessness and inaccuracy of much of the society's work (Benzie, *Dr F. J. Furnivall*, 124–25, 150–52).

43. Murray, *Caught in the Web of Words*, 143.

44. Terence Hawkes, "A Professor of Literary Theory Writes in to Disagree," *LRB*, 21 November 1985, 4. Hawkes's letter came in response to an article by Hough in *LRB*, 17 October 1985.

45. Tillyard, *The Muse Unchained*, 25.

46. Brian Doyle, *English and Englishness* (London: Routledge, 1989), 41.

47. John Dover Wilson, *Milestones on the Dover Road* (London: Faber and Faber, 1969), 97.

48. Ibid., 98. See also Matthews, *The Making of Middle English*, 189.

49. Quoted in Doyle, *English and Englishness*, 49.

50. Henry Newbolt, "The Poetry of Chaucer," *English Review* 15 (1913): 171.

51. Renate Haas notes that the first lecture course on Chaucer was offered in 1844 at the University of Berlin, while the first Chaucerian dissertation was presented at Bonn in 1847. Haas, "Lionesses Painting Lionesses? Chaucer's Women as Seen by Early Women Scholars and Academic Critics," in *A Wyf Ther Was: Essays in Honour of Paule Mertens-Fonck*, ed. Juliette Dor (Liège: Université de Liège, 1992), 179.

52. Furnivall to Henry Bradshaw, 17 October 1870, CUL, Addit. MS 2592, no. 239.

53. Donald C. Baker, "Frederick James Furnivall," in *Editing Chaucer: The Great Tradition*, ed. Paul Ruggiers (Norman, Okla.: Pilgrim Books, 1984), 158, 160, 279 n. 4.

54. Letter from S. O. Halliwell to Furnivall, 30 June 1866, Huntington Library, Furnivall Correspondence, box 11.

55. *The Poems of Geoffrey Chaucer, Modernized* (London: Whittaker, 1841), ix.

56. Henry Bradshaw to F. J. Furnivall, 9 January 1868, Huntington Library, Furnivall Correspondence, box 11. Furnivall makes the distinction himself in a letter to Bradshaw on 8 February 1871: "You're the man to edit Chaucer, if only you will. I'm the man to print the texts, if only you'll add your notes of MSS. to mine, or tell me what books to look in to find out the MSS." See Benzie, *Dr F. J. Furnivall*, 165. Baker comments: "One can admire Bradshaw's scholarship, but without Furnivall there would have been nothing" ("Frederick James Furnivall," 166).

57. Henry Bradshaw to Furnivall, 16 August 1867, CUL, Addit. MS 2591, no. 384a.

58. Matthews, *The Making of Middle English*, 173.

59. Henry Bradshaw to Furnivall, 25 September 1868, CUL Addit. MS 2591, no. 632.

60. Letters to Henry Bradshaw, 21 July 1866, CUL, Addit. MS 2591, no. 319; 1 January 1867, CUL, Addit. MS 2591, no. 344. Benzie also quotes Furnivall writing to Bradshaw on 16 July 1868: "I hope you'll die a horrible death if you persist in putting Chaucer into . . . uniform spelling. I believe now that the desire for uniformity proceeds from your being a ritualist & a Fellow. Such a being must be up to mischief." CUL, Addit. MS 2591, no. 590.

61. F. J. Furnivall and W. G. Stone, eds., *The Tale of Beryn, with a Prologue of the Merry Adventure of the Pardoner with a Tapster at Canterbury,* Chaucer Society (London: Trübner, 1887), x.

62. Furnivall to Henry Bradshaw, 24 December 1870, CUL, Addit. MS 2592, no. 258; 17 October 1870, CUL Addit. MS 2592, no. 239; 1 January 1871, CUL, Addit. MS 2592, no. 260.

63. Baker quotes this correspondence in "Frederick James Furnivall," 162.

64. Ibid., 163.

65. Bradshaw comments: "[Y]ou must allow that it is a matter in which there are two sides, & many agree with me in finding it easier to work honestly without having every single step of one's work & one's half-conclusions published to the world—and no doubt the determination on your part to adopt the puff system acted on me the wrong way in making me much less communicative than I had always been before." Henry Bradshaw to Furnivall, 7 August 1868, CUL, Addit. MS 2591, no. 609.

66. William K. Wimsatt Jr. and Cleanth Brooks, *Literary Criticism: A Short History* (London: Routledge and Kegan Paul, 1957), 533; also quoted by Benzie, *Dr F. J. Furnivall*, 175.

67. Baldick, *The Social Mission of English Criticism*, 73.

68. Ibid., 72–73.

69. In 1906, for example, the School of "English Language and Literature" at Oxford was bifurcated: the only texts to be examined by both sections were translations from Old and Middle English, Chaucer and Shakespeare. D. J. Palmer, *The Rise of English Studies* (London: Oxford University Press, 1965), 130. And at Cambridge, after 1926 it became possible "for a man to get a degree in English since Chaucer." Tillyard, *The Muse Unchained*, 109.

70. Palmer writes of Churton Collins: "English literature began with the Renaissance. Not only did he pour contempt on Anglo-Saxon and medieval literature as 'the barbarous and semi-barbarous experiments of the infancy of civilisation,' he also identified the subject with the philological method of study to which it was then confined: the very confusion against which he had warned others in defending the Classics" (Palmer, *The Rise of English Studies,* 86). Palmer also describes Sir Walter Raleigh's "unconsummated ambition to write his own book on Chaucer, to have included such a chapter as, 'What the Philologists should tell us about Chaucer and don't'" (ibid., 147).

71. John Churton Collins, *Study of English Literature: A Plea for Its Recognition and Organization at the Universities* (London: Macmillan, 1891), 31, 32.

72. Matthews, *The Making of Middle English,* 190.

73. Lee Patterson, *Negotiating the Past: The Historical Understanding of Medieval Literature* (Madison: University of Wisconsin Press, 1987), 19.

74. John Livingston Lowes, *Geoffrey Chaucer* (Oxford: Clarendon, 1934), 192.

75. Leigh Hunt, *Wit and Humour Selected from the English Poets, with an Illustrative Essay and Critical Comments* (London: Smith, Elder, 1848), 99.

76. W. P. Ker, *Essays on Medieval Literature* (London: Macmillan, 1905), 78. Later, he goes on, "Melibeus may be left out of account, as a portent too wonderful for mortal commentary: there are other problems and distresses in the Canterbury Tales, and they are singular enough, though not altogether inexplicable or 'out of all whooping,' like that insinuating 'little thing in prose' by which Sir Thopas was avenged on his detractors" (98).

77. Ibid., 95.

78. Caroline Spurgeon, ed., *Five Hundred Years of Chaucer Criticism and Allusion 1357–1900*, 3 vols. (London: Cambridge University Press, 1925), cxiv.

79. Ibid., cxxiv. On 14 June 1877, Thomas Arnold wrote to Furnivall from Oxford, similarly using the image of the clerk as a coded sign of familiarity with Furnivall's project: "[N]one can tell better than a 'clerk of Oxenford' what services Mr Furnivall has, by his indefatigable industry and love of our early literature rendered to the cause of English studies." Huntington Library, Furnivall Correspondence, box 7.

80. *Frederick James Furnivall: A Volume of Personal Record* (Oxford: Oxford University Press, 1911), 178–80.

81. Ibid., 11, 92.

82. Derek S. Brewer, "The Annual Chaucer Lecture: Furnivall and the Old Chaucer Society," *Chaucer Newsletter* 1, no. 2 (1979): 3.

83. E. T. Donaldson, "Chaucer the Pilgrim" (1954), reprinted in *Speaking of Chaucer* (London: Athlone, 1970), 2.

84. A. S. G. Edwards similarly aligns Furnivall's editorial practice with "the tradition of the scribes and early printers, one that remained . . . essentially pragmatic and unreflective." Edwards, "Middle English Literature," in *Scholarly Editing: A Guide to Research*, ed. D. C. Greetham (New York: Modern Language Association of America, 1995), 186.

85. Baker, "Frederick James Furnivall," 169. Baker gives Furnivall much credit for his enthusiasm and gratitude for the "accurate scholarship" of others. Yet his method of assembling the texts for this edition "combines those features which every scholar would approve with elements at which one can only stand aghast" (160). Finally, "As an editor, as I have remarked, his work cannot really be evaluated, for he never, in a sense, edited anything. He printed, but how fully, how gloriously, he printed!" (169).

86. Patterson, *Negotiating the Past*, 13.

87. Faulkner, "The Paths of Virtue," 157.

88. Kathleen Biddick, *The Shock of Medievalism* (Durham, N.C.: Duke University Press, 1998), 92. Biddick sees her own postcolonial reading of the EETS's imperial reach as a contrast to the traditional narratives of English studies, and so it may be for American readers. Yet her work makes no mention of the materialist studies of Baldick and Eagleton, which stress the importance of English studies across a range of nationalist agendas in the late nineteenth and early twentieth centuries, or the Foucauldian work of Ian Hunter, who reverses the dominant account to argue that the Newbolt Report's emphasis on literature, for example, derives from the cultural "machinery of social investigation and administration," already in place in English elementary schools. Hunter, *Culture and Government: The Emergence of Literary Education* (Houndmills: Macmillan, 1988), ix.

89. Antonia Ward, "'My Love for Chaucer': F. J. Furnivall and Homosociality in the Chaucer Society," *Studies in Medievalism* 9 (1999 [for 1997]): 45–57. This important essay nevertheless depends on a number of "applications" of the reading practices of Carolyn Dinshaw and Eve Sedgwick to Furnivall's own writings, applications Ward admits are methodologically contentious. In my view, her reading has the unfortunate effect of abstracting Furnivall's projects out from their very distinctive social contexts, despite her discussion of the work of the Chaucer Society. It also depends heavily on the troublesome metaphor of the text (in this case, Chaucer) as woman.

90. Julian N. Wasserman and Robert J. Blanch, eds., *Chaucer in the Eighties* (Syracuse, N.Y.: Syracuse University Press, 1986), xiii.

91. See Ian Hunter's summary of this process in *Culture and Government*, 121.

92. For a discussion of other "popular" Chaucerian studies of the first half of the twentieth century, see Steve Ellis, *Chaucer at Large*. I have singled out Woolf and Chesterton because they are consistently cited, but out of context, and depoliticized.

93. Virginia Woolf, *A Room of One's Own and Three Guineas*, ed. and introd. Morag Schiach (Oxford: Oxford University Press, 1992), 9.

94. For a discussion of Woolf's resistance to the "rigid division between amateur and professional—and its concomitant relegating of women to a leisure class—which went virtually unquestioned in her own world," see Juliet Dusinberre, *Virginia Woolf's Renaissance: Woman Reader or Common Reader?* (London: Macmillan, 1997), esp. 6–16. Dusinberre also sketches Woolf's contradictory impulses in defining herself as a professional.

95. Sheila Sullivan, ed., *Critics on Chaucer* (London: Allen and Unwin, 1970), 21.

96. Ibid.

97. Dusinberre, *Virginia Woolf's Renaissance*, 43–44. The trope of friendship with Chaucer is also deployed by Lady Anne Clifford in the seventeenth century, an important model of a woman reader for Woolf (ibid., 9–11, 74–75). The congenial company is not always depicted as exclusively masculine, though it is predominantly so.

98. Dusinberre discusses an early unpublished story by Woolf, "The Journal of Mistress Joan Martyn," whose central character, Rosamond Merridew, has an unconventional approach to writing medieval history: "Dame Elizabeth Partridge . . . wanted stockings! & no other need impresses you in quite the same way with the reality of mediaeval legs; & therefore with the reality of mediaeval bodies, & so, proceeding upward step by step, with the reality of mediaeval brains." The story dramatizes the stern response of conventional historians to her work as too digressive and lacking the proper sources. Dusinberre, *Virginia Woolf's Renaissance*, 20–21.

99. Virginia Woolf, "The Pastons and Chaucer," in *The Common Reader* (1925; reprint, London: Hogarth Press, 1984), 1:10.

100. Ibid., 11.

101. Susan Stanford Friedman, "Virginia Woolf's Pedagogical Scenes of Reading: *The Voyage Out, The Common Reader*, and Her 'Common Readers,'" *Modern Fiction Studies* 38 (1992): 119.

102. Elsie F. Mayer sketches out the feminist challenges to "masculinist" criticism that also facilitated the recuperation of Woolf for modern feminist literary studies in "Literary Criticism with a Human Face: Virginia Woolf and *The Common Reader*," in *Private Voices,*

Public Lives: Women Speak on the Literary Life, ed. Nancy Owen Nelson (Denton: University of North Texas Press, 1995), 283–97.

103. G. K. Chesterton, *Chaucer* (London: Faber and Faber, 1932; 2nd ed., 1948), 9.

104. Ibid., 14.

105. Ibid., 27.

106. Ibid., 20, 137.

107. Ibid., 10. "I should no more think of setting up to be an authority on Chaucer than an authority on Punch and Judy; or Pickwick; or the Christmas pantomime. These things are not studied, but appreciated" (227). Later, he describes himself as an "amateur, ignorant of all but human experience" (268).

108. Ibid., 11.

109. J. A. Burrow, ed., *Geoffrey Chaucer: A Critical Anthology* (Harmondsworth: Penguin, 1969), 113.

110. See Ian Boyd, "Chesterton's Medievalism," *Studies in Medievalism* 3 (1991): 243–55.

111. Chesterton, *Chaucer*, 10–11.

112. Ibid., 12.

113. Ibid., 12. Steve Ellis draws attention to Chesterton's criticism of Chaucer "for displaying that weakness of the 'clubbable fellow' or 'man's man' in putting comfort and sociability before political commitment" ("Popular Chaucer and the Academy," *Studies in Medievalism* 9 [1999, for 1997]: 29).

114. Chesterton, *Chaucer*, 35.

115. Ibid., 293.

116. Boyd contrasts Chesterton to both romantic medievalists ("with whom he has been so frequently identified") and "modern scientific medievalists, who wrote refutations of the work of their naive colleagues" ("Chesterton's Medievalism," 248).

117. See also Steve Ellis's discussion of some other more populist Chaucerians of this period in *Chaucer at Large*, 26–27. Ellis stresses the work of Nevill Coghill in popularizing Chaucer through his translations, broadcasts, and theatrical work.

7. Reforming the Chaucerian Community

1. See Lee Patterson, *Negotiating the Past: The Historical Understanding of Medieval Literature* (Madison: University of Wisconsin Press, 1987), 4–5 n. 4.

2. In addition to Patterson's very full account of the contradictions in exegetics in *Negotiating the Past*, see David Aers, "Reflections on the 'Allegory of the Theologians,' Ideology, and Piers Plowman," in *Medieval Literature: Criticism, Ideology, and History*, ed. Aers (Brighton: Harvester, 1986), 58–73; and in the same collection, Derek Pearsall, "Chaucer's Poetry and Its Modern Commentators: The Necessity of History," 123–47.

3. Laurie A. Finke and Martin B. Shichtman, eds., *Medieval Texts and Contemporary Readers* (Ithaca, N.Y.: Cornell University Press, 1987), viii.

4. Donald Rose, ed., *New Perspectives in Chaucer Criticism* (Norman, Okla.: Pilgrim Books, 1981), ix, x–xi.

5. Morton W. Bloomfield, "Contemporary Literary Theory and Chaucer," in *New Perspectives in Chaucer Criticism*, ed. Rose, 25, 35.

6. Ibid., 36.

7. Ibid., 35.

8. Alastair J. Minnis, "Chaucer and Comparative Literary Theory," in *New Perspectives in Chaucer Criticism*, ed. Rose, 69.

9. Alastair J. Minnis, *Medieval Theory of Authorship: Scholastic Literary Attitudes in the Later Middle Ages* (London: Scolar Press, 1984), 7.

10. Rose, ed., *New Perspectives in Chaucer Criticism*, ix.

11. David Aers, *Chaucer, Langland, and the Creative Imagination* (London: Routledge and Kegan Paul, 1980); Stephen Knight, "Chaucer and the Sociology of Literature," *SAC* 2 (1980): 15–51.

12. David Aers, *Chaucer* (Brighton: Harvester, 1986), vi.

13. Ibid., 8.

14. Ibid., 12–13.

15. Ibid., 29, 55, 57, 58, 72, 106 n. 17.

16. Ibid., 53, 55, 67.

17. David Aers, "The Good Shepherds of Medieval Criticism," *Southern Review* 20 (1987): 168, 180.

18. Ibid., 180. An earlier version of Aers's article was presented as a conference paper at the University of Melbourne in 1986 and published by South Australia's *Southern Review* in the following year. As the strongest anti-American statement of this period of Aers's writing, at least, it seems as if Australia might have provided a useful mediating point in the global context of Chaucer studies.

19. Stephen Knight, *Geoffrey Chaucer* (Oxford: Blackwell, 1986), 32.

20. Ibid., 1.

21. Ibid., 2.

22. Ibid., 4–5.

23. Bernard O'Donoghue, "David Aers, *Chaucer;* Stephen Knight, *Geoffrey Chaucer;* Roger Ellis, *Patterns of Religious Narrative in the Canterbury Tales;* C. David Benson, *Chaucer's Drama of Style*," *TLS* 29 May 1987, 587.

24. John Simons, "David Aers, *Chaucer;* Stephen Knight, *Geoffrey Chaucer;* Piero Boitani and Jill Mann, *The Cambridge Chaucer Companion;* Charles Muscatine, *The Old French Fabliaux*," *Literature and History* 14 (1988): 116.

25. Sheila Delany, "*Chaucer,* by David Aers; *Geoffrey Chaucer,* by Stephen Knight," *Science and Society* 52 (1988): 239.

26. Derek Pearsall, "*Chaucer,* by David Aers; *'The Miller's Tale' by Geoffrey Chaucer,* by Michael Alexander; *Techniques of Translation: Chaucer's 'Boece',* by Tim William Machan," *Modern Language Review* 84 (1989): 112.

27. T. L. Burton, "'Al is for to selle': Chaucer, Marx, and the 'New' Historicism," *Southern Review* 20 (1987): 193.

28. Carolyn Dinshaw, *Chaucer's Sexual Poetics* (Madison: University of Wisconsin Press, 1989), 15.

29. Ibid., 28–29.

30. Ibid., 35–36.

31. Ibid., 36.

32. Ibid., 37, 182.

33. Ibid., 29.

34. Helen Cooper, "*Chaucer's Sexual Poetics,* by Carolyn Dinshaw," *Review of English Studies,* n.s., 43 (1992): 258.

35. Peter L. Allen, "*Chaucer's Sexual Poetics,* by Carolyn Dinshaw," *Journal of the History of Sexuality* 2 (1992): 473.

36. Ibid.; see also Sheila Delany, "*Chaucer's Sexual Poetics.* Carolyn Dinshaw," *Women's Studies* 20 (1992): 356; Derek Pearsall, "Carolyn Dinshaw, *Chaucer's Sexual Poetics,*" *Speculum* 67 (1992): 136.

37. Dinshaw, *Chaucer's Sexual Poetics,* 36. Cooper comments, "It is not clear, in fact, that she herself altogether avoids 'reading like a man,' even if she does it in feminist terms" (*"Chaucer's Sexual Poetics,"* 258).

38. Pearsall, "Carolyn Dinshaw," 137.

39. Delany, *"Chaucer's Sexual Poetics,"* 355.

40. Ibid., 356.

41. See also Antonia Ward's brief discussion of gendered language in modern Chaucer studies, in "'My Love for Chaucer': F. J. Furnivall and Homosociality in the Chaucer Society," *Studies in Medievalism* 9 (1999 [for 1997]): 50. My most recent example comes from Douglas Moffat and Vincent P. McCarren, who, impervious to Dinshaw's devastating critique of this passage, describe Donaldson writing "amusingly" of the editor torn between two manuscripts as a man torn between two women. Moffat and McCarren, "A Bibliographical Essay on Editing Methods and Authorial and Scribal Intention," in *A Guide to Editing Middle English,* ed. Vincent P. McCarren and Douglas Moffatt (Ann Arbor: University of Michigan Press, 1998), 53.

42. Elaine Tuttle Hansen, *Chaucer and the Fictions of Gender* (Berkeley: University of California Press, 1992), 25.

43. Ibid., 17, 12.

44. Ibid., 7–9.

45. Ibid., 47.

46. Ibid., 45–49.

47. Marilynn Desmond, "*Chaucer and the Fictions of Gender* by Elaine Tuttle Hansen," *Journal of the History of Sexuality* 4 (1993): 297.

48. Kathryn Lynch, "Review of Elaine Tuttle Hansen, *Chaucer and the Fictions of Gender,*" *JEGP* 92 (1993): 431.

49. Jill Mann, "Elaine Tuttle Hansen, *Chaucer and the Fictions of Gender,*" *Medium Aevum* 62 (1993): 329.

50. David Wallace, "Elaine Tuttle Hansen, *Chaucer and the Fictions of Gender,*" *Speculum* 69 (1994): 157.

51. Hansen, *Chaucer and the Fictions of Gender,* 292.

52. Cheryl Glenn makes a similar point, describing Hansen as remaining Chaucer's friend through the very detail of her rereadings. Glenn, "Elaine Tuttle Hansen, *Chaucer and the Fictions of Gender,*" *College English* 56 (1994): 326.

53. Anne Laskaya, *Chaucer's Approach to Gender in "The Canterbury Tales"* (Cambridge: Brewer, 1995), 4.

54. Catherine S. Cox, *Gender and Language in Chaucer* (Gainesville: University Press of Florida, 1997).

55. Longman "Literature 98" catalog.

56. Gary Taylor, "The Renaissance and the End of Editing," in *Palimpsest: Editorial Theory in the Humanities*, ed. George Bornstein and Ralph G. Williams (Ann Arbor: University of Michigan Press, 1993), 132–33.

57. See Alcuin Blamires, *The Canterbury Tales* (Houndmills: Macmillan, 1987), 2–3.

58. Ibid., 47.

59. Jill Mann similarly refuses to define her feminist approach more precisely, in *Geoffrey Chaucer* (New York: Harvester Wheatsheaf, 1991). Priscilla Martin defends such eclecticism, labeled "magpieism" by David Aers at the 1990 Conference of the New Chaucer Society, in "Chaucer and Feminism: A Magpie View," in *A Wyf Ther Was: Essays in Honour of Paule Mertens-Fonck*, ed. Juliette Dor (Liège: Université de Liège, 1992), 235–46.

60. David Williams, *The Canterbury Tales: A Literary Pilgrimage* (Boston: Twayne, 1987), 101.

61. Ibid., 32, 42–45, 71.

62. Ibid., 102–3, 104.

63. Anne Rooney, *Geoffrey Chaucer* (Bedminster: Bristol Press, 1989), 14.

64. Peter Brown, *Chaucer at Work: The Making of the Canterbury Tales* (Harlow: Longman, 1994), 5–6.

65. Gail Ashton, *Chaucer: The Canterbury Tales* (London: Macmillan, 1998), 3.

66. Rooney, *Geoffrey Chaucer*, 44.

67. Rob Pope, *How to Study Chaucer* (London: Macmillan, 1988), 1–2.

68. Ibid., 21.

69. Ibid., 23.

70. Here, for example, are some of the sample questions Pope includes in his final chapter: "'Chaucer laughed at human weaknesses rather than denounced them.' Consider this remark with reference to *The General Prologue*"; or "'By contrast with the gods, the human actors acquire a certain tragic dignity.' Discuss this comment on the human and divine figures in *The Knight's Tale*." The ethical world invoked by these questions is preeminently a benign, humanist world.

71. Janette Dillon, *Geoffrey Chaucer* (London: Macmillan, 1993); Steve Ellis, *Geoffrey Chaucer* (Plymouth: Northcote House, 1996); S. H. Rigby, *Chaucer in Context: Society, Allegory, and Gender* (Manchester: Manchester University Press, 1996).

72. Clifton Hillegras, *Cliffs Notes, Inc.: Quality of Product . . . Service . . . Policy* (New York: Newcomen Society of the United States, 1985), 22.

73. Ibid., 21.

74. Tim William Machan, *Textual Criticism and Middle English Texts* (Charlottesville: University Press of Virginia, 1994), 190.

INDEX

philology, xix, 19, 137, 174–75; opposed to criticism, 11–13, 41, 152, 171, 178–79
pilgrims. *See* Chaucer, works
Plowman's Tale, The, 67, 85–86, 96, 136
Poets' Corner, 6
Pope, Rob, 225, 231–32
postfeminism, 221, 223
postmodernism, 1, 4, 18, 48–49, 54, 58–60, 79, 21
Potter, Russell, 13
print: and authorship, 49, 55, 57, 110, 141; and community, 111; culture, 115, 122–28, 135; and nationalism, 26, 172; printing clubs, 172–73; stigma of, 123, 130–31, 137, 140–41
professionalism, xxii, 44, 139, 156, 158, 185–87, 201, 237, 243 n.52
pseudo-Chaucerian writing, 41, 43, 80, 102–8, 109, 154
public sphere, 151, 158, 165, 176
Pynson, Richard, 16

queer theory, 221, 224

rape, 20, 36–39, 105, 219
readers. *See* Chaucer, readers of
reception. *See* Chaucer, reception history
Reinecke, George, 17
Rendall, Thomas, 108, 254 n.42
Renoir, Alain, 101, 254 n.32
Ricardian poetry, 51
Richmond, Velma Bourgeois, 226, 245 n.83
Ridley, Florence, 27, 241 n.20, 243 n.58
Rigby, S. H., 226, 232
Riverside Chaucer, xiii–xvii, xxiii, 11–13, 70
Robbins, Rossell Hope, xx–xxi
Robertson, D. W., 38, 198, 208, 210, 216–17, 219, 223
Robinson, F. N., 12, 16, 17, 184
Robinson, Peter, 14
Rollman, David, 257 n.23
romanticism, 207
Roney, Lois, 42

Rooney, Anne, 226, 228–29, 231
Root, R. K., 17, 180
Rorty, Richard, 24
Rose, Donald, 201–2, 205
Rowland, Beryl, xx
Rubin, Gayle, 219
Ruggiers, Paul, 16–17, 82
Rutter, Russell, 124

Saunders, J. W., 257 n.29
Sayce, Olive, 251 n.74
Scattergood, John, 29
Schibanoff, Susan, 79–80, 241 n.19
Schnapp, Jeffrey T., 247 n.15, 253 n.14
Schricker, Gale, 251 n.73
Scogan, Henry, xxi, 30–32
Sedgwick, Eve Kosofsky, 239 n.6, 267 n.89
Seymour, M. C., 248 n.28, 253 n.21
Shakespeare, 134–35, 154; criticism of, xxi, 10, 227, 243 n.47
Shichtman, Martin, 201
Shirley, John, 75, 112–15
Sidnam, Jonathon, 121
Sidney, Sir Philip, 141–42
signature, 41–42, 44–45, 87, 96, 118; and authorship, 57, 120; Chaucerian, xxii, 60, 62–64, 70–73, 79, 110. *See also* William Langland
Simons, John, 213–14, 264 n.38
Simpson, James, 24, 249 n.34
Sir Gawain and the Green Knight, 23
Skeat, W. W., 172, 174, 181–82, 256 n.2
Skelton, John, 111
Society of Antiquaries, 128
Spearing, A. C., 72–73, 99–101, 240 n.7, 254 n.30
Speculum, 23
Speght, Thomas, 16, 125, 129–39, 141, 143, 149
Speirs, John, 174, 206, 225
Spenser, Edmund, 57, 134–35, 142, 227, 240 n.9; imitates Chaucer's voice, 44, 109, 111, 139; inherits Chaucer's spirit, 22, 28, 146–47

Stephanie Trigg is senior lecturer at the University of Melbourne. Her publications include an edition of *Winner and Waster* for the Early English Text Society; two edited essay collections, *Medieval English Poetry* and *The Space of Poetry: Australian Essays on Contemporary Poetics;* and *Gwen Harwood.* She has published articles on medieval literature in *Exemplaria, Yearbook of Langland Studies,* and *Viator.*

MEDIEVAL CULTURES